THEORIZING TRANSITIONAL JUSTICE

Offers an exceptionally diverse array of normative theory and research relating to the evolving field of Transitional Justice.

Ruti Teitel, New York Law School, USA

Theorizing Transitional Justice

Edited by

CLAUDIO CORRADETTI
University of Oslo, Norway

NIR EISIKOVITS
Suffolk University, USA

JACK VOLPE ROTONDI
Suffolk University, USA

Routledge
Taylor & Francis Group
LONDON AND NEW YORK

First published 2015 by Ashgate Publishing

Published 2016 by Routledge
2 Park Square, Milton Park, Abingdon, Oxfordshire OX14 4RN
711 Third Avenue, New York, NY 10017, USA

First issued in paperback 2016

Routledge is an imprint of the Taylor & Francis Group, an informa business

British Library Cataloguing in Publication Data
A catalogue record for this book is available from the British Library

Library of Congress Cataloging-in-Publication Data
Theorizing transitional justice / by C. Corradetti, N. Eisikovits and J. Rotondi.
pages cm
Includes bibliographical references and index.
ISBN 978-1-4724-1829-6 (hardback) – ISBN 978-1-4724-1830-2 (ebook) – ISBN 978-1-4724-1831-9 (epub) 1. Transitional justice. I. Corradetti, Claudio, editor. II. Eisikovits, Nir, editor. III. Rotondi, Jack, editor.
K5250.T46 2014
320.01'1--dc23

2014029247

ISBN 13: 978-1-138-63761-0 (pbk)
ISBN 13: 978-1-4724-1829-6 (hbk)

Contents

List of Figures

Notes on Contributors

Sanja Bahun is Professor and Director of Graduate Studies in the Department of Literature, Film, and Theatre Studies at the University of Essex. She is also the Research Chair: Transitional Justice and the Arts, Gender and Children Focused Approaches, for the Essex Transitional Justice Network. Dr. Bahun's areas of expertise are international modernism and women's and gender studies, and her research interests related to transitional justice include the operation and representation of justice in oral culture, literature, and the visual and performing arts; gender and children's rights in transitional societies; and the role of the arts in the processes of reparation and recognition across the world. In addition to articles and book chapters on a variety of subjects concerning modernism, psychoanalysis, theory of the margin, and representation of the conflict-related trauma, Bahun is the author of *Modernism and Melancholia: Writing as Countermourning* (2013), and the joint editor of *The Avant-garde and the Margin* (2006), *Violence and Gender in the Globalized World* (2008; second, revised edition 2014), *From Word to Canvas* (2009), *Myth and Violence in the Contemporary Female Text* (2010), *Language, Ideology, and the Human* (2012), and *Cinema, State Socialism and Society in the Soviet Union and Eastern Europe, 1917–1989* (2014).

Claudia Card is Emma Goldman Professor of Philosophy, Affiliate Professor in Jewish Studies, LGBT Studies, Women's Studies and Affiliate Professor in Environmental Studies at the University of Wisconsin-Madison. She is author of *Confronting Evils: Terrorism, Torture, Genocide* (Cambridge, 2010), *The Atrocity Paradigm: A Theory of Evil* (Oxford, 2002), *The Unnatural Lottery: Character and Moral Luck* (Temple, 1996), *Lesbian Choices* (Columbia, 1995), and more than 100 articles and reviews. She is also editor of *Feminist Ethics* (Kansas, 1991), *Adventures in Lesbian Philosophy* (Indiana, 1994), *The Cambridge Companion to Simone de Beauvoir* (Cambridge, 2003), *On Feminist Ethics and Politics* (Kansas, 1999), *Genocide's Aftermath*, coedited with Armen Marsoobian (2007), and a special issue of *Hypatia: Journal of Feminist Philosophy* (1992). She is philosophy book review editor for the *Journal of Homosexuality* as well as a member of the editorial and review boards for *Social Theory and Practice, Hypatia, Ethics and the Environment*. She is the former chair of the APA Committee on the Status of Lesbian, Gay, Bisexual, and Transgendered People in the Profession (1997–2001) and Senior-Fellow at the Institute for Research in the Humanities (2002–2007). In 2008 she delivered the APA Dewey lecture; in 2011 she was President of the Central APA; and in 2016 she will deliver the Paul Carus lectures.

Claudio Corradetti is research and teaching fellow at the Faculty of Law, University of Oslo. Corradetti holds a doctorate in Political Theory from LUISS Rome, a Master of Philosophy from the University of London and a postgraduate Diploma in European Public Law from the European Group of Public Law, EPLO, Athens. He has been visiting at Cornell, Oxford, and the European University Institute, Florence. He was awarded a visiting research and teaching grant at McGill University, Montreal. He has published widely in books and international journals. Some of his most recent works include "What does cultural difference require of human rights?," in Cindy Holder and David A. Reidy (eds), *Human Rights: The Hard Questions*, Cambridge University

Press (2013), pp. 136–50; "Philosophical issues in transitional justice theory: A (provisional) balance," *Politica e Società,* Il Mulino, Bologna (2013): 185–220.

Nir Eisikovits received his Ph.D. in Legal and Political Philosophy from Boston University in 2005; prior to that he studied law in Tel Aviv. He is Associate Professor of Philosophy at Suffolk University in Boston where he co-founded and directs the Graduate Program in Ethics and Public Policy. He writes primarily on political reconciliation, transitional justice and the ethics of war. Eisikovits is author of *Sympathizing with the Enemy: Reconciliation, Transitional Justice, Negotiation* (Republic of Letters Publishing, 2010), as well as the forthcoming *Kill Me Tomorrow: A Theory of Truces* (Palgrave Macmillan, 2015). Recent articles include "Asymmetrical Warfare and Conscientious Objection" in the *International Journal of Applied Philosophy* (with Evan Feinhauer), "Peace versus Justice in Transitional Settings" in *Politica e Societa* and a thoroughly revised and updated entry on 'Transitional Justice' in the *Stanford Encyclopedia of Philosophy*. Nir will serve as guest editor of a forthcoming issue of *Theoria* on the "Idea of Peace in the Age of Asymmetrical Warfare." In addition to his scholarly work, Eisikovits writes often for American newspapers and magazines, primarily about the Middle East conflict. He has written for the *Boston Globe*, *Miami Herald*, *Christian Science Monitor*, *National Interest*, *Forward* and *Cognoscenti* among others.

Juan Espindola is Assistant Professor at the Center for Research and Teaching in Economics (CIDE) and holds a Ph.D. in Political Science from the University of Michigan. He is currently a postdoctoral fellow at the National University of Mexico's Institute for Social Research and formerly was a postdoctoral fellow at the University of Frankfurt (Centre for Advanced Studies *Justitia Amplificata*). He is currently completing a book on the moral and political dilemmas of the public exposure of Stasi collaborators in Germany, which will be published by Cambridge University Press. Some recent and forthcoming publications include "An Apology for Public Apologies? Transitional Justice and Respect in Germany," in *German Studies Review* 36(2), May 2013; "The Case for the Moral Permissibility of Amnesties: An Argument from Social Moral Epistemology," in *Ethical Theory and Moral Practice*; and "The Problem of Historical Rectification for Rawlsian Theory (with Moises Vaca)," *Res Publica,* August 2014, 20(3): pp 227–43

.

Paul Gowder is Associate Professor of Law at the University of Iowa College of Law. His research and teaching span a broad territory in constitutional law, ethics, normative and conceptual jurisprudence, political philosophy, democratic theory, and game theory. Currently, his primary research program is an exploration of the rule of law and its relationship to political and social equality, with various pieces of the overall project drawing on philosophical argument, historical research into the law in societies as diverse as seventeenth-century England and classical Athens, and political science formal modeling, all directed at the overall end of making sense of the idea of government under law and its application in real-world societies.

Grace Hunt is an Assistant Professor of Philosophy at Western Kentucky University. She specializes in nineteenth and twentieth-century Continental Philosophy, Social Philosophy, and Feminist Theory. Hunt is author of *Redeeming Resentment: Nietzsche's Affirmative Ripostes* (*American Dialectic*) and 2012 Winner of the *American Dialectic* Annual Dissertation Contest. She also wrote *Performing Dignity: The Restorative Value of Bodily Resentments for Women in Philosophy* (2010–11) as well as numerous other published papers.

Cheryl Lawther is a Lecturer in Criminology at Queen's University Belfast. She was previously a postdoctoral research fellow at the School of International Relations, University of St. Andrews and received her Ph.D. from the School of Law, Queen's University Belfast in 2010. Key publications include "Securing the Past: Policing and the Contest over Truth in Northern Ireland," in the *British Journal of Criminology*, (2010, 5(3): 455–73) and "Denial, Silence and the Politics of the Past: Unpicking the Opposition to Truth Recovery in Northern Ireland," in the *International Journal of Transitional Justice* (2013, 7(1): 157–77). The former article was awarded the Brian Williams Article Prize by the British Society of Criminology in July 2011. This award is made in recognition of the best sole authored journal article by a "new" scholar in the previous year. Her monograph *Truth, Denial and Transition: Northern Ireland and The Contested Past* was published by the Routledge Transitional Justice Series in early 2014.

Pádraig McAuliffe is a Lecturer at the School of Law, University of Dundee and a graduate of University College Cork. In 2009, he was awarded his doctorate for his research on the Special Panels for Serious Crimes in East Timor. He held a visiting research fellowship at the University of California, Los Angeles in 2007. From 2008 to 2009, Pádraig worked as a researcher in the Legal Division of the Irish Department of Foreign Affairs. In 2009 Pádraig was appointed to a lectureship in law at the University of Dundee. He is a contributor to the *Oxford Reports on International Criminal Law*. He has published one book, three book chapters and numerous articles.

Thaddeus Metz is the Humanities Research Professor and Head of the Philosophy Department at the University of Johannesburg. He earned his Ph.D. in Philosophy from Cornell University in 1997. Since then he has become recognized for his research on four major topics in value theory: using a principle of respect for human dignity to resolve moral controversies in law, politics, business and medicine; interpreting the African ethic of *ubuntu* in an analytic, rigorous way; addressing normative issues in higher education; and systematically developing and evaluating theoretical approaches to what makes a life meaningful. Metz has had more than 100 scholarly manuscripts accepted for publication, which include a book, *Meaning in Life: An Analytic Study* (Oxford University Press, 2013) and several dozen articles in journals such as *Ethics*, *Philosophy and Public Affairs*, *Religious Studies*, *Oxford Journal of Legal Studies*, *Law and Philosophy*, and *Journal of Political Philosophy*. Metz has also reviewed more than 100 manuscripts for presses and journals, supervised more than 50 postgraduate research projects, and taught more than 30 different courses. Recent recognition of his research includes an "A" rating President's Award from the South African National Research Foundation, and the Vice-Chancellor's Research Award from the University of Johannesburg.

Mihaela Mihai is the 50th Anniversary Lecturer in Politics at the University of York and Researcher, Centre for Social Studies, at the University of Coimbra. She holds a doctorate in Political Theory from the University of Toronto and a Master's degree in Government from the University of Manchester. Her research interests cut across political theory, political science and law. More precisely, she is interested in the affective dimension of politics, political judgment, transitional justice, historical injustice and the politics of memory. Her book manuscript, entitled *Rescuing Resentment and Indignation: The Democratic Potential of Negative Emotions for Transitional Justice*, is currently under review with a university press. She is also preparing, together with Mathias Thaler, an edited book on public apologies for past injustice. Her work has appeared in *Political Theory, Journal of Political Philosophy, Ratio Juris, Oxford Journal of Legal Studies,*

Parallax, and *European Journal of Political Theory*, among others. She is the co-editor of *On the Uses and Abuses of Political Apologies* (Palgrave, 2014).

Monica Mookherjee is a Senior Lecturer in Political Philosophy at Keele University. She is the author of *Women's Rights as Multicultural Claims: Reconfiguring Gender and Diversity in Political Philosophy* (Edinburgh University Press, 2009), and the editor of *Democracy, Religious Pluralism and the Liberal Dilemma of Accommodation* (Springer, 2010). In addition, she has published a number of articles on the themes of gender, feminism, postcolonialism and multiculturalism in political theory. The chapter herein is derived from a longer book-length project on reconciliation and multiculturalism in contemporary political theory.

Colleen Murphy is an Associate Professor of Philosophy and Law and the Director of the Women and Gender in Global Perspectives Program (WGGP) at the University of Illinois at Urbana-Champaign. Her research focuses on the moral dimensions of those disruptions to political communities that arise from repression, war, and natural disasters. She is the author of *The Conceptual Foundations of Transitional Justice* (Cambridge University Press, under contract) and *A Moral Theory of Political Reconciliation* (Cambridge University Press, 2010). Murphy was a Laurance S. Rockefeller Visiting Faculty Fellow at the Princeton University Center for Human Values, and her research has been supported by the National Endowment for the Humanities and the National Science Foundation.

Michael Phillips is Senior Lecturer in Law and a member of the Centre for Human Rights in Conflict at the University of East London. He completed his Ph.D. at the University of Sydney; his doctoral thesis was on the Politics and Theology of Aboriginal Reconciliation in Australia. He was awarded the Mayer Prize by the Australian Political Science Association in 2006. Prior to joining UEL in 2011, Michael was a commercial solicitor in Sydney and London. His current research interests are in the fields of religion and transitional justice.

Jack Volpe Rotondi is Assistant Vice President of Organizational Operations at the United Way of Massachusetts Bay and Merrimack Valley and has a 25-year tenure in non-profit operations, technology and process change. Rotondi (B.A., Cornell University) earned his Master of Science in Ethics and Public Policy at Suffolk University in 2014. His Master's thesis was entitled "WikiLeaks Byline: The First Amendment, the Fourth Estate, and Reporter's Privilege in the 21st Century." Jack is also a professional jazz vocalist and leader of the Jack Volpe Project band.

Krista K. Thomason is Assistant Professor of Philosophy at Swarthmore College. Thomason's areas of specialization are moral and political philosophy. Her research in political philosophy focuses on human rights and atrocity. She has presented research at American Philosophical Association meetings and International Social Philosophy conferences. Some of her work appears in *Philosophy and Phenomenological Research*, *The Journal of Southern Philosophy*, and the *Kantian Review.*

Lynne Tirrell is Associate Professor of Philosophy, Women's Studies, at UMass Boston. Tirrell's current work in philosophy of language focuses on the ways that linguistic practices enhance social justice or facilitate injustice. This has led to a deepening focus on the role of discursive practices in the 1994 genocide of the Tutsi in Rwanda and in Rwanda's recovery. Recent papers include *Genocidal Language Games* which uses inferential role semantics and speech act theory to explain the power of linguistic practices to shape social conditions that make genocide possible. Her *Apologizing for Atrocity: Rwanda and Recognition* analyzes the survivor's need for recognition and offers an analysis of U.S. President Clinton's apology to the people of Rwanda for his role in the international abandonment of Rwanda in 1994. *Studying Genocide: A Pragmatist Approach* digs into the philosophical underpinnings of Tirrell's approach. Following research trips to Rwanda and to the ICTR in Tanzania, she has been working on several papers about ICTR cases, and analyzing Rwanda's anti-divisionism law. Professor Tirrell is also working on a collaborative project with Alisa L. Carse on issues surrounding forgiveness and reconciliation. Tirrell's articles, on philosophy of language, aesthetics, feminist theory, and the politics of discourse, have appeared in numerous journals, including *The Journal of Philosophy, Noûs, The Journal of Aesthetics and Art Criticism,* and *Hypatia*, as well as in edited collections.

Margaret Urban Walker is Donald J. Schuenke Chair in Philosophy at Marquette University, and author of *Moral Repair: Reconstructing Moral Relations after Wrongdoing* (2006), *What is Reparative Justice?* (2010), and numerous articles on reparations and reparative truth-telling in the context of post-conflict and transitional justice. She is writing a book on reparations that integrates the roles of public truth-telling and remembrance with compensation, restitution, and reform in an expressive conception of reparations. Walker has contributed to research projects with the International Center for Transitional Justice on gendered violence and reparations and on truth commissions.

Introduction

The philosophical debate over transitional justice as a concept can be traced back to ancient Greece. Some of its most central problems were already addressed in Aeschylus's trilogy of *The Oresteia* where Athena played the transitional role of casting the decisive vote for pardoning Orestes and saving him from the Furies (the Erinnyes).[1] Yet, the linguistic expression "transitional justice" has been adopted for the first time in its technical sense by R. Teitel during late 1980s who then formulated the basic principles of this emerging discipline in her path-breaking work on the subject.[2]

Since its appearance, the term was immediately discussed and criticized due to its combination of two apparently irreconcilable elements: the idea of justice and the idea of change through time—transition. The skepticism accompanying the birth of transitional justice as a study area was thus characterized since the beginning by a continuous attempt of defining the field, an attempt which is even now far from having been completed.[3] Some views have challenged the notion of transitional justice as a form of compromise among contracting parties whereas others have instead considered it as a specific context of application of general normative principles independently justified (hence the proper interpretation of "transitional").[4]

The specific task for a normatively framed programme of justice in transition is the focus of some of the most influential literature in the field as, for instance, in R. Teitel (2003), where the author considers how twentieth-century institutional and legal developments of transitional justice revolved around three major historical events/phases: I) the post-Second World phase of the Nuremberg Trials prosecuting Nazis' generals, II) the post-Cold War phase which has modified the bipolar equilibrium and opened democratization processes, and finally, III) the steady-state phase of transitional justice.[5]

Whereas the first phase of the Nuremberg trials was characterized by a very limited scope dominated by criminal law, the post-Cold War phase moved beyond a mere retributive strategy and looked for social and interparty restoration. What emerged was a dichotomy between truth and justice, where truth commissions as *ad hoc* institutions favoring reconciliation were created. In addition to the trade of justice for truth, this second phase was characterized by the trade of justice for peace. A large amount of literature developed in relation to concepts of "forgiveness" or "reconciliation." Finally, phase II reinterpreted the universalist view on the rule of law typical of phase I and considered it as dependent on state-particularist perspective. Universality was therefore seen as embedded in contingent political contexts. Even if characterized by institutional innovation, the second phase was nevertheless limited by circumstances linked to nation-state transitions. Such constraints are now inadequate for the understanding of the global dimension, which is instead

---

1 On the transitional justice interpretations of *The Orestea*, see B. Leebaw, *Judging State-Sponsored Violence, Imagining Political Change*, Cambridge: Cambridge University Press 2011, 108 ff.

2 R. Teitel, *Transitional Justice*, New York, NY: Oxford University Press 2000.

3 In this regard, P. De Greiff has recently affirmed that: "Finally, and most surprising, there is no fully worked-out conception of transitional justice even in the most influential works in the field", P. De Greiff, "Theorizing Transitional Justice", in M.S. Williams, R. Nagy and J. Elster (eds), *Transitional Justice*, New York-London: New York University Press 2012: 32.

4 This latter thesis is defended by P. De Greiff, "Theorizing Transitional Justice," cit., p. 58 ff.

5 R. Teitel, "Transitional Justice Genealogy," cit.

typical of the third phase. This latter, indeed, due to the permanent action of investigation and prosecution assigned to the International Criminal Court has *normalized* the exceptionality of the special tribunals of Rwanda and Yugoslavia.[6] This process of normalization is also connected to the expected change of role of transitional justice into the politics of prevention and self-defense from terrorist attacks. The latter events have placed the scope of transitional justice strategies more directly into the field of economic and political transformations of the global world and raised the question of the opportunity of global rule of law.[7]

This collection of chapters aims to bring conceptual clarity to the study and practice of transitional justice. Theorists and practitioners of transitional justice are interested in the aftermath of conflict and large-scale human rights abuses: how do nations and political groups address past wrongs in order to create (sometimes recreate) a decent civil order? The question as noticed is very old and it is still very much with us in recent history: from the failure to account for the Armenian Genocide, through the Nuremberg Trials, denazification, lustration policies in Eastern Europe after the fall of communism, the creation of ad hoc and then a permanent International Criminal Tribunal, the South African Truth and Reconciliation Commission—all offered different answers. If the twentieth century was the nightmarish, barbaric century of genocide, it was also an epoch in which the question of how to account for mass crimes has been taken most seriously. Needless to say, the question is still relevant, as we consider how best to transition to sustainable democracy after years of authoritarian rule in Egypt, Libya and Syria, to pluck but a few names from recent headlines.

The study of transitional justice in recent decades has been interdisciplinary, running the gamut from philosophy through theology, sociology, anthropology, law and recently even neuroscience.[8] The field had its contemporary birth with the creation of the Nuremberg Tribunals after the Second World War, the first successful and effective trials for large-scale war crimes. But the concern with accountability for past wrongs went into a deep freeze with the Cold War and the inability of the two great powers to agree on the nature and orientation of international norms. Interest reemerged after the collapse of the Soviet Union. In the past several decades we have seen the creation of new ad hoc criminal tribunals (e.g., the former Yugoslavia, Rwanda and Cambodia) as well as the rise of Truth and Reconciliation Commissions (most famously in South Africa) and other semi-judicial bodies (e.g., Rwanda's Gacaca courts).[9]

In spite of the exponential growth of interest in this area, there have been surprisingly few attempts to provide a systematic conceptual grounding of the nature, aims and limitations of transitional justice. Perhaps this theoretical lack is due to the different contexts in which transitional policies are put into practice. One of the chapters herein suggests as much. Perhaps it is due to the vastly disparate scholarly methodologies employed by academics who take up such questions. Be that as it may, the collection before you seeks to fill this lacuna by asking a wide range of established, as well as up and coming writers, to "theorize" transitional justice—to reflect on how the interaction between moral, political, legal and conceptual questions shapes our practices after war. What kind of justice is transitional justice? What are the contradictions between its transitionality and

6 R. Teitel, "Transitional Justice Genealogy," cit.

7 These opening paragraphs are a revised extrapolation from Corradetti, C. 2013. "Philosophical Issues in Transitional Justice Theory: A (Provisional) Balance." *Politica e Società* 2/2013: 185–220.

8 See, e.g., a recent initiative to study the connection between neuroscience and post-conflict strategies inaugurated by *Beyond Conflict*, a non-profit organization based in Tufts University. A report on a recent conference organized by Beyond Conflict on this topic can be found here: Beyond Conflict. 2012. "Neuroscience and Social Conflict: Identifying New Approaches for the 21st Century." Accessed July 9, 2014. http://www.beyondconflictint.org/wp-content/uploads/2014/01/Neuroscience_Bro_v2_optimized.pdf.

9 For a discussion of different cases and strategies of reparation see Brooks, R.L. 1999. *When Sorry Isn't Enough: The Controversy over Apologies and Reparations for Human Injustice*. New York: New York University Press.

its justness? What are the operative assumptions that any state seriously engaging in transitional policies entertains? How do we understand the tensions between the desire to hold criminals responsible for what they have done and the need to generate political and economic stability for a new state? Are the major dilemmas of transitional justice themselves transitory, to be dispelled with the creation of a settled democracy, or do they continue to animate the political life of a state founded (as so many are) in great injustice? What is the potential of transitional justice to bring about social change? More specifically, how and when can it promote political reconciliation? How and when can it bring about significant structural and economic reform? What are the interactions between transitional justice practices and a new state's cultural life? Are some social-scientific and philosophical methodologies more promising than others in trying to address these questions? In regard to these questions the volume represents one of the few systematic attempts to take on the theory of transitional justice from a philosophical perspective given that as De Greiff has recently affirmed: at present " ... there is no fully worked-out conception of transitional justice even in the most influential works in the field."[10]

Absence in systematic philosophical literature in this field does not amount to a complete lack of engagement in some of the core themes by individual philosophers which sporadically, but significantly, contributed to the setting up of the discussion. This is for instance, the case of Adorno's contribution on what it means to "come to terms with the past" which expanded on Arendt's and Jaspers' opening of the debate about "the German Guilt," revived then once again by Habermas' and Minchnik's discussion of post-war reconciliation between Germany and Poland.[11]

More generally, some of the philosophical problems raised by transitional justice concern the reframing of the opposition between ideal versus non-ideal justice. This seems suggested by John Rawls' reference to improvements of the conditions for non-well-ordered and burdened societies as "questions of transition"—as he refers to them—but with no indication on the specific steps and institutions to adopt.[12] Another central area of philosophical debate to emerge recently has focused on the question of whether it is possible to define transitional justice as a form of special justice or if, instead, it has to be regarded as a form of normal justice.[13] This question is of central importance because if transitional justice is sui generis, it is far from clear that our best theories of justice apply to transitional settings. If, on the other hand, the question of justice in times of momentous political change is at bottom a question about ordinary justice, then many of the normative questions of transitional justice have already been addressed in previous theorizing. Other areas of interest include the opposition between forgiveness and forgetting as ways for transitional societies to confront the past; the understanding of the nature of evil; as well as the normativity of historical

10 De Greiff, P. 2014. "Theorizing Transitional Justice." In *Transitional Justice*, edited by M.S. Williams, R. Nagy and J. Elster. New York and London: New York University Press. An excellent collection of essays published in 2014: Buckley-Zistel, S., Beck, T., Braun, C., Mieth, F. (eds). 2014. *Transitional Justice Theories*. New York: Routledge. Provides outstanding methodological coverage but does not put equal emphasis on philosophical inquiry.

11 Adorno, T.W. 1986. "What Does Coming to Terms with the Past Mean?" In *Bitburg in Moral and Political Perspective*, edited by G.H. Harman. Bloomington, IN: Indiana University Press.

See also, Arendt, H. 1978. "Organised Guilt and Collective Responsibility [1945]." In *The Jew as Pariah: Jewish Identity and Politics in the Modern Age*, edited by R.H. Feldman. New York: Grove Press; Jaspers, K. 1961. *The Question of German Guilt*. New York: Capricorn Books; Habermas, J. and Michnik, A. 1994. "Overcoming the Past." *New Left Review* 1/203: 3–16.

12 Rawls, J. 1999. *The Law of Peoples*. Cambridge, MA: Harvard University Press. For a comprehensive overview of some of the crucial philosophical themes in transitional justice theory, see Corradetti, 2013: 185–220.

13 Posner, E.A. and Vermeule, A. 2003. "Transitional Justice as Ordinary Justice." In *Public Law and Legal Theory, Working Paper n. 40*. Chicago, IL: University of Chicago Press. http://www.law.uchicago.edu/files/files/40.eap-av.transitional.both_.pdf. Nir Eisikovits also takes up this question in his entry on Transitional Justice in the *Stanford Encyclopedia of Philosophy* (http://plato.stanford.edu/entries/justice-transitional) as well as in the recent essay Eisikovits, N. 2013. "Peace versus Justice in Transitional Settings." *Politica e Società* 2/2013: 221–36.

memory within time, etc. An especially important chapter by Jeremy Waldron merits noting in this context as it has raised the possibility that the force of claims for historical justice can fade over time. This discussion not only suggests an interesting and controversial relationship between the abstract claims of justice and the force of changed circumstances, it also constitutes a prime example of non-ideal philosophizing about transitional justice. It raises the possibility that non-ideal theory is perhaps especially well-suited for taking up the philosophical questions involved.[14] Other important work in the non-ideal theory of transitional justice has taken up the question of how international norms of transitional justice emerge. Thus, Kathryn Sikkink, in her major recent book, *The Justice Cascade*[15] has investigated how international prosecutions are becoming an international norm and expectation influencing both the prospects of transition and creating a potential for deterrence. In a similar vein, Michal Ben Josef's Hirsch's recent scholarship traces the growth and increasing acceptance of truth commissions as instruments of Transitional Justice.[16]

The unfinished project of transitional justice does not include simply the already mentioned abstract conceptualizations at the normative and metaethical level but it is reflected also in the classificatory criteria for the typological varieties of transitional justice processes. The phenomenology of transitional justice events has itself become more inclusive and moved far beyond the initial stage of post-conflict transitions. Now, one can speak also of transitional justice processes *within* democratic settings as well as of transitions in *non-transitional* contexts.[17] Today, there is even a further area of application, as it is the case for the so-called "transitional jurisprudence" of the European Court of Human Rights (ECtHR) in regard to the former Soviet states that are now members of the Council of Europe (CoE) and subject to the European Convention of Human Rights (ECHR).[18] In all these cases the ECtHR adopted the principle of "self-defending" or "militant democracy" as guidance for delimiting, on temporally constrained bases and mainly on issues concerning electoral participation of extremist parties, in order to favor the achievement of democratic stability.[19]

All considered and to a large extent, the more or less inclusiveness of transitional justice phenomena as part of a single coherent framework depends very much on whether a merely descriptive approach is confronted with a normative one; that is, one in which transformations are seen as oriented towards democratic advancement. If the first approach characterizes J. Elster's path-breaking work on transitions, the latter approach is significantly endorsed and developed by R. Teitel, the founder of the contemporary scholarship on transitional justice, as well as one of the most important scholars today on transitional justice.[20]

The book has seven sections. The first centers on the most basic assumption in the field—that political reconstruction requires a reckoning with past wrongs. Rotondi and Eisikovits question this "memory assumption," almost axiomatic in writings about transitional justice, which dictates that a violent past *must* be addressed in any process of transition. The received view underlying much of

14 Waldron, J. 2001. "Superseding Historical Injustice." *Ethics* 1/103: 4–28.

15 Sikkink, K. 2011. *The Justice Cascade*. New York: Norton.

16 See, for example, Ben-Josef Hirsch, M. 2012. "Ideational Change and the Emergence of the International Norm of Truth and Reconciliation Commissions." *European Journal of International Relations*. Accessed August 15, 2014. http://ejt.sagepub.com/content/early/2013/07/09/1354066113484344.full.pdf+html.

17 Hansen, T.O. 2011. "Transitional Justice: Toward a Differentiated Theory." *Oregon Review of International Law* 1: 10–13.

18 For a legal analysis of some of the most important cases in this respect see: Sweeney, J. 2012. *The European Court of Human Rights in the post-Cold War Era: Universality in Transition*. London: Routledge.

19 The historical antecedent of the self-defending democracy principle was the "*wehrhafte Demokratie*" principle adopted in the post-Nazi Gemany transition.

20 See respectively: Elster, J. 2004. *Closing the Books: Transitional Justice in Historical Perspective*. Cambridge: Cambridge University Press; Teitel, R. 2000. *Transitional Justice*. Oxford: Oxford University Press.

the literature is that impunity, burial of the past, unaccountability, not only impede transition but also exacerbate the divide between victims and oppressors. But is this always and unconditionally true? The authors argue that under specific circumstances, a (qualified) argument for not remembering can be formulated. They consider three cases in which the memory assumption is problematic:

1. post-conflict societies that evidence a widespread cultural ambivalence about policies of accountability for past wrongs;
2. conflicts where there is an immensely complicated division of guilt between the parties; and
3. political situations where an insistence on immediate commemoration and thorough accountability risks reigniting the conflict.

Like Rotondi and Eisikovits, Lawther is also interested in the possibility of a transition without addressing past wrongs. Based on over 40 semi-structured interviews conducted with groups and individuals involved in the decades-long conflict in Northern Ireland, Lawther wonders if it is possible to achieve peace without excavating the past. More importantly, can silencing the past be beneficial rather than detrimental to stability? The question is taken up in the Northern Irish context, where transitional justice mechanisms have been implemented in the absence of a clear truth process. Commenting insightfully about the role of trust in any policy of post-war truth-telling, the author provides both a set of interpretations for why truth-telling was neglected in the Northern Irish transition and of the possibilities that picking it up could generate.

The second part of the book takes up the subject of punishment (and refraining from punishment) in a process of transition. Espindola articulates a two-pronged attack on Carl Schmitt's famous argument for amnesties in the aftermath of World War II: Schmitt's defense fails to take into account the moral importance of retributive sentiments and the possibility of channeling them into productive responses by means of transitional policies. More devastatingly, Schmitt's support of amnesties is inconsistent with much else in his writing—primarily the insistence that political communities have the exclusive ability to identify who their own enemies are and treat them accordingly. As Espindola puts it: "Schmittian amnesties violate Schmitt's own principle of epistemic privilege of political communities with respect to the paradigmatic political decision about how the enemy should be dealt with."

Murphy's chapter provides us with a sophisticated and important comparison between the aims and scope of retributive and transitional justice. She argues that the retributive justification for punishment, quite coherent in settled contexts, does not hold up in circumstances of political transition. If, as part of our transitional policy, we are to punish those associated with a deposed authoritarian regime (and Murphy accepts that such punishments can be appropriate) the justification for punishment cannot be purely retributive. Murphy sets several tasks for any theory of punishment in transitional settings. Chief among these are determining how a perpetrator becomes liable for punishment (though the wrongs he is accused of may well have been legal at the time of commission), why the new state should try to punish under transitional circumstances and whether/how it can do so effectively.

Part III examines the potential (or lack thereof) of transitional policies to bring about lasting structural change and to truly mold a new polity's economic and constitutional institutions. Taking her bearings from Young's understanding of responsibility as based in structural injustices (i.e. we are responsible not only for our specific acts but also for participating in, benefiting from and upholding structural distortions in our political system), Thomason sketches a theory of transitional justice as structural justice. Her account focuses on the background conditions that led to strife in the first place rather than on particular acts of violence. As she puts it, "Structural injustice occurs when institutions and systems work in such a way to disadvantage large groups of people while allowing others to benefit. Structural justice, then, would require that institutions and systems work to ensure that large groups of people are not disadvantaged." The main task of transitional justice policies according to such a model is to end or prevent wide-scale disenfranchisement of certain groups. This involves identifying (and abolishing) the institutions and practices that contributed to the disenfranchisement in the past and constructing the kind of institutions that would be less likely to engage in it again.

Phillips argues, convincingly, that settler states, often created at terrible human and material cost to indigenous populations, must concentrate their transitional justice efforts on the political empowerment of the groups they have dispossessed. Transitional measures must "allow indigenous populations the right to participate, as an equal, in the resolution of justice claims." Such a commitment calls for looking beyond the relatively narrow focus of truth commissions, war crime trials, or compensation programs to claims about "political" or "constitutional" justice arising from the original wrongdoing and dispossession. Phillips considers two case studies and argues that Australia has failed to address such questions of political and constitutional justice when it comes to the status of the aboriginal population, while New Zealand's approach to the plight of the Maori shows far greater promise. The chapter is significant not only for its insistence on the centrality of political and constitutional justice but also for the implied argument expanding the scope of transitional justice to states (like Australia and New Zealand) no longer in the acute throws of a transition.

McAuliffe's chapter, an exemplary exercise in non-ideal theory, gives us an account of why transitional justice often falls short of its ambitions to effect structural change in new democracies. The belief that transitional justice can transform the pathological economic structures of countries undergoing transition depends on the flawed assumption that transitional policies can be lifted wholesale "from standard blueprints." And this, in spite of much scholarly work that supposes otherwise, cannot be done. McAuliffe's chapter seeks to explain why it is that transitional justice does not carry the kind of limitless potential for redistributing resources and ushering in an era of greater socioeconomic fairness. The explanation is solidly grounded in the political economy of transitions and among the chief reasons he identifies is the reluctance of old power elites to relinquish economic advantage (a reluctance bolstered by their lingering strength and leverage) and the difficulty, (see the case of Afghanistan) at least in some contexts, to extend central power beyond the capital city.

The next section explores the nature and limits of political reconciliation, which many consider as the telos or aim of transitional policies. Taking her bearings from the writings of Auschwitz survivor Jean Améry, Hunt provides a defense of resentment as a response to wrongdoing. She suggests that resentment can be interpreted as a source for victims' empowerment whenever the sentiment is acknowledged by a community of survivors. The author explores the paradoxical possibility of *reconcilable resentment*—a form of resentment that can be productive for political reconciliation. One possible avenue of understanding resentment along these lines is viewing it as one legitimate, non-exclusive option available in transition (alongside, e.g., forgiveness). Here the author is in dialogue with Brudholm's important work on the subject. The upshot of such a legitimization of resentment is that even in the case of an agreed policy of forgiveness, a "right to resent" must be recognized as a means of criticizing policies of normalization.

Metz offers a novel and important theory of national reconciliation based in African ideas about community. His version of communitarianism illuminates the relationship between different elements of political reconstruction, including truth-telling, apology, forgiveness, compensation and amnesty. For Metz the understanding of community (and, consequently, how to rebuild a community) turns on two relationships: "identity" and "solidarity." The former asks us to "share a way of life" with others; the latter requires that we be willing to act for the benefit of our compatriots.

Metz argues that the requirements of reconciliation are behavioral rather than attitudinal. Genuine community does not require us to *feel* like we forgive or love others. It just asks us to behave as if we are beginning to belong to the same group as they do.

Mookherjee puts forward an account of political reconciliation based on Sen's Capabilities Approach. Steering clear of the debate between a thick idea of political reconciliation, (unpalatable to most liberal theorists as it aggressively promotes a single idea of the good) and thin conceptions (based on the creation of civic trust where the goal is simply the institutionalization of impartiality), she offers a third possibility: Reconciliation-as-Agency. The approach adopted here aims at the re-imagination of all relevant actors as human beings who can pursue a plurality of goals beyond simple subsistence.

The fifth section of the book explores the relationship between transitional justice and artistic expressions and practices. Bahun's chapter provides us with a magisterial survey of how art interacts with transitional mechanisms. She argues that the arts can enhance the scope and impact of transitional justice efforts; she also insists that under some circumstances they can undermine these efforts. Beginning with the premise that art practices, formative of a nation's culture, can be both implicated in past abuses and crucial for future transformation, Bahun gives us a taxonomy of how different art forms interact with different types of transitional policies. The argument provides powerful evidence for the understudied force of the arts and how they represent past wrongs, highlight the weaknesses and absurdities in a process of transition and also contribute to the amelioration, and perhaps even eventual repair, of fraught social ties. Towards the end of her chapter, Bahun gives us useful methodological guidance for studying the role of the arts in transitions, stressing the importance of a comparative approach.

Mihai's chapter 'Democratic "Sacred Spaces": Public Architecture and Transitional Justice', considers how newly established democracies should deal with architecture created by a deposed authoritarian regime. Following Levinson's notion of "sacred space" as a structuring of the social order, the author takes up the problem of structures that were erected to aggrandize a troubling ideology or to communicate a sense of collective humiliation. Two cases are analyzed: South Africa's Voortrekker monument – a racist edifice celebrating the 'civilization' of the Zulus by the white Trekkers—and the Romanian Civic Centre, an architectural complex declaring the supremacy of Ceauşescu. The respective transitional polities are judged to have mishandled these old monuments, each failing to neutralize or sufficiently address the weight of humiliation that the structures carry.

Part VI offers philosophical accounts of key operative concepts pertaining to transitions: time, genocide, and political repair. Corradetti's "Transitional Times, Reflective Judgment and the 'Hōs mē' Condition" brings together Agamben's notion of temporality and Kant's idea of reflective judgment to demonstrate the essential interdependence of restorative and retributive justice in transitional societies. The synthesis of past and present implicit in Agamben's understanding of eschatological time suggests a more subtle conception of justice than a traditional chronological approach can provide. According to Corradetti, temporality as interpreted by Agamben offers a crucial, although mostly overlooked, framework for theories of transitional justice. Corradetti argues that Kant's notion of reflective judgment is particularly relevant in this temporal perspective because it is capable of addressing past wrongdoing while at the same time focusing on the future construction of identity. The larger aim of Corradetti's argument is to show that it is possible to maintain the normative aspect of justice while at the same time focusing on the complex circumstances that characterize political transitions.

Building on her previous work, Card asks us to think through the conceptual implications of understanding genocide as "social death" or the loss of social vitality. By social vitality is meant "the meanings, shapes, and contents given the lives of individuals by social relationships, personal and institutional, contemporary and inter-generational, that unite them into a people … " Her account poses a series of fascinating puzzles: does the elimination of an evil group like, for example the KKK, count as genocide (since its evil practices do impart meaning to the lives of its members)? Does the prosecution of groups constituted on specific attributes of the members (such as sexual orientation or gender) count as genocide (as these groupings also account for social vitality)? What does the social death thesis tell us about the relationship between the quantity of people killed and the quality of ties destroyed?

Walker's chapter provides an important philosophical account of the undertheorized and underutilized transitional instrument of reparations. The contemporary discussion of reparative justice lacks a clear terminology and seems to assume that repair for past wrongs is impossible. In practice, reparations are the least popular instrument of transitional justice, and when they are used very little attention is paid to the actual needs of victims. Walker offers a novel and compelling relational view of reparations. These must be "about demonstrating (rather than establishing) relations of accountability and reciprocity … " Any meaningful attempt at reparations should address the material needs of victims (and it is important that victims participate in defining these), acknowledge wrongs perpetrated, and signal willingness to base future relationships on mutual accountability and responsibility.

The book's seventh and last section takes up two case studies, one ancient, and the other contemporary, which provide a unique inductive perspective on how transitions should be shaped. Taking his bearings from the democratic reconstruction of Athens after the abortive rule of the Thirty Tyrants (403 BCE), Gowder argues that new democracies should stick to their original decisions about how to handle past crimes and must create the political institutions to help them do so. Such steadfastness cements public commitment to the rule of law and provides an outlet for lawful participation in political life. More precisely, for Gowder, the commitment to our post-war policies and the design of institutions necessary for carrying them out, are what it means to create the rule of law in a new democracy. And without signaling that the rule of law is to be taken seriously, the new state cannot protect itself against the resurgence of the old power elites that have just been ousted.

Building on her research into Rwanda's post genocide transition, Tirrell argues, compellingly, that a coherent and successful transition policy must focus on retributive justice, public truth-telling, focused reparations and economic development. Ultimately, it is the combination of these factors that can restore the dignity of victims and begin to mend what she has called, elsewhere, "recognition harm." Since these areas of focus are mutually enhancing, it is only their interdependence that has the potential to generate lasting and stable peace. As Tirrell puts it: "Punishment of offenders and material repair are each individually insufficient for this task, but when combined with economic development and enhanced protection of human rights, there are better odds of creating a social and political system in which all have a voice, one which offers a shared narrative that fosters mutual recognition."

All in all, these sections suggest key areas for further theoretical investigation where it is likely that a convergence of scholarly interest will occur in the near future. As mentioned, we are witness to a multiplicity of state and legal transformations which are not only affecting interstate relations, but also questioning the mission and the scope of competences for international organizations such as the UN and the EU policies, the Council of Europe's functions and internal power balancing or even the more prominent role that some regional organizations are assuming as a result of the proactive role of the International Criminal Court. The multiplicity of factors involved in state and regional transformations require a new understanding of justice in times of transition.[21] This

21 One of the pioneering books in this respect was Kritz, N.J. (ed.) 1995. *Transitional Justice. How Emerging Democracies Reckon with Former Regimes*. Washington D.C.: United States Institute of Peace Press.

is not only due to the numerous failures characterizing political responses to past atrocities but also the more complex dynamics now developing among different civil and institutional actors which contribute to formulate more adequate responses to the transformation of society and the rehabilitation of its basic conditions of fairness. Also, the methodological rethinking of justice in transitional times raises the question of what type of explanatory framework it aims to promote and also the question of "what do we expect" from a theory of transitional justice. Answers can vary but what cannot be ignored is that the international community is called to play an ever more decisive role in ending impunity and injustice. The fragility of transitions, the reversibility and tentativeness of any perceived "successes," as well as the growing complexity of interactions between local, international, modern and traditional institutions involved, requires that we achieve as much conceptual clarity as possible about transitions. We hope this volume answers some questions about how to understand transitional times and what can be expected, morally, practically and legally from post-war processes. As many of the chapters in this book argue, remaking a state is a thankless and all too often tragic task. To offer any assistance, however small, to those engaged in this Herculean task is a great reward indeed.

Boston-Oslo, July 2014

Claudio Corradetti, Nir Eisikovits, and Jack Volpe Rotondi

PART I

Is it Always Necessary to Account For Past Wrongs?

Chapter 1
Forgetting after War: A Qualified Defense

Jack Volpe Rotondi and Nir Eisikovits

Remembering: An Article of Faith

Milan Kundera's *The Book of Laughter and Forgetting* begins with a description of two communist party leaders, Gottwald and Clementis, standing next to each other on a porch in Prague. Gottwald is about to give a speech. It is winter and he does not have a hat. Clementis takes off his own hat and gives it to his comrade. A few years later, Clementis falls out of favor and is accused of treason. He is removed from official photographs. All that remains of him is the hat on Gottwald's head. "The struggle of man against power is the struggle of memory against forgetting," comments Mirek, Kundera's protagonist.[1]

The discipline of transitional justice focuses on the question of how nations can best own up to a past of political violence: once the killing subsides, what does it take for parties to account for their old crimes and make a transition to civil society? What are the institutional ways of dealing with the past? What are the legal, moral, and political problems involved in the operation of bodies such as truth commissions, war crime tribunals, or lustration panels? How is their efficacy to be assessed? What role should indigenous practices have in the design of transitional policies? And what about reparations? Who should pay? Who should receive the payments? What counts as payment in the first place? There is much disagreement about these questions. However, one thing the scholars and practitioners of transitional justice do agree about is that the past *must* be dealt with. We might call this "the memory assumption." With Mirek, they assume that forgetting, not dealing with the past, or, to paraphrase Cambodia's Prime Minister Hun Sen, digging a hole and burying the past, is toxic.[2] Such suppression, we are told, is an act of brute force. It solves nothing. It merely exacerbates injustice, fuels a culture of impunity, and creates a reservoir of unprocessed resentment on the part of victims and their families, always bubbling close to the surface, ready to explode at the first instance of political unrest.

This chapter takes up the question of forgetting after war. While acknowledging the powerful rationale for robust policies of transitional justice it will argue that remembering cannot be an article of faith. We will try to make a limited and qualified case for forgetting, or at least raise some questions about the axiomatic nature of the "memory assumption." First, however, let us briefly explore the case for that assumption.

The Case for Remembering

At least as far back as John Locke's famous account of personal identity in "An Essay Concerning Human Understanding," modern Western political thought has been committed to the view that

1 Milan Kundera, *The Book of Laughter and Forgetting* (New York: HarperCollins, 1999), 4.

2 Seth Mydans, "Cambodian Leader Resists Punishing Top Khmer Rouge," *New York Times*, December 29, 2001, http://www.nytimes.com/1998/12/29/world/cambodian-leader-resists-punishing-top-khmer-rouge.html?src=pm.

memory is central to our ability to perceive ourselves, as ourselves, through time. Our memories are constitutive of who we are and, as a result, it is crucial to have others listen to (and, ideally, acknowledge and reflect) our understanding of our past. Having our history suppressed, destroyed, or hidden amounts to severe violence against the core of our identity.[3]

In his essay "Superseding Historical Injustice," Jeremy Waldron makes one of the most compelling contemporary cases for the importance of memory in the face of historical injustice. He offers three reasons why we must, institutionally and otherwise, strive to memorialize what we have done to others and what they have done to us.[4] First, "our moral understanding of the past is often a way of bringing to imaginative life the full implications of principles to which we are already in theory committed."[5] Remembering allows us to take our moral principles seriously as it gives us a particular historical context to think about how they apply in practice. Rational but abstract moral "principles" are insufficient; a contextual sensibility which maps current "circumstances and entanglements" to representative past "temptations" is essential for living, breathing people to "face moral danger."[6]

Waldron then goes on to illuminate the relationship between "identity and contingency," suggesting that, "[w]hat happened might have been otherwise, and, just because of that, it is not something one can reason back to if what actually took place has been forgotten or concealed."[7] Quite simply, if the past is not remembered, there is no way of rationally reconstructing it on the basis of counterfactual reasoning. Once it is gone, it is gone. Deduction yields nothing about how Jews acted in the Warsaw ghetto, the participation of women in the Rwandan genocide or Native American ideas of property in the fifteenth century.

Finally, Waldron explains how forgetting can be implicated in the creation and perpetuation of unjust social relations:

> When we are told to let bygones be bygones, we need to bear in mind also that the forgetfulness urged on us is seldom the blank slate of historical oblivion. Thinking quickly fills up the vacuum with plausible tales of self-satisfaction, on the one side, and self-deprecation on the other. Those who as a matter of fact benefited from their ancestors' injustice will persuade themselves readily enough that their good fortune is due to the virtue of their race, while the descendants of their victims may too easily accept the story that they and their kind were always good for nothing. In the face of all this, only the deliberate enterprise of recollection (the enterprise we call "history"), coupled with the most determined sense that there is a difference between what happened and what we would like to think happened, can sustain the moral and cultural reality of self and community.[8]

In other words, a refusal to remember can create stereotypes and structures of subjugation. Without the benefit of history, those who find themselves disadvantaged lack the context to make sense of their predicament and may come to see it as reflective of some innate deficiency. Conversely,

3 John Locke, *An Essay Concerning Human Understanding* (Indianapolis, IN: Hackett, 1996). On the damage that lack of recognition of our history can entail see also: Charles Taylor, *Multiculturalism and the Politics of Recognition* (Princeton, NJ: Princeton University Press, 1992), 25.

4 Jeremy Waldron, "Superseding Historic Injustice," *Ethics*, 103(1) (1992): http://www.jstor.org/stable/2381493. It is important to note that this discussion of the importance of memory appears in the beginning of an essay that claims that historical entitlements can fade over time. But Waldron's innovative argument suggests that there is a distinction between the case for remembering and the political entitlements that have been compromised by historical injustice. While the latter may fade or become "superseded" this is not the case with the former.

5 Ibid., 5.

6 Ibid.

7 Ibid., 6.

8 Ibid.

those who find themselves on top may justify their fortunes by making reference to ahistorical abstractions and fantasies about "manifest destiny" or "natural right."[9]

Transitional justice scholars make the case for remembering after war in more concrete terms. We must, they insist, account for historical injustices because burying the past is a profound injustice to victims and because forgetting oppression perpetuates a culture of impunity. Martha Minow, in *Between Vengeance and Forgiveness*, ascribes the "most appalling goal" to the perpetrators of twentieth century atrocity: "the destruction of the remembrance of individuals as well as of their lives and dignity."[10] Intentional regime-sponsored forgetting as well as flawed transitional justice efforts have adversely affected discrete and very real human lives. Nir Eisikovits describes one such case in his *Sympathizing with the Enemy*. Forgetting, he writes:

> compounds the suffering of individuals by forcing them to watch their tormentors walk around freely, reenter politics, or maintain their posts in public service and the military. All of this takes place while their painful memories and traumas remain unacknowledged. Amanda Pike, a reporter for PBS' Frontline, tells a story which starkly demonstrates the cost of forgetfulness for individual victims. During a trip through the Cambodian province of Pailin, Pike came across Samrith Phum, whose husband was executed by the Khmer Rouge. Phum knows the murderer well. He is her neighbor and he operates a noodle shop across the street from her house. He was never arrested and never charged with her husband's murder. There is no procedure through which he can be sued for damages. Phum must simply get used to the idea that her husband's killer quietly manages his store next door.[11]

Transitional justice writers also share a broad consensus that some form of accountability helps nurture budding non-authoritarian institutions. In other words, forcing perpetrators of past human rights abuses to face their crimes allows a new democracy to start off on the right foot—such accounting conveys the message that from now on human lives are once again valuable enough to receive the law's attention—and this, in the transition from an authoritarian regime that did not display such respect—is a very important message to be sending.

Is Forgetting Ever Admissible?

To what extent do the philosophical and practical arguments sketched above support the strong presumption in favor of historical remembering? Are there cases where the possibility of not

9 The same commitment to memory as a moral project is evident in recent works by Avishai Margalit and Tony Judt. In *The Ethics of Memory*, though he cites the risk of memory-propagating institutions that are "bureaucratic and soulless," Margalit makes the case that "radical evil consists … of acts that undermine the very foundation of morality itself" and constitute "a direct onslaught on the very idea of shared humanity." While acknowledging that it is "immeasurably difficult" to build a credible universal shared memory, Margalit asserts that "gross crimes against humanity" should serve as "minimal shared moral memories." Judt decries the public treatment of twentieth century barbarity as "a pedagogically serviceable Chamber of Historical Horrors." Remembering in the wrong way might convince us "that all of *that* is now behind us, that its meaning is clear, and that we may now advance—unencumbered by past errors—into a different and better era." Nevertheless, though he warns against the fruitless memorialization of atrocity, his *Reappraisals* is a thoughtful paean to the "perennial complexity" and cardinal virtue of historical memory. Avishai Margalit, *The Ethics of Memory* (Cambridge, MA: Harvard University Press, 2002). Tony Judt, *Reappraisals: Reflections on the Forgotten Twentieth Century* (New York: Penguin, 2008).

10 Martha Minow, *Between Vengeance and Forgiveness: Facing History after Genocide and Mass Violence* (Boston, MA: Beacon, 1998), 1.

11 Nir Eisikovits, *Sympathizing with the Enemy: Reconciliation, Transitional Justice, Negotiation* (Dordrecht, the Netherlands, and St. Louis, MO: Republic of Letters Publishing, 2010), 37.

addressing the past needs to be taken more seriously? There are two ways of approaching these questions. The first is to undermine the rationale for remembering presented above. The second, more tentative and modest approach, is to identify some cases in which there is an argument for not remembering. We shall pursue the second strategy. While we think there are strong grounds for the memory assumption, it is important to avoid turning it into a dogma. Our concern is that much of the recent literature treats it as such. We propose to look at three cases in which the memory assumption is problematic: conflicts with significant cultural variance on the question of how best to deal with the past; conflicts where there is a complicated division of guilt between the parties; and political situations where an insistence on commemoration and thorough accountability risks reigniting the conflict.

In selecting these categories we draw on the work of Priscilla Hayner. In her canonical work on truth commissions, *Unspeakable Truths: Confronting State Terror and Atrocity*, Hayner outlines four components which "would account for this lack of desire to formally establish the truth."[12] The first involves "fear of negative consequences."[13] She defines this as "a perception that violence would increase, war could return, or that the current violence or war would not end, if old crimes were revisited."[14] Hayner's second and third categories are, respectively, *lack of political interest* ("little or no interest by the political leadership in truth-seeking and a lack of significant nongovernmental actors pushing them to do so") and *other urgent priorities* (including "extensive destruction resulting from the war or violence, widespread popular sentiment to focus on survival and rebuilding, and a lack of basic institutional structures that could support a truth-seeking process.")[15] Hayner's fourth and final category addresses "alternative mechanisms or preferences" and focuses on cultural variance about remembering.[16] She describes this as "indigenous national characteristics [which] may make truth-seeking unnecessary or undesirable, such as unofficial community-based mechanisms that respond to the recent violence or a culture that eschews confronting conflict directly."[17]

Hayner's first and fourth categories are important and useful. In what follows we expand on them and try to offer at least the beginning of a philosophical argument for the legitimacy of using them. To these we add the category of cases with a complicated division of guilt. While Hayner considers some such cases she does not view these circumstances as creating a separate argument to forego policies of transitional justice. Hayner's second and third categories, however, present significant problems and, as a result, cannot be included in a putative case for official forgetting. For one thing both categories raise the problem of political agreement. We shall have more to say about this in section 4, but let us provide a preview here: to justify foregoing efforts of transitional justice, there has to be a significant degree of social consensus about the lack of political interest and about the relative importance of alternative priorities. In other words, in such cases it is not enough that the political class has no interest in digging up the past (as its lack of interest may be due to the wrong reasons) or that it has decided that there are other more important things than digging up the past (again, because the priorities of the political class may be informed by problematic considerations). If these two categories are to *justify* foregoing efforts of transitional justice there must be substantive level of agreement about the judgments they

12 Priscilla Hayner, *Unspeakable Truths: Confronting State Terror and Atrocity* (New York: Routledge, 2001), 185–6. We are not seeking to equate "forgetting" with not "formally establish[ing] the truth"; however, some form of confronting the truth about heinous acts is found across the transitional justice toolbox continuum.

13 Ibid.

14 Ibid.

15 Ibid.

16 Ibid.

17 Ibid.

contain. Furthermore, the employment of the category of "other urgent priorities" presupposes that coming to terms with the past and tending to other priorities are mutually exclusive efforts. Two observations are in order about this assumption. First, some ways of addressing past wrongs are more expensive than others. War crime trials and truth commissions with limited mandates cost less to operate than those with expansive authority. Commissions of historical inquiry are cheaper to run than truth commissions. And so on. In other words, efforts to come to terms with the past can be designed in a cost sensitive manner with other priorities in mind (and with the awareness that a reduced effort will probably yield less comprehensive results). More importantly, there may well be a link between a commitment to truth-telling and the ability to build sustainable and legitimate institutions (even given countervailing risks as we shall explore). If foregoing transitional justice is likely to lead to resentment on the part of those victimized by the previous regime, such sentiments would undermine or threaten the viability of the new institutions that have been designated as a more urgent priority. In this sense, efforts of transitional justice and institution or nation-building are mutually enhancing. A government willing to address past wrongs may well enjoy more public trust when it begins to create new institutions. And its ability to create fair, competent and effective new institutions may help to gradually convince the public that the past really is in the past.

Cultural Variance about Remembering

Much of the appeal of the memory assumption lies in its usefulness for overcoming trauma. Remembering is said to be key because of the purported healing benefits of truth-telling and the airing out of the past.[18] Is this therapeutic understanding of memory, influenced as it is by the basic assumptions of psychodynamic theory, equally applicable in all cultural contexts?[19] Is it, in other words, a universal human truth that "the truth sets us free" (or at least helps us feel better and overcome trauma) or are there cultural contexts in which truth-telling and the public, open discussion of atrocities are viewed with more skepticism? In *Contemporary Conflict Resolution*, Ramsbotham, Woodhouse, and Miall maintain that "some societies seem able to 'forgive and forget' much more easily than others, and to achieve full reconstitution of relations between former enemies without having to go through the travails of justice, perhaps for cultural reasons—amnesia is the chosen path to reconciliation."[20] Hayner agrees that "there may be cases in which a 'truth always' recommendation is not appropriate, or at least in which a recommendation for a formal and official truth-telling project such as a truth commission might be inappropriate."[21]

Rosalind Shaw's 2005 "Special Report" on Sierra Leone, raises the difficulty thus: "Sierra Leone's TRC [Truth and Reconciliation Commission], like South Africa's ... valorized a particular kind of memory practice: 'truth-telling', the public recounting of memories of violence. This valorization, however, is based on deeply problematic assumptions about the purportedly universal

---

18 See Minow and Hayner among others cited here.

19 There is some disagreement about this assumption across multiple disciplines. Rosalind Shaw offers the following formulation rejecting the national-personal healing analogy: what, however, is national healing? The idea of healing a nation that is wounded or traumatized is primarily nation-building rhetoric that anthropomorphizes the nation as a feeling, suffering entity, as Brandon Hamber and Richard Wilson have noted. This notion derives from nineteenth-century models of society as akin to an organism that can be healthy or sick. Such biological models for societies have, however, long been discredited. While mass violence certainly disrupts and transforms social institutions and practices, it is not valid to conceptualize these changes in terms of a damaged collective national psyche that can be healed through a cathartic process of truth-telling [see note 16]. Also: Eisikovits, *Sympathizing with the Enemy*, 123–4.

20 Oliver Ramsbotham, Tom Woodhouse and Hugh Miall, *Contemporary Conflict Resolution* (Cambridge: Polity Press, 2005), 235.

21 Hayner, *Unspeakable Truths*, 184.

benefits of the verbal recounting of past violence."[22] She considers the genesis of this brand of remembering:

> Such commissions and the truth-telling that characterizes them became an especially significant weapon against human rights abuses in the 1970s and 1980s, most notably during the Reagan era. During this period certain repressive Latin American regimes that were U.S. allies knew that if they wished to retain U.S. support, they could not use overt forms of violence. Instead, they developed deniable forms of repression and violence, such as disappearances and death squads (as Aryeh Neier, among others, has noted). Truth-telling thus became a tool used against covert, state-sponsored crimes to reveal clandestine violence, to establish the accountability of political and military leaders, and to publicly acknowledge the previously silenced stories of victims. In such contexts, the public recounting of memories of violence was a redemptive process.[23]

This model, however, is not necessarily efficacious in every post-conflict scenario; further, it is also not necessarily accepted, and can be at loggerheads with indigenous cultural preferences:

> Different regions and localities, moreover, have their own memory practices and often their own techniques of social recovery that may have developed during the course of their own history. How do these practices intersect with public truth-telling during a truth commission? … In Sierra Leone, this question was especially important, since the imperative to remember violence during the TRC was at odds with widespread local techniques of healing and reintegration, which are based on the *social forgetting* of violence.[24]

In Mozambique such practices were similarly prevalent and widely accepted. In fact, compared to adjacent South Africa, Mozambique approached reconciliation in almost a diametrically opposed manner: "[I]f in South Africa there was a widely accepted position, at least at the beginning of its truth commission's operations, that 'the more truth, the more we talk about the past, then the more reconciliation', in Mozambique the accepted, though largely unstated belief was 'the less we dwell on the past, the more likely reconciliation will be'."[25] In Mozambique, the process of reconciliation was incredibly swift:

> Stories abound of how soldiers of the two warring sides put down weapons and greeted their opponents as brothers … [a]s the war ended, national and international organizations were concerned with creating mechanisms to reinforce peace at the local level, but found their initiatives were not needed … Jose Luis Cabaco, the former Frelimo government official [said] "our ideas were only confusing and stirring up trouble."[26]

Complications with Apportioning Guilt

The second case in which the memory assumption runs into difficulty involves conflicts with a complicated division of responsibility. Under these circumstances it may be practically impossible to

---

22 Rosalind Shaw, "Forgive and Forget: Rethinking Memory in Sierra Leone's Truth and Reconciliation Commission," United States Institute of Peace, presentation, April 29, 2004, http://www.usip.org/events/forgive-and-forget-rethinking-memory-sierra-leones-truth-and-reconciliation-commission.

23 Ibid.

24 Ibid.

25 Hayner, *Unspeakable Truths*, 187.

26 Ibid., 190–91.

provide an account of past wrongs because of the difficulty of figuring out who did what to whom. Perhaps more significantly, the very acknowledgment of such complexity –the knowledge that everyone did everything to everyone else– may impact the motivation of parties to come to terms with the past. When many of those involved understand that they or those close to them were both perpetrators and victims of massive atrocities, the drive to neatly sort out guilt and innocence may well diminish.

Consider, again, the aftermath of the civil war in Mozambique. Hayner tells us that "those who have watched Mozambique over the past twenty years describe it as experiencing one of the most brutal wars the world has seen."[27] But surprisingly, an accounting of past abuses was not countenanced: "In a country where some 1 million civilians were killed, thousands tortured, and some of the most gruesome acts of mutilation and barbarism documented, there have been virtually no calls on the national level for justice, accountability, punishment or banishment from public office … "[28] Why?

Roberto Luis, a Mozambican development specialist who works closely with rural communities, put it succinctly: "Who would retaliate against whom? There wasn't one group against another. Families and communities were put against each other. If it was one ethnic or language group against another, then maybe you could see it. But it's hard to think how retaliation would be mobilized. It was the Browns versus the Smiths—but even then families were split up."[29]

In other words, accounting for what happened during the war years in Mozambique was complicated by the particularly chaotic nature of that conflict. Any attempt at transitional justice would implicate a great number of people on all sides. It would require a tremendous amount of resources and time. It would tear families apart even further. And, most importantly, it would be unlikely to produce a legally or historically coherent narrative. In the rare cases when countries devolve so profoundly into the proverbial Hobbesian State of Nature that the very concepts of guilt, perpetrators and victims lose much of their meaning—how much force does the memory assumption hold? In her famous criticism of Jaspers' account of German "collective responsibility" for the Holocaust, Arendt wrote that "where all are guilty none is."[30] She meant that guilt had to be tied with individual agency and that the term was diminished if it was allowed to encompass those who simply stood by or were not aware of what they should have known. But what of cases where actual, individualized guilt is almost universal? When an incomprehensible number on all sides is actually guilty of specific acts? Does the rationale of carefully sorting out and documenting such acts still hold? It must be emphasized that we are speaking about an extreme case. Many post-war contexts present a complicated division of responsibility. The ANC committed acts of terrorism against South African civilians in the course of its struggle.[31] Paul Kagame's Tutsi militias committed atrocities as they made their bid to reclaim Rwanda.[32] But in both cases there was a historically coherent story that could and had to be told about who was the main instigator

27 Ibid., 187.

28 Ibid.

29 Ibid., 189.

30 Hannah Arendt, *On Violence* (San Diego, CA: Harcourt Brace & Co., 1970), 65. The exact quote is: "Where all are guilty, no one is; confessions of collective guilt are the best possible safeguard against the discovery of culprits, and the very magnitude of the crime the best excuse for doing nothing." also see: "Personal responsibility under dictatorship," *The Listener* 6 (1964): http://web.ics.purdue.edu/~other1/Hannah%20Arendt%20-%20Personal%20Responsibility%20Under%20Dictatorship.pdf.

31 Minow, *Between Vengeance and Forgiveness*, 52.

32 Richard Grant, "Paul Kagame: Rwanda's Redeemer or Ruthless Dictator?," *The Telegraph*, July 22, 2010, http://www.telegraph.co.uk/news/worldnews/africaandindianocean/rwanda/7900680/Paul-Kagame-Rwandas-redeemer-or-ruthless-dictator.html.

of the conflict and who committed crimes that were incidental to a legitimate struggle in the name of self-determination and self-defense.

Reigniting Violence

Finally, let us consider circumstances of extreme political volatility. Are there situations where politically sanctioned forgetting may be the only viable alternative to renewed bloodshed? Mirek, Kundera's protagonist, is mostly correct. Usually the desire to forget after war is based on the wish of the guilty to wash themselves clean (or at least channel public attention away from their crimes). But what of cases where remembering, and seeking to apportion blame for the crimes of the past, even if morally requisite, is genuinely dangerous? Such cases raise the famous "peace vs. justice" question in its most extreme form. Political transitions often require compromises—a gentle balancing act between the need to bring human rights violators to book and the desire to ensure peace and social stability. South Africa's Truth and Reconciliation Commission was such a compromise—between the African National Congress which wanted Nuremberg-style tribunals for the masterminds and operatives of apartheid and the still militarily powerful National Party, who insisted on blanket amnesties.

Here the balancing point was located somewhere between full accountability and impunity—apartheid operatives (and ANC militants) would receive full amnesty in return for full disclosure of their actions.[33] A similar debate between the requirements of justice and the requirements of stability arose in the push to indict Omar Bashir for genocide.[34] Surely, the perpetrators of mass killings must be put on trial. On the other hand, what if the decision to indict them results in the exacerbation of violence? Again, unlike the scholars and activists of transitional justice, politicians usually insist that it is best to "look forward" rather than focus on excavating past crimes. And often this insistence is self-serving—meant to either deflect attention from their own complicity or questionable past record or to ensure the political status quo. But are there cases where the politicians have a point?

The circumstances of post-Franco Spain are illustrative. After Franco's death, the Spaniards decided they would not address atrocities committed during the civil war or those perpetrated by the fascists under Franco. Although there were many who dissented from this *pacto del olvido*, there was in fact a high degree of public and governmental consensus around it. Moreover, it worked:

> Until 1977, when democracy was introduced in Spain, it was dangerous to talk about the civil war and its aftermath. After that came a "pact of silence" which was endorsed on all sides. Fears of a new civil war and the longing for reconciliation called for collective silence. Virtually the entire political class, communists and moderate Basques included, wished to turn over a new leaf. The archives of the secret police were sealed. History lessons maintained the gap in the collective memory, year after year. In addition, just about everyone remained in their jobs, even the most faithful supporters of Franco and his dictatorship. There was no question at all of any trials … This strategy appears able to work miracles. Spain slipped apparently effortlessly into the world of stable democracies.[35]

---

33 For an overview see: Martin Meredith, *Coming to Terms: South Africa's Search for Truth* (New York: Public Affairs, 1999).

34 Krishanu Sengupta, "Peace or Justice?: The Dilemma of the International Criminal Court," *Lethbridge Undergraduate Research Journal*, 2008, Volume 3, Number 1.

35 Luc Huyse, *All Things Pass Except the Past* (Diestsesteenweg 71a-3010 Kessel-Lo: Luc Huyse & Uitgeverij Van Halewyck, 2009), 127–8.

The "fears of a new civil war" were not without merit: "in the five years after Franco's death, more than a hundred demonstrators, left-wing activists, students and separatists were killed by the police and the 'ultras', on the far right. Many more were killed by ETA and other left-wing or separatist terrorist groups … "[36] And so:

> Year after year, government after government, the "plot of silence" did its work. The country looked itself in the mirror and saw that all was well. Until, that is, the first questions began to arise in the late 1990s. Was it still necessary to keep the collective memory locked down? Was Spain not mature enough to confront its past without fear? Had the time not come to hunt down some of the myths that had grown up?[37]

The scholar Carlos Closa documents four phases in Spain's transition: 1975–1978—"enabling democracy," 1978–2002—"material equality," 2002–2008—"moral recognition," and, since 2008, "unchartered waters."[38] He suggests that the Spanish case "defies the belief that transitional justice is necessary for a successful transition to democracy and democratic consolidation."[39]

At the very least it is fair to acknowledge, as Hayner does, that "[d]igging into the details of past conflicts can be dangerous and destabilizing … and may disrupt fragile relationships in local communities recently returned to peace."[40]

The three types of cases we have outlined do not set up neatly distinct categories legitimizing forgetting. Rather they bleed into and sometime reinforce each other. For example, the fact that the division of responsibility was difficult to trace in Mozambique was likely to make an insistence on tracing it politically dangerous. And, surely, the cultural legitimacy afforded to some forms of 'forgetting' in that country played a role in heeding these fears of renewed violence over a need for retributive justice. Our aim in describing these categories is not to provide a sharp analytical tool with which to dissect different historical cases. With Aristotle, we think that there is a limit to just how sharp political tools can be. The idea is, rather, to provide a set of intersecting reference points that renders the choice of amnesia after war more plausible.

The Problem of Agreement

It is important to note that the post-conflict cases considered here involve a significant degree of agreement not to pursue justice for the past. It is this consent that makes such cases *prima facie* plausible candidates for forgetting. But what is the nature of such agreement? What does it mean, for example, for parties to agree that there is a complicated division of guilt between them? What does it mean that there is a cultural agreement not to pursue historical justice? What does it mean that there is agreement to not account for the past because the situation is too volatile? Is the agreement of political elites sufficient or is a more broadly based consensus required? What would the nature of such a consensus be? A super-majority? A simple majority? How would the relevant questions be formulated? These questions raise the familiar and complicated problem of identifying and articulating group intentions. We will bracket these difficulties here and assume

36 Giles Tremlett, *Ghosts of Spain: Travels through Spain and its Silent Past* (New York: Walker & Company, 2006), 77.

37 Huyse, *All Things Pass Except the Past*, 128.

38 Carlos Closa, "Transitional Justice in Spain," (presentation to the Center for European Studies, Harvard University, March 25, 2011).

39 Ibid.

40 Hayner, *Unspeakable Truths*, 185.

that we are dealing with cases where real, widespread agreement is present (either because it is reached between elites that enjoy political legitimacy, or by means of referenda, or the agreement is simply obvious to any fair-minded observer of the culture). However, does agreement always suggest that we must adhere to what the involved parties agreed?

Let us consider an analogy to domestic criminal wrongdoing. In such cases a perpetrator and a victim cannot decide to stop the criminal process on their own. As Eisikovits puts it elsewhere:

> in the domestic context, the fact that two sides to a conflict agree to bury the hatchet does not preclude their prosecution by the criminal justice authorities. Thus, if two neighboring families become entangled in a massive brawl, during which property on both sides is destroyed, and some injuries are sustained, the District Attorney's Office may decide to issue indictments, even if all of those who did the fighting would like to put the whole incident behind them. The criminal law is not a private matter completely at the discretion of citizens. The public has a stake in upholding the criminal law, and is understood to be an interested party whenever it is broken. After all, in the example provided above, wider interests were compromised: traffic may have been disturbed by the fighting, the small children of other neighbors may have been watching, publicly funded hospitals may have been called on to treat the injured, reports of the fight may have made their way into the news media bringing down house prices, etc. In short, the fight, almost any fight, has repercussions for third parties. That is why, in important ways, such fights are everyone's business. And that is why criminal cases are typically titled Commonwealth vs. Jones rather than Smith vs. Jones.[41]

Now, if agreement is not sufficient domestically, is there an argument to be made, on similar grounds, that it should not be sufficient when it comes to war crimes as defined by international law? Is there a public interest in international contexts that should compel polities to come to terms with the past in spite of an agreement to the contrary? Eisikovits writes:

> Are there any third party interests that may justify some kind of reckoning with mass atrocity, even if all of those involved would freely choose to put the past behind them? … First, [we must ask] who are the third parties whose interests are implicated by a decision … to bury the past? Could we argue that … a failure to address massive violations of human rights in location *X* (for whatever reason) may endanger human rights in location *Y* (by, say, bolstering the confidence of would-be perpetrators)? If so, the third party could be described, vaguely, as the international community, a community with a serious interest in creating a robust culture of human rights wherein violations are documented and addressed rather than simply ignored.[42]

But, he cautions:

> When all is said and done, it appears that the main difference between the domestic and international cases has to do with the consequences of the decision whether to use the courts. While in the domestic arena a failure to prosecute can result in increased cynicism about the law (and eventually in a weakening of the rule of law), imposing accountability in the aftermath of war may, under some circumstances, reignite violence. Insisting on doing justice in such cases recalls Lord Mansfield's famous dictum in the 1772 Somerset case: that justice must be done "though the

41 Eisikovits, "Transitional Justice," *Stanford Encyclopedia of Philosophy*, first published January 26, 2009, http://plato.stanford.edu/entries/justice-transitional/.

42 Ibid.

> heavens may fall." The trouble, of course, with this Kantian pronouncement is that there is no one to reap the fruits of justice after the heavens have fallen.[43]

In other words, the dilemma between maintaining stability and doing justice is more acute in the aftermath of war than it is in the domestic criminal context. In the former setting, initial stability may well require compromises of justice. Domestic criminal law, on the other hand, usually presupposes such stability. In the domestic setting, failure to prosecute undermines whatever stability has been achieved. In the international context, insistence on prosecuting may mean that the stability required for functional domestic institutions is never reached. Thus, our non-Kantian conclusion is that agreement to refrain from coming to terms with the past in transitional contexts must be given much more weight than in regular domestic settings exactly because it is an agreement to try to create a regular domestic setting which, in the future, will conform to our basic ideas of the rule of law.

The cases that we have outlined present a real challenge to the memory assumption because they fit within a liberal framework that values the consent of the involved parties. It is not obvious that these cases are susceptible to Mirek's accusation. When we choose not to remember for the reasons we have outlined, are we really engaged in an attempt to rewrite or erase history- or are we, rather, consciously indicating that there are times when it is not as useful to reclaim it as is usually assumed?

Conclusion

Transitional justice thinkers generally agree that the past must be dealt with: we called this "the memory assumption." There are unequivocal philosophical and practical foundations to support some form of remembering after atrocities have been perpetrated. However, we posed the question "Is remembering sacrosanct?" and attempted to make a limited and qualified case for forgetting. We considered three cases in which the memory assumption is problematic.

Through the cases of Sierra Leone and Mozambique, we considered how some cultures do not share a belief in the assumed reconciliatory powers of truth-telling. There are situations where indigenous approaches to forgetting are both preferred and more successful than court or commission-sponsored remembering. Second, cases where there is an extremely complicated division of responsibility provide a challenge to the dogma of remembering. And third, we considered situations, as in Spain, where there were legitimate, largely non-cynical reasons for foregoing transitional justice due to rational fears of reinstating massive violence.

The qualified case for forgetting we make here has particular legal implications. The ICC (International Criminal Court) has residual authority; this means that it has a mandate to act if, and only if, it determines that a member country is not addressing an atrocity. For some, this has raised questions about whether the ICC has the authority to get involved if a country chooses to address past atrocities by means substantially less robust than a war crime trial. But what about a country that decides (however we characterize what it means to decide in this context) to do nothing to address the past for the reasons we have outlined? Would such a decision justify the ICC's intervention? Should the ICC have the authority to override a reasonable decision to forget?

More broadly, customary international law has moved closer in recent years to acknowledging an individual right to truth. Bodies such as the Inter American Court of Human Rights, The Inter American Commission on Human Rights and the European Court of Human Rights have increasingly

43 Ibid.

been willing to recognize a responsibility on the part of the state to provide full information to victims about the circumstances under which they were abused (in addition to general information about patterns of injustice). Thus, for example, the 1988 *Velásquez Rodríguez* case handed down by the Inter-American Court of Human Rights stated that: "Even in the hypothetical case that those individually responsible for crimes of this type cannot be legally punished under certain circumstances, the State is obligated to use the means at its disposal to inform the relatives of the fate of the victims and as may be the case, the location of their remains."[44] How is the emergence of such a right impacted by a plausible, qualified case for forgetting after war? We hope that the argument made in this paper will give rise to further discussion of these questions.

There is of course, a darker way of taking up the question of forgetting after war, which does seem to raise the specter Mirek fears. Some writers, most notably the French thinker Ernest Renan, claim that new nations emerging from prolonged war must engage in a conscious, deliberate attempt to forget in order to forge an attractive national identity. He writes:

> Forgetting, I would even go so far as to say historical error, is a crucial factor in the creation of a nation, which is why progress in historical studies often constitutes a danger for [the principle of] nationality. Indeed, historical enquiry brings to light deeds of violence which took place at the origin of all political formations, even of those whose consequences have been altogether beneficial.[45]

Burke's famous remarks about throwing "a politic, well-wrought veil" over some of the events in the Glorious Revolution and his other famous claim in the *Reflections* that "To make us love our country, our country ought to be lovely" follow very much in the same vein.[46] More recently, Tony Judt has argued that Europe's recovery after the Second World War depended on the selective erasure of parts of its past.[47] Tom Segev writes persuasively about how the Israelis refused to discuss the details of the extermination of Jews in the Holocaust because these events did not fit in with the ethos of new Jewish masculinity that they were trying to create until the Eichmann trial came and rubbed this bit of history in their face.[48] Examples can be multiplied: American, Turkish, Canadian and many other national identities were built on selective historiography. But this insight is best understood descriptively. There is no policy recommendation here; just an observation, from a distance, on how our ideas of national character are formed (and deformed).

To some extent the observation is reflective of the nature of memory in general—all remembering involves forgetting. Telling a story about the past—even a meticulously fair story, requires, for its very coherence, a degree of editing, of leaving out. A great deal has been written on this, largely in the continental tradition, and a detailed discussion goes far beyond the scope of this paper.[49] Suffice

---

44 *Velásquez Rodríguez Case*, Inter-Am.Ct.H.R. (Ser. C) No. 4 (1988), Inter-American Court of Human Rights (IACrtHR), July 29, 1988, available at: http://www.unhcr.org/refworld/docid/40279a9e4.html. For good overviews of the development of the right to truth see: Gloria Park, "Truth as Justice: Legal and Extralegal Development of the Right to Truth," *Harvard International Review*, February 1, 2010. Also, Yasmin Naqvi, "The Right to the Truth in International Law: Fact or Fiction?," *International Review of the Red Cross*, Volume 88, Number 862, June 2006.

45 Ernest Renan, "Qu'est-ce qu'une nation?" ("first delivered as a lecturer at the Sorbonne in 1882"). http://www.nationalismproject.org/what/renan.htm.

46 Edmund Burke, *Reflections on the Revolution in France* (Indianapolis, IN: Hackett, 1987), 17.

47 Tony Judt, *Post-war* (New York: Penguin Group, 2006).

48 Tom Segev, *The Seventh Million* (New York: Henry Holt & Company, 1991).

49 For example, expanding on Ricouer's famous discussion Miroslav Volf writes " … every narration inscribes forgetting into the activity of remembering. Given that we are finite beings with particular interests, if we tell a story, we must leave out events and episodes that, from the perspective of the narrator, seem unimportant. The possibility of telling a story differently is grounded on this selectivity, which makes active forgetting part of remembering itself. The same is true of the stories of our lives. Because narrative identities are always conferred a posteriori—after the events have happened—and from a particular vantage point, forgetting is an essential aspect of the work of identity-shaping recollection … "

it to say that he who remembers everything, like Borges' "Funes the Memorious" can communicate nothing.[50] He is relegated, indeed cursed into silence. And so, historical narratives do involve a process of weeding out. And that process is often animated by political reasons that gloss over the suffering of very real people. The history of post-war Europe largely ignored the suffering of German civilians who were killed by Allied air raids and completely ignored the plight of millions of Germans ethnically cleansed from Poland, Czechoslovakia and parts of the Soviet empire after the war ended. The war crime that was their removal was, as it were, swallowed up by the far greater war crimes committed.

But while the partial erasure of historical detail is inevitable, and while political and other circumstances (accessibility to archival materials, for example) dictate that some episodes will be remembered in greater detail than others, this does not amount to an argument to actively abuse history from the get-go. Renan, Judt and Segev provide reminders that no matter how hard we try to come to terms with the past, memory will find a way to trick us. But this should not be read as a license to forego the effort in the first place.

Bibliography

Agimi, Ilire, and Ilir Dugolli. "Transitional Justice in Kosovo." Kosovar Institute for Policy Research and Development, Policy Research Series, Prishtina, July 2009. http://www.kipred.net/site/documents/ToJ_eng.pdf [accessed September 11, 2011].

Andrieu, Kora. "Transitional Justice: A New Discipline in Human Rights." *Online Encyclopedia of Mass Violence*. 2010. http://www.massviolence.org/Transitional-Justice-A-New- Discipline-in-Human-Rights?cs=print [accessed September 11, 2011].

Arendt, Hannah. "Personal Responsibility under Dictatorship." *The Listener* 6 (1964). http://web.ics.purdue.edu/~other1/Hannah%20Arendt%20-%20Personal%20Responsibility%20 Under%20 Dictatorship.pdf [accessed September 11, 2011].

Arendt, Hannah. *On Violence*. San Diego, CA: Harcourt Brace & Co., 1970.

Betancourt, T.S., and A. Ettien. "Transitional Justice and Youth Formerly Associated with Armed Forces and Armed Groups: Acceptance, Marginalization and Psychosocial Adjustment." UNICEF, Innocenti Research Centre, Innocenti Working Paper, June 2010. http://www.unicef-irc.org/publications/pdf/iwp_2010_17.pdf [accessed September 11, 2011].

Borges, Jorge Luis. *Collected Fictions*. New York: Penguin Books, 1999.

Brahm, Eric. "Amnesty." In *Beyond Intractability*, edited by Guy Burgess and Heidi Burgess. Boulder, CO: University of Colorado, 2005.

Brandese, P.J. "Democratic Memory, Amnesty and Amnesia: Nietzschean Forgetting and South Africa's Truth and Reconciliation Commission." Essay prepared for the annual conference of the American Political Science Association, Washington D.C., September 1–3, 2005. http://www.allacademic.com/meta/p_mla_apa_research_citation/0/4/0/1/8/pages40182/p40182-1.php [accessed September 11, 2011].

Burke, Edmund. *Reflections on the Revolution in France*. Indianapolis, IN: Hackett, 1987.

Closa, Carlos. "Transitional Justice in Spain." presentation to the Center for European Studies, Harvard University, March 25, 2011.

50 Jorge Luis Borges, *Collected Fictions* (New York: Penguin Books, 1999).

Cobban, Helena. "Does telling (and hearing) the truth always heal?" forum post on Transitional Justice Forum. Comment posted June 19, 2006. http://tj-forum.org/archives/001992.html [accessed September 11, 2011].
De Greiff, Pablo, Ana Cutter Patel, and Lars Waldorf. *Disarming the Past: Transitional Justice and Ex-Combatants*. New York: Social Science Research Council, 2009.["This volume is the fourth in the *Advancing Transitional Justice Series*, a joint project of the International Center for Transitional Justice and the Social Science Research Council."]. http://www.ssrc.org/workspace /images/crm/new_publication_3/%7B465 ede38–0c0d- df11–9d32–001cc477ec70%7D.pdf [accessed September 11, 2011].
Doung, Viroth, and Sophal Ear. "Transitional Justice Dilemma: The Case of Cambodia." *The Peace and Conflict Review*, University of Peace, 4(1), Fall 2009. http://www.review.upeace.org/index.cfm?opcion=0&ejemplar=18&entrada=89 [accessed September 11, 2011].
Eisikovits, Nir. "Transitional Justice." *Stanford Encyclopedia of Philosophy*. 2009. http://plato.stanford.edu/entries/justice-transitional [accessed September 11, 2011].
Eisikovits, Nir. *Sympathizing with the Enemy: Reconciliation, Transitional Justice, Negotiation*. Dordrecht, the Netherlands, and St. Louis, MO: Republic of Letters Publishing, 2010.
Encarnación, Omar G. "Justice in Times of Transition: Lessons from the Iberian Experience." Center for European Studies Working Paper Series #173, 2009, http://aei.pitt.edu/11883 /01/CES_173.pdf [accessed September 11, 2011].
d'Entreves, Maurizio Passerin. "Hannah Arendt." *Stanford Encyclopedia of Philosophy*. 2006. http://plato.stanford.edu/archives/fall2008/entries/arendt [accessed September 11, 2011].
Galloway, Anne. "Collective Remembering and the Importance of Forgetting: A Critical Design Challenge." Dept. of Sociology & Anthropology, Carleton University, Ottawa, ON, http://www.purselipsquarejaw.org/papers/galloway_chi2006.pdf [accessed September 11, 2011].
Garrett, Stephen A. "Models of Transitional Justice: A Comparative Analysis." Columbia International Affairs Online, International Studies Association, 41st annual convention, Los Angeles, March 14–18, 2000. http://www.ciaonet.org/isa/gas02/gas02.html [accessed September 11, 2011].
Han, Sang Wook Daniel. "Transitional Justice: When Justice Strikes Back – Case Studies of Delayed Justice in Argentina and South Korea." *Houston Journal of International Law*, June 22, 2008. http://www.highbeam.com/doc/1G1-186516757.html [accessed September 11, 2011].
Hayner, Priscilla B. *Unspeakable Truths: Confronting State Terror and Atrocity*. New York: Routledge, 2001.
Hughes, Paul M. "Forgiveness." *Stanford Encyclopedia of Philosophy*. 2010. http://plato.stanford.edu/entries/forgiveness [accessed September 11, 2011].
Huyse, Luc. *All Things Pass Except the Past*. Diestsesteenweg 71a-3010 Kessel-Lo: Luc Huyse & Uitgeverij Van Halewyck, 2009.
Ignatieff, Michael. *The Warrior's Honor: Ethnic War and the Modern Conscience*. New York: Henry Holt & Co., 1997.
Judt, Tony. *Reappraisals: Reflections on the Forgotten Twentieth Century*. New York: Penguin, 2008.
Judt, Tony. *Post-war*. New York: Penguin Group, 2006.
Karstedt, Suzanne, ed. *Legal Institutions and Collective Memories*. Onati International Series in Law and Society. Portland, OR: Hart Publishing, 2009.
Kauffman, Craig. "Transitional Justice in Guatemala: Linking the Past and the Future." Paper prepared for the ISA-South Conference, Miami, FL, November 3–5, 2005. http://www6.miami.edu/maia/ISAS05/papers/Craig_Kauffman.pdf [accessed September 11, 2011].

Khan, Nadia, and Mary Pottanat. "Roma (Gypsies) and the Holocaust." Holocaust/Genocide Project, "An End to Intolerance," vol. 5 [June 1997]. http://www.iearn.org/hgp/aeti/aeti-1997/roma-in-holocaust.html [accessed September 11, 2011].

Kundera, Milan. *The Book of Laughter and Forgetting*. New York: HarperCollins, 1999.

Levy, Daniel, and Natan Sznaider. "Forgive and Not Forget: Reconciliation between Forgiveness and Resentment." In *Taking Wrongs Seriously: Apologies and Reconciliation*, edited by Elazar Barkan and Alexander Karn. Palo Alto, CA: Stanford University Press, 2005.

Locke, John. *An Essay Concerning Human Understanding*. Indianapolis, IN: Hackett, 1996.

Loraux, Nicole. *The Divided City: On Memory and Forgetting in Ancient Athens*. New York: Zone Books, 2002.

Maierean, Andreea. "The Unbearable Burden of Forgetting. Lustration in Post-Communist Romania." In: *Perspectives on Memory and Identity*, edited by B. Marrin and K. Hammerstein. Vienna: IWM Junior Visiting Fellows' Conferences, vol. 28, 2010. http://www.iwm.at/index.php?option=com_content&task=view&id=311&Itemid=125 [accessed September 11, 2011].

Mannergren Selimovic, Johanna. "Remembering and Forgetting after War: Narratives of Truth, Justice and Reconciliation in a Bosnian Town." PhD diss., University of Gothenburg, November 15, 2010. http://gupea.ub.gu.se: 8080/dspace/handle/2077/23838 [accessed September 11, 2011].

Margalit, Avishai. *The Ethics of Memory*. Cambridge, MA: First Harvard University Press, 2004.

Miall, Hugh, Oliver Ramsbotham, and Tom Woodhouse. *Contemporary Conflict Resolution*. Cambridge: Polity Press, 2005.

Minow, Martha. *Between Vengeance and Forgiveness: Facing History after Genocide and Mass Violence*. Boston, MA: Beacon, 1998.

Moroccan American Center for Policy. "Morocco's Truth & Reconciliation (IER) Commission." http://www.moroccanamericanpolicy.org/upload/documents/IER_factsheet_102507.pdf [accessed September 11, 2011].

Mydans, Seth. "Cambodian Leader Resists Punishing Top Khmer Rouge." *New York Times*, December 29, 2001. http://www.nytimes.com/1998/12/29/world/cambodian-leader-resists-punishing-top-khmer-rouge.html?src=pm [accessed September 11, 2011].

Renan, Ernest. "Qu'est-ce qu'une nation?"/"What Is a Nation?" ("first delivered as a lecturer at the Sorbonne in 1882") http://www.nationalismproject.org/what/renan.htm [accessed September 11, 2011].

Ricœur, Paul. *Memory, History, Forgetting*. Chicago, IL: The University of Chicago Press, 2006.

Ruiz, Alicia Garcia. "Interview with Enzo Traverso: History can be an 'arm of power'." *Barcelona Metropolis*. Winter (January—March 2010). http://www.barcelonametropolis. cat/en/page.asp?id=21&ui=333&prevNode=35&tagId=Alicia%20Garc%EDa%20Ruiz [accessed September 11, 2011].

Saffon, Maria Paula, and Rodrigo Uprimny. "Transitional Justice, Restorative Justice and Reconciliation: Some Insights from the Colombian Case." "Coming to Terms" with Reconciliation—Working Paper Library. http://global.wisc.edu/reconciliation/library/papers_open/saffon.pdf [accessed September 11, 2011].

Segev, Tom. *The Seventh Million*. New York: Henry Holt & Company, 1991.

Shaw, Rosalind. "Rethinking Truth and Reconciliation Commissions: Lessons from Sierra Leone." United States Institute of Peace, Special Report 130. http://www.usip.org/files/resources/sr130.pdf [accessed September 11, 2011].

Shaw, Rosalind. "Forgive and Forget: Rethinking Memory in Sierra Leone's Truth and Reconciliation Commission." Presentation at United States Institute of Peace, Washington,

D.C., April 29, 2004. http://www.usip.org/events/forgive-and-forget- rethinking-memory-sierra-leones-truth-and-reconciliation-commission [accessed September 11, 2011].

Sutton, John. "Memory." *Stanford Encyclopedia of Philosophy*. 2003. http://plato.stanford.edu/entries/memory [accessed September 11, 2011].

Taylor, Charles. *Multiculturalism and the Politics of Recognition*. Princeton, NJ: Princeton University Press, 1992.

Tremlett, Giles. *Ghosts of Spain: Travels through Spain and its Silent Past*. New York: Walker & Company, 2006.

Trusteeship Council, Peacebuilding Commission—Working Group on Lessons Learned. "Justice in Times of Transition." U.N. Peacebuilding Support Office, February 29, 2008, http://www.un.org/peace/peacebuilding/Working%20Group%20on%20Lessons%20Learned/Justice%20in%20Times%20of%20Transition%20(26.02.2008)/26.02.2008%20Chair%20Summary.pdf [accessed September 11, 2011].

Vanderginste, Stef. "Transitional Justice for Burundi: A Long and Winding Road." Crisis Management Initiative, International Conference—"Building a Future on Peace and Justice," Nuremberg, June 25–7, 2007, Workshop 10—Alternative Approaches to Dealing with the Past," http://www.peace-justice-conference.info/download/WS10-Vandeginste%20report.pdf [accessed September 11, 2011].

Vivian, Bradford. *Public Forgetting: The Rhetoric and Politics of Beginning Again*. University Park, PA: The Pennsylvania State University Press, 2010.

Volf, Miroslav. *The End of Memory: Remembering Rightly in a Violent World*. Grand Rapids, MI: Wm. B. Eerdmans Publishing Co., 2006.

Waldron, Jeremy. "Superseding Historic Injustice." *Ethics* 103(1) (1992). http://www.jstor.org/stable/2381493?origin=JSTOR-pdf&. [accessed September 11, 2011].

Chapter 2

Peace without the Past? Truth, Transition and the Northern Ireland Case

Cheryl Lawther

Introduction

Transitional justice is a field on an upward path. In recent decades, the norms and principles of transitional justice and, in particular, truth recovery, have moved from the exceptional and exotic to become an axiomatic element of post-conflict reconstruction and, latterly, to where notions of 'truth', 'reconciliation', and 'forgiveness' permeate contemporary social and political debates in 'settled' societies (Teitel 2000; Roht-Arriaza and Mariecurrena 2006; McEvoy 2007). As this collection ably demonstrates, increasing scholarly attention has been paid to different forms of transitional justice mechanisms, their intersection with human rights norms and to those case studies where 'dealing with the past' is firmly embedded in the transitional process. It has, variously, been suggested that dealing with the past, particularly recovering truth about past human rights violations, is essential to democratic consolidation; reaffirming the rule of law; responding to victims' needs; and challenging incompatible versions of the past in divided societies (Hayner 2011; Tutu 1999; Boraine 2000; Wielbelhaus-Brahm 2010).

Considerably less well explored and also under theorized are those sites where transitions from political violence have taken place in the absence of a formal investigation of the past, particularly the recovery of truth, via a truth commission or other similar mechanism. This absence leaves questions of whether 'peace' without the 'past' is a pragmatic political accommodation; to what extent recovering truth about the past is essential for political and social reconciliation; and why techniques of silence and denial appear to persist 'post conflict' unanswered. More fundamentally, and as is the focus of this chapter, as yet, transitional justice scholarship tells us little about *why* the purported benefits of truth recovery may be rejected and the practical, political and sociological influences which underpin such opposition.

This chapter draws on the Northern Ireland case study to begin to contribute to a more fully theorized understanding of opposition to truth recovery and transitional justice. While a variety of mechanisms which fall under the transitional justice rubric have played a part in Northern Ireland's transition from political violence, at the time of writing, a formal overarching truth process has not been established and remains hotly contested. As well explored elsewhere, the utility of establishing such a body has been the subject of a lengthy and ongoing debate (see for example: Hamber 1998; Northern Ireland Affairs Committee 2005; Healing Through Remembering 2006; Consultative Group on the Past 2009; Lundy 2010). The most sustained and public opposition to a truth process has been from pro-state political actors – unionist political elites, loyalist ex-combatants and representatives of the security forces. Based on the author's empirical research with these constituencies,[1] this chapter

1 Between March and October 2009, over 40 semi-structured interviews were conducted with elite level representatives of the main unionist political parties (the Democratic Unionist Party (DUP), the Ulster Unionist Party (UUP) and the Traditional Unionist Voice (TUV)), loyalist ex-combatants represented politically by the Ulster Political Research Group (UPRG) and the

sets out five thematic areas which can inform opposition to truth recovery. They are: competing interpretations of memory and blame(lessness); the politics of victimhood; the tension between trust and truth-telling; the need to honour – not betray – past sacrifices; and from a pragmatic perspective, the importance of maintaining political and social stability. Each is explored in turn below. This chapter argues that critically interrogating the motives and understandings of those who are opposed to truth recovery is essential to theoretically and empirically developing the transitional justice field.

Northern Ireland and the Trouble with Truth

While beyond the scope of this chapter, in brief, the Northern Ireland conflict, between unionists and loyalists, nationalists and republicans and the British and Irish states, lasted over 30 years, resulted in over 3,700 deaths and injured over 40,000 individuals (McKittrick et al. 2007). It has left a legacy of pain, division, socioeconomic deprivation and many unanswered questions. Despite, for example, making provision for the release and reintegration of political prisoners, the reform of the police force and the establishment of the Northern Ireland Human Rights Commission, the Belfast Agreement did not make reference to the need to establish a formal truth process (Northern Ireland Office 1998).

In this vacuum, a 'piecemeal' approach to truth recovery has taken place (Bell 2003: 1095). The main mechanisms include an array of high profile public inquiries – such as the Saville Inquiry into the events of Bloody Sunday, 30 January 1972; 'right to life' cases under Article 2 of the European Convention on Human Rights; police led truth recovery – facilitated by the Office of the Police Ombudsman for Northern Ireland[2] and the Historical Enquiries Team;[3] and victim-centred initiatives, such as the establishment of the Independent Commission on the Location of Victims' Remains, to help facilitate the recovery of the remains of those individuals murdered and 'disappeared' by the IRA (see for example: Saville, Hoyt and Toohey 2010; Anthony and Mageean 2007; HET undated; Healing Through Remembering 2006). The weaknesses and critiques of this approach to the past include the lack of effective response to victims' need to hear and tell their stories (where so desired); the selective nature and financial cost of public inquiries; concerns over the impartiality and operational independence of the HET and OPONI; and how, in the absence of a formal truth process, the past is continuing to haunt the present, destabilizing the political institutions and impeding the peace process (CVSNI 2012; Hegarty 2003; Rolston and Scraton 2005; Lundy 2009, 2012; Bell 2003).

The debate on establishing a formal truth process has, however, been long and protracted. Arguably the most significant development was the establishment of the Consultative Group on the Past (CGP) in June 2007. Co-chaired by Archbishop Robin Eames, the former Church of Ireland primate and Denis Bradley, the former vice-chairman of the Northern Ireland Policing Board (NIPB), its official terms of reference were:

> To consult across the community how Northern Ireland society can best approach the legacy of the events of the past 40 years; and to make recommendations, as appropriate, on any steps that might

---

Progressive Unionist Party (PUP), and representatives of the security forces, including the Police Service of Northern Ireland (PSNI), the Office of the Police Ombudsman for Northern Ireland (OPONI), the Historical Enquiries Team (HET) and the Northern Ireland Retired Police Officers Association (NIRPOA).

2 The Office of the Police Ombudsman for Northern Ireland has responsibility for investigating historical complaints against the conduct of the Royal Ulster Constabulary during the conflict.

3 The Historical Enquiries Team is re-examining 3,286 deaths associated with the conflict and with the aim of bringing a measure of resolution to victims' families (HET undated).

be taken to support Northern Ireland society in building a shared future that is not overshadowed by the events of the past. (CGP 2009: 3)

Following a public consultation process, the Group published its Report in January 2009. One of its key recommendations was for the creation of a 'Legacy Commission', which, based on the three strands of 'Review and Investigation', 'Information Recovery' and 'Thematic Examination', was, essentially, a bespoke truth commission type body (CGP 2009). While the Report immediately faulted on the proposal that a 'Recognition Payment' of £12,000 would be paid to all victims of the conflict – civilians and former members of paramilitary organizations, there has been little progress on its other recommendations. At the time of writing, the former US envoy to Northern Ireland, Richard Haass, has recently been appointed to facilitate talks on issues related to flags, parades and the past (Northern Ireland Office 2013). His conclusions are due to be published by the end of 2013 and will undoubtedly involve further consideration on the establishment of a truth commission type body.

In the main, support for a formal truth process has fallen on sharp political divisions. Ostensibly at least, the main nationalist and republican political parties, the Social Democratic and Labour Party (SDLP) and Sinn Fein (SF), have publicly supported the establishment of a formal truth process. The SDLP for example have advocated for an 'ethical' approach to the past and the necessity of a 'robust truth process', while SF have consistently called for the establishment of an independent international truth commission, to which parties to the conflict would be accountable (SDLP 2012; SF 2003, 2013). In contrast, unionist political elites (the Democratic Unionist Party (DUP), Ulster Unionist Party (UUP) and the Traditional Unionist Voice (TUV)), loyalist ex-combatants and representatives of the security forces have remained opposed to the truth recovery debate and the establishment of a formal truth process. Key arguments include that a truth process would become 'a Brit bashing session' and provide an opportunity for republican politicians to 're-write' the past, legitimizing their actions and that it would retraumatize bereaved families and victims (DUP 2003; UUP 2009; NIRPOA 2009). Their objections are the focus of this chapter.

Truth, Identity and the Past

Defined by Cohen (2001: 25) as 'the need to be innocent of a troubling recognition', the capacity of a truth process to challenge contested versions of the past is one of the most compelling and challenging features of transitional justice. The objective, in theory at least, is often to broaden ownership and responsibility for the past, inculcating the idea that 'all sides in the struggle did bad things' and complicating simple and polarized histories (Lawther 2014). The South African Truth and Reconciliation Commission for example, has been praised for the manner in which it held sectoral hearings into the role of the business, medical, legal, religious and prison communities during the apartheid era and, via the media, brought apartheid into the living rooms of white South Africans who could no longer say 'I didn't know' (Dyzenhaus 1998; Boraine 1999, cited in Rolston 2002: 96).

Yet, conversely, for once and still powerful actors and where competing interpretations of blame and responsibility for the conflict continue to dominate the post-conflict landscape, a truth process may be rejected on the grounds that it challenges their identity and preferred reading of the past. In Northern Ireland, unionist political elite's reluctance to countenance the idea that their actions or inactions, or those of the state, played a role in the causes or consequences of the conflict has been instrumental in shaping their opposition to a truth process. The CGP made several attempts to encourage unionists to begin to accommodate the idea that wrongs were committed by all parties to the conflict. An early speech by the Group's co-chairs Archbishop Eames and Denis Bradley noted that while it is difficult, unionists need to consider their own 'ugly truths', including the fact that the state, at times, acted outside the law (Eames and Bradley 2008). Eames argued, 'This is one of the crucial issues facing us as a Group, difficult as it may be for some in our society to hear that elements of the State, on occasions, acted outside the law' (Eames and Bradley 2008). Such arguments were not well received. Pointing a highly polarized view of the conflict and a narrative of blamelessness, senior unionist figures have critiqued the Report of the CGP and therefore the idea of a truth process as 'promoting the view that it is the fault of unionism from 1921' and based on the assumption of 'too much guilt' (UUP 2009; Birnie 2009).

These objections also link to a highly stratified understanding of the relationship between truth recovery and the notion of blame. For Ignatieff (1998), the very point of a truth recovery exercise is to leave no one untarnished – the contribution of such a venture is to expose the myth of blamelessness. Rejecting the need to broaden ownership and responsibility for the conflict, unionists have made two distinct arguments. First is that a truth process would be used to 'blame' unionists and members of the security forces for the conflict, and second is that a truth process should be used to place all responsibility for the conflict with republican paramilitaries.[4] Speaking to a determination to apportion 'right' and 'wrong' and a mirroring of the lines of the conflict, a truth process may be interpreted as part of this battle. As this example illustrates, the contested nature of the past can directly map onto and structure opposition to a formal truth process (Lawther 2014).

Truth and the Politics of Victimhood

As well set out by Bouris (2007) and Borer (2003), in the aftermath of violent conflict, the definition of a 'victim' or 'perpetrator' is inherently politicized. Daniel Bar-Tal (2003: 78) notes that groups in conflict tend to form selective 'collective memories' of violence that focus mainly on the other side's responsibility for the outbreak and continuation of the conflict and its misdeeds, violence and atrocities while at the same time 'concentrating on their own self-justification, self-righteousness, glorification and victimization'. In this contest, articulating a narrative of victimhood has been interpreted as a way of garnering support and sympathy, and, based on the argument that 'in as far as they are victims, they are devoid of volition or intent', can be used to claim legitimacy for past actions (Gilligan 2003: 30; Cohen 2001). As Marie Breen Smyth (2003: 126–7) argues, for those who participated in the violence of the past, without the status of victimhood, 'their violence becomes too naked, politically inexplicable, and morally indefensible'. By implication, to be outside this categorization of victimhood is to be aligned with notions of guilt, illegitimacy and complicity. It may also involve a reluctance to countenance the victimhood of the 'other', which as Nadler and Schnabel (2008, cited in Aiken 2010: 181) warn, is a common danger in post-conflict societies where a sense of 'double victimhood' prevails and in which each identity group perceives itself to be the sole legitimate victim of past violence and expects its enemies to accept responsibility for past wrongdoing (Brewer 2010).

The politicization of victimhood in Northern Ireland has had a direct bearing on attitudes to truth recovery. Particularly problematic for unionists and forming the backdrop to much of their opposition to a truth process is the statutory definition of a victim contained in the Victims and Survivors (Northern Ireland) Order 2006. As an 'inclusive' definition, the Order includes victims, former combatants and their families. Adhering to a highly polarized definition of victimhood, unionists have sought to maintain a sharp demarcation between victims and combatants and the associated concepts of 'innocence' and 'guilt' and 'good' and 'evil' (DUP 2007, 2011; UUP 2011;

4 Interview, Gregory Campbell, DUP, 12 May 2009; Interview, Maurice Morrow, DUP, 20 April 2009; Interview, Tom Elliott, UUP, 20 April 2009.

Lawther 2013, 2014). Privileging a hierarchal conception of victimhood and the identity of the 'real' and 'innocent' victims of the conflict, to challenge or complicate these categories as the Victims and Survivors (Northern Ireland) Order 2006 does, is perceived as offering justification and legitimacy to the actions of paramilitary organizations (DUP 2007, 2011; UUP 2011; Lawther 2014). It has also been perceived to deny and exacerbate the Protestant community's memories of loss and 'disproportionate' victimization (Hayward and Mitchell 2003).

Against this backdrop, unionists and representatives of the security forces have consistently argued that a formal truth process would seek to create or imply 'moral equivalence' between the actions of victims and combatants (Williams and Scharf 2002; Birnie 2009; Patterson 2009; McAdam 2012; NIRPOA 2009).[5] This critique has been manifested in a number of ways and is illustrative of the competing narratives which attempt to explain the causes of the conflict. One of the strongest of these, and made in the light of the publication of the Report of the CGP (2009), was made by a member of the TUV who argued that the entire purpose of a truth process would be to create moral equivalence, treating all narratives of the past with equal validity and respect (Lawther 2013).[6] Equally problematic is the question of whether an amnesty or limited immunity should be offered to aid and incentivize truth recovery. Not without precedent in Northern Ireland and given the decreasing possibility of achieving large numbers of criminal prosecutions, a form of limited immunity was recommended by the Consultative Group on the Past (CGP 2009; Bell 2003; Duffy 2010; McEvoy and Mallinder 2008). This recommendation was opposed by unionist political elites and members of the security forces who have variously described an amnesty as 'sickening and unacceptable', 'immoral', and a 'betrayal' of innocent victims (*News Letter* 2008). Perceived to blur the line between *innocence* and *intent*, these factors illustrate how the mechanics of a truth process can be interpreted as challenging a claim to 'innocent' victimhood and by implication (as explored below), the meaning of death and sacrifice.[7] Where the meta-conflict is continuing, such discourses can provide a ready source of mobilization against truth recovery.

Trust and Truth-Telling

Seeking to preserve narratives of loss and claims to victimhood is also related to trust, or a lack of trust in the process of truth recovery. While Ignatieff (1996: 113) argues that a truth process can 'narrow the range of permissible lies' and examine abuses on all sides, doing so requires a level of trust in the bona fides of the truth process itself and in the 'truths' of the 'other side' (Misztal 2011; Hunt 2004). That trust may be in short supply in the aftermath of violent conflict is not unexpected or uncommon and may directly map on to a lack of trust in the truth process itself and in the capacity of all parties to the conflict to participate and play a full role in that process. A related concern is that 'truths' may be used in a partial and selective manner to 're-write' the past from a particular political vantage point (Brewer 2010; Hayner 2011).

These concerns can be identified in Northern Ireland and are a direct result of unionists' experience during the conflict – a period which saw approximately 3,739 people killed, 2,167 of whom were killed by republican paramilitary organizations – and the peace process which many unionist political elites believe to be structurally predisposed towards a nationalist/republican interpretation of the conflict (McKittrick and McVea 2012; Hayes and McAlister 2004). A direct read across can be made

5 Interview, Nelson McCausland, DUP, 3 April 2009.

6 Interview, Jim Allister, TUV, 20 March 2009.

7 Interview, Tom Elliott, UUP, 20 April 2009; Interview, Maurice Morrow, DUP, 20 April 2009; Interview, Jim McDonald, Royal Ulster Constabulary George Cross Foundation, 10 August 2009.

in terms of unionists' lack of trust in existing mechanisms of truth recovery and in the prospect of a formal truth process. The most visible forms of truth recovery in Northern Ireland have been facilitated by public inquiries, the OPONI and the HET. Public inquiries and the OPONI have largely, though not exclusively, investigated allegations of state misconduct during the conflict. In the case of public inquiries, as noted above, this has included the Saville Inquiry which found that British Army paratroopers shot dead 13 civilians, 'none of whom was posing a threat of causing death or injury' (Saville et al. 2010: 58). In respect to the OPONI, the 2007 'Operation Ballast' investigation found clear evidence of collusion between loyalist paramilitary informers and members of the security forces (OPONI 2007). That these inquiries have largely stemmed from and/or responded to nationalist and republican campaigns for truth and justice and have been 'state centric' in focus, has fed the perception that truth recovery is 'anti-state' and is contributing to the creation of a selective memory of the conflict (see for example: DUP 2009; UUP 2012). The resulting perception is that a formal truth process would provide a forum from which republicans could 're-write' the history of the conflict and ensure that only the state and its security forces are held to account (Lawther 2011).[8]

Secondly, there is considerable mistrust amongst many unionists and loyalists over republicans' willingness to honestly participate in a truth process. This is a significant concern in any transitional jurisdiction, as Ricœur (1999: 9) argues, 'To share testimony is to exchange trust. Beyond this we cannot go'. In this vein, leading unionists, the former UUP leader Tom Elliott and the DUP leader and First Minister Peter Robinson have respectively stated that 'You just wouldn't get the truth' and 'What would be the purpose of having a Truth Commission when we know without a doubt that the terrorists will not be coming forward to tell the truth' (UTV News 2011; McAdam 2012). As I have argued elsewhere, a number of themes have dominated unionists' discussions on truth – the IRA's responsibility for the majority of the Disappeared and the conduct of two senior SF figures – the Deputy First Minister Martin McGuinness and SF President Gerry Adams (Lawther 2011, 2014). Given that space prevents an exhaustive examination of each, Martin McGuinness's evidence to the Saville Inquiry is useful for illustrative purposes. When under cross-examination, McGuinness made frequent reference to a republican 'code of honour' and used the strictures of this code as a way to evade questions concerning the conduct or identity of other IRA members at that time.[9] Such instances further embed unionists' lack of trust in republicans' commitment to truth-telling and their opposition to the truth recovery debate.[10] As these examples have illustrated, without trust in the mechanics of truth recovery; in the truths that are uncovered; and in the capacity for truth-telling, there is little opportunity for a truth process to succeed.

Truth and the Sacrifices of the Past

The maintenance of life is one of the most sacred and universal values in human culture and, in the aftermath of violent conflict, there is often a 'desire to keep faith with the dead, to honour their memory' (Bar-Tal 2003; Ignatieff 1998: 188). Part of this equation may involve the quest for truth and justice – functions that participating in a truth process may fulfil. Equally, given that the meaning of a victim's death is often linked to societal beliefs about the conflict, including the delegitimization of the opponent and the legitimization of the self, unpicking past actions can be interpreted as betraying the sacrifices that have been made during the conflict (Winter 1995; Hamber 2009).

---

8 Interview, Ian Paisley Junior, DUP, 12 September 2009; Interview, Esmond Birnie, UUP, 19 May 2009.

9 Bloody Sunday Inquiry Transcript, Day 391, 5 November 2003. Available at: http://webarchive.nationalarchives.gov.uk/20101103103930/http://report.bloody-sunday-inquiry.org/transcripts/Archive/Ts391.htm (accessed on 11 June 2013).

10 Interview, Nelson McCausland, DUP, 3 April 2009; Interview, Billy McQuiston, UPRG, 18 June 2009.

A narrative of sacrifice – often by way of physical loss – has been particularly strongly associated with the police force which served during the conflict in Northern Ireland, the Royal Ulster Constabulary. From a unionist and security force perspective, this discourse focuses on the death of 305 police officers and those who were injured and their willingness to pay the ultimate sacrifice – death – in the quest to promote peace and to defend the Northern Ireland state and union with Great Britain (Mulcahy 2006; Ryder 2000). As is detailed above, there is a profound sense that throughout the period of conflict transformation, the British government has been too ready to meet republicans' demands over and above the sacrifice and memory of the security forces commitment to peacekeeping (Ryder 2000). One immediate objection is that the British government has and will continue to prioritize republicans' demands for truth concerning state abuse to the neglect of hurt and loss among policing communities (NIRPOA 2009; PFNI 2009). That the main truth recovery mechanisms have, to date, been state centric, has done little to allay this concern while the 'dust of neglect' is gathering on the unsolved files of more than 200 police officers who were murdered during the conflict.[11] For many, this is a fundamental betrayal of their loyalty. There is also a sense, on the part of the security forces at least, that their sacrifice has been subsumed by the demands of political expediency – 'The lack of activity regarding the murders of our colleagues is a sad indictment of this government who seem only too happy, for reasons of political expediency, to pump millions into the deaths of a select few' (PFNI 2003).

For many unionists and representatives of the security forces, re-examining the past, or how the past has been re-examined, has also called the meaning of their death into question. Of particular concern and in keeping with the claim to innocent victimhood detailed above, members of the security forces have consistently rejected the suggestion that their actions implicitly or explicitly played a role in the conflict (Lawther 2010, 2014). The discourse of sacrifice has often been used as a shield of legitimacy. To call aspects of the past into question therefore challenges their identity and organizational memory and betrays the significance and meaning of that loss. The reaction of members of the security forces to the allegation that collusion with loyalist paramilitaries played a role in the death of members of the nationalist and republican community bears out this case. The DUP's Jeffrey Donaldson for example argued that allegations of collusion have been interpreted as 'a betrayal of the brave men and women who served in the security forces'.[12] Prominent unionist victims' campaigner Willie Frazer has similarly pointed to how keeping faith with the dead – in this case those individuals who lost their lives while on duty, and the broader memory of the RUC, is to continue to remember, respect and uphold their values in the face of challenge – 'If I go back on my opinion and change what they believed in, I'd be degrading their memory' (cited in Dawson 2007: 281; Lawther 2014). As these sentiments suggest, in certain circumstances, dealing with the past may therefore not be interpreted as honouring victims' memory and sacrifice, but as a betrayal of their identity and the meaning of their physical loss. The Northern Ireland example indicates that this perspective can provide firm grounds for opposition to truth recovery.

Truth and Practical Peacemaking

The final area this chapter considers is the practical arguments against truth recovery – that, for example, unpicking the past may be politically, socially or individually retraumatizing (Mendeloff 2004). As Hayner (2011: 196) notes, there may be cases in which a 'truth always' recommendation is not appropriate, or at least, in which a recommendation for a formal truth recovery project might

11 Interview, Lady Sylvia Hermon, 3 April 2009.

12 Interview, Jeffrey Donaldson, DUP, 11 May 2009.

be inappropriate. The Spanish transition following the civil war of 1936–39 during which 500,000 citizens were killed, and latterly, the dictatorial rule of General Francisco Franco until 1975, is commonly presented as a textbook illustration of a transition from violence during which the demands of peacemaking appeared to have taken precedence over the need to address the abuses of the past. The 'Pacto del Olvido', the pact of forgetting, operated on two levels (Davies 2005). For Spanish political elites, fears of a right-wing coup or return to civil war led to the prioritization of peace, order and democratic consolidation over the examination of the past (Aguilar 2001). There was also a broad social consensus on the need for silence, whereby for those communities most affected by violence and disappearances, 'the traumatic memory of a fratricidal conflict' and a fear of a return to totalitarianism offset many victims' demands for truth and the return of the bodies of the disappeared (Aguilar 2001: 132; Farran and Amago 2010).

In Northern Ireland, the preponderance of arguments of a practical nature have come from unionist sources, although arguably of significance to all parties to the conflict. Concerns as to the effect of a truth process on political stability were made by a number of unionist politicians. Leebaw (2008) argues that this tension between the objectives of challenging denial and exposing the extent of complicity on one hand, and protecting political compromise on the other, is inherent to transitional justice. A number of themes can be identified. One of the most common arguments made to the author was that uncovering the 'dirty details' of the past would poison and polarize political relationships.[13] The assertion that 'it would be very very difficult for the devolved institutions to function in a positive and productive way if you have that backcloth literally every week' was similarly strongly stated (NIRPOA 2009; PFNI 2009).[14] These arguments also speak to the perception that a truth process would become another site of the conflict, or, as expressed by one interviewee, that the process or the final report would 'become a running sore' (Lundy and McGovern 2008; Healing Through Remembering 2006).[15] These arguments are also reflective of a clear lack of confidence in the ability of the political institutions to withstand an investigation of the past. Equally compelling and often closely related, are concerns as to the potential impact on social stability. In Northern Ireland, as elsewhere, it has, for example, been suggested that unearthing the past could heighten community tensions and encourage recruitment to paramilitary groups; that ex-combatants may become a target for scapegoating; and that Northern Ireland is 'too small' for truth recovery, suggesting that the relationship between the intimacy of the conflict and the cost of recovering truth about that period is too high (EPIC 2004).[16]

In other cases, and as to be expected given the personal and collective impact of the conflict, the potential for retraumatization has been highlighted (Hamber 2009; Hayner 2011). The argument that members of the security forces and unionists have been disproportionately victimized throughout the conflict and peace process and the claim that they have 'suffered enough' also fits within this framework (Mulcahy 2000; Dawson 2007). Of particular interest and of relevance to other transitional sites, several loyalist ex-combatants suggested that for those with a close proximity to violence and in the absence of available counselling, a 'self-medicating' approach to drugs and alcohol has been adopted – 'a lot of the usage of drink and drugs are related to coping with the conflict, they can't cope with what they done, with what happened and they don't want to

13 Interview, Sir Reg Empey, UUP, 17 April 2009; Interview, Danny Kennedy, UUP, 5 May 2009.

14 Interview, Richard Bullick, DUP, 25 March 2009.

15 Ibid.

16 Reflecting the small size and close knit nature of Northern Ireland, by 1998 approximately 1 in 5 reported having had a family member or close relative killed or injured, and more than half personally knew someone who had been similarly affected (Hayes and McAllister 2001). Interview, Frankie Gallagher, UPRG, 11 June 2009; Interview, Sir Reg Empey, UUP, 17 April 2009; Interview, Tom Roberts, Ex-Prisoners Interpretive Centre, 28 April 2009; Interview, Jim Allister, TUV, 20 March 2009.

revisit it' (see also: Jamieson, Shirlow and Grounds 2010).[17] In their opinion, to establish a truth process in this context could be catastrophic for individuals and communities. Collectively, these arguments point to the continued importance of managing social and political stability post-conflict and protecting those most affected by the violence of the past.

Conclusion

This chapter has sought to develop the theorization of transitional justice by shifting the focus onto those sites where a formal truth recovery process has not played a role in the transition from violent conflict. At the time of writing, Northern Ireland is one such jurisdiction. Indicators suggest that it is likely to remain so for the foreseeable future. Using Northern Ireland as a case study, this chapter has begun to tease out five broad thematic areas which motivate opposition to truth recovery. Encompassing political, sociological and practical objections, this chapter has highlighted the importance of memory and identity; competing notions of victimhood; the impact of a continued legacy of mistrust; the importance of honouring past sacrifices; and from a practical peacemaking perspective, the need to maintain political and social stability. Understanding the objections of those opposed to truth recovery and broadening its appeal in any transitional jurisdiction requires a critical interrogation and, appreciation of these challenges.

Bibliography

Aguilar, Paloma. 2001. 'Justice, Politics and Memory in the Spanish Transition'. In *The Politics of Memory: Transitional Justice in Democratizing Societies*, edited by Alexandra Barahona de Brito, Carmen Gonzalez-Enriquez and Paloma Aguilar, 92–118. Oxford: Oxford University Press.

Aiken, Nevin. 2010. 'Learning to Live Together: Transitional Justice and Intergroup Reconciliation in Northern Ireland'. *International Journal of Transitional Justice* 4: 166–88.

Anthony, Gordon, and Paul Mageean. 2007. 'Habits of Mind and "Truth Telling": Article 2 ECHR in Post Conflict Northern Ireland'. In *Judges, Human Rights and Transition: Essays in Honour of Stephen Livingstone*, edited by John Morison, Kieran McEvoy and Gordon Anthony, 181–200. Oxford: Oxford University Press.

Bar-Tal, Daniel. 2003. 'Collective Memory of Physical Violence: Its Contribution to the Culture of Violence'. In *The Role of Memory in Ethnic Conflict*, edited by Ed Cairns and Micheal Roe, 77–93. Houndmills: Palgrave Macmillan.

Bell, Christine. 2003. 'Dealing with the Past in Northern Ireland'. *Fordham International Law Journal* 26: 1095–147.

Birnie, Esmond. 2009. *Evaluation of the Report of the Consultative Group on the Past – Eames Bradley*. Copy on file with author.

Boraine, Alex. 2000. *A Country Unmasked: Inside South Africa's Truth and Reconciliation Commission*. Oxford: Oxford University Press.

Borer, Tristan Anne. 2003. 'A Taxonomy of Victims and Perpetrators: Human Rights and Reconciliation in South Africa'. *Human Rights Quarterly* 25: 1088–116.

17 In Northern Ireland, the prescription rate for antidepressants is twice that of the prescription rate in England and has been linked to the psychological legacy of the conflict. See: *BBC News*. 2010. 'Antidepressants "twice more common in Northern Ireland."' *BBC News*, 8 June.

Bouris, Erica. 2007. *Complex Political Victims*. Bloomfield, CN: Kumarian.

Brewer, John. 2010. *Peace Processes: A Sociological Approach*. Cambridge: Polity.

Cohen, Stanley. 2001. *States of Denial*. Cambridge: Polity Press.

Commission for Victims and Survivors Northern Ireland. 2012. *Comprehensive Needs Assessment*. Belfast: Commission for Victims and Survivors Northern Ireland.

Consultative Group on the Past. 2009. *Report of the Consultative Group on the Past*. Belfast: Consultative Group on the Past.

Davies, Madeleine. 2005. 'Is Spain Recovering its Memory? Breaking the Pacto del Olvido'. *Human Rights Quarterly* 27: 858–880.

Dawson, Graham. 2007. *Making Peace with the Past? Memory, Trauma and the Irish Troubles*. Manchester: Manchester University Press.

Democratic Unionist Party. 2003. *A Voice for Victims: The Democratic Unionist Party's policy on Innocent victims of terrorism*. Belfast: Democratic Unionist Party.

Democratic Unionist Party. 2007. 'Distinction between the Innocent and Guilty Must be Maintained'. Press Release, 22 June 2007.

Democratic Unionist Party. 2009. *Dealing with the Past in Northern Ireland*. Belfast: Democratic Unionist Party.

Democratic Unionist Party. 2011. *Moving Forward; Manifesto 2011*. Belfast: Democratic Unionist Party

Duffy, Aoife. 2010. 'A Truth Commission for Northern Ireland?' *International Journal of Transitional Justice* 4: 26–46.

Dyzenhaus, David. 1998. *Judging the Judges: Judging Ourselves*. Oxford: Hart.

Eames, Robin, and Denis Bradley. 2008. 'Eames: The Speech in Full'. *Belfast Telegraph*, 29 May.

Ex-Prisoners Interpretative Centre. 2004. *Truth Recovery: A Contribution from within Loyalism*. Belfast: Ex-Prisoners Interpretive Centre.

Farran, Carlos, and Samuel Amago. 2010. *Unearthing Franco's Legacy: Mass Graves and the Recovery of Historical Memory in Spain*. Notre Dame, IN: University of Notre Dame Press.

Gilligan, Chris. 2003. 'Constant Crisis/Permanent Process: Diminished Agency and Weak Structures in the Northern Ireland Peace Process'. *The Global Review of Ethnopolitics* 3: 22–37.

Hamber, Brandon. 1998. 'Remembering to Forget: Issues to Consider when Establishing Structures for Dealing with the Past'. In *Past Imperfect: Dealing with the Past in Northern Ireland and South Africa*, edited by Brandon Hamber, 56–78. Londonderry: INCORE/University of Ulster.

Hamber, Brandon. 2009. *Transforming Societies after Political Violence. Truth, Reconciliation and Mental Health*. New York: Springer.

Hayes, Bernadette, and Ian McAllister. 2004. 'Protestant Disillusionment with the Northern Ireland Peace Agreement'. *Irish Journal of Sociology* 13: 109–25.

Hayner, Priscilla. 2011. *Unspeakable Truths: Transitional Justice and the Challenge of Truth Commissions*. London: Routledge.

Hayward, Katy, and Claire Mitchell. 2003. 'Discourses of Equality in Post-Agreement Northern Ireland'. *Contemporary Politics* 9: 293–312.

Healing Through Remembering. 2006. *Making Peace with the Past: Options for Truth Recovery Regarding the Conflict in and about Northern Ireland*. Belfast: Healing Through Remembering.

Hegarty, Angela. 2003. 'The Government of Memory: Public Inquiries and the Limits of Justice in Northern Ireland'. *Fordham International Law Journal* 26: 1148–92.

Historical Enquiries Team. Undated. *Policing the Past: Introducing the Work of the Historical Enquiries Team*. Belfast: Police Service of Northern Ireland.

Hunt, Tristram. 2004. 'Whose Truth? Objective Truth and a Challenge for History'. *Criminal Law Forum* 15: 193–8.

Ignatieff, Michael. 1996. 'Articles of Faith'. *Index on Censorship* 25: 110–22.

Ignatieff, Michael. 1998. *The Warrior's Honour: Ethnic War and the Modern Conscience*. New York: Henry Holt & Co.

Jamieson, Ruth, Peter Shirlow and Adrian Grounds. 2010. *Ageing and Social Exclusion among Former Politically Motivated Prisoners in Northern Ireland and the Border Region of Ireland*. Belfast: The Community Foundation for Northern Ireland.

Lawther, Cheryl. 2010. '"Securing" the Past: Policing and the Contest over Truth in Northern Ireland'. *British Journal of Criminology* 50: 455–73.

Lawther, Cheryl. 2011. 'Unionism, Truth Recovery and the Fearful Past'. *Irish Political Studies* 26: 361–82.

Lawther, Cheryl. 2013. 'Denial, Silence and the Politics of the Past: Unpicking the Opposition to Truth Recovery in Northern Ireland'. *International Journal of Transitional Justice* 7: 157–77.

Lawther, Cheryl. 2014. *Truth, Denial and Transition: Northern Ireland and the Contested Past*. London: Routledge.

Leebaw, Bronwyn. 2008. 'The Irreconcilable Goals of Transitional Justice'. *Human Rights Quarterly* 30: 95–118.

Lundy, Patricia. 2009. 'Can the Past be Policed? Lessons from the Historical Enquiries Team Northern Ireland'. *Law and Social Challenges* 11: 109–71.

Lundy, Patricia. 2010. 'Commissioning the Past in Northern Ireland'. *Review of International Affairs* LX: 101–33.

Lundy, Patricia. 2012. *Research Brief: Assessment of the Historical Enquiries Team (HET) Review Processes and Procedures in Royal Military Police (RMP) Investigation Cases*. Available at: http://www.socsci.ulst.ac.uk/sociology/profiles/p.lundy/research.phtml (accessed on 14 May 2013).

Lundy, Patricia, and Mark McGovern. 2008. 'A Trojan Horse? Unionism, Trust and Truth Telling in Northern Ireland'. *International Journal of Transitional Justice* 2: 42–62.

McAdam, Noel. 2012. 'Troubles Amnesty and Truth Commission are Ruled out by Robinson'. *Belfast Telegraph*, 27 February.

McEvoy, Kieran. 2007. 'Beyond Legalism: Towards a Thicker Understanding of Transitional Justice'. *Journal of Law and Society* 34: 411–40.

McEvoy, Kieran, and Louise Mallinder. 2008. *Article Two Compliant Truth Recovery and Guarantees of Non-Prosecution*. Submission to the Consultative Group on the Past. Belfast: Queen's University Belfast.

McKittrick, David, and David McVea. 2012. *Making Sense of the Troubles: A History of the Northern Ireland Conflict*. London: Penguin Books.

McKittrick, David, Seamus Kelters, Brian Feeney, Chris Thornton and David McVea. 2007. *Lost Lives: The Stories of the Men, Women and Children Who Died as a Result of the Northern Ireland Troubles*. Edinburgh: Mainstream.

Misztal, Barbara. 2011. 'Forgiveness and the Construction of New Conditions for a Common Life'. *Contemporary Social Science* 6: 39–53.

Mulcahy, Aogan. 2000. 'Policing History: The Official Discourse and Organisational Memory of the Royal Ulster Constabulary'. *British Journal of Criminology* 40: 68–87.

Mulcahy, Aogan. 2006. *Policing Northern Ireland: Conflict, Legitimacy and Reform*. Cullompton: Willan Publishing.

News Letter. 2008. 'Victims Anger at "Amnesty for Terrorists"'. *News Letter*, 9 January.

Northern Ireland Affairs Committee. 2005. *Ways of Dealing with Northern Ireland's Past: Interim Report – Victims and Survivors*. London: The Stationery Office.
Northern Ireland Office. 1998. *The Belfast Agreement: An Agreement Reached at the Multi-Party Talks on Northern Ireland*. London: The Stationery Office.
Northern Ireland Office. 2013. 'Dr Richard Haass to Chair All-Party Talks'. Press Release, 9 July.
Northern Ireland Retired Police Officers Association. 2009. *Response to the Northern Ireland Office Consultation Paper on the Report of the Consultative Group on the Past (Eames–Bradley)*. Belfast: Northern Ireland Retired Police Officers Association.
Office of the Police Ombudsman for Northern Ireland. 2007. *Statement by the Police Ombudsman for Northern Ireland on Her Investigation into the Circumstances Surrounding the Death of Raymond McCord Junior and Related Matters*. Belfast: Office of the Police Ombudsman for Northern Ireland.
Patterson, Henry. 2009. 'Truth and Reconciliation in NI? Not Much Hope of Either'. *Parliamentary Brief*, 9 February. Available at: http://www.parliamentarybrief.com/articles/1/new/truth-and-969_67_0.html (accessed on 10 February 2009).
Police Federation for Northern Ireland. 2003. 'Federation Dismisses Idea of Truth and Reconciliation Commission'. Press Release, 20 June.
Police Federation for Northern Ireland. 2009. 'Eames-Bradley: A view by Terry Spence Chairman of Police Federation for Northern Ireland'. Press Release, 2 February.
Ricœur, Paul. 1999. 'Memory and Forgetting'. In *Questioning Ethics: Contemporary Debates in Continental Philosophy*, edited by Richard Kearney and Mark Dooley, 5–11. London: Routledge.
Roht-Arriaza, Naomi, and Javier Mariezcurrena. 2006. *Transitional Justice in the Twenty First Century: Beyond Truth versus Justice*. Cambridge: Cambridge University Press.
Rolston, Bill. 2002. 'Assembling the Jigsaw: Truth, Justice and Transition in the North of Ireland'. *Race and Class* 44: 87–106.
Rolston, Bill, and Phil Scraton. 2005. 'In the Full Glare of English Politics: Ireland, Inquiries and the British State'. *British Journal of Criminology* 45: 547–64.
Ryder, C. 2000. *The RUC 1922–2000: A Force under Fire*. London: Arrow.
Saville, Mark, William Hoyt and John Toohey. 2010. *Report of the Bloody Sunday Inquiry*. Vol. 1: Principle Conclusions and Overall Assessment of the Bloody Sunday Inquiry. London: The Stationery Office.
Sinn Fein. 2003. *Truth: A Sinn Fein Discussion Document*. Belfast: Sinn Fein.
Sinn Fein. 2013. 'Adams calls for Truth Commission'. Press Release, 31 March.
Smyth, Marie. 2003. 'Truth, Partial Truth and Irreconcilable Truths: Reflections on the Prospects for Truth Recovery in Northern Ireland'. *Smith Studies in Social Work* 73: 205–25.
Social Democratic and Labour Party. 2012. *Addressing the Past: A Comprehensive Truth Process and the Ethical Way Forward*. Belfast: Social Democratic and Labour Party.
Teitel, Ruti. 2000. *Transitional Justice*. Oxford: Oxford University Press.
Tutu, Desmond. 2000. *No Future without Forgiveness*. London: Rider.
Ulster Unionist Party. 2009. 'Reject Eames-Bradley Says Elliott'. Press Release, 30 January.
Ulster Unionist Party. 2011. *Victims' Charter*. Belfast: Ulster Unionist Party.
UTV News. 2011. 'Paterson Rules out Truth Commission'. *UTV News*, 4 October. Online. Available at: http://www.u.tv/News/Paterson-rules-out-NI-truth-commission/1276eec3-3c13-4982-90f1-3fc369ccb624 (accessed on 4 October 2011).
Wiebelhaus-Brahm, Eric. 2010. *Truth Commissions and Transitional Societies: The Impact on Human Rights and Democracy*. London: Routledge.

Williams, Paul, and Michael Scharf. 2002. *Peace with Justice: War Crimes and Accountability in the Former Yugoslavia*. New York: Rowman & Littlefield.

Winter, Jay. 1995. *Sites of Memory, Sites of Mourning: The Great War in European Cultural History*. Cambridge: Cambridge University Press.

PART II
Punishing after War

Chapter 3

The Force of Forgetting or Forced Forgetting? Schmittian Amnesties and Transitional Justice[1]

Juan Espindola

In the aftermath of the Second World War, Carl Schmitt wrote an extremely short albeit provocative piece advocating the use of amnesties in the context of Germany's post-war criminal prosecutions: "Amnesty or the Power of Forgetting" (Schmitt 1995). This apology for amnesties should come as no surprise given his early sympathies with the Nazi regime. The main goal of this chapter is to argue that Schmitt's defense of amnesties is objectionable and even inconsistent with some strands of his political theory. The chapter moves on two methodological levels. The central one articulates a *criticism* of Schmittian amnesties, based among other things on what recent literature on transitional justice has to say about coming to terms with the past in post-conflict scenarios. Admittedly, it is an exercise in Schmitt bashing, a quite common and well-established practice in contemporary scholarship (Holmes 1993; Lilla 2001; Manin 2003, among many others), but one that nevertheless has a very strong counterpart in a large number of Anglo-American scholars whose goal is to "recover" and revitalize Schmitt's political theory (for instance Mouffe 1999). The second level presents a *critique*, rather than a criticism, of Schmitt's defense of amnesties. This means that instead of trying to challenge Schmitt based on a set of previously and independently defined values and categories, one is to proceed immanently to Schmitt's theory, from within his own terms and categories in order to show how they relate to one another, and whether they are mutually consistent (McCormick 1997: 6–7).

Engaging with Schmitt's advocacy of amnesties is important not only for the sake of coming to grips with his political thought. More importantly, he should be taken as an author who challenges the paradigm of individual accountability for serious crimes, and with it the consolidation of an anti-amnesty that has been crystallizing in the last decades (Sikkink 2012). There is a growing, although by no means absolute, consensus on the part of international bodies like the United Nations, as well as international non-governmental organizations and academics, that amnesties for international crimes, such as genocide, torture, war crimes, and crimes against humanity, should be removed from the transitional justice toolkit. Despite its appeal, the anti-amnesty position is yet to develop more solid foundations, both legal (Freeman 2009; Freeman and Pensky 2012; Trumbull 2007), and moral (Pensky 2008; Ryberg 2010). Some of Schmitt's arguments were quite successful in his time and country (Frei 2002), and even hold currency today. Addressing these arguments, then, can contribute in the task of constructing a compelling position with regards to the use of amnesties. I do not believe that an *absolute* ban on amnesties is a defensible position. It is also not a popular one, based on the increment in the use of amnesties worldwide (Mallinder 2012). The challenge is to develop *principled* criteria on the use of amnesty. This chapter does not undertake the work of laying out these criteria, but it shows why Schmitt's defense of the use of amnesties is not a good referent, and even, to put it bluntly, why it is not even Schmittian in spirit.

1 This chapter was presented at the Western Political Science Association, 2013, and at the Institute for Philosophical Research at the National University of Mexico in the same year.

The chapter discusses a rather unconventional case in the growing amnesty scholarship: Athena's "amnesty" in the epic *The Odyssey*. In "Amnestie oder die Kraft des Vergessens" (AKV), Schmitt references this literary example in extolling the benefits of amnesties. The reason to focus on this example is that it allows one to peel away the added layers of complexity that usually come along with real life scenarios such as civil wars or interstate conflict. These layers of complexity oftentimes complicate normative evaluation. By contrast, "Odysseus war" is relatively transparent, thus leaving exposed the core normative principles behind pro-amnesty positions such as Schmitt's.

The chapter is divided into three sections. Section one presents Schmitt's views on amnesties in AKV, as well as in other parts of his corpus. The next two sections criticize these views. The second section argues that Schmitt's understanding of reconciliation, as well as his prescription that reactive emotions in post-conflict scenarios should be suppressed, is highly unconvincing. The third section criticizes Schmitt's lack of a standard to evaluate the causes of conflict, and the manner in which conflict is carried out. Schmitt defends an unrestricted right of political communities to go to war. But his position is not defensible, neither from the perspective of just war theory nor from his own perspective in other writings, and this undermines his case for amnesties. The fourth section concludes.

The Force of Forgetting

The first version of AKV appeared in 1949. The text was published several times with minor revisions, in different places, and with different titles ("Amnestie—Urform des Rechts," "Amnestie ist die Kraft des Vergessens," "Das Ende des kalten Bürgerkrieges—Im Zirkel der tödlichen Rechthaberei"). It was even plagiarized once in the German weekly *Die Zeit*. AKV is only six paragraphs long. Despite its brevity and its abundant rhetorical flurries, it is premised on deeper Schmittian themes. The crux of its argument is as follows. Amnesties are the only mechanisms available to societies for stopping potentially endless cycles of violence resulting from post-war revenge. Punishing the losing side in a war is always an instance of victor's justice—the expression of petty vindictiveness, or even of imperialistic hubris. The reluctance to offer amnesties signals the ushering of a new era in which war is considered to be a crime, not legitimate combat; and belligerent parties are regarded as "criminals or gangsters," not as legitimate opponents. But let me develop the argument at greater length.

Schmitt sets the stage for AKV by noting a transformation in the character of war, and lamenting this change. War, he claims, is no longer a clash between two disciplined armies, but a struggle where opponents fight each other with all the means at their disposal. Furthermore, the cessation of war does not give way to peace, but to "civil war," by which he means that even after one of the combatants has won the war, violence is perpetuated through petty desire for revenge and its conclusion is the complete annihilation of the enemy. The distinguishing feature of civil wars, Schmitt says, is that they treat individuals in the losing side as "criminals, murderers, saboteurs, and gangsters," not as worthy opponents or legitimate belligerents. Civil war is, in other words, a form of victor's justice and a *just war*, a term that in Schmitt's conceptual map has a negative connotation, not a positive one as is usually the case in the tradition of Saint Augustine and in contemporary philosophy. Thus Schmitt writes: "In an eerie sense, the civil war is a just war, because each of the parties sits on his right as on spoil [of war]. Each takes revenge in the name of law. How is it possible to get out of this state of cold war to one of peace? How can this circle of dogmatism/self-righteousness be broken? How can the cold war come to an end?" (2005: 218). Schmitt continues his line of reasoning by posing a (false) dichotomy—he contends that there are only two strategies for bringing a civil war to an end. One is the "communist way," the complete annihilation of "the other." The alternative is to implement an amnesty, and he goes on to define it in the following way: "The word amnesty means forgetting. and not only forgetting, but also the strict prohibition to rummage in the past, and finding occasion there to further acts of revenge and further compensation" (2005: 218).

Schmitt's defense of amnesties in AKV is consistent with two major dimensions of his political theory—his understanding of sovereignty as the prerogative to declare the state of exception (what I call internal sovereignty), and more interestingly, his anti-cosmopolitan criticism of post-Westphalian political and legal order, a criticism that comes along with an affirmation of the value of a political community's sovereignty vis-à-vis other political communities (external sovereignty). The remainder of the section connects the justifications for amnesties in AKV to Schmitt's conceptions of internal and external sovereignty.

Internal Sovereignty

In *Political Theology*, Schmitt summarizes his understanding of sovereignty in a lapidary fashion: the sovereign is he who decides the state of exception. Even this succinct formulation has given rise to multiple interpretations, and it is the most radical expression of Schmittian sovereignty. The standard interpretation should suffice for the moment—exceptional situations call for the emergence of a potentially all-powerful agent who must not only rescue constitutional order from any given crisis, but also charismatically deliver it from its own constitutional procedure, which Schmitt pejoratively describes as mechanical. This agent is the sovereign. Given this standard interpretation of Schmitt's conception of sovereignty, his plea for post-Nazi amnesties would seem to be no surprise. Amnesties suspend ordinary course of criminal law. They could be seen as an expression of the state's sovereign power to declare an exception to the normal parameters of the rule of law as a way of furthering some other political end. Thus, in *Political Theology*, Schmitt (2005: 38) refers to amnesties as examples of the "omnipotence of the modern law giver."

External Sovereignty

The Nomos of the Earth (2006), arguably Schmitt's most ambitious work, stands in the background of AKV; in fact, it was published in 1950, just about a year after AKV. This work presents Schmitt's broader criticism of some of the transformations of international law. *Nomos* is a paean to the *Jus Publicum Europaeum* (JPE), the framework of international law prevailing between the birth of sovereign states to the beginning of the First World War. What Schmitt has to say in this work about international law follows from his conception of politics.

I start by unpacking what Schmitt takes to be the basis of politics, or as he called it somewhat idiosyncratically, "the political." Schmitt seeks to find an *independent* criterion appropriate to politics for justifying political actions and motives. Just like morality has a criterion based on the distinction between good and bad, and aesthetics has a criterion based on the distinction between beauty and ugliness, so politics has a criterion: the distinction between friend and enemy. Enmity, in particular, is a relation that arises when I recognize that a group of persons are "existentially something different and alien" to me and represent "the other." Enmity is for Schmitt a public enemy (*hostis*), not a *private* one (*inimicus*). A collectivity is a political body only to the extent that it has enemies. Defining one's public enemy means also defining one's collective self. In a phrase, distinguishing one's enemies from oneself is the essence of politics.

This conception of politics, grounded on the friend-enemy distinction, implies that every true political community must claim an unrestricted right to go to war (*jus ad bellum*) based on what it judges to be just and necessary. Were the decision whether to declare war in a concrete situation no longer up to the political community but to some third party—say, an international organization like the United Nations—the group would lose its existence as an independent political community (1996: 45–53). This implies a condition of the legitimacy of international order—a legitimate international order must recognize that all political communities have a legitimate claim to *jus ad bellum*.

According to Schmitt in *Nomos*, JPE lived up to his criteria of legitimacy. All independent states were recognized to possess the right to go to war on the basis of their own judgment of justice and necessity. The legal order of JPE, indeed one of its highest achievements, was to move away from the medieval notion of "just war" (*gerechter Krieg*), which as we saw Schmitt alludes to in AKV. JPE did not distinguish between just and unjust war. Under JPE, the just cause for a war was not to be determined by moral arguments and natural law (the "just cause" of medieval times), as was the case in the Middle Ages, but the equal sovereignty of states. All sovereign states in a given conflict were by default recognized as legitimate belligerents (2006: 140–71). JPE drove a wedge between the *inimicus* and the *justus hostis*, the private from the just public enemy. The *justus hostis* is not one with whom one has an existential conflict, but simply a conflict of interests. This was Schmitt's idea of a non-punitive war among states, in his terms, a "non-discriminatory concept of war." War is not waged by criminals, but by worthy opponents with conflicting interests.

Schmitt believes that international law between 1919 and 1939 undermined JPE, and laments this historical development. Under the new paradigm, any war opposed to the new international legal order, which outlawed wars of aggression and expanded international law to include crimes against humanity, became unjust wars, and the enemy became a criminal. Schmitt thinks that one of the consequences of the criminalization of war is the transformation of the institution of amnesties. Before interstate war was a crime, peace treaties implied amnesties. Belligerent parties would not be treated as criminals; amnestying those who had fought a war was understood to be a "practice of peace between two mutually recognized partners." This was the appropriate method, according to Schmitt, who on this point (but not in others) quotes Kant approvingly: "The concept of a peace treaty already contains the provision that an amnesty goes along with it" (2006: 171). This understanding changes with the demise of JPE. In his typically apocalyptic tone, Schmitt writes: "amnesty was destroyed by a discrimination against the vanquished" (2006: 262); "a vanquished state was obligated to turn over to the enemy state its *own* citizens who committed war crimes" (2006: 261).

With this background in mind, let us turn back to AKV. In that piece, Schmitt mentions several historical instances in which some form of amnesty was used to put an end to civil conflict. He includes the paradigmatic amnesty of 403 B.C. in Athens after the Peloponnesian War, which he describes as a "fraternal war." He also mentions the Indemnity and Oblivion Act ("Act of free and general pardon, indemnity, and oblivion") that ended Cromwell's English Revolution in 1660. Schmitt's use of these examples is extremely problematic on many levels. Against what he believes, in both cases war was criminalized and the belligerent parties on the losing side were treated like "gangsters and criminals"; in Athens, the Thirty Tyrants were executed; in England, those who ordered the execution of Charles I were sentenced to death (even Cromwell was posthumously executed: his body was exhumed and then hanged). But in this chapter I will focus on a different example of AKV. In some of its versions, Schmitt refers to Odysseus' return to Ithaca, where he and his son Telemachus initiate a battle that, so Schmitt argues, would have degenerated into an endless spiral of violence but for the timely intervention of the goddess Athena. Schmitt tells the conclusion of the epic in a way that is partial to the lesson he wants to draw. However, far from supporting his views, a richer account of the *Odyssey* actually undercuts the very point that Schmitt is trying to make.

The story of Odysseus' homecoming is well known. After 20 years of expatriation, he makes his way back to Ithaca, where all but his wife and son had lost faith that he would return. Upon arriving Odysseus finds out that the suitors of his wife Penelope have wreaked havoc on his estate. The suitors have abused Penelope's hospitality and broken guest rules. At the same time, however, it should be noted that they linger in Odysseus' home because Penelope, who has pledged to marry one of them after she finishes weaving a shroud for Odysseus' father, cunningly postpones her decision by unweaving at night what she weaves during the day. Odysseus is enraged at the behavior of the suitors, and in retaliation starts a blood bath. Violence spirals, until Athena, who instigated Odysseus' wrath in the first place, now wonders how to proceed to curb violence and asks Zeus for guidance. Schmitt quotes Zeus' reply:

> "My child," Zeus who marshals the thunderheads replied,
> "why do you pry and probe me so intently? Come now,
> wasn't the plan your own? You conceived it yourself.
> Odysseus should return and pay the traitors back.
> Do as your heart desires—
> but let me tell you how it should be done.
> Now that royal Odysseus has taken his revenge,
> let both sides seal their pacts that he shall reign for life,
> and let us purge their memories of the bloody slaughter
> of their brothers and sons. Let them be friends,
> devoted as in the old days. Let peace and wealth
> come cresting through the land.

This is the only direct reference that AKV makes to the *Odyssey*. Sympathetic to Zeus' diagnosis of the situation, Schmitt says about cycles of vengeance such as this one: "this kind of political cleansing could ruin the whole nation" (AKV, 220).

The literary reference seems to be in line with Schmitt's decisionism. Zeus, the almighty god, dictates what is to be done, and Athena follows his commands. She addresses all the parties and imposes a form of amnesty: "Hold back, you men of Ithaca, back from brutal war!/Break off—shed no more blood—make peace at once" (584–5). And as Homer puts it, she "hands down" her "pacts of peace between both sides for all the years to come" (599/600).

I now turn to show the weaknesses in Schmitt's defense of amnesties.

Forgetting Reconciliation and Reactive Emotions

One of the problems with AKV is common to many a defense of amnesties—it characterizes retributive emotions (such as resentment and anger of victims) as utterly destructive and at the same time as easily suppressible, as if they were an obstacle that needs to be removed because it clogs efforts towards reconciliation. There is a tension between these two views, because the alleged destructiveness of retributive emotions would suggest that these will not be easy to root out. Regardless, Schmitt believes that it is desirable to build reconciliation through a commitment to erase old grievances, and to not act upon them. In his view, the state should discourage the vindictiveness of those who have been harmed during conflict, because reactive attitudes like revenge do not have any positive value.

The title of Schmitt's piece already foreshadows one of the problems with the argument—its reliance on an unacceptably *thin* normative theory of reconciliation (Murphy 2010 reviews the strengths and weaknesses of several conceptions of reconciliation). AKV equates amnesty to a mere act of oblivion, one in which former belligerents draw a line under the past and move ahead with their lives. It is obvious that this understanding of reconciliation rules out accountability, individual or collective, for crimes committed in the course of the conflagration. Even non-criminal mechanisms for holding perpetrators accountable for past crime, such as requiring a public apology from them, seem to be excluded in this account. To be sure, the notion of amnesty is conceptually independent of moral acts such as apologies. The term amnesty may be understood simply as a "prescribed forgetting" (Weinrich 2004). Despite this conceptual independence, however, many scholars and activists agree that a normative connection should be drawn between amnesties and apologies. In transitional justice settings, innovative institutions such as the South African Truth and Reconciliation Commission thrived on the idea that (public) apologies and repentance from perpetrators are a precondition for amnesties. The goal, according to one of its main architects, Desmond Tutu, was to promote historical clarification and to consolidate an ideal of social harmony. This does not mean that victims *must* forgive after an apology has been given; forgiveness is after all an imperfect duty (Digeser 2001: 78–9); it just means that perpetrator apologies should be considered as a necessary if not sufficient condition for amnestying perpetrators.

The connection between apology and amnesty is one that escapes Schmitt's normative horizon among other reasons because he believes that war does not raise issues of *moral* responsibility for combatants (Sitze 2007). In fact he altogether rejects the victim/perpetrator dichotomy in war contexts. But accountability for crimes committed in war is impossible without such a central dichotomy.

Apart but related to reconciliation is the issue of retributive emotions. Consider a passage in the *Odyssey* that Schmitt does not reference or quote. It precedes the epic's resolution, just before Athena addresses the relatives of the suitors. In a mourning spirit, Euphites, father of the first suitor to be slain by Odysseus, addresses the grief-stricken relatives, who belong to the most important families of Ithaca, in this manner:

> My friends, what a mortal blow this man has dealt
> to all our island people! Those fighters, many and brave,
> he led away in his curved ships—he lost the ships
> and he lost the men and back he comes again
> to kill the best of our Cephallenian princes.
> Quick, after him! Before he flees to Pylos
> or holy Elis, where Epeans rule in power—
> up, attack! Or we'll hang our heads forever,
> all disgraced, even by generations down the years,
> if we don't punish the murderers of our brothers and our sons!
> Why, life would lose its relish—for me, at least—
> I'd rather die at once and go among the dead.
> Attack—before the assassins cross the sea
> and leave us in their wake. (471–84)

This is precisely the kind of discourse that deserves Schmitt's rejection because it perpetuates cycles of vengeance. AKV devalues the worth of retributive emotions present in post-violence contexts. The piece characterizes them as "acts of revenge" (*Racheakten*), and puts blame on them for contributing to the perpetuation of conflict.

But it is one thing to acknowledge the combustible nature of these emotions, and their contribution to increasing the likelihood of sustained conflict, and another to stigmatize them and wish them away. Schmitt expects that the relatives of the suitors will lay down their arms simply because Zeus and Athena say so. But in settings where the gods cannot enforce amnesties by erasing the grievances from the memories of vindictive parties, it seems like retributive emotions cannot and should not be repressed.

Most measures whose goal is to suppress vindictive emotions of victims are problematic in prudential and moral terms, especially when the state sponsors it. In prudential terms, the problem is that, if repressed those emotions can fester and reemerge later on, maybe even with increased strength; and because attempts at repression can give rise to vigilantism in lieu of state-administered punishment, which is a more reliable mechanism for administering justice. For example, in a post-genocide transitional justice scenario like contemporary Rwanda, amnesty was ruled out right from the beginning because "it would inflame many genocide survivors' perceived desire for vengeance" (Clark 216). Moreover, since unrecognized negative feelings oftentimes travel across generations, the stability of the political regime would be constantly threatened if retributive emotions were not acknowledged.

More importantly, there are moral grounds to believe that retributive emotions ought not to be suppressed but channeled. There is ample evidence suggesting that simply "forgetting" past injustice is neither possible nor desirable, both from a psychological and a social perspective. Many victims involved in past violence often experience traumatic experiences that need to be properly addressed. Granted that the line between revenge and retribution is a thin one. However, retributive emotions do not necessarily play a destructive role in settings coming out of episodes of violence. In fact, acknowledging their existence may be at once a moral obligation and a strategic move in reconstituting political and social relationships. As Mihaela Mihai (2010: 195–8) points out, one should not be blind towards the moral affirmation inherent in retributive emotions. Take the case of resentment. Resentment, she argues, is an emotional marker: it signals the capacity to recognize injustice towards oneself and is therefore an "inalienable right" (others like Borneman 2005; 1997 argue along similar lines). Within post-oppression contexts, Mihai continues, these affective reactions are linked to the expectation of having political and moral equality re-established. Should victims be denied this after having suffered harm, the injury and the insult towards victims would be doubled, and the integrity of the democratic normative regime imperiled. Such emotions, therefore, should be properly channeled, not suppressed. Mihai suggests that one of the reasons why resentment has been stigmatized for political theory is the influence of Nietzsche's account of the genealogy of morals and the central place *ressentiment* occupies within it. Its resilience, obsession with the past and association with weakness and envy have relegated resentment to that category of emotions in need of suppression or silencing. Recall that in Nietzsche's *On the Genealogy of Morals* (1989), noble characters should be quick to forget any offense done to them because they should never be in the grip of a base emotion like revenge. This is especially true if the offender is one's inferior (a slave); such an offender would be neither worthy of equal respect nor likely to engage in an honest dispute.

A final observation about Schmittian amnesties is in order before turning to the next section. Literary analogies can be treacherous as is certainly the one deployed by Schmitt. Aristotelians should have strong reservations about the literary resource that Homer deploys in this passage.

In the *Poetics* (1454a33–1454b9), Aristotle characterizes it as a *deus ex machina*, the god in the machine. This resource is among the most harshly criticized in Aristotelian literary theory, signaling an impoverished literary craft incapable of offering an apt way to give resolution to the narrative. Aristotle discredits the resource mainly because it fails to respect the internal logic of the story. In the case of the *Odyssey*, the "pacts of peace" that Athena hands down are perhaps a more palatable end to the story, but they do not flow from the course of events.

The *deus ex machina* of the *Odyssey* is not only unsatisfactory from the literary point of view; it is also politically puzzling. Athena's "pacts of peace" are "handed down" by an actor from the outside, as it were; a prescient actor who applies the "provision" that is already "contained" in the concept of a "peace treaty," to paraphrase Schmitt's quote of Kant. But amnesties such as these, which are for Schmitt a sign of the omnipotence of the law-giver, are not an organic process involving the belligerent parties. Athena's amnesty does apply to both sides in the conflict, which is a promising albeit insufficient sign that it is not designed to promote the impunity of, say, the ruling class. But on the other hand an amnesty like the one defended by Schmitt in the *Odyssey* is an exercise of authoritarian force. Amnesties designed and enforced through an authoritarian use of force are not desirable, and probably not even plausible. As McEvoy and Mallinder (2012: 38) argue:

> the power relations at work in contemporary amnesties are much more complex than simply an expression of the will of the sovereign [i.e. the ruler]. Amnesties usually come in the wake of a direct challenge to the state's monopoly on the use of force. In such contexts, the exercise of power may be fragile, contingent, and certainly contested. Indeed, in such contexts, amnesties may be more an effort to garner or consolidate state power rather than an expression of dominance.

Even the shape and the content of amnesties are never a reflection of the will of the ruler, but the result of a host of other factors, many of which have to do with local power relations. McEvoy and Mallinder (2012: 440) further argue that amnesties:

> represent an attempt to turn what was historically untrammeled power into a creature of law. Amnesties usually require legislation, they must be compliant with international law, they often entail the creation of some kind of commission that must make decisions against declared criteria, they may be subject to judicial scrutiny, and so forth.

This view of amnesties suggests that not all amnesties should be removed from the transitional justice toolkit, but Schmittian amnesties should.

Forgetting *Jus ad Bellum*

In a scenario as strikingly simple as the *Odyssey*, it should be relatively easy to cast judgment on the validity of the causes of conflict. Real life cases, one could contend, are difficult to assess because the motivations of the actors are oftentimes hidden, and the particularities of each conflict are so difficult to fathom that the possibility of drawing conclusions of any kind is extremely complex. Things are less obscure in the case of the *Odyssey*, however. Yet Schmitt does not step back and cast judgment upon the causes of the conflict in Ithaca, or upon the manner in which Odysseus wages his "war." He proposes amnesties as the solution to stop hostilities regardless of what ignited them, and of how the conflagration was fought. Put crudely, Schmitt recommends the use of amnesty too lightly. For there is a growing consensus that amnesties should not be offered to combatants who commit international crimes (*how* combatants fight a war is relevant for the question of amnesties). That is, there is a connection between the principles of what the just war tradition calls *jus in bello* and the permissibility of the use of amnesties. Furthermore, if a war is just, then it would be unjust to try to stop it by invoking amnesty as a way to defuse conflict. That is, there is a connection between *jus ad bellum* and the permissibility of the use of amnesties. Schmitt rejects, or does not fully address, neither of these two points, and where he scantly touches on these issues, what he has to say does not seem quite consistent with some of the key insights of his theory.

Schmitt's position with respect to the morality of war is what one might call political realism. On his view, war falls outside the scope of morality and is therefore not constrained by it. A different theory holds that war is sometimes but not always morally permissible, and that a set of moral constraints must regulate the conduct of war (Jeff McMahan 1996). Schmitt is a political realist according to these categories. He rejects the notion of the just war and of the just enemy, a move that is motivated by several factors, like his belief that ethics in the realm of international relations simply mask imperialistic interests. This move might also reflect what some scholars view as his proclivity to violence.

Consider just war theory tradition. The theory draws a distinction between the principles that govern the resort to war (*jus ad bellum*) and those that govern conduct in war (*jus in bello*). These principles establish requirements that must be met if a war or an act of war is to be considered permissible. One *jus ad bellum* principle is the just cause principle, which as we saw previously Schmitt rejects. It states that there must be a sufficiently strong cause to justify the awful actions that war inevitably produces. What counts as just cause in just war theory is subject to much controversy. One common interpretation is that just war is always reactive; that is, it is the response of a collectivity to the violation of a right. But shifts between restrictive and expanded accounts of just cause have accompanied the tradition of just war theory. The reactive reading of the just cause principle would seem to suggest that the relatives of the suitors are justified in repealing Odysseus' offensive with violence. As Herzog (2006: 16) points out, Odysseus' behavior can be interpreted in two ways. A backward-looking interpretation suggests that his actions are plain vengefulness. By contrast, a forward-looking reading points towards the idea that his wrath is a strategy to build a reputation as a ruthless leader; after many years absent from Ithaca, he needs to reestablish his authority (in the descriptive, not normative sense). On any of these readings, the relatives of the suitors have reasons to worry; spiteful or merciless rulers seem to be a legitimate target for collective violence. In other words, the suitors, and the collectivity they represent, have a just cause for waging a war. Stopping it through an "imposed" amnesty would be unjust—yet another decision foisted on them. They are undertaking *collective* action against a tyrant. This point takes me to Schmitt's political theory.

Schmitt was particularly adamant in his belief that each community has an unrestricted right to go to war based on its own judgment of necessity and justice. As was previously explained, this is because Schmitt attributes value to the survival and integrity of distinct political communities (particularly states), and therefore to state sovereignty, which is for him the supreme value. He does not even seem to concede that a state's sovereignty may legitimately be overridden to stop it from committing atrocities against its own citizens, as his minimal engagement with the theme of the Holocaust suggests.

It would seem as if within Schmittian parameters the suitors would be justified in reacting violently to Odysseus' attack. Through his actions, Odysseus has become a *justus hostis*. To see why, consider Euphites' words, included in the previous subsection. Euphites' arguments, I contend, do not only provide an argument for the use of force that is both compelling and consistent with just war theory. They are even Schmittian in spirit. Euphites says that "life would lose its relish" and be disgraced if he does not "punish" the murderers of his kin; he makes an existential assertion of the kind Schmitt praises. More importantly, note that Euphites begins by framing the conflict in terms of public enmity; thus, he claims to speak on behalf of "our island people," and he casts Odysseus as enemy of Ithaca, and rightly so. Ten years after his mysterious absence (the war lasted another 10 years), Odysseus has become an outsider, who is now threatening the preservation of the collectivity (Herzog 2006: 15–37). In other words, beyond his personal grievance, Euphites' plea to his fellow citizens to "attack" the "assassins" (a term describing politically motivated murder) has political bases. As I have already shown, in *The Concept of the Political* Schmitt argues that for a political community to exist it takes a group of people to be willing to engage in political life by setting themselves apart from outsiders; they should, in other words, be able to make a distinction between friends and enemies (Schmitt 1996: 38, 43–4). According to Schmitt, drawing the distinction between friend and enemy does not require that the group has already assumed a formal organization that allows for rule-governed collective decision-making. A people's existence is prior to all legal form so long as there is a sense of shared identity strong enough to motivate its members to fight and die for the preservation of the group. This, it seems to me, is what the people of Ithaca are doing, before Athena steps in to prevent it.

Schmitt also insists that political communities have what might be termed an epistemic advantage in deciding whether they should or should not use self-defensive violence against a public enemy that threatens its existence. Only the members of the group in question, so Schmitt argues in many of his works, are in a position to decide whether "the other" poses an existential threat to the collectivity and must therefore be fought, even through violent means. They know better than any external party. The decision whether another group constitutes a threat to the existence of one's own, and the decision whether it is necessary to use reactive or even pre-emptive violence to remove or to escape that threat, should not be delegated to a third agent (Schmitt 1996: 45–53). In Schmitt's words: "Thus, a politically existing people (*Volk*) cannot refrain from distinguishing, on its own (*durch eigene Bestimmung*) and at its own risk, between friend and enemy" (Schmitt 1932: 79).

This is the main tension in Schmitt's justification for amnesties. On the one hand, he thinks a political community should determine on its own who the internal enemy is, and whether it should reactively or even pre-emptively strike in order to secure its preservation; no other party should make that decision. On the other hand, when a political group like Euphites and the people of Ithaca do precisely that, Schmitt thinks it is acceptable that Athena intervenes with a "pact of peace" preventing the group from exercising its own judgment about whether, when, and through which means it is appropriate to fight the existential other. Schmittian amnesties violate Schmitt's own principle of epistemic privilege of political communities with respect to the paradigmatic political decision about how the enemy should be dealt with. In other words, some amnesties can be unjust if their aim is to stop a just war.

In sum, if the suitors are justified in their reaction against Odysseus, then they have a "right" to go to war by Schmittian standards. By the standard of just war theory, their use of violence against Odysseus is also justified. The relatives of suitors have legitimate reasons for pursuing their fight further. In either case, they have grounds for rejecting Athena's amnesty.

Now let us look at things from the perspective of Odysseus, again according to both just war theory and Schmittian standards. According to the standard of just war theory, even if we remain agnostic about the justice of the cause of the war, another *jus ad bellum* principle should be considered—proportionality (McMahan 2010). To put it shortly, the point is one of lesser evils: the harms that war inevitable generates should not exceed those that the war is trying to eliminate. Even by the standards of his time, Odysseus' wrath is excessive in that it destabilizes for the sake of the obscure motives of the absent king. It is quite clear that the "punishment" he metes out to the suitors is by all means disproportionate. He even commits deeds that are disproportionate in the *jus in bello* sense, that is, some of the *specific* actions he takes in his already disproportionately violent campaign are, to put it mildly, cruel. Consider how he punishes some of the servants who had been "receptive" to the suitors. Some servant girls had made themselves sexually available to them. Odysseus has them hanged in the yard after they have cleaned up the gore left behind during the domestic battle where Odysseus massacres the suitors. Another servant, who had mistreated Odysseus when he was disguised as a beggar, is dismembered, and his genitals are cut off and fed to the dogs. Odysseus' actions are disproportionate through and through. In such a context a general amnesty like the one Schmitt seems to have in mind turns a blind eye on actions such as these.

The evaluation of Odysseus' deed would be similarly negative from a Schmittian perspective. We saw that admittedly Odysseus had a legitimate grievance against the suitors—they were ruining his estate and contending with him, as it were, to fill the political vacuum that Odysseus had left behind upon leaving for Troy. Therefore, one could argue, he had a reason to take offense. One could even contend that following the norms of the time, he had the "right" to challenge the suitors on account of this offense. His revenge is a duel writ large, and duels are a socially sanctioned practice at the time. War, Schmitt thinks, is like a duel (2006: 411–13). He writes in *Nomos*:

> Where duel as an institution is recognized, the justice of it is based similarly on the sharp distinction between *justa causa* and the form ... a duel is not "just" because the just side always wins, but because there are certain guarantees in the preservation of the *form*—in the quality of the parties to the conflict as agents, in the adherence to a specific procedure ... and, especially, in the inclusion of witnesses on an equal footing ... here, men of honor have found a satisfactory means of dealing with a matter of honor in a prescribed form and before impartial witnesses. Thus, a challenge to a duel (*défi*) was neither aggression nor a crime, any more than was a declaration of war. (Schmitt 2006: 412)

Brunkhorst (2004: 514) argues that Schmitt's notion of "duel wars" would have met with Kant's full disapproval, since for Kant the duel is the consummate symbol of the continuing state of nature.

According to these standards, Odysseus' actions cannot be analogized to a duel. His anger is rather amorphous—it spills over to individuals who were not a threat to him, if any were to begin with; it is not restrained by any procedure whatsoever; and there is no impartial witness in sight, only a rather capricious goddess who is so partial to Odysseus that during the battle she deflects the spears of the suitors to protect him. It is a dishonorable fight indeed. If the backward-looking interpretation of Odysseus' actions is correct, then his overpowering vengefulness respects no boundaries; he is not dueling honorably. If the forward-looking version is on point, then his strategy for ruling Ithaca is premised precisely on appearing to be a Machiavellian ruler who if need be pays no heed to pre-established forms, but imposes his own.

In sum, by the standards of Schmitt's political realism or by those of just war theory, Odysseus is not justified in starting a conflict like the one he initiates. In view of this scenario, amnesty does not seem to be a desirable solution to the conflict: it is neither politically sensitive nor morally permissible.

At this point it should be useful to compare Schmitt's thoughts regarding war to those of an author like Kant. Both Schmitt and Kant agree that morally motivated just war is unacceptable and should be overcome through the *legalization* of war. Both draw a sharp distinction between law and morality, between legal and just war, the latter being the greater evil (Brunkhorst 2004: 513–16). However, their agreement ends there. In *Nomos*, Schmitt takes issue with Kant's use and development of the notion of the unjust enemy. As mentioned before, Schmitt believes that the category of a just enemy is a regression towards the view of war as a just cause, and of the enemy, the *hostis*, as a criminal. In Kant's *The Metaphysical Elements of Justice*, the unjust enemy is "an enemy whose publicly expressed will (whether by word or deed) reveals a maxim by which, if it were made a universal rule, any condition of peace among nations would be impossible and instead a state of nature would be perpetuated" Benhabib (2012: 697) adds that, following Kant's earlier "Towards Perpetual Peace," the unjust enemy should be understood as an agent who would reject the three definitive principles of perpetual peace, particularly his insistence that nations should enter a "pacific federation," one that establishes the conditions of lawful coexistence with each other such that war is kept to a minimum, if not eliminated. All of this shows that for Kant war is an absolute evil inflicting harm on people, and therefore an event that can and should be avoided at all costs. By contrast, Schmitt thinks war, or at least the possibility thereof, is inevitable; and that an arrangement of the kind proposed by Kant is implausible and undesirable. This, I think, is the source of Schmitt's freewheeling invocation of amnesties.

In response to the foregoing discussion, a Schmittian might retort that if the predicted outcome of a conflagration is the annihilation of all parties involved, then what is the point of thinking about the causes of the war? Amnesties are the only mechanism to avert the extermination of all combatants, and therefore thinking about the etiology of the conflict in that context is beside the point. Before concluding this section, let me address this objection. Put briefly, Schmitt's argument here is that the interests of peace and justice compete for priority, and for him the latter carry the day. This is a consequentialist argument through and through. But consequentialist arguments have problems. First, consequentialist justifications rely heavily on inductive arguments; they must therefore bear the burden of demonstrating the causal effect of amnesties (their "force," to use Schmitt's term) in achieving or consolidating peace. The problem is that in conflict and post-conflict contexts, producing a satisfactory amount and quality of information is extremely hard. Second, no empirical evidence can show that but for the amnesty, peace or stability will not be achieved. Third, it is an open question whether amnesties help resolve social fractures in the case of "fraternal wars," as Schmitt assumes, or if they in fact simply postpone, maintain or even aggravate those fractures (Elster 2004). More importantly, Schmitt's argument takes stability as a context-independent *summum bonum*, but provides no consequence-independent standard to rule out alternative accounts of what the best outcome for a society torn by civil war should be. One could argue that nothing short of stability "for the right reasons" as opposed to stability in the short run, which is what amnesties commonly produce, is an acceptable outcome for those affected by ongoing conflict; and that they prefer the continuation of hostilities to stability of the second kind (Pensky 2008; Ryberg 2010). I repeat that Schmitt believes that political communities have an epistemic privilege over the decisions that regard them. It is up to them to decide whether they accept an amnesty or not.

Conclusion

I have tried to show why Schmitt's rationale for defending amnesties rests on very weak foundations. Schmitt's ideas about the use of amnesties directly contradict contemporary legal and political developments at the international level, such as the internationalization of criminal law, embodied in institutions like the universal jurisdiction or the International Criminal Court (ICC). Before the creation of the ICC, it was up to each sovereign state to decide whether it would offer an amnesty (or something equivalent) to its citizens in the context of internal conflict or even interstate war. In the present situation, by contrast, some crimes (war crimes, genocide, crimes against humanity, and so on) fall within the jurisdiction of the court according to the Rome Treaty, which governs it, and may be prosecuted without the consent of the sovereign state. This means that the ICC may rescind domestic amnesties offered by the members who are party to the Treaty, and can even prosecute individuals of states who are not parties to the statute if they committed one of the crimes listed before within a country that is a signatory to the Treaty. This means the end (or more modestly, the beginning of the end) of sovereignty in the realm of criminal justice, an outcome that a Schmittian framework would discourage.

Bibliography

Benhabib, Seyla. 2012. "Carl Schmitt's Critique of Kant: Sovereignty and International Law." *Political Theory* 40(6): 688–713.

Borneman, John. 1997. *Settling Accounts: Violence, Justice, and Accountability in Postsocialist Europe*. Princeton, NJ: Princeton University Press.

———. 2005. "Public Apologies as Performative Redress." *SAIS* 25(2): 53–66.

Brunkhorst, Hauke. 2004. "The Right to War: Hegemonial Geopolitics or Civic Constitutionalism?" *Constellations* 11(4): 512–26.

Clark, Phil. 2012. "*Creeks of Justice*: Debating Post-Atrocity Accountability in Rwanda and Uganda." In *Amnesty in the Age of Human Rights Accountability: Comparative and International Perspectives*, edited by Francesca Lessa and Leigh A. Payne, 210–13. New York: Cambridge University Press.

Digeser, Peter. 2001. *Political Forgiveness*. New York: Cornell University Press.

Elster, Jon. 2004. *Closing the Books: Transitional Justice in Historical Perspective*. New York: Cambridge University Press.

Freeman, Mark. 2009. *Necessary Evils: Amnesties and the Search for Justice*. Cambridge: Cambridge University Press.

Freeman, Mark, and Max Pensky. 2012. "The Amnesty Controversy in International Law." In *Amnesty in the Age of Human Rights Accountability. Comparative and International Perspectives*. Cambridge: Cambridge University Press.

Frei, Norbert. 2002. *Adenauer's Germany and the Nazi Past: The Politics of Amnesty and Integration*. New York: Columbia University Press.

Habermas, Jürgen. 1991. *The New Conservatism: Cultural Criticism and the Historian's Debate*. Cambridge, MA: MIT Press.

Herzog, Don. 2006. *Cunning*. Princeton, NJ: Princeton University Press.

Holmes, Stephen. 1993. *The Anatomy of Antiliberalism*. Cambridge, MA: Harvard University Press.

Lessa, Francesca. 2012. "Barriers to Justice: The Ley de Caducidad and Impunity in Uruguay." In *Amnesty in the Age of Human Rights Accountability: Comparative and International Perspectives*.

Lilla, Mark. 2001. *The Reckless Mind: Intellectuals and Politics*. New York: New York Review Books.

McCormick, John P. 1997. *Carl Schmitt's Critique of Liberalism: Against Politics as Technology*. Cambridge: Cambridge University Press.

McMahan, Jeff. 1996. "Realism, Morality, and War." In *The Ethics of War and Peace: Religious and Secular Perspectives*, edited by Terry Nardin, 78–92. Princeton, NJ: Princeton University Press.

McMahan, Jeffrey. 2010. "Humanitarian Intervention, Consent, and Proportionality." In *Ethics and Humanity: Themes from the Philosophy of Jonathan Glover*, N. Ann Davis, Richard Keshen, and Jeff McMahan. New York: Oxford University Press.
Mallinder, Louise. 2012. "Amnesties' Challenge to the Global Accountability Norm? Interpreting Regional and International Trends in Amnesty Enactment." In *Amnesty in the Age of Human Rights Accountability: Comparative and International Perspectives*.
Mallinder, Louise, and Kieran McEvoy. 2012. "Amnesties in Transition: Punishment, Restoration, and the Governance of Mercy." *Journal of Law and Society* 39(3): 410–40.
Manin, Bernard. 2003. "Libéralisme et Puissance de l'État 'Étatance de lManquée de Carl Schmitt." In *Être Gouverné. Études En L'honneur de Jean Leca*, edited by P. Havre et al. Paris: Presses de Sciences-Po.
May, Larry. 2004. *Crimes against Humanity: A Normative Account*. New York: Cambridge University Press.
Meier, Heinrich. 2006. *Carl Schmitt and Leo Strauss: The Hidden Dialogue*. Chicago, IL: University of Chicago Press.
———. 2011. *The Lesson of Carl Schmitt: Four Chapters on the Distinction between Political Theology and Political Philosophy Expanded Edition*. Chicago, IL: The University of Chicago Press.
Mihai, Mihaela. 2010. "Transitional Justice and the Quest for Democracy: A Contribution to a Political Theory of Democratic Transformations." *Ratio Juris* 23(2): 183–204.
Mouffe, Chantal. 1999. *The Challenge of Carl Schmitt*. New York: Verso.
Murphy, Colleen. 2010. *A Moral Theory of Political Reconciliation*. Cambridge: Cambridge University Press.
Nietzsche, Friedrich. 1989. *On the Genealogy of Morals*. New York: Vintage.
Pensky, Max. 2008. "Amnesty on Trial: Impunity, Accountability, and the Norms of International Law." *Ethics & Global Politics* 1(1–2): 1–40.
Ryberg, Jesper. 2010. "Mass Atrocities, Retributivism, and the Threshold Challenge." *Res Publica* 16(2) (May 1): 169–79. doi: 10.1007/s11158-010-9113-3.
Schmitt, Carl. 1932. *Der Begriff Des Politischen*. Munich: Duncker & Humblot.
———. 1995. *Staat, Großraum, Nomos: Arbeiten Aus Den Jahren 1916 Bis 1969*. Berlin: Duncker & Humblot.
———. 1996. *The Concept of the Political*. Chicago, IL: University of Chicago Press.
———. 2005. *Political Theology, Four Chapters on the Concept of Sovereignty*. Chicago, IL: University of Chicago Press.
———. 2006. *The Nomos of the Earth*. New York: Telos.
Sikkink, Kathryn. 2012. "The Age of Accountability: The Rise of Individual Criminal Accountability." In *Amnesty in the Age of Human Rights Accountability: Comparative and International Perspectives*.
Sitze, Adam. 2007. "Keeping the Peace." In *Forgiveness, Mercy, and Clemency*. Stanford, CA: Stanford University Press.
Trumbull, Charles P. 2007. "Giving Amnesties a Second Chance." *Berkeley Journal of International Affairs* 25(2): 283–345.
Weinrich, Harald. 2004. *Lethe: The Art and Critique of Forgetting*. Ithaca, NY: Cornell University Press.
Wolin, Richard. 1992. "Carl Schmitt: The Conservative Revolutionary Habitus and the Aesthetics of Horror." *Political Theory* 20 (3): 424–47.

Chapter 4

Transitional Justice, Retributive Justice and Accountability for Wrongdoing

Colleen Murphy

Introduction

It is widely recognized that communities should respond to wrongdoing. One standard response, commonly taken to satisfy the demands of justice, is the trial, conviction, and legal punishment of perpetrators. Legal punishment involves the intentional infliction of something burdensome by the state, which communicates condemnation of a criminal action. However, legal punishment is fraught politically and morally in paradigm transitional contexts. Transitional contexts refer to societies emerging from an extended period of conflict and/or repression and engaging in the process of democratization. South Africa following the end of apartheid, Guatemala after its extended civil war, and Egypt in the aftermath of the toppling of Hosni Mubarak are a few of the paradigm examples of societies in transition.

Punishment in the context of a transition is often difficult, given that those responsible for wrongdoing may still wield influence and threaten a transition if prosecuted; evidence may have been destroyed by state agents prior to a transition which diminishes the likelihood of a successful prosecution; and the number of potential cases to pursue overwhelms the capacity of criminal justice systems. The difficulties surrounding punishment have led many transitional societies to adopt alternative processes for dealing with past wrongs (e.g., truth commissions, reparations and/ or programs of lustration). However, the moral status of alternative practices, and in particular whether they satisfy the demands of justice, is the subject of ongoing dispute. According to theories of retributive justice, perpetrators of wrongdoing deserve to be punished. Insofar as this is what justice demands, alternatives that do not entail the imposition of punishment seem to be merely second-best alternatives, necessary to adopt in transitional contexts because of the pragmatic obstacles to successful conviction and punishment.

I argue in this chapter that it is a mistake to use the standards of retributive justice to evaluate the justice of responses to wrongdoing, including punishment, in transitional contexts. Establishing the justice of any response to wrongdoing is always a context-dependent exercise. The case for punishment offered by theories of retributive justice is compelling in the circumstances of justice characterizing reasonably just and stable democracies. However, the circumstances of justice that typify such societies are importantly different from the circumstances that typify transitional communities. In the circumstances of transition, the rationale for punishment offered by theories of retributive justice is not persuasive. Punishment may be just in such contexts, but it will not be just for the reasons retributive theories offer. Nor is it obvious that punishment is the only response that will satisfy what justice demands in terms of how perpetrators of wrongdoing should be held accountable for their actions.

There are three sections to this chapter. In the first section, I provide an overview of the standard, retributive account of the justice of punishment. I emphasize the reasons given for why punishment is controversial and in need of justification, and on the contextual circumstances of justice implicitly or explicitly assumed to make punishment controversial in these ways. The second section then argues that the contextual circumstances assumed to hold in the standard retributive account of punishment do not obtain in paradigm transitional contexts. I lay out four alternative circumstances that characterize transitional societies, and the implications of these circumstances for the plausibility of the standard retributive justification of punishment. In short, the retributive rationale for punishment is not compelling in the circumstances of a transition. This is not to suggest that punishment is not justified in transitional contexts. Rather, the rationale for the justifiability of punishment will need to be different, given the variations in the context in which it is being implemented. The third and final section articulates desiderata for an adequate theory of punishment for transitional contexts. These desiderata suggest that responses other than punishment may be not only justifiable but also better suited as ways to hold perpetrators accountable for wrongdoing in the circumstances of transitions.

Standard Account of Punishment

Retributive theories of punishment answer the question: why is punishment by the state just? Principles of justice articulate especially demanding deontological constraints on action.[1] I take deontological constraints to specify in part what is needed to recognize the basic, irrevocable, and equal dignity of individuals. Such constraints ground claims that individuals have on other individuals, institutions, or agents, claims that give rise to obligations or duties of justice of such individuals, institutions, or agents. Such duties are legally and socially enforceable by society. In this section, I lay out four basic assumptions of theoretical accounts of retributive justice, before going on to explain why punishment is morally controversial given these assumptions and how theories of retributive justice respond.

Accounts of retributive justice that explain why punishment is just assume that there is nothing especially suspect or problematic about either criminal law or the state. That is, criminal law is as it should be; that is, the sorts of behavior that should be criminalized are criminalized. Criminal behavior is wrongful behavior. Behavior proscribed in the criminal law roughly captures or coheres with the public's views about what sorts of behavior are wrong and what sorts of wrongs should be prohibited by the state. Citizens are—and are generally recognized to be—equals. That is, they enjoy an equal status in the political community, and this is reflected in the criminal law. Theorists thus assume what I will call *limited structural injustice*. Limited structural injustice reflects the recognition by theorists of the possibility of the existence of structural injustice even in reasonably just states. However, the overall institutional system is such that it does not undermine or threaten the legitimacy of the institutional order.

The state is also taken to have political authority. The state, in other words, has the right to govern, setting norms for interaction and enforcing those norms. The state maintains its authority by respecting the limits on what it is authorized to do.[2] Theories of retributive justice thus typically

1 For a similar conceptualization of the demandingness constraint shared by principles of justice see Mathias Risse, *Global Justice* (Princeton, NJ: Princeton University Press, 2012). He writes, "It is commonly agreed, though, that obligations of justice are not the only sorts of moral obligation, and that among moral obligations, obligations of justice are especially stringent" (p. 5). For the articulation of the other dimensions of principles of justice I am grateful to Linda Radzik for discussions of this issue.

2 Theories of punishment do not always make explicit the normative view of the criminal law that is endorsed or the nature and limits of the authority of the state. On this point see Anthony Duff, "Legal Punishment," *Stanford Encyclopedia of Philosophy* (http://plato.stanford.edu/entries/legal-punishment).

assume the condition of what I will call *narrow uncertainty about authority*. Particular questions may arise in practice as to the authority of a particular government official, given for instance his or her complicity in wrongdoing. Or disputes may arise as to which branch of government has the authority to deal with a particular issue or question. However, the basic authority of the state to set out norms governing conduct and enforce those norms is not in dispute, and the limits on the state's authority are generally respected.

The state in which punishment is being considered is also taken to be relatively stable. The condition of what I call *minimal existential uncertainty* obtains. That is, there is a clear political trajectory for a given political community, one in which the basic institutional structure is maintained and continues to structure the community.

Against this background punishment is morally controversial because of a possible tension between the intentional infliction of something burdensome on citizens and the respect owed to all citizens. Punishment characteristically includes the loss of liberty. One worry is that such a loss of liberty renders a citizen unequal in terms of the standing she enjoys within the state; the question arises, "How is punishment consistent with, or even expressive of, the respect that citizens owe to each other?"[3] A more general utilitarian worry is that the infliction of something unpleasant serves no purpose, and so causes needless suffering.

Theories of punishment respond to both kinds of worries, establishing how someone becomes liable to the infliction of something burdensome by committing a crime, why this imposition is compatible with equal citizenship, and what moral purpose punishment serves.[4] In particular, theories of negative retributivism explain how individuals become liable to punishment and its compatibility with equal citizenship. Such theories establish the moral permissibility of punishment; it is something that states may permissibly do. Theories of positive retributivism explain why there are good moral reasons to inflict punishment on those who are so eligible. In particular, such accounts provide a rationale for instituting a system of criminal law, where the rationale is based fundamentally on the claims that it is important for the state to give people what they deserve and that this is what punishment for perpetrators does. "'Positive' retributivism is typically expressed in the language of penal desert … penal desert constitutes not just a necessary, but an in principle sufficient reason for punishment."[5]

To illustrate how a set of circumstances of justice affect the justification of principles of retributive justice, consider the theory of retributive justice developed by Jean Hampton.[6] My aim in discussing Hampton is not to challenge her defense of the core positive retributive intuition; to the contrary, against the background context that is implicitly assumed, Hampton's defense of the basic principle of retributive justice is quite compelling.

At their most general level, theories of retributive justice offer an account of what constitutes the just treatment of a perpetrator of wrongdoing. In particular, retributive theories explain why justice demands that perpetrators of wrongdoing suffer, characteristically via punishment. All wrongful actions involve the violation of a moral standard for conduct, and often that violation results in wrongful harm to an individual. However, according to Hampton, only a specific category of wrongful action deserves a retributive response. Some wrongful actions insult a victim's dignity

3 Ibid.

4 Ibid.

5 Ibid.

6 Jean Hampton, "Correcting Harms versus Righting Wrongs: The Goal of Retribution," *UCLA Law Review* 39 (1992): 1659–702.

and inflict moral injury on victims by damaging his or her ability to realize her value and have that value acknowledged.[7]

To explain the moral injury inflicted by some kinds of wrongdoing, Hampton first assumes a Kantian theory of moral worth, according to which all individuals have equal moral value by virtue of our humanity. This value is not something that other individuals can alter through their actions. However, all individuals are vulnerable to being diminished. Human behavior is communicative and can express views about the value of others.[8] Some wrongful conduct communicates a message about the value of the victim, a message that is "'read off of'" the action.[9] In particular, in committing some wrongs a perpetrator falsely declares that he is superior to the victim in value and is permitted to treat the victim in the manner constitutive of the wrong done; the victim is entitled to no better treatment. An individual is diminished if she is the target of behavior or treatment that falsely communicates her relative inferiority. Illustrating with the example of rape, Hampton writes, "The action—in both its commission and in its results—representing the rapist as master and the victim as inferior object … accounts for its being wrongful."[10]

Though victims are not in fact less valuable than perpetrators and do not lose value through such treatment, they can be injured by such wrongdoing in two ways. First, such treatment damages the acknowledgement of a victim's value. The act of wrongdoing itself failed to acknowledge the victim's value. Moreover, that failure by the perpetrator makes a victim vulnerable to similar treatment by others and potentially reinforces an incorrect understanding of an individual's value among others, including the victim. Second, wrongdoing impairs a victim's ability to realize her value. Having a certain value generates entitlements to make claims on others, including claims to be treated in particular ways. To be intentionally treated in a way that violates these claims, often by being subject to certain harm, is to deny an individual's ability to have her value respected through the actions of others. In Hampton's words, "harms anger us not merely because they cause suffering we have to see in others, but also because we see their inflictions as *violative of the victim's entitlements given her value*."[11]

In Hampton's view, justice demands that this false claim expressed in wrongdoing be countered and that the moral equality of perpetrator and victim be reasserted. More specifically, to repair the injury involved in wrongdoing it is necessary to annul the act of diminishment. Annulling the act and asserting the moral truth cannot be accomplished through words alone.

Verbally asserting or communicating the worth of the victim is insufficient because the evidence of the inferiority of the victim is still out there; the action did not simply assert the superiority of the victim and relative diminishment of the victim, but tried to achieve that diminishment.[12] To annul wrongdoing the social world must be "remade" such that the situation the wrongdoing tried to create with his or her action is repudiated.

Retribution, or retributive suffering, remakes the social world, according to Hampton, by denying the claimed superiority of the perpetrator and repairing the damage to the acknowledgement of a victim's value and ability to realize her value.[13] Suffering repudiates the superiority of the perpetrator by defeating him or her. The intentional infliction of suffering involves a form of mastery over another individual. By being put in a position where he cannot do what he wishes,

7 Ibid., 1666 and 1679.

8 Ibid., 1670.

9 Ibid., 1674. In Hampton's view the message implicit in an action is objective; it is not a function or product of the psychological responses of a victim to certain treatment. Individuals with a distorted sense of self-worth (undervalued or exaggerated) may not be bothered by objectively injurious actions or be bothered by actions that are not in fact injurious.

10 Ibid., 1684.

11 Ibid., 1678.

12 Ibid., 1687.

13 Ibid., 1686.

the perpetrator experiences the state of no longer being a master of another. This directly counters the wrongdoing in the same language as the wrong itself. By punishing the perpetrator on behalf of the victim the state affirms the victim's importance, acknowledging her value and affirming the central importance of having her claims on others respected. Given the overarching objective of punishment, the amount of punishment to be inflicted must be proportional to the suffering needed to repudiate the message of superiority implicit in the action thereby reestablishing the equality of the victim.

Hampton establishes why it is appropriate for the state to inflict such suffering and what such suffering by the state represents. The state is assumed in such contexts to be the moral representative of our values. As Hampton writes:

> some crimes are so serious that we cannot imagine any person or institution sufficing as an adequate agent other than the state. As Hegel appreciated, the modern state is the citizenry's moral representative; in the face of pluralism and religious controversy, it is the only institutional voice of the community's shared moral values. Serious crimes represent serious attacks on those moral views, and in particular, on the conception of worth animating those views, and thus the state is the only institution that can speak and act on behalf of the community against the diminishment accomplished by the crime.[14]

The suffering inflicted via punishment emphatically denies the permissibility of violating the norms for treatment defining this general context. In addition, the state is supposed to be impartial with respect to the victim and perpetrator. Because of this neutrality, the state can focus on what is morally relevant in determining how the perpetrator should be treated given his action and basic humanity, and similarly what is needed to reaffirm the victim's value.

A fourth assumption implicit in Hampton's analysis, which is worth highlighting, concerns the kind of wrongdoing to which retributive responses provide an answer. Wrongdoing is presumed to be largely *individual and personal*. Wrongdoing is not political; it is not committed with the sanction of the state, formally or informally, and is not committed in order to further political ends or objectives. Rather, individual reasons and objectives motivate criminal action. Moreover, wrongdoing occurs against a background of broad compliance with the criminal law; it is the structurally condemned exception and not the rule.[15] In these circumstances the moral equality of the victim is generally affirmed and respected. Wrongdoing is the exception and not the rule. Wrongdoing thus represents an isolated action by an individual in violation of the entitlement of the victim. Inflicting suffering on the perpetrator by the state addresses the source of the violation of the victim's entitlements.

Circumstances of Transitional Justice

Hampton's justification of the core retributive claim is plausible in a particular set of circumstances, namely, those defining reasonably just, stable democracies outlined in the previous section: *limited and localized structural injustice, minimal existential uncertainty, limited uncertainty about authority*, and *individual and personal wrongdoing*. In this section I describe a different set of circumstances of justice, circumstances characterizing societies in transition. My aim is to show how the persuasiveness of Hampton's explanation diminishes when the background circumstances

14 Ibid., 1694.

15 A few exceptions to this general picture may exist in a given community. For example, in the United States purchasing alcohol while underage is criminal behavior that is the norm rather than the exception.

are altered. Importantly for my purposes, the persuasiveness diminishes when the background circumstances of transitional justice are introduced. My discussion highlights the need to develop an alternative explanation of the justice of punishment in transitional contexts.

No community perfectly satisfies the demands of justice, and so every community is transitional in the sense of continually striving to better fulfill the demands of justice. However, the injustice with which communities must deal varies. *Pervasive Structural Injustice* has two important characteristics. First, structural injustice is so severe and prevalent that it undermines the legitimacy of the institutional order. Institutional structures, and not just infractions of legal norms, can be considered criminal. Second, efforts to enact reform or change within the existing legal order have a low probability of success.

Collective and Political Wrongdoing occurs when wrongdoing becomes commonplace and is no longer exceptional. Wrongdoing has become normalized. Wrongdoing is collective in the sense it is committed by groups and often is targeted against groups. It is political in two senses. First, wrongs are done for the sake of fulfilling and achieving political objectives. Second, wrongdoing is committed by agents of the state, by individuals acting with the authorization of the state, or by groups contesting the authority of the state. One consequence of the political character of wrongdoing is that what should be criminalized is not criminalized, formally or informally, by the state. Wrongdoing thus does not involve the violation of a generally recognized demand of equality, but takes place in a context in which the moral standing of (some) citizens is challenged.

The third circumstance characteristic of transitional societies is *moderately severe existential uncertainty*. This refers to the fact that the political future of a community can be or become deeply unclear. In such a context, the larger narrative into which a given event figures is indeterminate at the moment the event occurs. It is not obvious whether an election is the ushering in of a new era of political decision-making or is an anomaly. Cooperative interaction leading to a temporary pause in fighting is often fragile, and is vulnerable to being disrupted. The data on transitions to democracy reinforce the reasonableness of such narrative uncertainty. Transitions to democracy often fail; successful transitions are the exception and not the rule. Thus, the likelihood of actually achieving the consolidation of democratic institutions is low. Citizens and policy experts often also share the subjective skepticism about the likelihood of success for a transition.

Finally, any use of coercive power by the state raises questions of authority; questions, that is, about the standing of the state. Given the moral equality of all persons, it is not obvious why one individual has the right to compel another individual to act in certain ways and respond coercively if not obeyed. In contexts of *fundamental uncertainty about authority* the standing of the state to punish is especially fraught. The state is characteristically implicated in the wrongdoing to which individuals are being called to account. Moreover, the institutional framework of the government is by definition in flux, with democratic norms and processes in the process of being consolidated but not yet actually in place. Thus, standard accounts of the nature of democratic authority cannot be applied directly to such contexts.

In circumstances of pervasive structural injustice and collective, political wrongdoing, there is no prior baseline of equal standing among all citizens, which the infliction of punishment threatens to disrupt. The rights and liberties enjoyed by citizens vary. Thus, punishment occurs in a context in which some citizens or group of citizens have a lower recognized standing or status in the political community than others. Insofar as punishment is *prima facie* morally controversial and the liability of perpetrators of wrongdoing to punishment is in doubt, then, it is not for the same reason offered in stable democratic contexts. That is, the question is not how punishment is compatible with recognizing the equal status of all in a community, and the respect owed to all citizens by the state given our moral equality. In transitional contexts there is no prior situation of equality or equal respect that could be threatened. Indeed, it is precisely a context of equal respect that is in need of cultivation.

Rather, punishment is controversial because individual perpetrators do not violate norms that others were respecting in general. Violations of basic norms of conduct are common and widespread, so that an act of rape is one of many acts of its kind in contexts where sexual violence becomes a tool of warfare. The fact that the actions that are now the subject of punishment were not criminalized formally or in practice and that individual perpetrators are characteristically acting in collaboration with many others, working collectively to achieve a broader political goal, challenges the core claim of negative retributivism; namely, that a person who commits a wrong thereby becomes liable to punishment. The moral question becomes: why is it permissible and fair to punish an individual for an action that was not socially and/or legally proscribed at the time it was committed and that was committed (in many cases) by an individual who was following orders issued by a superior?

The rationale for positive desert, for why suffering is what perpetrators of wrongdoing deserve and should be a priority for the state to pursue, is also less persuasive in the circumstances of transition. In short, this is because punishment is not going to be effective in achieving its putative retributive purpose.

Acts of wrongdoing in circumstances of transition are not isolated violations of the entitlements of specific citizens. Rather, individual acts of wrongdoing form part of a broad pattern of action and institutional structures that systematically diminishes the status of certain individuals or groups. Being subjected to ongoing violence, or under the threat of violence given membership in a group, is one important way of undermining the status of individuals in communities. For implicit in violence, especially when widespread and systematic, is the permissibility of treating individuals with contempt and disrespect. Individual acts of wrongdoing thus cumulatively attempt to establish and maintain the relative inferiority of certain members. Moreover, the state is intimately involved in this process of diminishment by committing or condoning acts that have this purpose.

Against this background, addressing the message implicit in an isolated act of wrongdoing will fail to reassert the moral truth about the moral standing of the victim, because it does not address fully the source of the challenge to the victim's status. The diminishment to which individuals or groups are targeted by, for example, violence, is not simply a function of one act of violence committed by a single individual. Rather, it is a function of an act, often committed as part of a broad pattern of treatment towards members of a targeted group, and moreover sanctioned, committed, and/or ordered by government officials. It is this collective and political character of the wrongdoing that leads to the systematic diminishment of individuals. This is most obvious in cases of genocide. Genocide is a collective endeavor, and it is only possible to identify an act as an act of genocide when the actions of many individuals are considered together. Victims are subject to treatment that is taken to be de facto permissible. The message implicit in wrongdoing is thus not just that a single individual perpetrator believes that he/she is superior to the victim. It is that this individual, along with many others within the community, hold such a view. Moreover, in cases of collective and political wrongdoing victims are not only subject to harmful and disrespectful treatment, they cannot use official channels to protest since those channels are complicit in the wrongdoing.

The infliction of punishment on a single perpetrator leaves untouched the actions of others or the broader institutional context in which wrongdoing occurred. Unaddressed are the other actions of violence, or the official figures that gave the orders to those inflicting torture or participating in genocide. In a context in which there was a systematic and institutionally structured denial of this equality, insofar as there is a message of the equality of the victim implicit in the suffering of punishment, it is not likely to be powerful enough to counter the broader institutional context in which unequal treatment was and often still is sanctioned and justified.[16] If an individual act of punishment expresses the moral equality of the victim that an individual act of wrongdoing denied, this isolated message, absent other responses or structural change, stands little chance of countering the history of messages of the inequality of victims expressed by the actions of other individuals and the structure of institutions.

Moreover, it is not obvious that the social meaning of punishment is the same in the circumstances of transitional justice than in the circumstances of a just and stable democracy. Given the complicity of the state in wrongdoing, the message of equality at the core of punishment could be seen as insincerely expressed by the state, given its recent history. Criminal trials may become merely the victor's justice rather than attempts at retributive justice. At a minimum, it is not clear that the conventional social meaning that is at the core of Hampton's account of retributive suffering can plausibly be attributed to suffering inflicted by the state in transitional circumstances.

Finally, Hampton's explanation of why the state should punish is also unconvincing in transitional contexts. The reason why the state is especially effective in achieving punishment's purpose in stable democratic contexts cannot be offered in transitional contexts. In circumstances of structural injustice and political wrongdoing, the state is *not* the moral exemplar of a community's values. Rather, in a number of ways it is the exemplar of values in need of repudiation. Moreover, since the state is implicated in wrongdoing, it is not morally impartial and so not necessarily in the best position to ensure the appropriate punishment is given. More fundamentally, the basic standing of the state to inflict punishment is in need of justification. Given the complicity of the state in wrongdoing and the pervasive structural injustice in the background of such wrongdoing, the basic authority of the state to order citizens to act in certain ways and to punish infractions of norms for behavior is in doubt.

Lastly, the very norms that have been violated, the violation of which is the subject of punishment, are often not norms that the state recognized and enforced. A basic principle of the rule of law is that individuals be punished for actions that were criminal at the time they were committed. However, that norm seems to be violated in many cases where punishment is inflicted in transitional contexts, for the actions that become the subject of punishment were not proscribed formally or informally in practice that the time they were committed. For example, torture may have been ordered or encouraged by officials. The state acts outside the scope of any authority it may have, insofar as the state must violate this norm to inflict punishment.

Responding to Wrongdoing in Transitional Contexts

Punishment may be justified in transitional contexts. Perpetrators of wrongdoing may become liable to punishment through their actions, there may be an important moral purpose facilitated by the state through punishment, and the state may have or acquire both the standing to mete out punishment and the characteristics that would make it an especially effective agent in achieving punishment's purpose. However, I claimed in the previous section, the arguments for these conclusions will be fundamentally different in transitional contexts. The explanation for why an individual is liable to punishment cannot simply demonstrate how punishment is compatible with the respect owed to individuals. The rationale for why punishment should be pursued cannot be based on an account of the social function of punishment appropriate for contexts in which structural injustice is limited and criminal wrongdoing is isolated. And the account of the standing and efficacy of the state to

16 Pablo de Greiff, "Theorizing Transitional Justice," in Rosemary Nagy, Jon Elster and Melissa Williams (eds), *NOMOS LI: Transitional Justice* (New York: New York University Press, 2012), 31–77.

inflict punishment cannot presuppose that the state is legitimate. So what should an account of punishment in transitional contexts look like? I want to end by summarizing the desiderata for an adequate theory of punishment in such contexts. Such a theory would establish the justice of punishment in transitional contexts.

The first task for a theory of punishment in the circumstances of transition is to explain how perpetrators of wrongdoing become liable to punishment. This explanation must confront directly the question of the legal status of the wrongdoing subject to punishment at the time the wrong was committed. It cannot be assumed that the actions subject to punishment were criminalized formally by declared rules and/or were proscribed by customary practice as many candidate wrongs for punishment during a transition were not. Pursuing punishment of actions that were legally sanctioned at the time they were committed violates a basic principle of the rule of law. Thus, the explanation of the eligibility of a perpetrator to punishment must account for the permissibility of pursuing punishment despite the violation of this tenet or explain how this tenet is not violated. Discussions in the legal philosophy literature of the permissibility of punishing so-called grudge informers provide resources for dealing with this issue.[17] Grudge informers refer to individuals who report personal enemies to authorities during periods of conflict and/or repression in order to get rid of them. Some grudge informers from Nazi Germany were put on trial following the end of World War II. Philosophical discussions of the justification for the punishment of such informers directly grappled with the question of whether punishment was permissible, given that such informers were acting within the legal framework at the time they reported their personal enemies.

One question that discussions of the case of grudge informers raise, but do not directly take up, is whether and in what way the fact that individuals were acting for personal and not political reasons impacts their liability to punishment. In South Africa following the end of apartheid and transition to democracy, only individuals who were acting for political reasons were permitted to apply for amnesty as part of the Truth and Reconciliation Commission proceedings. Individuals who committed acts of killing, abduction, torture and severe ill treatment who were not acting for such reasons remained liable to punishment. Thus, we find differences in treatment of those who did wrong following the end of Nazi Germany and the end of apartheid, based on whether political objectives or personal objectives were being pursued. One philosophical question this variation raises is the moral salience of the political dimensions of action for determining how perpetrators of wrongdoing should be treated following the end of conflict and repression. A related issue concerns the fact that wrongdoing is often collective, committed by groups and targeting groups. A fundamental issue raised by this collective character concerns the fairness of prosecuting an individual for a crime for which he or she was jointly responsible.

After addressing the liability of a perpetrator to punishment, a theory of punishment in the circumstances of transition must explain why punishment is an important objective for the state to pursue. Here it will be critical to understand the social function of punishment in such circumstances. As the discussion of Hampton's account of retributivism highlighted, this social function will not be the same as in stable democratic contexts. What an isolated instance of wrongdoing does during conflict and repression is not just assert a false claim that is otherwise accepted. It reinforces a false claim that is widely accepted and institutionally endorsed. An account of the social good facilitated by punishment must begin from this understanding of wrongdoing and then make the case that punishment is fitting and effective as a way to respond to wrongdoing of this kind. My discussion of Hampton demonstrated that there are compelling reasons to think that punishment

17 See D. Dyzenhaus, "The Grudge Informer Case Revisited," *New York University Law Review* 83 (2008): 1000–34; L. Fuller, "Positivism and Fidelity to Law: A Reply to Professor Hart," *Harvard Law Review* 71(4) (1958): 630–72; H.L.A. Hart, "Positivism and the Separation of Law and Morals," *Harvard Law Review* 71(4) (1958): 593–629.

is not sufficient to counter a message of inequality implicit in wrongdoing, nor is it addressed in a context in which that message is broadly accepted. Thus, considered in isolation, punishment cannot be defended in the way that retributive theories such as Hampton's do. Perhaps punishment is still a fitting response.

Finally, in explaining what important moral good is facilitated by punishment, a theory of punishment in transitions must make the case that the state is an effective agent to facilitate this good. The efficacy of the state in achieving punishment's purpose becomes an issue because the state is implicated in past wrongdoing. Thus, the state is not a neutral or impartial party to wrongdoing that occurred and has not symbolized and institutionally endorsed values underpinning a just and legitimate institutional order. This alters the social meaning that actions of the state can have. Moreover, it severely challenges the authority of the state to deal with past wrongs. Part of what a theory of punishment must explain is how the state has or can acquire the authority to deal with past wrongs.

These desiderata suggest that the case for the justifiability of punishment in the circumstances of transition will not be easy to satisfy. Indeed, the case for punishment in circumstances of transitions may turn out to be conditional in the sense that the justifiability of punishment in any particular transitional context depends on what actions or reforms the transitional government is (or is not) taking. For example, given the collective character of wrongdoing, the appropriateness or fittingness of punishing an individual may be influenced by how other individuals complicit in the wrongs done are treated. To the extent that others are held accountable, this may enhance the fairness of punishing any given individual. Or the efficacy of punishment in achieving its particular social function may be enhanced by other way(s) that the state deals with past wrongs. Insofar as the trial and punishment of perpetrators is not an isolated response, but part of a broader program for dealing with extant structural injustice and past wrongs, the sincerity of the message being communicated by the state through punishment or the state's purpose in punishment may be enhanced.

Alternatively, the desiderata for an adequate theory of punishment in transitions may more radically suggest that punishment is not the appropriate way to hold perpetrators accountable for past wrongs in transitional contexts. It may be the case that the turn to other kinds of responses to wrongdoing, such as policies of lustration or truth commissions, reflects not just the constraints imposed by transitional circumstances. Such responses may in fact be better suited to dealing with wrongs that have a collective and political character and are being dealt with by a state whose authority must be (re-) established. A theory of transitional justice that articulates the basic principles to be satisfied by responses to wrongdoing will provide resources for understanding whether this is the case.

PART III
Transitional Justice as a Vehicle of Structural and Institutional Change

Chapter 5

Transitional Justice as Structural Justice

Krista K. Thomason

Philosophical scholarship on transitional justice has largely focused on adjudicating between retributive or restorative justice in post-conflict societies (Mani 2002: 5–6; Arbour 2007: 5–6; Nagy 2008: 276–8). The primary question is usually as follows: do we properly achieve justice by arresting and prosecuting the perpetrators of genocide and mass atrocity, or do we properly achieve justice by reconciliation between victims and perpetrators in favor of establishing peace? The debate over retributive and restorative justice has been the focus of recent criticism. Some scholars have begun to urge theorists of transitional justice to take into account the economic, cultural, and social realities of post-conflict nations (Arbour 2007; Nagy 2008; Dicklitch and Malik 2010; Millar 2011). This objection raises an important question for scholarship on transitional justice: exactly how do we take into account the particularities of post-conflict nations while still exploring transitional justice at the level of theory? In what follows, I propose an answer to this question. Using Young's concept of structural injustice, I construct a theoretical framework of transitional justice as what I call *structural justice* (Young 2011). Transitional justice as structural justice focuses primarily on the political, social, and economic institutions that give rise to violence. It aims to (a) revise or abolish the original institutions that contributed to the violence and (b) implement new institutions that prevent economic, social, or political disenfranchisement. I argue that structural justice is a theoretical framework of transitional justice that can accommodate economic and social issues of particular post-conflict nations.

The Importance of Theories of Transitional Justice

Literature in transitional justice spans both theoretical and empirical realms. A great deal of work has been done on the empirical issues of transitional justice by anthropologists, sociologists, historians, and journalists (Crocker 1999: 45–6). Political theory, legal theory, and philosophy have contributed to the theoretical side. One might wonder, however, why transitional justice needs much theorizing. Each transitional society is different and as such one could argue that the empirical study of particular nations is much more crucial to the process of transition than abstract theory. Even among theorists, there seems to be little consensus about the components of any particular theory of transitional justice and where consensus exists, it is thin (de Greiff 2012: 32). If theories of transitional justice are disparate, it is unclear how work in the theoretical realm aids in actual processes of transitional justice. One might reasonably wonder if there is anything to be gained from such theorizing.

Philosophers who work in transitional justice have responded to challenges like these in several ways. First, as de Greiff argues, theory can help guide action. It can help us to "understand what we are committing ourselves to" (de Greiff 2012: 33). If, for instance, one thinks that the primary aim of transitional justice is to achieve lasting peace, then theorizing can clarify just what lasting peace is and how it is achieved. Additionally, theorizing helps to provide societies with a broader perspective on the transitional process. Theorizing about transitional justice apart from any particular cases of it can draw attention to common problems. Paying too strict attention to the particularities of individual cases of transitional justice is likely to miss deeper issues. Transitional justice that focuses too closely on the immediate situation is likely to be "ad hoc, ineffective, inconsistent, and unstable" (Crocker 1999: 63). Finally, theories of transitional justice deal explicitly with the normative aims of transitional justice (de Greiff 2012; Crocker 1999). While empirical study focuses on the details of what has happened or is happening in transitional societies, theory investigates what ought to have happened or what ought to happen in the future. Explicit attention to the normative aspect of transitional justice is one of the primary purposes of theory. Articulating what transitional justice ought to be or ought to achieve is an indispensable guide to transitional policies, laws, and procedures (de Greiff 2012: 33).

A Challenge for Theories of Transitional Justice

Despite the importance of transitional justice theory, it faces a substantive challenge. More recently, scholarship in transitional justice raises the worry that too often Western conceptions of justice dominate the process of post-conflict reconciliation (Mani 2002; Arbour 2007; Nagy 2008; Corntassel and Holder 2008; Dicklitch and Malik 2010; Millar 2011). This concern arises both at the level of practice and at the level of theory. With regard to practice, tribunals and truth commissions are often organized and funded by international institutions and Western nations (Nagy 2008: 278; Dicklitch and Malik 2010: 520–21; Hoogenboom and Vieille 2010: 189–90). Thus the paradigm for transitional justice tends to resemble a Western legalistic model. Even though truth commissions are thought to be more conducive to reconciliation than tribunals, they still share many of the same legalistic elements: witness testimony, gathering evidence, and cross-examination by members of the truth commission (Nagy 2008: 278–9). The parties involved in implementing transitional justice believe that reconciliation ought to reflect the values, beliefs, and commitments particular to the nation in transition. Desmond Tutu argues, for example, that the Truth and Reconciliation Commission of South Africa was rooted in the African concept of *Ubuntu*, which captured the commitments and attitudes of South Africa better than a tribunal (Tutu 1999: 31).

Those who raise the worry about Western influence suggest that it is important that transitional justice incorporate and address the particular concerns of the members of the transitional society because they should experience the process as just. Millar points out, for instance, that local people in Makeni expected that the transitional justice process in Sierra Leone would help amputees with access to health care, but it did not (Millar 2010: 525). As such, they perceive the TRC as failing to provide justice because victims of the war are unable to meet their basic needs. If the members of a transitional society do not experience truth commissions or tribunals as accomplishing justice, transitional justice is ultimately "alien and distant to those who actually have to live together after atrocity" (Nagy 2008: 275). This raises two serious worries. First, if transitional justice is experienced as alien, the peace supposedly brokered by truth commissions and tribunals may not be sustainable. The local people may not feel any ownership or connection to the peace and thus be unmotivated to maintain it. Second, the failures of the truth commissions and tribunals may be harming the societies they are supposed to help. The victims of the conflict might feel wronged by the perpetrators of violence and then feel wronged a second time when their concerns are ignored by the truth commissions and tribunals. This second worry is often compounded by the political involvement that Western nations may have had in the original conflict. The fact that the UN, for instance, gave a seat in the General Assembly to the "Coalition Government of Democratic Kampuchea," which gave international recognition to the rule of the Khmer Rouge, gives the people of Cambodia little faith in the good intentions of the UN-backed tribunal (Dicklitch and Malik 2010: 518). To address these worries, scholars urge that special attention be paid to the particular features of each transitional society in the implementation of transitional justice.

The problem of a dominant paradigm arises at the level of scholarship as well. Millar notes that most scholarship on transitional justice is written by Western scholars, and scholars question whether the absence of non-Western voices shapes the debate:

> Because the currently dominant paradigms of transitional justice place the emphasis on either individuated retribution (in the form of criminal tribunals) or collective truth telling (in the form of Truth Commissions), and the application of transitional justice is dominated by Western and relatively privileged intellectuals, these more basic needs for economic and social justice are commonly overlooked or disparaged in the ongoing discourse. (Millar 2011: 531)

A large portion of the literature on transitional justice focuses on the debate between types of justice, mainly retribution and reconciliation (Little 1999: 66–7; Dicklitch and Malik 2010: 518). This debate resembles the more classical debates in political philosophy about justifications of punishment (Arbour 2007: 4–6; Nagy 2003: 278–9). As such, there is a tendency to fit the problems of transitional justice into an existing model that is based on issues in the Western legal tradition. Scholars suggest that in spite of its growth over the last two decade, the literature on transitional justice has been myopically concentrated on a small handful of theoretical issues that largely ignore problems facing particular transitioning societies.

Theorists might reasonably respond that many of the current theories of transitional justice can be amended to include some of the issues that critics raise. Current work in transitional justice has begun to include issues like fair distribution of goods (de Greiff 2012; Fuller 2012), gender-based violence (Oosterveld 2009; Buckley-Zistel and Stanley 2012), and reparations or memorialization (Walker 2010; Blustein 2012) as essential components to transition. Although widening the scope of transitional justice to include things like economic concerns and gender-based violence is surely a step forward, merely casting a wider net does not solve a deeper theoretical tension uncovered by the challenge above. Retributive and restorative models have in common a narrow focus on the particular violent event or particular violent regime: retributive justice claims such events must be punished and restorative justice claims that the society must heal from these events. In both cases, transitional justice is that which "bridges a violent or repressive past and a peaceful, democratic future" (Nagy 2008: 289). Even if we think of transitional justice as including more, it is still conceived as that which mends a rift or heals a wound. Including memorialization or reparations as essential to transition merely reinforces the paradigm of transitional justice as a response to massive violence or some particular regime. But thinking in this way ultimately undermines the project of trying to accommodate the specifics of post-conflict societies.

The particular conflicts that are a focus of trials and truth commissions are often closely tied to a longer history of conflict in the society. But the violence and conflicts are seen as deviations from the norm: they are "dark times" in an otherwise peaceful nation. This conception does not allow for the examination of previous policies and historical legacies that may have led to or fueled the violence. The challenge from scholars like Nagy, Millar, and Arbour precisely is to argue that scholarship in transitional justice ought not to see a genocide, mass atrocity, or violent regime as a deviation from a society's otherwise peaceful and unproblematic history. There were many incidents of violence during South African apartheid committed by both the police force and the resistance movements, but apartheid itself was the result of several laws and policies. Apartheid was implemented over several years, which means that its policies were at some point the norm and not the deviation. Additionally, the 1994 violence of the Rwandan genocide was extreme and immediate, but given the long-standing historical tensions between the Hutus and the Tutsis as well as the rampant and well-known violence of Dutch colonial rule, it is not as though the genocide was an *ex nihilo* disruption in an otherwise harmonious state of affairs (Hochschild 1999; Mamdani 2001). Similarly, the violence against the Maya in Guatemala is part of a long history of tensions between the Maya and Ladino people over the economic future and national identity of Guatemala (Handy 2003). Even though the massacre in Panzos was appalling, it was "not surprising" given the reinvigorated guerilla movements in the 1960s (Handy 2003: 285–6). The point here is not to downplay the outbreaks of violence or mass atrocity in these cases, but rather to show that—horrifying though they are—seeing them as deviations from the norm misses the extent to which background conditions of the societies in which they take place contributed to them. The scholars who challenge the legalistic model of transitional justice are suggesting that sustainable peace and reconciliation are only possible if these background conditions are addressed in the process of transition.

The charge of Western dominance in both the theory and practice of transitional justice is a serious one. How are we to balance the importance and need for theory with the corrective value of paying attention to the "facts on the ground" in individual cases? I offer a theoretical model for transitional justice that avoids the pitfalls of Western dominance. In what follows, I argue that Iris Young's account of structural injustice can be modified to provide an account of structural justice. Transitional justice can be, as I will argue, thought of as structural justice. I will illustrate how transitional justice as structural justice might work by analyzing particular cases of transitioning societies. Structural justice can be a model of transitional justice that avoids the overly legalistic elements of other theories.

Young's Structural Injustice

Young defines structural injustice this way:

> Structural injustice occurs when social processes put large groups of persons under systematic threat of domination or deprivation of the means to develop and exercise their capacities, at the same time that these processes enable others to dominate or to have a wide range of opportunities for developing and exercising capabilities available to them. (Young 2011: 52)

She provides an example of housing deprivation in the US to illustrate: people often lack access to affordable housing due to a number of factors beyond their control (Young 2011:45). Landlords sell older buildings to developers forcing tenants to move. These former tenants are forced to seek apartments elsewhere, even though affordable housing is at a premium. The apartments they can afford are often too far from their jobs, which would require them to buy a car that they cannot afford. Or affordable housing is in unsafe neighborhoods where families with children are afraid to move (Young 2011: 43). As a result, many families face the prospect of homelessness–not because they have been the victim of a crime or the victim of discrimination, but simply because a complex set of laws, policies, and social structures interact in ways that disadvantage them (Young 2011: 52). In spite of the fact that there is no nefarious actor who threatens families with homelessness, Young contends that being vulnerable to homelessness is a wrong because "some people's options are unfairly constrained and they are threatened with deprivation while others derive significant benefits" (Young 2011: 52). Lacking affordable housing wrongs the people who are disadvantaged in this system because their lives and plans are unfairly limited because of the position they occupy in the system. In cases of structural injustice, no one person or group of persons is the cause of the injustice. It is the system—a set of overlapping social forces, laws, and policies—rather than people or groups that is unjust.

Because structural injustice arises in this way, traditional accounts of responsibility cannot adequately explain what ought to be done about it (Young 2011: 74). Traditional conceptions of moral and legal responsibility rely heavily on the notion of liability: those whose actions can be shown to cause or contribute to the harm done are held responsible for it (Young 2011: 97). Thinking about vulnerability to homelessness on the liability model, some person or group must be said to cause the lack of affordable housing and thus blamed for the injustice. The trouble with this model is twofold. First, vast numbers of people contribute to the lack of housing: landlords who sell their older buildings, developers building luxury houses, and wealthier people who can afford pricier rent and so drive up its cost all in some sense "cause" the lack of affordable housing. But none of these actors intend or foresee that their actions cause other families to be vulnerable to homelessness. Traditional models of responsibility usually require that agents must foresee or intend the actions that lead to a wrong in order to be blameworthy for that wrong (Young 2011: 100). In structural injustice, that is not the case. Additionally, the actions of those who cause structural injustice are well within acceptable legal and moral parameters. Wealthier renters are free to choose luxury apartments and landlords are free to sell their property. An agent who acts within her legal and moral rights is traditionally not seen as blameworthy even if her actions cause something bad. An agent acting in self-defense, for instance, is not blameworthy for the death of her attacker even though she kills him. Since the people who cause or contribute to the lack of affordable housing are pursuing their own interests in a morally and legally permissible way, the liability model will hold that they cannot be responsible for the injustice that results (Young 2011: 100).

Given the problems of the liability model of responsibility, Young argues instead for a "social connection" model of responsibility (Young 2011: 96). The social connection model emphasizes the ways in which individuals and nations are connected through complex social relations and dynamic institutions (Young 2006: 119). In contrast to the liability model, it separates responsibility from guilt or blame: agents can be held responsible for contributing to structural injustice even if they cannot be blamed for their particular actions (Young 2011: 104). As such, the social connection model highlights the background conditions in which agents act rather than their individual actions: saying that structural injustices exist is precisely to claim that the structures in which agents act are unjust or unacceptable (Young 2011: 107). We can be held responsible for these injustices because of our participation in and contribution to the systems that bring that injustice about. As Young writes, "Our responsibility derives from our belonging together with others in a system of interdependent processes of cooperation and competition though which we seek benefits and aim to realize projects" (Young 2011: 105). Because the social connection model of responsibility focuses on ways in which individuals and groups contribute to the systems they belong to, responsibility is shared rather than isolated. Although a wealthy renter might be responsible for structural injustice produced by her choice of a luxury apartment, she is not solely responsible for that injustice. All participants in the system that cause injustice are responsible for the injustice in a forward-looking way: they are responsible for altering the system in such a way that alleviates the injustice (Young 2011: 109). The social connection model thus explains what can be done about structural injustice even though it does not result from the bad acts of a person or group.

Young's account has several features that are attractive for transitional justice. Scholars in transitional justice struggle with questions of complicity and collective responsibility precisely because the violence and conflict that takes place during mass atrocity does not neatly fit the liability model of responsibility. As Nagy points out, violence and conflict often spill across borders: rebel groups often take refuge in neighboring nations and parties to conflict are sometimes funded by outside organizations (Young 2008: 283). Since conflict is neither isolated nor directly tied to one group, Young's social connection model can accommodate this kind of fluidity. One of the features of Young's account of structural injustice that is in my view most relevant to developing a theory of transitional justice is the importance of background conditions. In what follows, I use this feature to sketch an account of transitional justice as structural justice.

Structural Justice

My suggestion here is that we can use Young's definition of structural injustice to construct an account of transitional justice as *structural justice*. Structural injustice occurs when institutions and systems work in such a way to disadvantage large groups of people while allowing others to benefit. Structural justice, then, would require that institutions and systems work to ensure that large groups of people are not disadvantaged. People can be disadvantaged by structural injustice in a number of ways: they might lack access to basic goods, they might be denied economic opportunities, or they may be ostracized from social life. In order to accommodate the variety of disadvantages, I argue that the primary concern for transitional societies is best understood as the prevention of disenfranchisement. With regard to transitional societies, disenfranchisement would mean that some groups are barred from or unable to fully participate in the process of transition and subsequently in the society's transformation moving forward. Although achieving structural justice is a monumental task and not one easily accomplished even by wealthier industrialized nations, it serves the normative aim of transitional justice theory. Thinking of transitional justice as structural justice provides a standard that helps both to guide the process of transition and to evaluate its success. Ideal transitional justice, in other words, should aim at achieving structural justice. In order to prevent disenfranchisement, the systems and institutions of the transitioning society must be evaluated in two ways. First, the structures that contributed to the conflict or violence must be examined and likely repealed or abolished. Second, the new structures that are put into place must ensure that groups are not disenfranchised moving forward. I will explain each of these evaluation processes.

Transitional justice as structural justice takes as its starting point an evaluation of the institutions that contributed to the original conflict. As Young argues, to claim that structural injustice exists is precisely to claim that the institutions themselves are morally problematic (Young 2011: 107). This approach requires seeing violence or conflict not as the "crime" that has to be either prosecuted or reconciled, but rather as part of the system or institutions out of which is arises. The escalating violence in South Africa during the 1980s and 1990s, for example, was at least in part a response to the inauguration of the tricameral parliament where blacks were not represented, the increased militarization of the National Party, and the ban of the African National Congress (ANC) (Lötter 1997: 52–9). Thinking about the connection between institutions and violence does not entail that the perpetrators of that violence are merely cogs in a larger machine rather than responsible agents. It simply situates conflict in its larger context in order to show how that larger context is unjust. Transitional justice as structural justice also does not rule out the establishment of tribunals or truth commissions. Addressing instances of violence is an important part of the transition process, but it is not sufficient. Addressing the systematic and institutional issues is the main focus of transitional justice as structural justice, and tribunals and truth commissions can operate in the service of this larger goal.

One might object that the structures that give rise to events like apartheid, the Rwandan genocide, and the rule of the Khmer Rouge could potentially be traced to the transitioning society's earliest history.[1] If this is true, how can transitional justice as structural justice address these historical legacies? The process of transition will require addressing the institutions that are most pressing and most disenfranchising. Deciding which policies to address will depend on the particular cases, and transitional justice as structural justice allows for these kinds of contextualized decisions. In South Africa, for instance, apartheid itself was the most pressing system to be addressed: lifting the ban on the ANC and freeing Mandela paved the way for substantive negotiations. Cambodia, by contrast, has been politically unstable since the Vietnamese invaded in 1979 and government corruption is rampant (Dicklitch and Malik 2010: 517–18). Indeed, because of the political instability and corruption, the Cambodian tribunals have largely stalemated (Dicklitch and Malik 520–1). Reforming the political process seems to be an immediate step for Cambodia to take. This may include, given their still-powerful influence, banning former Khmer Rouge officials from holding public office. The systems that are current and powerful hindrances to the process of transition should be addressed first even if there are historical legacies that gave rise to them. It is true that many of the unjust structures emanate from a society's long history and that history cannot be changed. But it is a strength of transitional justice as structural justice that it is able to consider the events in a transitioning society's history. A successful transition and a sustainable peace may require addressing some of the historical injustices that went unaddressed for too long. Although the wrongs cannot be undone, memorializing them and acknowledging them as part of the society's history—and as linked to the recent violence—may better facilitate reconciliation than simply treating those wrongs as unrelated.[2]

In addition to evaluating the institutions that led to conflict and violence, transitional justice as structural justice requires ensuring that the new or restored institutions that will be put in place will not disenfranchise groups in the society. Arbour (2007), Nagy (2008), and Millar (2011) specifically call attention to the need for issues of economic and social justice to be included in transitional justice. Transitional justice as structural justice is uniquely able to accommodate these concerns. Both the transitions of Guatemala and Sierra Leone illustrate unaddressed economic and social issues. The violence against the Maya was due in no small part to the conception of Guatemalan nationalism supported by non-Mayans, which was largely European and capitalist (Corntassel and Holder 2008: 483–5; Handy 2003: 280–1). This vision of Guatemala did not include any aspects of traditional Mayan culture, and it helped facilitate and justify the violence against the Mayan population (Corntassel and Holder 2008: 484; Handy 2003: 282). Although the truth commission was able to acknowledge this long-standing tension, Corntassel and Holder argue that the truth commission in Guatemala has not led to proper reconciliation because it did nothing to address indigenous self-determination (2008: 467). Even though the commission recommended reparations to the victims as a measure of restorative justice, it did not address the status of Mayan culture moving forward (Corntassel and Holder 2008: 485). Reparations and memorials, in other words, recognize the Maya as victims, but not as participants in the future of Guatemala. Transitional justice as structural justice would seek to remedy the possible disenfranchisement that can stem from the failure to integrate Mayan culture into the identity of Guatemala. Implementing policies that specifically aim at supporting Mayan self-determination would be one way to guard against this kind of structural injustice.

With regard to Sierra Leone, Millar notes that the truth commission offered victims an opportunity to tell their stories in a public forum, but local populations expected far more (Millar 2011: 524). The war in Sierra Leone decimated much of the nation's infrastructure: homes were burned, hundreds of thousands of people were displaced, and many people were maimed during the actual episodes of violence (Millar 2011: 518). Although right after the war, many people saw the work of the truth

1 Unlike many truth commissions, the truth commission in Guatemala was able to take into account its nation's history of racism (Corntassel and Holder 2008: 483).

2 Blustein articulates the way in which memorialization can aid in reconciliation (Blustein 2012: 22).

commission as important, a few years after the commission finished its work, local experiences told a different story. Years later, many victims of the violence still had no assistance from the government for their basic needs. Despite the fact that amputees were unable to work, they did not receive help with medical care for their children (Millar 2011: 525–6). As such, as Millar argues, the victims of the war did not experience the TRC as just (Millar 2011: 529). Given that the background conditions of poverty were a contributing factor to the situation of the war victims, transitional justice as structural justice would take those conditions into account. Rather than focusing on restorative justice as addressing the violence and its immediate aftermath, transitional justice as structural justice focuses on ensuring that the victims of the war are able to participate in the reconciliation process long into the future. They are unable to fully participate if they lack basic means of subsistence. An important part of the transition process in Sierra Leone would have to be rebuilding the government assistance programs to ensure that victims have a viable voice in the transitional society.

The sketch of structural justice I have given here is brief and much more could be said about it, but we can see its main elements. Transitional justice as structural justice takes as its main task the (a) evaluation, revision, or abolition of the systems that led to violence or conflict and (b) implementing new systems that prevent groups from being disenfranchised in the transition process. Transitional justice as structural justice can do this precisely because—unlike a retributive or restorative model—it does not see the violence or conflict as the primary issue to be addressed in transition. Tensions that lead to violence arise out of or as a response to various social and political institutions. Although the violent incidents should be taken seriously, addressing them fully will likely require serious consideration of the conditions that led to them, particularly when violence is perpetrated by multiple parties. In South Africa, the police, the resistance, and private citizens all engaged in violent acts. Because transitional justice as structural justice evaluates systems and institutions rather than the actions of particular agents, it can more fully respond to cases where violence is widespread in this way. In addition, transitional justice as structural justice is forward-looking as well as backward-looking. Retributive justice is often criticized for being too backward-looking since it is focused on rectifying past acts. But restorative justice is criticized for being too forward-looking and glossing over the past in favor of a brighter future. Transitional justice as structural justice evaluates and reforms past unjust institutions so that future institutions do not suffer from the same problems. It is not enough to revise or abolish unjust policies, but new policies have to be informed by the mistakes of the past. Finally, if peace is to be sustainable, all groups must have a role to play in the society's future. One of the main aims of transitional justice as structural justice is to ensure that all groups in the society are able to participate as fully as they wish in the transition. While retributive and restorative justice see victims and perpetrators, structural justice sees a complex set of structures that gave rise to violence as an extreme form of structural injustice.

Responding to the Challenge

Transitional justice as structural justice is able to respond to the challenge that transitional justice theories are too often dominated by Western legalistic elements. First, it does not posit the primary task of transitional justice to be redress for violence or reconciliation from violence. Accounts of transitional justice that focus primarily on the violence or conflict fall too easily into conceiving of that violence or conflict as a "crime" that must be prosecuted or from which the victims must heal. Even though retributive and restorative accounts advocate for very different kinds of responses to the violence (tribunals versus truth commissions), the violence itself remains the thing that must be responded to. The background conditions that led to the conflict might be seen as important for understanding the conflict, but they are still seen as secondary to the conflict itself. As such, since retributive and restorative accounts posit the conflict as the primary thing to address, transitional justice as structural justice better avoids the legalistic paradigm of the violence as a crime.

Additionally, transitional justice as structural justice is better able to take account of the particular issues involved in each society. First, transitional justice as structural justice will require a comprehensive understanding of the background conditions in order to evaluate and revise those that led to the conflict. These institutions will be different for every post-conflict nation: the long-standing conflict, for instance, between Maya and non-Maya over national identity provides a set of background conditions that is unique to Guatemala. Understanding (and ultimately addressing) this issue cannot be achieved simply by interviewing the survivors and perpetrators of violence about the details of the conflict. Because each transitional society will have different systems to evaluate, transitional justice as structural justice will require a great deal of information gathering. This information gathering specifically aims at the "facts on the ground" not just about the violence or conflict, but about the fabric of the nation itself. Thus the process will be tailored to the individual society from the start.

Since transitional justice as structural justice has to deal with the particular features of each transitioning nation, there is less of a risk that the members of that nation will experience the transition as alien or external. According to locals interviewed, both the tribunals in Bosnia and truth commission in Sierra Leone failed to reflect the concerns of many of the members of the transitioning nations (Hoogenboom and Vieille 2010; Millar 2011). Because the tribunal and truth commission are primarily concerned with violent events, they see the groups involved as victims of the war. But the war affects these groups not just as survivors of violence, but as members of the society in crisis. The amputees in Sierra Leone are literal victims of the violence (in being maimed), but they are also "victims" in a wider sense because the nation in which they live is in crisis. These kinds of concerns are not addressed if the victims are only thought of as survivors of violence. Tribunals and truth commissions are experienced as external or alien because they do not see the victims as part of the social and economic network that they exist in. The amputees in Sierra Leone do not see themselves as just amputees; they see themselves as members of a war-torn nation whose government assistance programs are unable to help them (Millar 2011: 526). Transitional justice as structural justice addresses the concerns of the victims as members of a society in crisis, not just as survivors of a particular violent event. If structural justice focuses on the victims as members of a community, the risk that they will feel alienated during transition is alleviated.

Finally, economic and social issues will not be mere add-ons to transitional justice as structural justice. Scholars like Arbour and Nagy have called for economic and social issues to be at the center of transitional justice, not simply in its periphery (Arbour 2007; Nagy 2008). For example, even though the truth commission in South Africa is widely considered a success, economic issues that are directly related to racial discrimination have yet to be properly addressed (Nagy 2008: 280). The TRC was only mandated to deal with the most egregious violence and thus any attention paid to economic issues had to be secondary (Nagy 2008: 284). Transitional justice as structural justice, unlike other models, puts these issues at the forefront of transition. Young conceives of structural injustice as starting from an individual's social or economic position and determining whether that position is either advantaged or disadvantaged (Young 2012: 57). Social positions are determined by a number of factors, such as gender, education, ethnicity, and community membership. Since addressing structural injustice requires knowing how different social positions fair in the society, transitional justice as structural justice will deal directly with issues like access to education or gender discrimination. In order to ensure that groups are not disenfranchised in the process of transition, the disadvantages of social positions will have to be remedied or addressed before or as the society moves forward. Because transitional justice as structural justice requires this attention to social as well as economic institutions, it is better able to accommodate differing cultural contexts, which can avoid the problem of "one-size-fits-all" solutions.

References

Arbour, Louise. 2007. "Economic and Social Justice for Societies in Transition." *International Law and Politics* 40: 1–27.

Blustein, Jeffery. 2012. "Human Rights and the Internalization of Memory." *Journal of Social Philosophy* 43(1): 19–32.

Buckley-Zistel, Susanne, and Stanley, Ruth, eds. 2012. *Gender in Transitional Justice*. Basingstoke: Palgrave Macmillan.

Corntassel, Jeff and Holder, Cindy. 2008. "Who's Sorry Now? Government Apologies, Truth Commissions, and Indigenous Self-Determination in Australia, Canada, Guatemala, and Peru." *Human Rights Review* 9: 465–89.

Crocker, David A. 1999. "Reckoning with Past Wrongs: A Normative Framework." *Ethics and International Affairs* 13(1): 43–64.

Dicklitch, Susan and Malik, Aditi. 2010. "Justice, Human Rights, and Reconciliation in Postconflict Cambodia." *Human Rights Review* 11: 515–30.

Fuller, Lisa L. 2012. "Burdened Societies." *Ethical Theory and Moral Practice* 25: 369–86.

de Greiff, Pablo. 2012. "Theorizing Transitional Justice." In *Transitional Justice*, edited by Melissa S. Williams, Rosemary Nagy, and John Elster. New York: NYU Press.

Handy, Jim. 2003. "Reimagining Guatemala: Reconciliation and the Indigenous Accords." In *Dilemmas of Reconciliation: Cases and Concepts*, edited by Trudy Govier. Waterloo, ON: Wilfrid Laurier University Press.

Hoogenboom, David and Vieille, Stephanie. 2010. "Rebuilding Social Fabric in Failed States: Examining Transitional Justice in Bosnia." *Human Rights Review* 11: 183–98.

Hochschild, Adam. 1999. *King Leopold's Ghost: A Story of Greed, Terror, and Heroism in Colonial Africa*. Boston, MA: Houghton Mifflin Harcourt.

Little, David. 1999. "A Different Kind of Justice: Dealing with Human Rights Violations in Transitional Societies." *Ethics and International Affairs* 13(1): 65–80.

Lötter, Hennie P.P. 1997. *Injustice, Violence, and Peace: The Case of South Africa*. Amsterdam: Rodopi.

Mani, Rama. 2002. *Beyond Retribution: Seeking Justice in the Shadows of War*. Malden, MA: Polity.

Mamdani, Mahmood. 2001. *When Victims Become Killers: Colonialism, Nativism, and Genocide in Rwanda*. Princeton, NJ: Princeton University Press.

Millar, Geroid. 2011. "Local Evaluations of Justice through Truth Telling in Sierra Leone: Postwar Needs and Transitional Justice." *Human Rights Review* 12: 515–35.

Nagy, Rosemary. 2008. "Transitional Justice as Global Project: Critical Reflections." *Third World Quarterly* 29: 275–89.

Oosterveld, Valerie. 2009. "The Special Court for Sierra Leone's Consideration of Gender-based Violence: Contributing to Transitional Justice?" *Human Rights Review* 10: 73–98.

Tutu, Desmond. 1999. *No Future without Forgiveness*. New York: Doubleday Press.

Walker, Margaret Urban. 2010. "Truth Telling as Reparations." *Metaphilosophy* 41(1): 525–45.

Young, Iris Marion. 2006. "Responsibility and Global Justice: A Social Connection Model." *Social Philosophy and Policy* 23: 102–30.

Young, Iris Marion. 2011. *Responsibility for Justice*. New York: Oxford University Press.

Chapter 6

Justice-Seeking in Settler States: A Model for Thinking about 'Justice' in Transitional Societies

Michael Phillips

In transitional justice studies the question of justice is often, and for good reason, conceived of as one involving trade-offs between justice and other important values, such as peace, stability and truth.[1] Some scholars have attempted to square the circle by arguing that criminal justice, for example, ultimately contributes to a stable peace.[2] Other scholars, such as Jeremy Webber, have tried to give a nuanced account of the internal structure of the concept of justice itself, and in doing so have clarified the way in which justice claims, although advanced under the same label, may take rather different, and at times conflicting, forms. In this chapter I argue that it is also helpful to think of justice in terms of the activity of justice-seeking, an activity defined by two key features: the making of justice claims, and the resolution or determination of those claims. Indigenous peoples' claims for political or constitutional justice are first order justice claims insofar as they go to the identity of indigenous peoples as political constituencies, and hence to their ability to make, waive and settle other justice claims, such as rights to land and self-government, through agreement with the state. At bottom, this means that transitional justice mechanisms in settler democracies should be structured in ways that enable indigenous people to participate in those processes as political constituencies, with the right to be consulted and to enter into agreements with the state on matters affecting their key interests. It follows that the agenda of reconciliation must extend beyond 'hearts and minds' to issues of treaty rights, native title and self-determination and related issues. My focus in this chapter is particularly on Australia in comparison with New Zealand and, to a lesser extent, Canada.

1 Williams, M. and Nagy, M., Introduction, *Transitional Justice*, New York: NYU Press 2012, p. 5; Leebaw, B.A. 'The Irreconcilable Goals of Transitional Justice', *Human Rights Quarterly*, 2008, 30(1): 95–118; Corradetti, C., 'Philosophy of Transitional Justice: Conceptual Problems and Political Perspectives', University of Oslo Faculty of Law Legal Studies Research Paper Series, no. 2013-08, p. 9; Baker, R.B., 'Towards a New Transitional Justice Model: Assessing the Serbian Case', *San Diego Int'l L.J.*, 2009, 11(171): 174; Aloyo, E., 'Transitional Justice Trade-Offs: A Partially Democratic Theory of Transitional Justice', One Earth Future Foundation Discussion Paper, March 2010; Sooka, Y., 'Dealing with the Past and Transitional Justice: Building Peace with Accountability', *International Review of the Red Cross*, 2006, 88(862): 312; Tietel, R, 'Transitional Justice: Postwar Legacies', *Cardozo Law Review*, 2006, 27(4): 1617.

2 International Centre for Transitional Justice: A False Dilemma, http://ictj.org/news/peace-versus-justice-false-dilemma, accessed 13 April 2012; Guinn, D., 'Human Rights Education: The Third Leg of Post-Conflict/Transitional Justice', International Human Rights Law Institute Working Paper, http://ssrn.com/author=199608, p. 1; Sharp, D., 'Beyond the Post-Conflict Checklist: Linking Peace-building and Transitional Justice through the Lens of Critique', *Chicago J. Int'l Law* 14, 165, 2013; Corradetti, C., 'Philosophy of Transitional Justice: Conceptual Problems and Political Perspectives', University of Oslo Faculty of Law Legal Studies Research Paper Series, no. 2013-08, p. 28. On the rise of the two paradigms of transitional justice and peace-building, and their overlap, see Vandeginste, S. and Sriram, C.L., 'Power Sharing and Transitional Justice: A Clash of Paradigms?' *Global Governance*, 2011, 17(4): 489.

Outline

In the first part of this chapter I argue that it is useful to think of justice-seeking as an activity constituted by the making of justice claims i.e., normative claims to fair treatment based on either substantive or procedural goals or standards. This model has important implications for how we think about both the emergence of justice claims and the relationship amongst justice claims. In the second part I argue that in settler democracies the demands of 'political' or 'constitutional' justice are first order justice claims which are conceptually prior to other justice claims, in the sense described above. In the third part I discuss this argument with reference to two settler states, Australia and New Zealand, and argue that whereas the Aboriginal Reconciliation process in Australia failed to adequately deal with the claims of Aboriginal Australians for political and constitutional justice, the approach taken in New Zealand through the Treaty of Waitangi claims process is far more promising. In Australia the dormant treaty process should be reactivated if real headway is to be made on transitional justice issues in that country.

Justice as Claim-Making

Jeremy Webber's article on the 'forms of transitional justice' provides a useful starting point for my discussion of justice in this chapter. Webber distinguishes three different conceptions of justice evident in arguments about transitional justice – 'retrospective', 'prospective', and 'the adjustment of contending legal and political orders'. Retrospective justice is the form of justice most readily understood within liberal polities, and derives from Aristotle's concept of 'corrective' or 'rectificatory' justice.[3] Prospective justice is a broader form of justice invoked when the parties 'are concerned not simply with repairing past events but rather with changing their society for the future, reconstructing it on different – and, ideally, more just – foundations'. Prospective justice 'tends to be the very essence of transition. The parties seek to arrange relations within society so that each party is treated appropriately from now on'.[4] Prospective justice has affinities to restorative justice, such as the need to repair and maintain a community into the future.[5] This is most evident in truth commissions, but also in official apologies, which 'are designed not to fix the past, but rather to repudiate it, dissociating the current regime from the past and making clear that the new regime intends to base its actions on new principles'.[6]

Webber describes a third form of justice invoked in the transitional justice literature as the 'adjustment of contending legal and political orders'. This form of justice goes to 'the framework within which justice is to be done'.[7] It involves a determination of the boundaries of the society and its membership. It may also include questions regarding the localization of justice into a particular vernacular, described by Webber as 'a set of terms, concepts, exemplifications, and points of reference'.[8] Included here are questions regarding the constitutional make-up of the state, including questions of secession, federalism and regional autonomy. Indigenous claims to land, often expressed and understood in terms of retrospective justice arising out of a prior wrong, namely dispossession, are also often claims to autonomy and fall within this third form of justice.[9]

3 Webber, J., 'Forms of Transitional Justice', in Williams and Nagy, *Transitional Justice*, p. 102.
4 Ibid., p. 103.
5 Ibid., p. 104.
6 Ibid., p. 105.
7 Ibid., p. 108.
8 Ibid.
9 Ibid., pp. 111–12.

To press Webber's point further, one implication of his view that justice claims may extend to claims made *between* legal and political orders is that such claims are potentially unsolvable on a conceptual level. This is because there is no third reference point of adjudication between the contending orders except if the parties agree to one, but it is precisely such agreement on common reference points that is missing. This is true of debates about the effect of legal documents, such as the Treaty of Waitangi, drafted in more than one language. This is an illustration of the larger problem that in conditions of cultural pluralism different persons and groups are likely to frame justice claims differently in response to their different experiences and normative expectations, themselves derived from their own cultures, history and politics. Hence Andrew Sharp, author of *Justice for the Maori*, has observed that 'there can be no permanent settlement of particular cases or agreement on conceptions of justice. The content of justice is contingent on what particular societies take to be good for people and what activities are being considered'.[10] This extends to claims for reparative justice because of the 'presence of fundamentally distinct and competing ethnic conceptions of what things were (and are) wrong and as to how individual and group identity and responsibility for actions persist through time'.[11]

The presence of a wider claim regarding what Webber has termed the adjustment of legal and political orders is likely to make resolution of other justice claims impossible on a conceptual level. Putting aside the use of force or structural violence, in such cases justice claims may only be waived, set aside, or determined in a manner that the claimant and the object of the claim regard as acceptable, or not. In settler democracies, transitional justice mechanisms should be structured in ways that, as far as practically possible, give institutional shape to this claim. This implies that transitional justice mechanisms in settler states must go beyond truth commissions and compensation packages, and should include processes which allow indigenous peoples to participate as political constituencies with the right to make decisions and reach agreements with the settler state on matters affecting their key interests. I will return to this matter below.

Implicit in this argument is a view of justice as a form of activity constituted by the making of claims by justice-seeking subjects. One of the most notable aspects of justice-talk is its ready accessibility and wide use in political and legal debate by ordinary people acting without philosophical or legal training. For most people, justice is not a philosophical term of art, but a claim to fair and proper treatment derived from an experience of human life that offends existing normative expectations.[12] That is, the universality of justice might be located not in its meaning but in the way in which it is deployed by justice-seeking claimants, or in the technical language of political sociology, 'subjects'.[13] On this view, the experience of injustice is prior to the claim for justice.[14]

Justice claims arise out of real human experience and specific social, political and economic contexts, and are therefore highly localized, even when expressed in universalist terms. An element of such universality is a second claim standing behind the first claim. This is the claim that the claimant is entitled to have their claim answered and, ultimately, resolved by a legitimate

10 Sharp, A., *Justice and the Maori: Maori Claims in New Zealand Political Argument in the 1980s*, 1st edn, Auckland: Oxford University Press, 1990, p. 30.

11 Ibid., p. 23.

12 Renault, E, 'Struggles of Justice: Political Discourses, Experiences and Claims', in Balibar, E., Mezzadra, S. and Samaddar, R. (eds), *The Borders of Justice*, Philadelphia, PA: Temple University Press, 2012, pp. 108–11.

13 Samaddar, R, 'The Justice Seeking Subject', in Balibar, Mezzadra and Samaddar, *The Borders of Justice*, pp. 146–166.

14 See Balibar, E, 'Justice and Equality: A Political Dilemma? Pascal, Plato, Marx', in Balibar, Mezzadra and Samaddar, *The Borders of Justice*, pp. 26–7.

authority.[15] Claims going to the identity of that authority are a special kind of justice claim, and are most recognizable in claims by indigenous peoples to sovereignty, in the exercise of which they claim to be entitled to determine other justice claims. Not all claims reach this last point of abstraction, but some do, and it is important to recognize them as such. In this chapter I call these claims 'political' or 'constitutional' justice claims, and they substantially overlap with the content of Webber's third form of transitional justice, described by Webber as the 'adjustment of contending legal and political orders'.

For example, under Australia's native title regime indigenous claimant groups must demonstrate title to land under Aboriginal customary law, that their title has not been superseded by an inconsistent act of state such as a grant of freehold over the land, and that the claimant group has maintained its connection to the land in question to the present day. Although the acquisition of sovereignty by the British Crown is not justiciable in Australian law under the 'act of state' doctrine, this formulation of the structure of native title points back, ultimately, to Aboriginal law as the source of native title. In turn, this points to the existence of Aboriginal peoples as politically organized constituencies with the right to make, litigate, waive and settle justice claims in respect of native title. In that sense, when indigenous peoples make native title claims they are also making a first order claim that they are political constituencies with rights derived from Aboriginal law and prior occupation and as such are entitled to both assert and settle other justice claims. As I argue below, the right to settle claims on terms acceptable to the claimant group is as important as the right to assert the claims in the first place, and supports the common practice of resolving native title claims through agreement rather than through litigation and judicial determination. A similar logic applies to other justice claims made by indigenous peoples as such, including rights to self-government, to cultural heritage and access to minerals and development. Such a claim is also recognized whenever the state engages with indigenous peoples in treaty negotiations directed at the resolution of these matters.

Political or constitutional justice claims are not always prior to other forms of justice claims. Much will depend on context. In many cases such claims will not arise, or will have already been answered. However, at least in the context of transitional justice processes in settler democracies, political or constitutional justice claims are first order justice claims because settler democracies are built upon the political exclusion of indigenous peoples, through various forms of dispossession of both land and the power of self-government, either absolutely (as is the case in Australia) or through violation of treaty rights (as in the case of New Zealand, Canada and the United States). In my view, this means that transitional justice mechanisms in settler democracies must be structured in ways that allow indigenous peoples to participate as organized political constituencies, with the right to make second order justice claims, and to enter into agreements with the state on the resolution of those claims. Typically, this will involve some kind of treaty process directed to agreement between indigenous peoples and the state on land rights, cultural heritage and various forms of self-government, and to the relationship between such treaty rights and liberal citizenship rights, such as rights to health, education and welfare as well as civil and political rights.[16]

---

15 Sharp observes that 'The language [of justice] was *chosen* by the Maori. It was chosen to express difference, separate interests and rights. It was chosen to express the passions that the injustice of their denial arouses. It was also chosen because justice demands – it does not merely suggest – that its dictates be acted upon'. Sharp, *Justice and the Maori*, p. 41.

16 To limit transitional justice mechanisms in settler democracies to liberal citizenship rights or to human rights is problematic, as Jung argues, 'an ethically loaded project that may reinforce liberal and neoliberal paradigms that indigenous peoples often reject'. Jung, C, 'Canada and the Legacy of the Indian Residential Schools: Transitional Justice for Indigenous Peoples in a Nontransitional Society', in Paige, A. (ed.), *Identities in Transition: Challenges for Transitional Justice in Divided Societies*, New York: Cambridge University Press, 2011, p. 217.

Transitional Justice in Settler Democracies

There is a debate in the literature about whether the field of transitional justice extends to transitions within 'advanced' or 'consolidated' democracies. Hansen, includes 'consolidated democracies' in his differentiated theory of transitional justice,[17] and lists Australia, Canada, New Zealand, Germany, and Belgium as consolidated democracies that have engaged in some kind of transitional justice process.[18] According to Hansen, limiting transitional justice to societies in a state of radical change 'implies a moral differentiation' where poor countries are seen as having endemic human rights problems whilst rich Western countries 'are implied to be free of such mess and only have a need to come to terms with practices that took place in a relatively distant past'.[19] In other work Hansen has described the process of expansion of the transitional justice field, and noted that truth-seeking and reparations measures in Australia and Canada, though discussed as transitional justice measures, 'do not seem to aim at achieving a fundamental political or peaceful transition'.[20] Hansen argues that such measures are important because they offer the potential to provide redress to victims, even in the absence of a fundamental transition.[21]

Joanna Quinn has observed that the field is 'more and more home to discussions of transitional justice mechanisms that have been appointed in pre-transitional societies and in those societies that show little evidence of any transition whatsoever'.[22] Quinn places Canada in the latter category. The 'Statement of Apology' by the Canadian Prime Minister to Canadian Aboriginal peoples for the consequences of the Indian Residential Schools policy, together with the associated compensation agreement, '*in no way marks a transition of any kind* in Canadian society'.[23] One of the key normative questions raised by the use of transitional justice in settler states is whether such mechanisms resolve historic injustices, or whether they contribute to the continuing colonial project of legitimizing settler democracies. This is the key political question identified by Courtney Jung in her discussion of the use of transitional justice mechanisms in Canada. Jung argues that governments may attempt to use transitional justice to 'draw a line through history and legitimate present policy' and to 'reassert their sovereign and legal authority'.[24] As Jung also notes, such claims are likely to be contested by indigenous peoples acting both within and without transitional justice mechanisms.[25] Whether transitional justice measures legitimate the settler state or have a transformational capacity depends in part, according to Jung, on the wider political context in which they operate.[26]

Each of these authors problematizes transitional justice processes in settler democracies by questioning whether such states are undergoing a transition, conceived of as a fundamental change in the structure of settler democracies. These critiques of transitional justice in settler democracies suggest that something is amiss. It does not seem right to talk about particular mechanisms as

---

17 Hansen, T.O., 'Transitional Justice: Towards a Differentiated Theory', *Oregon Review of International Law*, 2011, 13(1): 38.

18 Ibid., pp. 38–39 and n.144.

19 Ibid., p. 40.

20 Hansen, T.O., 'The Horizontal and Vertical Expansions of Transitional Justice: Explanations and Implications for a Contested Field', p. 8, in Buckley-Zistel, S., Beck, T.K., Christian B. and Mieth, F. (eds), *Transitional Justice Theories*, Routledge, 2014.

21 Ibid.

22 Quinn, J, 'Whither the "Transition" in "Transitional Justice"', paper presented at the Annual General Meeting of the Canadian Political Science Association, 16 May 2011, p. 1.

23 Ibid., p. 18, original emphasis.

24 Jung, C, 'Canada and the Legacy of the Indian Residential Schools', pp. 217–18.

25 Ibid., p. 218.

26 Ibid., p. 217.

being transitional justice mechanisms where they do not aim at any fundamental transformation. However, the picture looks different if we need to move the focus of inquiry. The debate is better looked at in terms of whether the process adopted includes the kinds of justice claims I have described in this chapter as political or constitutional justice. On that view, the measures commonly described as transitional justice measures in settler democracies tend to be second order transitional justice measures. The really significant activities in these countries are happening not so much within truth and reconciliation commissions as in the field of land rights, self-government and treaty making. These processes are transitional justice initiatives in so far as they are animated by what I have described in this chapter as claims for political or constitutional justice, or in the terms used by Webber, they are claims for the adjustment of contending legal and political orders.

Aboriginal Reconciliation in Australia

The Aboriginal Reconciliation process in Australia demonstrates that settler democracies that do not engage with indigenous peoples' claims to political or constitutional justice are likely to be frustrated in their attempts to obtain any kind of national 'reconciliation' as part of a transitional justice strategy. Despite a decade-long 'Reconciliation' process and a national apology to Aboriginal peoples, the structural position of indigenous peoples within the Australian Commonwealth remains largely the same today as it was in 1991, when the Reconciliation process commenced. The questions not taken up by the reconciliation process, at least formally, were the claims of Aboriginal peoples to political and constitutional justice, that is, of Aboriginal sovereignty and the treaty process.

The Aboriginal Reconciliation process was conducted in the decade 1991–2001 under the auspices of the Council for Aboriginal Reconciliation, a wholly appointed statutory body comprising eminent citizens and chaired throughout by an Aboriginal person, first Patrick Dodson and subsequently Evelyn Scott. However, the idea that Australia should seek a formal 'reconciliation' with its Aboriginal peoples was first proposed by a coalition of churches in 1988, the bicentenary of white settlement in Australia.[27] The churches were hoping to break the impasse in national politics generated by disagreements about proposed national land rights legislation and calls for an Aboriginal treaty or treaties.

Although intended to calm the political waters, reconciliation in turn became a matter of heated political debate throughout the 1990s and the early to mid 2000s.[28] The conservative government of John Howard, in office from 1996 to 2007, was opposed to an apology, and also strongly opposed the concept of a treaty with indigenous peoples. The Howard government also legislated to amend the Racial Discrimination Act to enable partial extinguishment of native title after the High Court's decision in the *Wik* case recognizing that native title could coexist with pastoral leases, and generally attempted to reduce the concept of reconciliation to 'practical reconciliation'. In its dying days the Howard government also authorized the national intervention into Aboriginal communities in the Northern Territory, a policy continued by the Rudd-Gillard Labor government since 2007.

---

27 The heads of 14 Australian churches had released a statement 'Towards Reconciliation in Australian Society' in 1988, and the parliamentary motion of reconciliation in that year was based on the text of the pamphlet: see statement of Robert Hawke, Prime Minister, *Hansard*, 23 August 1988, p. 137.

28 See generally Short, D., *Reconciliation and Colonial Power: Indigenous Rights in Australia*, Aldershot: Ashgate, 2008.

On one level, the reconciliation process was brought to an end by the national parliamentary apology moved by Labor Prime Minister Kevin Rudd in 2008.[29] The apology closed the chapter on what had been the most heated political debate in the field of Aboriginal affairs for the last decade. The apology was warmly welcomed by many Aboriginal people who regarded it as long overdue recognition of the wrongs done to them. However, it would be quite wrong to suggest that the apology has resolved any of the larger and long-standing problems in the field of Aboriginal affairs policy in Australia. Damian Short has argued that the reconciliation process 'is best understood as a legitimizing 'post-colonial' obfuscation of contemporary dispossession, cultural assimilation and the maintenance of colonial structures' which failed to address the problem of the ongoing internal colonization of indigenous peoples in Australia.[30] My own view is that politics of the reconciliation process were subtler and more complex than Short's assessment may imply, in that Aboriginal people and their supporters did attempt to pursue justice claims within the context of reconciliation.[31] Those claims extended to the type of political or constitutional justice claims described in the first part of this chapter. However, I would agree with Short in so far as, in overall terms, the reconciliation did not itself lead to any fundamental transition in Australia.

In my view, this was at least in part because the institutional set-up of the Reconciliation process, which reflected its limited mandate, did not allow for the resolution of the claims made by Aboriginal people to political or constitutional justice. The failure of the reconciliation process to achieve a transition was inscribed in the institutional set-up of the Council, which was not a representative body and had no mandate to engage in any negotiations with the government on such matters as land title, self-government or sovereignty. The great weakness of the reconciliation process was that it did not include the kinds of institutions or forms of representation conducive to formulating, discussing and resolving claims to political and constitutional justice made by Aboriginal Australians and their supporters. The Council primarily saw its task as one of promoting 'hearts and minds' reconciliation at the community and personal level. The treaty debate was deferred by a requirement for the Council to report on whether the Commonwealth should adopt a 'document of reconciliation' at the conclusion of the reconciliation process. The Council's draft document of reconciliation is perhaps anodyne although, in view of its limited mandate, this criticism is perhaps unfair.[32] The Council was established to circumvent or defer the treaty debate, not to solve it. The Council did its best within the limited terms of its mandate.

By the late 1990s and through to 2008, the Aboriginal Reconciliation process was narrowed down in the public debate to the question of the apology to the Stolen Generations. The entire process came to be seen through the prism of an interminable and hopeless debate on the meaning of the word 'sorry', the main objection to this not being that it was unedifying, but that it crowded out other important claims. The wider reconciliation process, with its heavy focus on truth-telling, apology and national unity, arguably had more to do with the needs of non-Aboriginal Australia to obtain a moral release for the history of injustice which marked the foundations of this settler society. This criticism resonates with Jung's observation that the Canadian reconciliation process has more to do with shoring up the legitimacy of the Canadian state than achieving justice for indigenous peoples.

---

29 The motion read, in part, 'We apologise for the laws and policies of successive Parliaments and governments that have inflicted profound grief, suffering and loss on these our fellow Australians'. http://australia.gov.au/about-australia/our-country/our-people/apology-to-australias-indigenous-peoples, accessed 12 April 2013.

30 Short, *Reconciliation and Colonial Power*, p. 8.

31 See Phillips, M, 'Aboriginal Reconciliation as Religious Politics: Secularisation in Australia', *Australian Journal of Political Science*, 2005, 40(1): 111–24.

32 See *Reconciliation: Australia's Challenge, Final Report of the Council for Aboriginal Reconciliation*, December 2000, Appendix 1, http://www.austlii.edu.au/au/other/IndigLRes/car/2000/16/appendices01.htm, accessed 13 April 2013.

As a result, the overarching questions of Australian law and jurisprudence remain the questions posed by Aboriginal people and their supporters. At present, the situation is confused. On the one hand, the Australia state remains, in its basic legal and constitutional structure, to a large extent a colonial state. The acquisition of sovereignty by the British Crown is non-justiciable in the Australian courts. No colonial or Australian government has ever negotiated a treaty with any indigenous people. Indigenous people do not have any dedicated representation in the Australian or state parliaments, do not have rights of self-government, and are not the subject of any special or protective provisions in the Australian Constitution. On the other hand, Australian law and administrative practice refers to Indigenous Australians both as a 'population' and as 'peoples'. The two formulations entail different logics of administration and different conceptions of social justice. Whereas a population is a subject of statistical measurement and administrative intervention, a people has a right of self-determination and is a negotiating partner with whom justice claims can be settled. Tim Rowse has written:

> The idiom of 'people-hood' implies that social justice comes from a resolution of differences between political entities, between peoples; in the idiom of 'population', there are not two (or three) peoples, there are many individuals and households within an Australian population categorised by self-assigned 'race' or 'ethnic identity', and the task of social justice is to ensure that the inequalities among those individuals and households do not correspond to such characteristics as their self-identified 'ethnicity'.[33]

The political debate over the meaning of Aboriginal Reconciliation featured these two different conceptions of Indigenous Australians, and included a kind of treaty politics by another name. Nevertheless, the Aboriginal Reconciliation process indicates that the shape of institutions matter because institutions which have the power to reach political settlements over justice claims embody or enact a particular view about who is entitled to participate in the resolution of those claims. Institutions that lack political authority and are armed only with the power of persuasion, as was the Council for Aboriginal Authority, are unlikely to be effective forums for these kinds of transitional justice processes. Any future transitional justice programme in Australia must avoid the mistakes of the Aboriginal Reconciliation Process. In my view, Australian governments should look again at the treaty question, and enter good faith negotiations with indigenous peoples to reach agreement on key questions extending beyond the protection of basic citizenship rights and extending into the claims for political and constitutional justice.

New Zealand: The Waitangi Tribunal

My focus in the remainder of this chapter is on the manner in which New Zealand has dealt with the ongoing legacy of colonization in the same period as discussed in relation to Australia in this chapter, that is, from the 1980s to the present day. New Zealand has charted a much more promising path than Australia and as a result has progressed further towards recognizing the claims for political justice made by the Maori. Sadly, this model appears to have reached its high point in the early 2000s, and since that time has been under threat from a conservative 'one law for all' discourse which is the antithesis of an approach which attempts, in Webber's terminology, to adjust the contending legal and political orders of New Zealand.

---

33 Rowse, T, *Rethinking Social Justice: From 'Peoples' to 'Populations'*, Canberra: Aboriginal Studies Press, 2012, p. 7.

The key development in New Zealand was the revival of the Treaty of Waitangi as a framework for resolving justice claims between the Maori and the New Zealand state.[34] The Treaty, which had sometimes been scorned as not worth the paper it was written on,[35] had been signed by over 500 Maori chiefs and Captain William Hobson as the representative of the British Crown in 1840. Much of the debate on the Treaty in the 1970s and 1980s focused on inconsistencies in the Maori and English versions of the Treaty.[36] In its English version the Treaty recognized British 'sovereignty', yet in Article 2 guaranteed to the Maori the 'full exclusive and undisturbed possession of their Lands and Estates Forests Fisheries and other possessions so long as it is their wish and desire to retain the same in their possession'.[37] The Maori version of the Treaty was significantly different and spoke of the Crown protecting, on one translation, the full, true, chieftainship, or authority of the Maori.[38]

Andrew Sharp, reflecting on the emergence of conflicting justice claims between Maori and Pakeha in New Zealand in the 1970s and 1980s, observed that in the midst of disagreement about what justice entailed, 'the inevitable occurred: appeals were made to sovereignty'.[39] The revival of the Treaty in the 1980s offered a plausible solution to a conceptual and political impasse resulting from divergent conceptions of justice and conflicting sovereignty claims: a model of justice based in contract and reparation.[40] Starting in the 1970s and then with increasing urgency in the 1980s, the Maori made the Treaty the 'standard of justice' between Maori and Pekeha, and between Maori and the state.[41] After a slow beginning, the Tribunal from 1984 'magnetically attracted Maori claims'.[42] For Sharp, the work of the Tribunal was animated by an idea whose time had come:

> What vivified the Tribunal was the idea of reparation for breach of contract. It was the new importance given the Treaty as expressing Maori rights, the spread of indignation at the injustice of violating those rights and the demand for reparation that came together in the story of its birth, reformings and activity.[43]

The Tribunal developed a jurisprudence of reparative justice based in contractualist thinking with the terms of the Treaty at its core. The appeal to contract, which is an appeal ultimately to agreement, offered a way out of the dilemmas of defining the precise content of justice in general terms. However, sitting behind the reparative jurisprudence of the Tribunal were a number of foundational beliefs, one of which was an appreciation of the virtue of compromise and settlement in the pursuit of wider social goals:

> that justice is not the whole political virtue, that the unmitigated pursuit of justice (especially reparative justice) is indeed a vice, and that in any case reparative justice might not well bring

34 Sharp, *Justice and the Maori*, p. 74.
35 Ibid., p. 97.
36 Ibid., p. 15.
37 Ibid., p. 16.
38 Ibid., p. 17. Debates as to the proper interpretation of the competing texts are ongoing; see for example Margaret Mutu, 'Constitutional Intentions: The Treaty of Waitangi Texts', in Mullholland, M. and Tawhai, V. (eds), *Weeping Waters: The Treaty of Waitangi and Constitutional Change*, Wellington: Huia Publishers, 2010, pp. 13–40.
39 Sharp, *Justice and the Maori*, p. 1.
40 Ibid., p. 33.
41 Ibid., p. 73.
42 Ibid., p. 77.
43 Ibid., p. 85.

> about the distribution of social goods that other ideals of justice required and that other ideals of a good future suggested.[44]

Sharp also refers to the Tribunal's future oriented, 'oracular' jurisprudence which 'sought retrospectively to construct a "fundamental law" for New Zealand based on the transactions of 1840'.[45] This jurisprudence sought to extract principles from the Treaty, over and above the letter of its provisions, derived from the 'spirit' in which it was signed. The motive in developing this jurisprudence was to promote negotiation and conciliation,[46] and it rested on an assumption that justice was due to the Maori because of their special status and to the history of their dealings with the British Crown. This jurisprudence 'captured what many Maori felt', signifying as it did both the recognition of their special status and their willingness to negotiate and compromise.[47]

There are indications that the Treaty is continuing to live its strange after-life as a model for a future-oriented jurisprudence. Professor Sir Mason Durie has written that 'there has been recognition that the Treaty of Waitangi provides a touch-stone upon which two world views, two sets of traditions, and two understandings can create a society where indigeneity and modern democratic practices can meet'.[48] A recent text on public policy in New Zealand describes the Treaty as 'always speaking'; 'the Treaty is a foundation for public policy in Aotearoa New Zealand, and that development begins with a commitment to its intentions, provisions and principles'.[49] Matthew Palmer, formerly Deputy Secretary for Justice (Public Law) in the New Zealand government, describes the shared objectives between Maori, Pakeha and 'other New Zealanders' as the desire that 'ongoing relationships between these three groups should be healthy. This is a simple but powerful concept. It reflects the conception of the Treaty as interpreted by our institutions exercising public power over the past 25 years. It is a way of understanding the purpose of the Treaty of Waitangi'.[50]

These statements are indicative of a public policy framework developed in New Zealand which came to be known as 'biculturalism'. David-Ives, in her work on the reworking of New Zealand's historical narratives by the Tribunal, describes how the Tribunal very soon began to operate within a bicultural framework, as evidenced by the use of oral historical evidence which is itself a political statement.[51] David-Ives argues that the use of a bicultural framework was an attempt by the Tribunal 'to shift the dominant perspective towards the Maori cultural sphere as a whole'.[52] This reframing of the historical narrative amounted to 'a phenomenon of "indigenisation" of New Zealand's identity … The negative polarization between colonized and colonizer has been re-deployed as a juxtaposition of the two cultures and frames of reference'.[53]

Sharp devoted a chapter of his book to what he described as a Pakeha ideology of equality, a kind of one nation nationalism reminiscent of the views of Pauline Hanson and her One Nation

44 Ibid., p. 163.

45 Ibid., p. 167.

46 Ibid., p. 168.

47 Ibid., p. 171.

48 Durie, Professor Sir Mason, Foreword, *Always Speaking: The Treaty of Waitangi and Public Policy*, edited by Tawhai, Veronika Mh, and Gray-Sharp, Katarina, Wellington: Huai Publishers, 2011, p. ix.

49 Tawhai and Gray-Sharp, *Always Speaking*, p. 2.

50 Palmer, Matthew S.R., *The Treaty of Waitangi in New Zealand's Law and Constitution*, Victoria University Press, Wellington, 2008, p. 297.

51 David-Ives, Corrine, 'The Waitangi Tribunal and the Reconstruction of the Narrative of National Identity in New Zealand', in Ryan-Fazilleau, Sue (ed.), *New Zealand and Australia: Narrative, History and Representation*, Kakapo Books, Centre for New Zealand Studies, Birkbeck, University of London, 2008, pp. 9–22, pp. 15–16.

52 Ibid., p. 16.

53 Ibid., p. 17.

Party in Australia. This ideology formed the basis for the political reaction against the politics of biculturalism in the second half of the 2000s.[54] As O'Sullivan has argued, the Brash National Party government attempted to move discussion of Maori-Pakeha relations onto the plane of individualism and a narrower conception of democracy and justice:

> The defining characteristic of contemporary Maori policy debate became the clash between self-determination, which gives theoretical articulation to the politics of indigeneity, and the re-emergence of assimilation as a subtle although not explicit policy objective.[55]

O'Sullivan argues that biculturalism remains a colonial relationship insofar as it positions Maori as the junior partner in an unequal relationship. O'Sullivan proposes a model of self-determination in preference to biculturalism.[56] In my view, O'Sullivan's critique of biculturalism has merit; however, it is O'Sullivan's comments on compromise that I find most interesting for the purposes of this chapter. Noting that the New Zealand state does not have sufficient resources to make full reparation for Treaty claims, he describes Maori willingness to settle such claims as a 'major pragmatic concession to the integrity of the nation state, to a true "nationhood" when iwu and hapu reach settlements with the Crown at levels well below what full reparation would demand'.[57]

I would go further than O'Sullivan on this point, and argue that settlement through negotiation is not just pragmatic, but also, under the right conditions, principled. Settlement is necessary not only for the financial reasons described by O'Sullivan. As discussed in the first part of this chapter, deciding what justice requires in settler states is not just a question of tallying up the losses. Justice claims will inevitably need to compromised or settled through negotiation, and the question is whether settler democracies are willing to recognize indigenous peoples as negotiating partners. And whilst negotiation and settlement are essential virtues of political life and association, they depend on an answer to a first question: who is entitled to settle a justice claim? When that right is recognized as inhering in indigenous peoples it is a response to the kinds of claims for political and constitutional justice described in the first part of this chapter.

This structure is evident in the conduct of land claims negotiations between settler democracies and indigenous peoples. When governments engage in land claim negotiations as a matter of policy they make a choice about how best to deal with those claims that has distinct normative foundations. As Christa Scholtz has argued, to negotiate land claims involves a prior conclusion that the state 'will recognize indigenous special land and political rights claims by enshrining the principle of indigenous consent in the policy process'.[58] In settler states this choice has highly significant implications for the way in which the polity is conceived, a concern which Scholtz articulates in the idiom of citizenship but which could just as well be formulated in terms of claims to political or constitutional justice, in the sense used in this chapter:

> The recognition of indigenous collective rights, at the heart of the negotiation choice, challenges deeply held notions of national citizenship … At any given point in time, the story of indigenous

---

54 See for example Robinson, John: 'We should resist all calls to move away from equality to privilege based on the accident of birth, a direction that leaves so many Maori trapped in a suffering underclass', *The Corruption of New Zealand Democracy: A Treaty Overview*, Wellington: Tross Publishing, 2011, p. 8.

55 O'Sullivan, D., *Beyond Biculturalism: The Politics of an Indigenous Minority*, Wellington: Huia Publishers, 2007, p. 1.

56 Ibid., p. 3.

57 Ibid., p. 215.

58 Scholtz, C., *Negotiating Claims: The Emergence of Indigenous Land Claim Negotiation Policies in Australia, Canada, New Zealand and the United States*, New York: Routledge, 2006, p. 2.

> land claims shows that policy responses are reflective of how government actors believe aboriginal people and the rights they claim can fit within a national dialogue on citizenship.[59]

Conclusion

History must make us cautious about the implications of a view of political justice that entails negotiated settlements. Canadian governments have recognized an indigenous right of self-government extending at least as far as the power to extinguish sovereignty claims through the treaty process.[60] In the *Mabo* decision the Australian High Court both recognized native title and confirmed that it could be extinguished by an inconsistent act of the Crown. Mark Hickford, writing on a broader historical canvass, suggests that nineteenth century British imperial practice in New Zealand included recognition of Maori property rights, but this practice 'tended to domesticate Maori politics in intra-anglophone terms':

> At the very least, as a strategy, it implicated Maori politics in the genres of colonization, internalizing Maori politics within the colonial polity through genres of jurisdiction, property rights, and subjecthood. Under this approach customary authority could be reduced to customary law to manage indigenous relations inter se or as an attribute or incident of a property right, such as the power to alienate land or to allocate its use to others for a brief time (leasing or licensing).[61]

Transitional justice processes in settler democracies must engage with indigenous peoples' claims to political and constitutional justice if they are to have any chance of achieving a transformation of those states on terms acceptable to both indigenous and non-indigenous peoples who, one way or another, must find a way to equitably share the territories in which they will continue to live. The Australian reconciliation process failed to transform relations between indigenous peoples and the Australian state, and with hindsight, it is clear that this failure was built into the structure of the reconciliation process itself. The idea of reconciliation was broad enough to provide Aboriginal Australians and their supporters with a language in which to advance justice claims. Yet the institutional structure of the process was flawed because it did not recognize the first order claims by Aboriginal Australians that they were entitled to make and settle justice claims with the Australian state, that is, that they are political constituencies with rights flowing from Aboriginal law and prior occupation of Australia. The hard questions associated with Australian treaty politics of the 1980s were dodged and deferred. Treaty negotiations are not a panacea and also pose risks for indigenous peoples, particularly where the settler state, as in some Canadian instances, pursues treaty negotiations in order to extinguish the rights of indigenous peoples. However, as New Zealand's recent experience with the Treaty of Waitangi shows, a well-structured treaty process which recognizes the political status of indigenous peoples and which provides a framework for the ongoing resolution of second order justice claims, offers a way forward for settler democracies, and it is to be hoped that this opportunity is revisited by Australia in the near future.

---

59 Ibid., p. 3. According to Scholtz, Australia 'represents a case of halted and gradual negotiation' and the United States represents the 'non-negotiation case'; p. 4.

60 See Dalton, J.E., 'Aboriginal Title and Self-Government in Canada: What is the True Scope of Comprehensive Land Claims Agreements?' *Windsor Rev. Legal & Soc.*, 2006, 22(29):. 29–78.

61 Hickford, M., *Lords of the Land: Indigenous Property Rights and the Jurisprudence of Empire*, Oxford: Oxford University Press, 2011, p. 461.

Chapter 7

Structural Causes of Conflict and the Superficiality of Transition

Pádraig McAuliffe

Introduction

Issues of socioeconomic justice played a marginal role in transitional justice in its first two decades as a policy concept and as a topic of mainstream academic study. Scholars and policy-makers in the field concentrated more on violations of civil and political rights than on structural violence, defined herein as the phenomenon whereby the structure of a society manifests unequal power relationships which lead to unequal life chances, harming people by preventing them from meeting their basic needs.[1] Inequalities and deprivation are closely related to the causes and dynamics of conflict, even if the precise causal relationship between inequality or socioeconomic rights deprivations and conflict are disputed. Even if inequality and poverty did not cause conflict, they may have constituted an aggravating factor or flowed from the conflict. Overall, as Aguilar and Gomez Isa argue, '[d]eeply embedded inequalities and discrimination very often pre-exist and exacerbate acts of direct violence against the poorest and most marginalized, and these inequalities translate into new forms of violence in the aftermath'.[2] Over time, a concern emerged that the overriding preoccupation with bodily integrity abuses in traditional transitional justice discourse would inevitably result in these inequalities being left in place, albeit in a more palatable, democratizing environment. Approaches that tackle historically constructed socioeconomic inequalities began to find favour in transitional justice in the last 10 years. It is argued that military action and political settlement alone cannot guarantee a successful transition, because as long as grievances and inequalities persist, new conflict entrepreneurs will be able to mobilize support. Scholars now routinely argue that mass poverty should be recognized as an object of justice[3] and that the mechanisms of transitional justice should be applied to transforming oppressive economic arrangements that disenfranchise and exclude vulnerable and resentful segments of society.[4] This distributive approach would conceptualize justice as equality to complement the traditional transitional justice preoccupation with liberty, and serve more forward looking-purposes than the ostensibly backward-looking emphasis of earlier approaches.[5] This change in emphasis in transitional justice has occurred in a supportive environment. The field itself increasingly embraces holistic, integrated strategies that combine retributive, restorative and distributive justice. Transitional justice also embraces other

1 Johan Galtung, 'Violence, Peace and Research', *Journal of Peace Research* 6 (1969): 167–91.

2 Gaby Ore Aguilar and Felipe Gomez Isa, 'Introduction', in *Rethinking Transitions: Equality and Social Justice in Societies Emerging from Conflict*, ed. Gaby Ore Aguilar and Felipe Gomez Isa (Portland, OR: Intersentia 2011), 1–11, at 1.

3 Ruben Carranza, 'Plunder and Pain: Should Transitional Justice Engage with Corruption and Crime?' *International Journal of Transitional Justice* 2 (2008): 310–30, at 315.

4 Ismael Muvingi, 'Sitting on Powder Kegs: Socio-Economic Rights in Transitional Societies', *International Journal of Transitional Justice* 3 (2009): 163–82, at 181.

5 Ibid., 166.

disciplines such as peace-building and security which are conceptualized with greater frequency in terms of human security and collective well-being.[6]

The most forceful advocacy for a re-orientation of transitional justice from a limited concept of conflict prevention to socioeconomic metamorphosis is found in a widely cited speech in 2006 by the then-UN High Commissioner for Human Rights Louise Arbour, who argued that transitional justice 'must' have the ambition of assisting the transformation of oppressed societies into free ones by exposing discriminatory practices and violations of economic, social and cultural rights before and during conflict.[7] This would yield a deeper and more substantive justice than the activities of development actors alone could generate.[8] Different suggestions have emerged as to how transitional justice can satisfy these ambitions. Aguirre and Pietropaoli contend that it should assure outcomes based on the third generation right to development,[9] while Mani argues for an explicitly distributive approach geared towards equity in resources and power.[10] Miller argues that transitional justice should aspire towards what she calls 'economic justice', which would address the economic roots of conflict, temper economic liberalization with redistribution, and impact on the transitional government's development plans.[11] African scholars have argued that transitional justice can and must 'elaborate remedial actions that comprehensively address grievances in societies emerging from conflict'.[12] By contrast, Duthie argues transitional justice measures are not a development strategy but should be designed in ways that are 'development sensitive',[13] but this is an unusually guarded vision of transitional justice's potential effect on post-conflict or post-authoritarian society. The presumption is that virtuous circles would emerge, of justice, development and democracy mutually reinforcing each other.[14]

Most arguments about the relation of transitional justice to socioeconomic rights are startlingly ambitious, and presume it can thoroughly transform unjust arrangements in a manner that war, democracy, development and aid have not. To this can be added a ratcheting-up of the surrounding rhetoric. It is argued that reconciliation without economic justice 'is cheap and spurious'[15] and that ignoring inequalities will inevitably lead to a recurrence of conflict,[16] notwithstanding the plethora of transitions in states like Mozambique, Angola, Guatemala and Sierra Leone which appear highly durable notwithstanding the absence of any real distributive justice. Others go even further, arguing that transitional justice's emphasis on civil and political rights deprivations serves to protect the

---

6 Most notably UN Secretary-General, *Report of the UN Secretary-General: In Larger Freedom: Towards Development, Security and Human Rights for All*, UN Doc. A/59/2005 of 21 March 2005.

7 Louise Arbour, 'Economic and Social Justice for Societies in Transition', *NYU Journal of Law and Politics* 40 (2007): 1–27, at 3.

8 Ibid., 20.

9 Daniel Aguirre and Irene Pietropaoli, 'Gender Equality, Development and Transitional Justice: The Case of Nepal', *International Journal of Transitional Justice* 2 (2008): 356–77, at 356.

10 Rama Mani, *Beyond Retribution: Seeking Justice in the Shadows of War* (Cambridge: Polity Press, 2002), 10.

11 Zinaida Miller, 'Effects of Invisibility: In Search of the "Economic" in Transitional Justice', *International Journal of Transitional Justice* 2 (2008): 266–91.

12 Japan International Cooperation Agency and International Center for Transitional Justice, 'Enhancing Socio-Economic Justice in Societies in Transition: Case Studies on the African Continent' (2008). Accessed 30 April 2013. http://ictj.org/sites/default/files/ICTJ-JICA-Africa-Justice-Development-2008-English.pdf, 7.

13 Roger Duthie, 'Towards a Development-Sensitive Approach to Transitional Justice', *International Journal of Transitional Justice* 2 (2008): 292–309.

14 Pablo de Greiff, 'Articulating the Links between Transitional Justice and Development: Justice and Social Integration', in *Transitional Justice and Development: Making Connections*, ed. Pablo de Greiff and Roger Duthie (New York: SSRC, 2009), 28–75, at 28.

15 Alex Boraine, *A Country Unmasked: Inside South Africa's Truth and Reconciliation Commission* (Oxford: Oxford University Press, 2000), 357.

16 Miller, 'Effects of Invisibility', 287 (cited in note 11).

interests of the privileged at the expense of the poor,[17] actively perpetuates the position of existing economic elites instead of empowering the marginalized,[18] and serves as an enabling context for free markets.[19] The field as a whole is deemed to risk losing credibility overall,[20] or being conceived of as nothing but a series of inconsequential events,[21] unless it improves overall living conditions for citizens in the transitional state.

What explains this degree of ambition and certainty of belief? It may appear puzzling given that development actors by and large ignore transitional justice and discount its centrality.[22] The answer may lie in the traditional optimism of scholars in the field regarding the potency of transition for reconceiving the premises on which a conflict-ridden society is based. Aguirre and Pietropaoli, for example, assert that transitions are rare periods of rupture 'that offer opportunities to reconceive the social meaning of past conflicts in an attempt to reconstruct their present and future effects'.[23] Similarly, Muvingi argues the transitional phase creates space for redistribution and the construction of a more just order.[24] However, this ambitiousness coexists with a surprising tepidity when it comes to actually proposing concrete ways in which transitional justice actors can take advantage of this window of opportunity to achieve these aspirations. Notwithstanding the seemingly boundless confidence scholars have in transitional justice to aid development or redistribution, even the most optimistic works ultimately acknowledge that thus far all we have are a series of hypothetical connections to be further researched,[25] 'points of possible interconnection',[26] underdeveloped concepts and boundaries.[27] Suggested activities ('exposing' discriminatory practices,[28] 'reaching' for deeper justice,[29] 'making connections')[30] exist in the sphere of the inspirational, at some causal remove from constituting a solid policy basis. Because these incitements to action have yet to be implemented, there is no established theoretical or empirical base on which to build. This has served not to undermine confidence in the emancipatory potential of the field, but rather appears to have boosted it.

The Limited Conception of Justice as an Explanation for Marginalization

In explaining the underdevelopment of theory and lack of impact in practice, scholars have primarily focused on the narrowness of the concept of justice in transition. Arbour argues that the neglect of structural inequalities is symptomatic of a 'deep ambivalence within justice systems about social justice'. She attributes this omission from transitional justice discourse to

17 Muvingi, 'Sitting on Powder Kegs', 182 (cited in note 4).

18 Aguirre and Pietropaoli, 'Gender Equality, Development and Transitional Justice', 367 (cited in note 9).

19 Paul Gready, 'Reconceptualising Transitional Justice: Embedded and Distanced Justice', *Conflict, Security and Development* 5 (2005): 3–21, at 5.

20 Rama Mani, 'Editorial: Dilemmas of Expanding Transitional Justice, or Forging the Nexus between Transitional Justice and Development', *International Journal of Transitional Justice* 2 (2008): 253–65, at 253–4.

21 De Greiff, 'Articulating the Links between Transitional Justice and Development', 30 (cited in note 14).

22 Duthie, 'Towards a Development-Sensitive Approach to Transitional Justice', 292–309 (cited in note 13).

23 Aguirre and Pietropaoli, 'Gender Equality, Development and Transitional Justice', 357 (cited in note 9).

24 Muvingi, 'Sitting on Powder Kegs', 178 (cited in note 4).

25 Christopher Colvin, 'Purity and Planning: Shared Logistics of Transitional Justice and Development', *International Journal of Transitional Justice* 2 (2008): 412–25, at 414.

26 Ibid.

27 Lisa Hecht and Sabine Michalowski, 'The Economic Dimensions of Transitional Justice'. Accessed 30 April 2013. http://www.essex.ac.uk/tjn/documents/TheeconomicandsocialdimensionsofTJ.pdf, 1.

28 Arbour, 'Economic and Social Justice for Societies in Transition', 3 (cited in note 7).

29 Tafadzwa Pasipanodya, 'A Deeper Justice: Economic and Social Justice as Transitional Justice in Nepal', *International Journal of Transitional Justice* 2 (2008): 378–97, 397.

30 De Greiff and Duthie, *Transitional Justice and Development*, 28–75 (cited in note 14).

the mistaken presumptions that they are less egregious than civil and political rights abuses or that their programmatic nature makes them less conducive to judicial or quasi-judicial action.[31] Others have argued that the traditional concern of transitional justice with the cessation of violence and handover of power has marginalized questions of socioeconomic development.[32] Along similar lines, it is alleged that progress is stymied by the field's building-blocks approach wherein justice mediates political transition after which larger problems can be addressed by the polity or the market.[33] As Arthur argues, when transitions were being conceptualized during the wave of democratic revolutions in South America and Europe in the 1970s and 1980s, they were envisaged as relatively short-term episodes of legal-institutional reconstruction, as opposed to longer-term, deeper socioeconomic transformation. This view of transition in turn coloured the conception of justice as retributive or restorative, as opposed to distributive.[34] As such, it is argued that transitional justice replicates the subservience of collective, future-oriented socioeconomic rights to individual, backward-looking civil and political rights in human rights discourse and practice.[35] Others take the argument one step further, arguing that because transitional justice is an integral part of the liberal peace-building model,[36] it must therefore promote neoliberal market-based economics antithetical to redistribution of wealth or economic equality.[37] Makau Mutua, for example, sees transitional justice reproducing the assumption of global human rights of the naturalness of the market and the inevitability of capitalist relationships.[38] Nagy contends that transitional justice is open to the accusation of attempting to 'produce subjects and truths that align with market democracy and are blind to gender and social justice'.[39] In this view, there is nothing natural or inevitable about the distance between transitional justice and socioeconomic injustice. It is simply a convenient 'constructed invisibility' on the part of the international community keen to embrace electoral democracy and the rule of law to further globalization, but less enamoured of equitable distribution of the wealth it may generate.[40]

Neoliberal capitalism often has an injurious effect on post-conflict societies by encouraging damaging competition and whittling away the resource base on which redevelopment and welfare could be based, among other reasons. However, it is necessary to examine critically the extent to which the limited impact of transitional justice on socioeconomic reform is explained by any acceptance of the rightness of the neoliberal free market paradigm on the part of practitioners and scholars. On the basis of a survey of writings on transitional justice since the late 1980s, it is hard to identify any theorist in the field explicitly arguing in favour of neoliberal capitalist economies. It is significant that none of the writers above cite any scholars in the field who do so. The very few scholars who explicitly oppose

31 Arbour, 'Economic and Social Justice for Societies in Transition', 5 and 10–11 (cited in note 7).

32 Muvingi, 'Sitting on Powder Kegs', 167 (cited in note 4).

33 Carranza, 'Plunder and Pain', 8 (cited in note 3); Arbour, 'Economic and Social Justice for Societies in Transition', 4 (cited in note 7).

34 Paige Arthur, 'How "Transitions" Reshaped Human Rights: A Conceptual History of Transitional Justice', *Human Rights Quarterly* 31 (2009): 321–67, 326.

35 Colvin, 'Purity and Planning', 418 (cited in note 25).

36 Chandra Lekha Sriram, 'Justice as Peace? Liberal Peacebuilding and Strategies of Transitional Justice', *Global Society* 21 (2007): 579–91.

37 e.g., Sandra Rubli, *Transitional Justice: Justice by Bureaucratic Means?* (Berne: SwissPeace 2012), 3; Patricia Lundy and Mark McGovern, 'The Role of Community in Participatory Transitional Justice', in *Transitional Justice from Below: Grassroots Activism and the Struggle for Change*, ed. Kieran McEvoy and Lorna McGregor (Portland, OR: Hart Publishing, 2008), 99–121 at 104.

38 Makau Mutua, 'A Critique of Rights in Transitional Justice: The African Experience', in Aguilar and Gomez Isa, *Rethinking Transitions*, 31–47, at 36–7 (cited in note 2).

39 Rosemary Nagy, 'Transitional Justice as a Global Project: Critical Reflections', *Third World Quarterly* 29 (2008): 275–89, 275–6.

40 Miller, 'Effects of Invisibility', 268 (cited in note 11).

a role for transitional justice in directly addressing socioeconomic wrongs do so not on the basis of opposition to redistribution, but on the basis that the available mechanisms of transitional justice are unsuited to doing so or risk being over-taxed.[41] By contrast, transitional justice generally rallies reformist forces and progressive elements who might be expected to support socioeconomic justice.[42] Traditional transitional justice discourse has always concentrated on how transitional justice can facilitate progress towards a liberal political agenda of electoral politics, the rule of law, responsive governance and constitutionalism, but demonstrates ambivalence about a liberal economic order. Transitional justice aspires towards a stable society, but not necessarily a capitalist one. Transitional justice is certainly guilty of under-analysing its potential in stimulating socioeconomic reform, a matter which is slowly being redressed. However, under-analysis of the potential to catalyze socioeconomic reform should not be confused with opposition. To assume transitional justice is a willing stalking-horse for neoliberal economic reforms is to make an ultimately unconvincing 'those who are not with us are against us' argument from omission. Transitional justice is not synonymous with all elements of the liberal peace-building agenda and scepticism over its distributive potential owes less to concerns over legitimacy of the aims, but to their feasibility.

Even these feasibility concerns are muted. It is difficult to find transitional justice scholars who either accept the argument that adjudicating violations of socioeconomic rights is outright impossible or who reject the indivisibility of rights. Certainly, there is force in the argument that the neglect of economic justice might owe to the complex nature of structural violence which the resources, size or capacity of transitional justice mechanisms are unsuited to grappling with.[43] Undoubtedly, transitional justice can identify a violator (the physical perpetrator and the government/military figure who gave the order) and a remedy (criminal punishment, guarantee of non-repetition by the democratizing state) for bodily integrity abuses like torture or crimes against humanity with greater ease than it can diagnose the reasons for, and ways to rectify, the unequal macro-level economic organization of society.[44] However, examples like the bills of rights in South Africa, Nepal and India demonstrate that socioeconomic rights can be enforceable by law, while truth commissions in the likes of Sierra Leone, Liberia and South Africa have outlined structural causes of conflict and made broad suggestion about possible reforms. On similarly practical lines, some suggest that the dearth of resources available to transitional justice limit its distributive impact,[45] while others argue the short life-spans of transitional justice mechanisms undermine their potential.[46] These explanations based on practicalities are reasonable but ultimately inconclusive. If transitional justice could realize even a fragment of the promise advocates hold out for it in redressing socioeconomic wrongs, any funding shortfalls could surely be overcome by international aid, while the case for extending, or even making permanent, mechanisms so evidently ameliorative would be incontestable.

---

41 Duthie, 'Towards a Development-Sensitive Approach to Transitional Justice', 292–309 (cited in note 13); Lars Waldorf, 'Anticipating the Past: Transitional Justice and Socio-Economic Wrongs', *Social & Legal Studies* 21 (2012): 1–16.

42 Godfrey Musila, 'Accountability Debate in Kenya in Near Policy Vacuum and Ethnic Tension', in *Oxford Transitional Justice Research: Debating International Justice in Africa*, ed. Phil Clark (Oxford: Foundation for Law, Justice and Society, 2010), 104–6, at 105.

43 Duthie, 'Towards a Development-Sensitive Approach to Transitional Justice', 306 (cited in note 13); Hecht and Michalowski, 'The Economic Dimensions of Transitional Justice', 5 (cited in note 27).

44 Kenneth Roth, 'Defending Economic, Social and Cultural Rights: Practical Issues Faced by an International Human Rights Organization', *Human Rights Quarterly* 26 (2004): 63–73.

45 Tony Addison, 'The Political Economy of the Transition from Authoritarianism', in De Greiff and Duthie, *Transitional Justice and Development*, 11–141, at 114.

46 Waldorf, 'Anticipating the Past', 6–7 (cited in note 41).

Laying the Blame – Transition or Justice?

Ideology therefore cannot explain the apparent under-performance of transitional justice in relation to addressing the structural causes of conflict. Both optimists and pessimists accept that unjust economic structures kill more than bullets and bombs[47] and that internal conflict operates as a form of 'development in reverse'.[48] Surveys of survivor populations overwhelmingly demonstrate that socioeconomic concerns trump the desire for criminal justice or truth in transitions.[49] If the conception of *justice*, therefore, does not explain the lack of impact of transitional justice on socioeconomic rights, development, or inequality, it is worthwhile switching attention to the other composite element of the concept, namely the *transitional*. As noted earlier, advocates of distributive transitional justice rely on the presumption that the sheer fact of transition is conducive to achieving their ambitious aims. This exemplifies what Colvin describes as transitional justice's technocratic and utopian imperative, relying heavily on a logic of project management in which the right combination of technique and planning will accomplish the goals set for any given mechanism.[50] This 'toolbox' approach tends to assume the universality of the norms underlying transitional justice as applicable in all contexts, an optimism that inevitably disregards local political, social, cultural and historical contexts and seemingly operates immune to local power struggles and political instrumentalization.[51] Consequently, 'vague statements' and 'received wisdom' 'are produced about what transitional justice is and how the aims of it can be achieved'.[52] In this manner, broad generalized statements about how transitional justice as a concept can achieve socioeconomic justice (or heal the traumatized, or end centuries-old cycles of violence) achieve widespread acceptability within the field without any attention to the inevitably idiosyncratic and difficult conditions it will be applied in.

The idea that law can displace politics and resolve conflict is tempting and one that has animated transitional justice from the beginning.[53] However, it relies on the presumption that a change from war or authoritarianism to peace and democracy automatically imports sufficient emancipatory momentum to achieving these ambitious aims, which is rarely the case. As the next section will illustrate, the political economy of even relatively straightforward transitions to democracy seldom conduces to distributive justice or socioeconomic reform – incoming democratic regimes may not organize their political programmes on this basis, the outgoing regime may only do so to the extent civil-political power is traded for the retention of economic power, power-sharing among elites may be preferred to distributive justice for the communities they purport to represent, or peace may rest on a structurally unequal status quo. Forms of state reconstruction are negotiated before, during, and after the transition, and rarely manifest the linear narrative presumed in transitional justice discourse. Optimistic accounts of transitional justice's distributive potential exaggerate the ability

47 Hecht and Michalowski, 'The Economic Dimensions of Transitional Justice', 1 (cited in note 27); Kader Asmal, 'Truth, Reconciliation and Justice: The South African Experience in Perspective', *Modern Law Review* 63 (2000): 1–24, at 16.

48 Paul Collier, V.L. Elliott, Håvard Hegre, Anke Hoeffler, Marta Reynal-Querol, and Nicholas Sambanis, *Breaking the Conflict Trap* (Oxford: Oxford University Press, 2003), i.

49 e.g., P. Pham, *P.* Vinck, M. Wierda, E. Stover and A. di Giovanni, *Forgotten Voices: A Population-Based Survey of Attitudes about Peace and Justice in Northern Uganda* (UC Berkeley, CA: International Center for Transitional Justice & Human Rights Center, 2005), 25; Simon Robins, *'To Live as Other Kenyans Do': A Study of the Reparative Demands of Kenyan Victims of Human Rights Violations* (New York: International Center for Transitional Justice, 2011), 28.

50 Colvin, 'Purity and Planning', 412–25 (cited in note 25).

51 Rubli, *Transitional Justice*, 9 (cited in note 37).

52 Ibid., citing Laurent Goetschel and Tobias Hagmann, 'Civilian Peacebuilding: Peace by Bureaucratic Means?' *Conflict, Security and Development* 9 (2009): 55–73.

53 Ruti Teitel, 'Humanity's Law: Rule of Law for the New Global Politics', *Cornell International Law Journal* 35 (2003): 356–87, at 385.

of transitional justice to 'set the tone' for future governance[54] – political transition is continuously negotiated by dynamic, non-teleological relations of control and consent, power and authority among multiple power poles, some of whom will be the inevitable (and extremely reluctant) losers in any distributive process and therefore resist it.[55] Transitional justice therefore is a game of relatives not absolutes: achievable goals should be determined not merely by the mechanisms available but also the opposition to be faced in a mediated state.

The Political Economy of Transition

Belief that transitional justice can significantly impact the macro-economic structures of all transitional states everywhere can only emerge if the proposed mechanisms are applied from standard blueprints and if insufficient reflection is given to contextual relevance and appropriateness, as transitional justice is regrettably wont to do.[56] The primary impediment to distributive justice is the same as that to retributive justice, namely the precariousness of transition generally. As Addison argues, while some transitions from authoritarianism to democracy have been successful, 'others remain tentative, and some have been reversed with either a relapse into full dictatorship or with the trappings of democracy used to cloak semi-authoritarianism'.[57] Periods of transition in partially democratized countries are those when risk of state failure is greatest.[58] Post-conflict states are even more insecure – 44 per cent of post-war states see a resumption of conflict within five years and 50 per cent revert back to war in their first decade.[59] Though the literature surveyed above assumes transition creates a window of opportunity in which new social compacts are arranged, before anything can be done in this regard many states have already degenerated into old patterns of poor governance and factional favouritism that caused the initial conflict.[60]

Even where a relatively stable transition is to a government committed at least minimally to democracy and human rights, it is important to recognize that the widening of political opportunity does not automatically mean there has been any economic opening in the spheres of production, distribution, consumption, or transfer of wealth. Transition is often a form of belligerent power-sharing where those formerly in power try to maximize their economic gains even where political power is conceded. This should come as no surprise – oppressive regimes install themselves in order to pursue certain economic policies that sustain their rule. If the violent suppression of underprivileged groups to safeguard economic power led to pre-transitional war or repression, the threat of its renewal remains pertinent in anything but the rare case of total defeat. Where internal or global power relations compel the removal of that regime, the military and security apparatus and economic interests and investments made might endure long beyond the return to democracy. As Addison concludes, 'where authoritarianism created a distorted economy and high inequality,

54 Aguirre and Pietropaoli, 'Gender Equality, Development and Transitional Justice', 375 (cited in note 9) argue it can do this.

55 Tobias Hagmann and Didier Peclard, 'Negotiating Statehood: Dynamics of Power and Domination in Africa', *Development and Change* 41 (2010): 539–62, at 542–5.

56 Colleen Duggan, 'Editorial Note', *International Journal of Transitional Justice* 4(2010): 315–28, at 317.

57 Addison, *Political Economy of the Transition*, 111 (cited in note 45).

58 Jack Goldstone, Monty G. Marshall and Hilton Root, 'It's All about State Structure: New Findings on Revolutionary Origins from Global Data', *Homo Oeconomicus* 21 (2004): 429–55, at 438–9.

59 Gerd Junne and Willemijn Verkoren, 'The Challenges of Post-Conflict Development', in *Post-Conflict Development: Meeting New Challenges*, ed. Gerd Junne and Willemijn Verkoren (Boulder, CO: Lynne Rienner, 2005), 1–18, at 1.

60 Michael Doyle and Nicholas Sambanis, *Making War and Building Peace: United Nations Peace Operations* (Princeton, NJ: Princeton University Press, 2006), 63–8.

democrats might find this hard to change'.[61] Many transitions will resemble that of Guatemala where those who signed the peace agreement (the liberal-conservative ruling party and the rebels) and those who supported it (civil society) were vastly outweighed in strength by the outgoing armed forces regime and the business elites who profited from past structural violence.[62] While progress could be conceded on issues like civil rights, identity, cultural diversity, education reform, participation, and political reform, socioeconomic reform aimed at reducing horizontal inequalities stalled.[63] Similar examples are legion – the militaries of Chile and Indonesia retained control of important enterprises within the state like copper mining and food distribution, respectively, even where they lost political control,[64] while the outgoing white elites could retain significant control of land in Zimbabwe and South Africa.[65] Transition to Maoist rule in democratic Nepal did little to alter the wealth of the deposed king.[66] In these environments, attempts to expand the focus of transitional justice to economic crimes or redistribution would incur the same types of automatic political resistance by privileged groups that non-transitional bids to tackle corruption or inequality have traditionally incurred.[67] Certain behaviours persist after transition such as unproductive expenditures on agencies such as the army, undisciplined rent seeking and macro-economic destabilization like capital flight which stiffen the will to resist even minimal socioeconomic justice.[68] The maintenance of the state in a low-equilibrium trap may be highly attractive to economic elites who may operate as both economic spoilers and governance spoilers if transition jeopardizes their wealth.[69]

Even transitions to ostensibly social-democratic governments rarely see considerations of equality trump power politics or discourses of entitlement based on participation in the pre-transitional struggle. Formal democratization in Mozambique and Angola has seen the leftist Frelimo and MPLA factions build single-party systems to tightly control state resources through and for their own structures.[70] Democracy itself can have adverse implications for development by providing systematic, long-term incentives to purchase state influence, collect rents to finance campaigns, and distribute resources to supporters.[71] Some transitions are to popularly elected centrist or centre-right governments whose policies are markedly different from the redistributive and developmental policies transitional justice scholars assume truth commissions and reparations programmes will recommend. In Africa, for example, instead of a focus on systematic redistribution and equality of opportunity, civil society and political parties typically embrace a limited social compact framed by the precepts of the liberal tradition like rule of law, political freedoms, property rights and separation of powers.[72] Committed advocates of wider reform are usually a minority and struggle to marshal enough political resources to overcome the residual power of *ancien regime* figures.[73] There is a presumption in the transitional justice literature that government legitimacy 'is inextricably linked to redistribution and redress

---

61 Addison, 'The Political Economy of the Transition from Authoritarianism', 111 (cited in note 45).

62 Graham K. Brown and Corinne Caumartin, 'Horizontal Inequalities in Post-Conflict Reconstruction: Guatemala and Nepal', in Aguilar and Gomez Isa, *Rethinking Transitions*, 114 (cited in note 2).

63 Ibid., 107.

64 Addison, 'The Political Economy of the Transition from Authoritarianism', 123 (cited in note 45).

65 Muvingi, 'Sitting on Powder Kegs', 163 (cited in note 4); Lungisile Ntsebeza and Ruth Hall (eds), *The Land Question in South Africa: The Challenge of Transformation and Redistribution* (Pretoria: HSRC Press 2006).

66 Aguirre and Pietropaoli, 'Gender Equality, Development and Transitional Justice', 361 (cited in note 9).

67 Madalene O'Donnell, 'Corruption: A Rule of Law Agenda', in *Civil War and the Rule of Law: Security, Development and Human Rights*, ed. Agnes Hurwitz and Reyko Huang (Boulder, CO: Lynne Rienner Publishers, 2008), 22–259.

68 Addison, 'The Political Economy of the Transition from Authoritarianism', 119 (cited in note 45).

69 O'Donnell, 'Corruption', 226 (cited in note 67).

70 Hagmann and Peclard, 'Negotiating Statehood', 548–9 (cited in note 55).

71 O'Donnell, 'Corruption', 241 (cited in note 67).

72 Mutua, 'A Critique of Rights in Transitional Justice', 34–5 (cited in note 38).

73 Ibid., 42.

of patterns of discrimination'.[74] However, this is open to the criticism that development is being examined through an overly Western lens in which welfare ranks much higher on the list of priorities than it does when viewed through the lens of the domestic political culture of the transitional society itself, where no such expectation may ever have attached to the state.[75] Redistributive or welfarist states are the product of unique historical and social processes. By contrast, in many states where the state has behaved in a predatory or abusive manner in the past, basic security and local autonomy may top the hierarchy of goods the state is expected to provide. Of course one can argue these centrist/centre-right programmes are not freely adopted given the neoliberal-capitalist demands of the world economy and Bretton Woods institutions if the state is to receive funding or participate in world trade,[76] but it does beg the question of whether the temporary, ad hoc, and cash-strapped institutions of transitional justice can ever do much more than challenge, resist, or recommend reconfigurations of externally imposed policies.

Because the rhetoric of redistribution and equality focuses on meta-level games of state-wide economic justice, it neglects the nested games embedded within this general meta-game.[77] While transitional justice scholars focus on this one overarching game, other games are being played simultaneously by actors (of revanchism, entitlement of the old opposition, centrist politics, global neo-liberalism) that serve to constrain efforts to this end and are so complex that the standard encomiums of transitional justice scholarship to *do something* appear unduly simplistic. Nevertheless, few advocates of a maximal role for transitional justice acknowledge these limitations. The best that may be achieved is a highly constrained optimum.

Antipathy to the State

Any interaction of transitional justice with developmental concerns will inevitably be state-centred and organized conceptually along the lines of the nation state because only the state has the resource base, coercive capacity and administrative capacity to make significant inroads into reducing inequalities.[78] However, any state that can achieve what some advocates argue transitional justice may catalyse, betrays ideal-typical visions of the state as the monopolist of physical violence, as bureaucratically capable, as the aggregate of individual references and as a legitimate political-territorial entity that is wildly at odds with the typical transitional state in the developing world. The tendency of transitional justice to 'see like the state' has operated to oversimplify dilemmas of transition and has failed to engage with local power structures, thereby encouraging grass-roots resistance.[79] Non-state political orders may operate parallel to, or independently of, a state with minimal capacity to restore a unified polity.[80] Distributive justice is not simply about conceiving justice holistically enough or calibrating institutions sufficiently – it is about resolving collective action problems where those who gain and lose power in transition are unable or unwilling to

74 Aguirre and Pietropaoli, 'Gender Equality, Development and Transitional Justice', 371 (cited in note 9).

75 Junne and Verkoren, 'The Challenges of Post-Conflict Development', 9–10 (cited in note 59).

76 Lisa Laplante, 'Transitional Justice and Peace Building: Diagnosing and Addressing the Socioeconomic Roots of Violence through a Human Rights Framework', *International Journal of Transitional Justice* 2 (2008): 331–55, at 338.

77 On meta-level games and nested games see Christopher Coyne, 'Reconstructing Weak and Failed States: Foreign Intervention and the Nirvana Fallacy', *Foreign Policy Analysis* 2 (2006): 343–60.

78 Colvin, 'Purity and Planning', 416 (cited in note 25).

79 Kieran McEvoy, 'Beyond Legalism: Towards a Thicker Understanding of Transitional Justice', *Journal of Law & Society* 34 (2007): 411–40, at 424.

80 Trutz Von Trotha and Georg Klute, 'From Small War to Parastatal Peace in the North of Mali', in *Healing the Wounds: Essays on the Reconstruction of Societies after War*, ed. Trutz Von Trotha and Marie-Claire Foblets (Oxford: Hart Publishing, 2004), 109–29, at 109.

work towards the goals of development and equality. Solutions premised on the effectiveness and legitimacy of the state in question, or those based on the assumption that all states generally should function the same way, may struggle to attain the emancipatory potential assigned to them in textbook discussions.

The primary reason for this is that state failure or the loss by the state of control over the political and economic space is often extremely profitably for special interests even if it imposes significant costs on ordinary people.[81] As Bøås points out:

> Most international interventions in fact overlook the deliberate aspect of state failure: the extent to which regimes allow and enable state recession in order to serve their own financial and security interests, regardless of the best interests of the people ... These interventions are therefore severely compromised, insofar as they are trying to 'fix' that which is probably broken for a reason. Even where this programming occurs in the context of post-conflict peace-building operations, the fact of ... regime shift does not necessarily change the incentives for continued state recession and informalisation, as the pathologies that created these incentives typically remain intact.[82]

Scholars generally accept that extractive, coercive and/or illegal war economies can prosper without the state and that war can be a sustainable system of economic organization.[83] Public goods once provided by the state, like security or health, become privatized by non-state actors, natural resources like mines or the sea can be captured, while political, ethnic or religious factions can establish areas of control where they can levy taxes. Though transition may end the conflict which permitted these activities, these spoilers may reject the state-building process even where weapons have been laid down:

> because they believe it poses a fundamental threat to their political or economic interests. This can include so-called warlords for whom the return of the rule of law could result in their marginalization ... businesspeople whose activities are illicit, and whole clans that have benefitted from armed occupation of valuable real estate during the war.[84]

Even after a successful transition, effective government control may not extend beyond the limits of the capital city. Political orders, institutions, and economies may have developed at a local level in the absence of the central government that may not trust the bona fides of a national government or transitional justice system.[85] These orders may acquiesce to political change at the state level but interference with wealth accumulated in conflict might shift their incentives in a manner unanticipated by those who see interference by the state in the distribution of wealth as an uncontroversial, unqualified good. The state, no less than the transition, may be a far more

---

81 Robert I. Rotberg, 'The Failure and Collapse of Nation-States: Breakdown, Prevention, and Repair', in *When States Fail: Causes and Consequences*, ed. Robert I. Rotberg (Princeton, NJ: Princeton University Press, 2003), 1–49, at 8.

82 Morten Bøås, 'Returning to Realities: A Building-Block Approach to State and Statecraft in Eastern Congo and Somalia', *Conflict, Security and Development* 10 (2010): 443–64, at 444.

83 Sabrina Grosse-Kettler, *External Actors in Stateless Somalia: A War Economy and its Promoters* (Bonn: Bonn International Center for Conversion, 2004), 2.

84 Ken Menkhaus, 'Governance without Government in Somalia: Spoilers, State-Building, and the Politics of Coping', *International Security* 31 (2007): 74–106, at 96.

85 Alice Bellagamba and Georg Klute, 'Tracing Emergent Powers in Contemporary Africa: Introduction', in *Beside the State: Emergent Powers in Contemporary Africa*, ed. Alice Bellagamba and Georg Klute (Cologne: Rüdiger Köppe Verlag, 2008), 7–22, at 6.

superficial phenomenon than advocates for an expansive role for transitional justice may be willing to concede.

Conclusion: Acknowledging the Superficiality of Transition

Much of transitional justice discourse in relation to economic justice is based on the cyclical relationship between conflict and pervasive poverty in which the latter makes societies more vulnerable to the former, which then in turn exacerbates poverty. Advocates of a more distributive justice approach should bear in mind the necessary corollary of this vicious circle, namely that redressing this poverty is inherently conflictive and exponentially more difficult than it is in peaceful developing states. Critics of the heretofore-dominant liberal-legalist paradigm in relation to civil and political rights in transitional justice argue that it denies the quintessentially political nature of rights and unduly simplifies the complexity of life in conflicted societies.[86] However, a similar accusation can be levelled at the philosophically unobjectionable language of equality, indivisibility of rights and distributive justice when applied as a blanket prescription for what transitional justice should aspire to or be judged on. Without attention to the dynamics of transition and the weakness of the state, arguments that transitional justice should 'facilitate change and provide the moral basis for development'[87] or formulate a 'holistic and comprehensive settlement addressing the foundational problems' that unleashed conflict[88] risk degenerating into the simplistic rhetoric and sloganeering that tarnish much-needed debates on the global protection of socioeconomic rights.[89]

The problem is not that justice has been defined too narrowly or that civil and political rights have been elevated to a higher plane than socioeconomic ones. The problem is instead the transition itself, which is regrettably but invariably a matter of elite bargaining over political and institutional reforms. One of the recurrent complaints in the literature is that these top-down peace agreements ignore victims and seldom address socioeconomic rights.[90] This trend is something that transitional justice is ill-placed to affect. As Wilson notes:

> The area of justice is the one in which civil groups are usually the least effective in shaping the course of talks, and where the two protagonists in the conflict act most expediently to protect their interests. It is one of the most elitist of all the issues in transitional negotiations, and the one in which leaders are most likely to reach a deal over the heads of ordinary people.[91]

After transition, even the best-designed and best-supported measures of justice may clash with the competing interests of domestic democratic constituencies (not all of whom will be reform-minded), revanchists and the dictates of the global economy. Transitional justice can provide a symbolic repertoire of justice, human rights, democracy, development and equality to mobilize support for distributive justice or to challenge existing power relations. However, it cannot be assumed that

---

86 McEvoy, 'Beyond Legalism', 418–19 (cited in note 79).

87 Muvingi, 'Sitting on Powder Kegs', 180–81 (cited in note 4).

88 Mutua, 'A Critique of Rights in Transitional Justice', 39 (cited in note 38).

89 Roth, 'Defending Economic, Social and Cultural Rights', 63, 65 (cited in note 44).

90 e.g., Aguirre and Pietropaoli, 'Gender Equality, Development and Transitional Justice', 372 (cited in note 9).

91 Richard A. Wilson, 'Justice and Legitimacy in the South African Transition', in *The Politics of Memory: Transitional Justice in Democratizing Societies*, ed. Alexandra Barahona de Brito, Carmen González-Enríquez and Paloma Aguilar (New York: Oxford University Press, 2001), 190–217, at 198.

this repertoire can automatically impact upon the dispersal of material resources that individuals and organized interest groups have at their disposal – money, land, skills, knowledge, violence.[92]

> Contrary to commonsensical assumptions, negotiation does not occur between co-equal parties or in an inclusive manner. Rather it engages heterogeneous groups with highly differentiated assets, entitlements, legitimacy and styles of expression. Not everything is or can be negotiated and not everyone takes part in negotiating statehood. But the political configurations and institutional arrangements that result from such negotiation processes must be seen as imprints of domination by the more powerful over weaker groups.[93]

Even assuming the questionable proposition that a programme of reparations or a truth commission could catalyze even moderate economic transformation, the typical transitional political ecology belies the Panglossian optimism in the literature about transitional justice's potential in this regard. The aspiration for transitional justice to influence development or enhance socioeconomic rights insists on an essential unity and competence the reconstructing state does not have and may never have. The distributive transitional justice envisaged by its advocates must inevitably become a bootstrapping process, a somehow self-sustaining process of social transformation that would proceed with minimal or zero resources or internal support from the country's main power-brokers and indifference (at best) from powerful international actors in the globalized neoliberal economy. Applying these generalized one-aspiration-fits-all expectations to post-conflict states like Somalia or the Ivory Coast reveals what Colvin describes as the naïve technicism of transitional justice in assuming 'that societies can be understood and manipulated, and people behave rationally or at least predictably'.[94]

This is not to counsel hopelessness about the prospects of redressing long-term patterns of inequality in transitional states, but rather modesty about what can be achieved in the radically imperfect ecology of a weak and divided failed state. It may be wiser to postpone highly contentious, *potentially* transformative transitional justice policies lest they undermine the delicate balance of power and compromise that the transition represents. Stability, after all, is a prerequisite for the type of growth the economy needs and the type of security needed to reassure those who benefited in conflict that their interests are not best served by resort to the gun. Even without economic transformation or massive redistribution, the construction of roads, schools or health clinics or the channelling of conflict entrepreneurs into legitimate economic activity can help ameliorate poverty. Development and socioeconomic justice are not matters of one-off intervention, but are rather continuous processes of critical dialogue with an expanding set of groups and interests to ensure that engagements undertaken reflect the needs and interests of at least some of these groups, regrettably including those who benefited from past injustice. It can also be argued that because of the sensitivity of local political factors and the need for some form of democratic accountability, a short-term intervention like transitional justice is less apt to address structural injustice than whatever state emerges in the longer-term.[95]

Peace without attention to structural injustices may not be durable in the long-term, but it may be an unavoidable necessity in the immediate future. Indeed, scholars now acknowledge that transitional justice processes in post-conflict states may need to unfold over periods of time of a decade and

---

92 On the distinction between symbolic repertoires and material resources in this context, see Hagmann and Peclard, 'Negotiating Statehood', 547 (cited in note 55).

93 Ibid., 545.

94 Colvin, 'Purity and Planning', 423 (cited in note 25).

95 Rhodri Williams, *The Contemporary Right to Property Restitution in the Context of Transition* (New York: International Center for Transitional Justice, 2007), 49.

longer.[96] As Waldorf contends, 'the reduction of longstanding inequality is necessarily 'post-transition' – something to be accomplished as part of creating an new and hopefully more democratic order',[97] though Arbour is certainly correct to argue that development of socioeconomic rights cannot be assumed to flow automatically from positive developments in terms of democratization and institutionalization.[98] However, this incremental, politically sensitive approach is more realistic than the overpromising regards transitional justice's transformative macro-economic impact than can only lead to the loss of hope in justice overall.[99] Scholarship consistently and commendably urges transitional justice to embrace a deeper appreciation of the sources of conflict.[100] However, the seemingly unshakeable confidence that this knowledge can automatically translate into beneficial change relies upon a very shallow appreciation of the dynamics of transition.

---

96 David Backer, 'Watching a Bargain Unravel? A Panel Study of Victims' Attitudes about Transitional Justice in Cape Town, South Africa', *International Journal of Transitional Justice* 4 (2010): 443–57, at 444.

97 Waldorf, 'Anticipating the Past', 9 (cited in note 41).

98 Arbour, 'Economic and Social Justice for Societies in Transition', 10 (cited in note 7).

99 Addison, 'The Political Economy of the Transition from Authoritarianism', 111 (cited in note 45); Duthie, 'Towards a Development-sensitive Approach to Transitional Justice', 306 (cited in note 13).

100 e.g., Japan International Cooperation Agency and International Center for Transitional Justice, 'Enhancing Socio-Economic Justice in Societies in Transition', 7 (cited in note 12); Muvingi, 'Sitting on Powder Kegs', 168–9 (cited in note 4).

PART IV
Transitional Justice and Political Reconciliation

Chapter 8
Reconcilable Resentments? Jean Amery's Critique of Forgiveness in the Aftermath of Atrocity

Grace Hunt

> What happened, happened. But that it happened cannot be so easily accepted. I rebel: against my past, against history, and against a present that places the incomprehensible in the cold storage of history and thus falsifies it in a revolting way. Nothing has healed, and what perhaps was already on the point of healing in 1964 is bursting open again as an infected wound. Emotions? For all I care, yes. Where is it decreed that enlightenment must be free of emotion? To me the opposite seems to be true. (Jean Améry, *At the Mind's Limits*)

Taking up Jean Améry's tormented defense of his right to resent Germany 20 years after his release from Auschwitz, this chapter examines the value of resentment in the aftermath of atrocity. As the epigraph suggests, Améry understands reactive emotions as part of the reconciliation process. My work focuses on a question that has been central to reconciliation efforts since the 1960s: how can the resentments so prevalent in testimonies of survivors contribute to state-authorized reconciliation in a way that is both empowering and politically productive for the survivors? How, in other words, might transitional justice square the reality of resentment with the ideal of reconciliation?

Well-documented criminal trials and reconciliation commissions have produced extensive testimony describing extraordinary crimes against human flourishing. The magnitude of the crimes has provoked growing suspicion that the overarching goal of reconciliation via forgiveness remains at odds with survivors who are not yet ready to move on. My work suggests that with its sights set on reconciliation, transitional justice risks marginalizing the testimonies driven by resentment. Against the tendency to view resentment as an angry fixation on private feelings linked to the past or an excessively hard-hearted refusal to forgive, I argue that resentment can be source of empowerment for survivors only when it is acknowledged and respected by the survivor's community. The upshot of my work is that respect for persons in the aftermath of atrocity need not demand anything like interpersonal forgiveness from survivors.

To this end, I turn to Jean Améry—a self-described "surviving Resistance fighter, Jew, victim of persecution by a universally hated regime"—and his book of essays that recounts the intellectual's experience of camp life (1980: 64).[1] Améry's work—which had until recently remained largely

---

1 Améry was born in 1912 as Hans Mayer and raised by his Catholic mother; his Jewish father died when Améry was a child. Améry studied philosophy and literature in Vienna and aspired to be a writer. He participated in the local resistance in Belgium until he was captured in 1943 by the Gestapo. Améry was tortured (and recounts this experience in detail in *At the Mind's Limits*) and afterwards detained in Auschwitz, Buchenwald, and Bergen-Belsen before being liberated in 1945. Shortly after his release, publicly renouncing his Austrian heritage, he changed his name to Jean Améry. His experience of torture and his time spent in concentration camps are the focus of his reflective essays, which combine survivor testimony and philosophical reflection on the moral meaning available to survivors. The essays were published in 1966 under the title *Jenseits von Schuld und Sühne: Bewältigungversuche eines Überwältigten* [Beyond Guilt and Atonement: Coping Attempts of the Overwhelmed] and translated into English in 1980 with the title taken from the first chapter's title, "At the Mind's Limits." The focus of my work falls on another chapter, titled "Resentments."

unknown to the Anglo-American world—has been revisited through a recent resurgence in discussions of his work and the value of forgiveness and resentment more generally within the context of reconciliation commissions.[2] Améry famously defended his resentments during a period of state-sanctioned reconciliation as a "principled revolt" against mandated forgiveness and the social complacency which it seems to bring (1980, xi and 72). In his essay "Resentments," Améry argues that a moral community, with its sights on forgiveness, remains unperceptive to the inherent vulnerability of the human condition (70, 71).

The political conflict between collective progress and survivors' struggle with the past is at the heart of Améry's work. This conflict suggests that the central struggle faced by victims of massive moral injury is between their particular needs for recognition and a societal desire for reconciliation.[3] For Améry, the more others forgive, the more he resents. His resentment reacts to a politically sanctioned program of forgiveness guided by commonality.[4] Political reconciliation premised on the willingness of survivors to forgive places undo pressure on victims of violence to overcome, repress, or otherwise deny affects that are necessarily part of the recovery process.[5] Framed within the conflict between victims unready to forgive, and a society too willing to forget, Améry's essay offers one of the most compelling and vehement defenses of the right to resent against the political privileging of forgiveness (Améry 1980: 64). The political pressure to forgive itself is immoral for Améry (Améry 1980: 72).

Améry's Critique of Forgiveness

Améry's essay is a testimony to the immense sense of betrayal and loneliness survivors experience as a result of political communities rapidly shifting from autocratic rule to democratic governance. During this swift transformation into democracy, many unspeakable wrongs were left unpunished. Within the reconciliatory climate, "Germans," Hannah Arendt explained, "for such a long time refused to prosecute even the murderers among themselves" (2003: 56). By the late 1950s, Améry had become a minority with his unrelenting resentment against Germany. He held the entire country responsible for Hitler's 12-year rule (Améry 1980: 67). Developed over time, his resentment resisted forgiving and interrupted forgetting in order to remember moral harm.

Améry's self-proclaimed "retrospective grudge" and "retroactive rancor" expresses what he calls his moral status as a victim (Améry 1980 63, 81). He preserves this grudge as a testament to the ongoing reality of his victimization, not at the hands of the Gestapo, but presently at the will of a society prepared to reconcile *on his behalf*. He expresses his resentment in spite of a world "now gushing over reconciliation … and converted to tolerance" (Améry 1980: 67):

> Whoever submerges his individuality in society and is able to comprehend himself only as a function of the social, that is, the insensitive and indifferent person, really does forgive. He calmly allows what happened to him to remain what it was. As the popular saying goes, he lets time heal his wounds. His time-sense is not dis-ordered, that is to say, it has not moved out of the biological and social sphere into the moral sphere. (Améry 1980: 71)

2 See Magdalena Zolkos, Editor, *On Jean Améry: Philosophy of Catastrophe* (Lanham, MD: Lexington Books, 2011) and Thomas Brudholm, *Resentment's Virtue: Jean Améry and the Refusal to Forgive* (Philadelphia, PA: Temple University Press, 2008).

3 cf. Magdalena Zolkos' *Reconciling Community with Subjective Life* (New York: Continuum, 2011).

4 Améry, like Nietzsche and Arendt, is extremely suspicious of appeals to mass culture to solve moral problems.

5 See Sonali Chakravarti, "Agonism and Victim Testimony", in Alexander Hirsch's *Theorizing Post-Conflict Reconciliation: Agonism, Restitution and Repair* (New York: Routledge, 2012).

Améry seeks to redeem his suffering by looking to the past. But the imagery in Améry's writing calls to mind Nietzsche's character of *ressentiment* who tears open his wound to keep it from healing.[6] Améry defines resentment as his "personal protection against the anti-moral natural process of healing that time brings about" (Améry 1980: 77). But what are we to make of the righteous character of resentment? How might it be distinguished from the spirit of revenge? On the one hand, Améry's resentment seems totally justified given the harm he suffered at the hands of his torturers, and the fact that Germans refused to prosecute known torturers and murderers.[7] On the other hand, however, Améry's resentments demand the impossible: they make what he calls "the genuinely humane and absurd demand that time be turned back" (Améry 1980: 77).[8] If we listen carefully to Améry's definition of resentment, we find that it serves a moral function. In a culture too ready to move on and rebuild, Améry's resentments linger and press for collective memory.

Margdalena Zolkos describes Améry as being deeply troubled by the "time-engineering" of reconciliation (2007: 29). The pressure to forgive is compelled by an illegitimate privileging of a time-sense that understands psychological and moral healing as analogous to the healing of physical wounds. Early in the essay, Améry admits that his resentment is both unnatural and logically inconsistent, and lists a number of problems that recall Arendt's concern regarding vengeance in the *Human Condition* (1958: 236–43). Améry says, "Absurdly, [resentment] demands that the irreversible be turned around, that the event be undone. Resentment blocks the exit to the genuine human condition, the future" (Améry 1980: 68). But Améry's understanding of what is natural and unnatural is counterintuitive and deserves a closer look. Améry believes that the sense of time that governs the Christian concept of forgiving is analogous to the physiological process of "wound-healing" (Améry 1980: 72). Améry's resentment is therefore a *moral* injunction against positivist/reductionist tendency to consider moral healing a matter of healing physical wounds. Aleida Assmann observes that for Améry:

> The political rehabilitation of Germany is accompanied by a new sense of time. This sense of time, which Améry calls "natural," "biological" or "social" time, is oriented towards forgetting. It is the time in which life goes on, wounds are healed and grass eventually covers everything. This shape of time enforces the law of life, not of truth. Its opposite is "moral" time … where there can be no forgiving and forgetting, but only a remorseless return to the crimes and the wish for their public acknowledgement. (2003: 125)

Améry's *moral* time remembers and returns to the past as a way to integrate the past while calling into question the social pressure placed on survivors to forgive. When Améry says he wishes

6 See, *On the Genealogy of Morals*, Third Book, sections 13–15. This worry is not only Nietzsche's. Anthropologists Didier Fassin and Richard Rechtman describe the "wounded eyes" through which we look back on history. Whereas "our gaze on the past was once a celebration of days of triumph," "our view of the future … has turned to disenchantment" (275). Society therefore experiences time differently, tragically. See *The Empire of Trauma: An Inquiry into the Condition of Victimhood,* translated by Rachel Gomme, Princeton, NJ: Princeton University Press, 2009.

7 Arendt, *Responsibility and Judgment*, 2003: 56.

8 That trauma has a disordered temporal structure at odds with the futural quality of linear time can be seen in the work of Vladimir Jankélévitch. He also speaks of time being "out of joint" in two senses that add to Améry's work. Jankélévitch distinguishes between irrevocable and irreversible time. Irrevocable time refers to actions that, "having been done", cannot be undone. Passed actions are irrevocable in that they cannot be annihilated. Irreversible time refers to agents, who cannot return to the past. Améry suffers from both irrevocable time in that he cannot undo have has been done to him, and irreversibility: he cannot return to the past in order to change what happened. Ironically, the irrevocable and irreversible character of time keeps Améry fixated on the past in such a way that he appears "stuck in the past." See Vladimir Jankélévitch, *L'Irréversible et la Nostalgie*, 1974. See also Paul Ricœur's beautiful analysis of Jankélévitch's concepts in *History, Memory, Forgetting,* 2006.

to "reverse the irreversible," he is expressing a wish and a worry: the past must be integrated, and yet this goal is made impossible according to the progressive time-sense of reconciliatory politics.[9] Negative affects such as resentment, in other words, do not "fit" within the progressive and normalizing period of reconciliatory politics and transitional justice.[10]

Reconcilable Resentments?

Although forgiveness was celebrated in the 1980s and 1990s as the cardinal virtue of truth and reconciliation commissions (see Archbishop Desmond Tutu's *No Future Without Forgiveness*, for instance), philosophers and legal theorists committed to agonistic pluralism have recently embraced backward-looking emotions as central to meaningful testimony and narration.

Améry explicitly dismisses politics as a hegemonic realm from within which his resentment became coded as objectively intelligible (Améry 1980: 63–4). Despite the oppositional character of Améry's resentment, one political theorist has suggested that Améry's defense can be useful even towards reconciliatory goals. Thomas Brudholm situates his interpretation of the political value of Améry's resentment within the greater context of transitional justice, which he defines as "the kind of justice or, more broadly speaking, the range of societal responses that can be found in phases of political transition from violence and instability to democracy, the rule of law, and reconciliation" (2008: 185n2). In the very definition of transitional justice we find the antagonistic relationship between undemocratic violence and democratic reconciliation. Transitional justice literature exemplifies a widespread privileging of this purported political dichotomy. Brudholm's work attempts to validate resentment despite its long-standing political opposition to forgiveness.

Brudholm says, "Political leaders, commissioners, and presidents of criminal tribunals often talk of the goal of 'closure': the shutting of the door on the past in order to move into a more 'glorious' future." The policies that accompany or reflect reconciliatory politics are therefore directed by particular goals while avoiding what Brudholm calls "emotional remainders." The entire scholarly field of transitional justice and its conceptual ideals of reconciliation, forgiveness and conflict resolution, Brudholm argues, "is guided by the possibility of restoration of trust and hope in the wake of mass atrocity" (2008: 7). In response to the boosterism of forgiveness within transitional justice literature, Brudholm's work aims to reorient our thinking towards the negative emotional remainders of mass conflict, particularly resentment. His work, to put it differently, tries to square resentment with reconciliation, and he turns to Améry as a case in point. Brudholm ultimately argues that neglecting the moral significance of survivors' negative affects post-atrocity is unfair and deeply offensive (2008: 4).

Accordingly, Brudholm is critical of those who assume in advance the priority and virtue of forgiveness.[11] Brudholm addresses resentment first in the context of the South African Truth and

9 There is more to be said here about history and trauma. See Walter Benjamin's Angel of History—a being who is propelled into the future even though he is unable to take his eyes off the past—in his essay "Theses on the Philosophy of History" from *Illuminations* (New York: Harcourt, Brace & World, 1968) and Rebecca Comay's *Mourning Sickness: Hegel and the French Revolution* (Stanford, CA: Stanford University Press, 2011)—wherein she develops a theory of trauma as a temporal category.

10 Chakravarti (2012) criticizes reconciliatory commitments by turning to the problem of anger, which as part of testimony is essential to reconciliation committees and yet is itself merely subjective and apolitical. She suggests that anger emerging from testimony often pathologized by the commission because anger is "immediately at odds with expectations for political discourse" insofar as anger "disrupts the temporal narrative suggested by liberal political institutions, a narrative marked by progress and greater efficacy and objectivity. The expression of anger often brings aspects of the past into the present in way that does not fit with an optimistic view of the future" (10).

11 See Brudholm's criticism of Desmond Tutu (2008: 42–56).

Reconciliation Commission and argues that in order for forgiveness to be deemed a legitimate choice within a democracy, it cannot be the only choice. Brudholm ascertains that "the TRC should have been obliged to acknowledge the legitimacy of anger and demands of retributive justice, just as government should acknowledge the legitimacy of conscientious objections to its efforts to mobilize its citizens to participate in a ... just war" (2008: 44). Forgiveness only gains legitimacy within transitional justice when it can be considered an option alongside other options.

Resentment, therefore, must be included, acknowledged, and validated alongside current valuations of forgiveness within the reconciliation process. But given that the aim of transitional justice is reconciliation, questions remain as to whether expressions of anger and resentment (seen as an unwillingness to forgive) are suited to this goal and whether they can be acknowledged and respected alongside the more forgiving attitudes[12] Are Améry's resentments best understood as compatible with reconciliatory collective goals?[13]

Within the arena of transitional justice, Brudholm brings legitimacy to Améry's defense of resentment as a kind of conscientious objection to the political view that forgiveness is the only legitimate response to moral atrocity. The question remains as to whether expressions of resentment are possible without the reconciliation process normalizing the traumatic remainders resentment carries for Amery.

Brudholm frames his defense of resentment within the realm of reconciliatory politics precisely because that is where we currently find the staunchest defenders of forgiveness. Forgiveness as a policy within reconciliatory politics is itself intolerant to residual suffering and negative affect, as Brudholm himself admits. The problem with modeling political reconciliation on an ideal of interpersonal forgiveness is that although there are at times face-to-face encounters within court testimony, ultimately it is the state that authorizes the reconciliation. The political application of an interpersonal event has the effect of forsaking the needs and demands of the victim; needs and demands, Brudholm argues, that are morally and politically necessary for justice. Améry seems to be suggesting that those demands and needs are at odds with the reconciliatory project itself.

The upshot of Brudholm's approach is that it dovetails with pluralistic and democratic theorizations of the value of negativity; those who study the political value of Améry's resentments are quick to point out that affects such as rage, despair, contempt, and resentment must be given a place within reconciliatory politics in order to promote the latter as democratic. The ongoing discussion of Améry within the realm of transitional justice is a much-needed counterbalance to what Brudholm calls the continued boosterism of forgiveness (2008: 50–56).

---

12 In her illuminating critique of the desire for politically sanctioned reconciliation and the sense of closure it claims to bring with it, Martha Minow acknowledges that even testimonies of violence "lack of closure and the impossibility of balance and satisfaction, in the face of incomprehensible human violence" (24). She claims that the importance of testimony is not its capacity to deliver universal truth, but rather to reveal indeterminate and elusive remainders of collective horrors. See *Between Vengeance and Forgiveness: Facing History after Genocide and Mass Violence*, Boston, MA: Beacon Press, 1998.

13 Echoing both Strawson and Nietzsche at once, philosopher Arne Johan Vetlesen maintains that resentment is human, all too human, and "to point out that it often proves counter-productive and discomforting to all involved is no argument against its essential humanness" (2006: 40). The humanness of resentment, characterized by its subjective and interpersonal characteristics (it is a personal experience that addresses others) may serve, according to Vetlesen, "as an experiential precondition for the identification of affliction-involving situations, situations involving others." In this way, Vetlesen continues, "far from diminishing the moral domain, resentment carries a potential to enlarge it" (42). To his credit, Brudholm turns to Strawson in order to show the necessity of negative affect in interpersonal life. One of Strawson's main claims is that resentment is paradigmatic of inter-subjectively constituted understandings of human responsibility ("Freedom and Resentment" 79). [For a contemporary and Kantian rendition of the moral import of Strawson's "reactive attitudes" see Stephen Darwall's *Second Person Standpoint* (Cambridge MA: Harvard University Press, 2006)]. Brudholm brings us to this point and then concludes that "a social life bereft of resentment is impossible, and insofar as it is imaginable, impoverished life" (2008: 11). It is one thing to agree with Strawson that resentment is expressive of an intersubjective engagement, but it is another to then say, as Brudholm does, that resentment can expand or inform the political sphere.

Many political theorists remain skeptical of this move to read Améry's work within the context of current transitional justice debates. Zolkos, for instance, argues that Brudholm's reading of resentment is itself teleological insofar as he believes that "the goal of the encounter of victim and perpetrator is to validate and/or 'objectify' the knowledge that derives from the subjective experience of victimhood" (2007: 30). Rendering the unintelligible desires of resentment *intelligible* is a prevalent practice within the political culture of reconciliation. Although Brudholm has the best intentions in attempting to explain the reasonableness of Améry's resentment in order to make it more widely understandable, he risks normalizing and thereby neutralizing unpopular but morally potent expressions of suffering.

Whereas political theorist like Brudholm remain hopeful that Améry's resentments can be welcomed into the reconciliatory process, Zolkos reads Améry's resentments as disrupting "the very discourse of 'normalization'" (2007: 27).[14] The progressive time characteristic of post-genocidal periods, Zolkos points out, "is construed as *the return to normalcy*."[15] Within transitional politics, the progressive time-sense brings unchallenged legitimacy to forgiveness. If Zolkos is correct that transitional justice is based on the assumption that some kind of resolution will be found through objectifying subjective experience, then its goal of reconciliation is at odds with Améry's project. Améry's essay can be interpreted as illustrating this very point.

I suggest that we understand Améry's resentments as a moral-psychological attempt to defend against political appropriations of suffering. Améry's vehement defense of resentment against politically sanctioned forgiveness offered in 1966 what would later become a standard worry within political theory regarding reconciliatory politics. Namely, that reconciliation is a device for "enforced commonality" that necessarily omits survivors' particular understandings of suffering and injustice. This section tries to make sense of why Améry's work, groundbreaking in its defense of the oppressed person's "right to resent"—failed to motivate the moral revolution Améry so desperately sought. Despite his denouncement of politics as an inadequate response to the properly moral transgressions of the Third Reich, Améry's writings reveal a deep political critique of the ideological character of reconciliation. His essay "Resentments" expresses a principled suspicion of the post-war climate wherein certain affects sediment into politicized customs and institutions. Specifically, Améry's resentments can be understood as a staunch mistrust of the privileging of forgiveness and its underlying affects (resignation, pity, kindness, sympathy, charity) as the guiding principle of reconciliation.

Ideological Reconciliation

Despite Améry's denouncement of politics as an inadequate response to the moral transgressions of the Third Reich (he says it is a moral, not political problem) (Améry 1980: 63), his writings reveal a deep political critique of the ideological character of reconciliation. His essay "Resentments" expresses a principled suspicion of the post-war climate wherein certain affects sediment into politicized customs and institutions; specifically, forgiveness and its underlying affects guide the *telos* and time of reconciliation. Political theorist Alexander Hirsch couches the problem of reconciliation as ideology in terms of the tension between negativity and transitional justice. Having whole-heartedly adopted reconciliation, transitional justice has been criticized for eliding the purely negative expressions in reaction to harm. Hirsch says:

14 Panu Minkkinen is also critical of the goals of transitional justice, additionally claims "with every attempt at a practical social arrangement for reconciliation contradicting the moral right of the victim to resent, the possibilities of transitional justice would seem to be very limited." See "Ressentiment as Suffering," 526.

15 "Jean Améry's Concept of Resentment," 27.

> Traditionally, transitional justice has referred to that field of theoretical scholarship that proffers recuperative strategies for political societies divided by a history of violence. Through the establishment of truth commissions, public confessionals and reparative measures, transitional justice regimes have sought to establish restorative conditions that might help reconcile historical antagonists both to each other and to the trauma of their shared past. Because of some of the theoretical lapses in this scholarship some have turned recently to the field of radical democratic and "new pluralist" thought—and especially to agonistic literature—to foreground a theory of post-conflict reconciliation based not on the principles of the *sublimation of difference*, but rather the perpetual deferral of accord. (2011: 166)

Said more strongly, Stewart Motha reminds us, "reconciliation and responsibility constitute a double move: both emancipatory demand and device by which an enforced commonality can be re-inscribed." Where reconciliation amounts to mere re-inscription of commonality, Motha maintains that reconciliation amounts to nothing less than domination (2007: 88). Motha's worries are precipitated by Améry's anxiety about the complacency state-sanctioned forgiveness instills in survivors. I think we can praise Améry's critical awareness while still being weary of his move to view reconciliation as merely a tool for domination.

Whereas traditionally transitional justice has been concerned with reconciliation based in the overcoming of difference, a recent radical movement has turned to agonism as a necessary condition for developing civil relations post-atrocity. What I'd like to suggest here, however, is that Améry's deep suspicion of political efforts to cure what is essentially a moral dilemma is the result of his own hasty conceptualization of politics as having both a teleological temporal structure (captured in a commitment to "progress") and enforced commonality (necessitated by state-sanctioned forgiveness). But do all political conceptualizations of reconciliation serve hegemonic and homogenizing functions? Or can dissidence be protected within the reconciliation process?

In his exploration of non-ideological conceptualizations of reconciliation, Andrew Schaap suggests that reconciliation as a concept can be non-controversially defined as "a public reckoning with a history of political violence and oppression in order to enable people divided by that past to coexist within one political community and to recognize the legitimacy of its law." As an ideal, the concept is difficult to oppose; public reckoning as a way towards peaceful coexistence is too vague to discount. It is rather according to its varied realizations or conceptualizations that reconciliation has been criticized. Schaap argues that the meaning of the concept of reconciliation became over-determined in the 1990s according to the dominant competing conceptions of reconciliation (2008: 250).

Schaap draws upon three conceptions that emerged in public debates in Australia when the Council for Aboriginal Reconciliation was founded in the 1990s by the Howard government. This program of reconciliation was created in response to the fact that there had been no formal steps to reconciling indigenous peoples with the colonizing ruling class. I bring up this case only to give context to three conceptualizations that have emerged from the attempt to reconcile the oppressed and its oppressors. Schaap points out that the two competing conceptualizations—a practical conception favored by the government in power at the time that focused on redistribution of socioeconomic resources, and the more symbolic approach based on reparative justice as collective responsibility—over-shadowed a third option, favored by oppressed persons themselves. The alternative was based on the democratic ideal of *self-determination* and "emphasized the importance of a treaty, indigenous rights, Aboriginal sovereignty and constitutional recognition" (2008: 250). Améry's resistance to reconciliation is based on a worry about diminishing self-determination (this is implicit in his claim about the moral particularity of the victim).

What his worry lacks is an articulated demand. Schaap helpfully brings to the table a properly political conceptualization of that self-determination would look like. I have turned to Schaap to point out that not all reconciliatory efforts are derived from an ideological or one-sided commitment to enforced commonality, and to provoke the worry that Améry employs only the ideological definition of reconciliation, a move that restricts the emancipatory purchase of his defense of resentment.

Andrew Schaap acknowledges the legitimacy of the concern that reconciliation might be a conservative device of enforced commonality, but also thinks "it might a strategic error to concede the ideological capture of the concept of reconciliation entirely to its conservative appropriators" (2008: 249). Améry, for better or for worse, adopted merely skeptical view of reconciliation as ideology. On the one hand, his mistrust of reconciliation provoked his valuable—if not systematized—critique of post-war forgiveness and his defense of resentment. On the other hand, his unwavering rejection of reconciliation amounts to a rejection of the very concept that could, if conceived differently, redeem his resentment. Améry's resentment names the conservative appropriation of the ideal, but struggles to fully articulate the emancipatory possibilities of reconciliation.

Améry's narrative-testimony of persecution offers those political theorists concerned with the status of resentment—an emotion all too common within the context of transitional justice—an account of how the refusal to forgive during periods of state-sanctioned reconciliation amounts to a principled revolt against the social complacency expressed in mandated forgiveness. In this respect, we have a great deal to learn from Améry in regards to a central tension within transitional justice between the demands of peace and justice.

References

Améry, Jean. 1980. *At the Mind's Limits: Contemplations of a Survivor of Auschwitz and its Realities*. Translated by Sidney and Stella Rosenfeld. Bloomington, IN: Indiana University Press.

Arendt, Hannah. 2003. *Responsibility and Judgment*. Edited by Jerome Kohn. New York: Schocken Books.

Assmann, Aleida. 2003. "Two Forms of Resentment: Jean Améry, Martin Walser and German Memorial Culture" in *New German Critique* 90: Autumn, 123–33.

Ben Shai, Roy. 2007. "*Reductio ad Moralem*: On Victim Morality in the Work of Jean Améry" in *The European Legacy* 12(7): 835–51.

Brudholm, Thomas. 2008. *Resentment's Virtue: Jean Améry and the Refusal to Forgive*. Philadelphia, PA: Temple University Press.

Darwall, Stephen. 2006. *The Second Person Standpoint: Morality, Respect, and Accountability*. Cambridge, MA: Harvard University Press.

Fassin, Didier, and Richard Rechtman. 2009. *The Empire of Trauma: An Inquiry into the Condition of Victimhood*. Translated by Rachel Gomme. Princeton, NJ: Princeton University Press.

Goodheart, Eugene. 1994. "The Passion of Reason: Reflections on Primo Levi and Jean Améry" in *Dissent Magazine* 14: 518–27.

Hirsch, Alexander. 2011. "Fugitive Reconciliation: The Agonistics of Respect, Resentment and Responsibility in Post-Conflict Society" in *Contemporary Political Theory* 10(2): 166–89.

Hirsch, Alexander, Editor. 2012. "Agonism and Victim Testimony" in *Theorizing Post-Conflict Reconciliation: Agonism, Restitution and Repair*. New York: Routledge.

Holmgren, Margaret R. 2012. *Forgiveness and Retribution: Responding to Wrongdoing*. New York: Cambridge University Press.

Jankélévitch, Vladimir. 1996. "Should We Pardon Them?" translated by Ann Hobart, in *Critical Inquiry*, 22 (Spring).
Jankélévitch, Vladimir. 2005. *Forgiveness*. Translated by Andrew Kelly. Chicago, IL: University of Chicago Press.
Jankélévitch, Vladimir. 2010. *L'Irréversible et la Nostalgie*. Paris: Flammarion.
MacLachlan, Alice. 2010. "Resentment and Moral Judgment in Smith and Butler" in *Adam Smith Review* 5: 161–77.
MacLachlan, Alice. 2010. "Unreasonable Resentments" in *Journal of Social Philosophy* 41(4): 422–41.
Minkkinen, Panu. 2007. "*Ressentiment* as Suffering: On Transitional Justice and the Impossibility of Forgiveness" in *Law and Literature* 19(3): 513–31.
Minow, Martha. 1998. *Between Vengeance and Forgiveness: Facing History After Genocide and Mass Violence*. Boston, MA: Beacon Press.
Motha, Stewart. 2007. "Reconciliation as Domination" in *Law and the Politics of Reconciliation*. Edited by Scott Veitch. Burlington, VT: Ashgate Publishing.
Murphy, Jeffrie. 1999. "Moral Epistemology, the Retributive Emotions, and the 'Clumsy Moral Philosophy' of Jesus Christ" in *The Passions of Law*. New York: New York University Press.
Murphy, Jeffrie. 2003. *Getting Even: Forgiveness and its Limits*. Oxford: Oxford University Press.
Murphy, Jeffrie, and Jean Hampton. 1988. *Forgiveness and Mercy*. New York: Cambridge University Press.
Nietzsche, Friedrich. 1989. *On the Genealogy of Morals and Ecce Homo*. Translated by Walter Kaufmann and R.J. Hollingdale. New York: Vintage Books.
Ricœur, Paul. 2006. *Memory, Forgetting*. Translated by Kathleen Blamey and David Pellauer. Chicago, IL: University of Chicago Press.
Rigby, Andrew. 2001. *Justice and Reconciliation: After the Violence*. Boulder, CO: Lynne Reiner Publications.
Schaap, Andrew. 2008. "Reconciliation as Ideology and Politics" in *Constellations* 15(2): 249–64.
Sebald, W.G. 2003. *On the Natural History of Destruction*. Translated by Anthea Bell. NewYork: Random House.
Stauffer, Jill. 2010. "'The Experience of an Extreme Loneliness': Resentment and Reconciliation in the thought of Levinas and Améry" presented at Pomona College. Forthcoming as *Ethical Loneliness*.
Strawson, Peter. 2003. "Freedom and Resentment" in *Free Will*. Edited by Gary Watson. Oxford: Oxford University Press.
Tutu, Desmond. 2000. *No Future without Forgiveness*. New York: Double Day.
Vetlesen, Arne Johan. 2006. "A Case for Resentment: Jean Améry versus Primo Levi" in *Journal of Human Rights* 5(1): 27–44.
Wilke, Christiane. 2007. "Recognizing Victimhood: Narratives and the Politics of Rehabilitation in Germany" in *Journal of Human Rights* 6: 479–96.
Zolkos, Magdalena. 2007. "Jean Améry's Concept of Resentment at the Crossroads of Ethics and Politics" in *European Legacy* 12(1): 23–38.
Zolkos, Magdalena. 2010. *Reconciling Community with Subjective Life: Trauma Testimony as Political Theorizing in the Work of Jean Améry and Imre Kertész*. New York: Continuum.
Zolkos, Magdalena, Editor. 2011. *On Jean Améry: Philosophy of Catastrophe*. Lanham, MD: Lexington Books.

Chapter 9

A Theory of National Reconciliation: Some Insights from Africa

Thaddeus Metz

Unifying Judgments about Reconciliation

In this chapter, I consider how best to construe the essential nature of an attractive sort of national reconciliation. Supposing that national, or political, reconciliation is something to be sought consequent to a period of intense social conflict, what are its necessary and sufficient conditions, or at least its salient recurrent properties, and how do they account for a variety of widely and firmly held views about the subject? An answer to this question is a theory of national reconciliation, something I aim to articulate and defend here.

In advancing a theory of *national reconciliation*, I focus strictly on that concept, considering related ideals such as restorative justice and transitional justice merely in passing. In addition, I am not out to capture just anything that might be fairly called "national reconciliation," but rather a desirable instance of it, one that particularly merits pursuit. Still more, I am interested in what a good form of national reconciliation is, not what is likely to bring it about or how it can be done so permissibly; my question is strictly about what constitutes national reconciliation, though I will address other issues when necessary to answer it.

In seeking a *theory* of national reconciliation, I do not spend much time reflecting on imprecise definitions of it that one commonly finds in the literature. For instance, I pass over, or rather intend to surpass, not only vague, first-pass definitions, such as that national reconciliation is a matter of "rebuilding damaged relationships," "establishing improved relationships," or "achieving stable peace," but also metaphorical characterizations about coming to "share the same symbolic and political space" (Moosa 2000: 119), to "build bridges" (de Gruchy 2002: 184), or to "renew damaged social capital" (Huyse 2008b: 188; Quinn 2009: 183). In addition, taking a theoretical approach to the topic means considering neither one or two examples of it in detail, which already pepper the literature, nor one or two piecemeal facets of it, say, insofar as it bears on forgiveness (Helmick and Petersen 2001), apology (Barkan and Karn 2006), or acknowledgment (Govier 2009b).

In contrast, my aim in this chapter is to be clear and comprehensive; I propose a basic principle capturing the "underlying structure" of an attractive sort of national reconciliation that entails and plausibly explains a wide array of disparate judgments about the subject. Such a theory would provide specific and systematic guidance about the myriad things that states, institutions and individuals should aim for when seeking to promote national reconciliation, and it would, one hopes, provide strong evidence that the category of reconciliation is a useful one for normative and descriptive analyses, and is not merely "little more than a buzzword, an amenable but loose framework for different contents, depending on the user … " (Hermann 2004: 41).

There are extant theories of national reconciliation in the literature, most of are which informed by Kantian, liberal-democratic and similar perspectives (e.g., Gutman and Thompson 2000; Crocker

2002; Moellendorf 2007).[1] In contrast to those accounts, I spell out one grounded on a comparatively underexplored sub-Saharan ethic. As I and others have been working to show recently (Bujo 2001; Ikuenobe 2006; Metz and Gaie 2010), there are communal approaches to morality prominent in sub-Saharan worldviews that should be taken no less seriously than Kantianism, utilitarianism, contractualism and the like. My foremost aim here is to demonstrate how African ideals about community, still largely unfamiliar to an international audience, do a promising job of providing a unified foundation for the roles of truth-telling, apology, forgiveness, compensation, amnesty, and related practices often associated with national reconciliation. A systematic comparison and defence of the Afro-communitarian principle with competitors must wait for another occasion.

I begin by spelling out what nearly all those who have reflected on national reconciliation would agree is inherent to it, my aim being to articulate an uncontested core that clarifies the subject of enquiry and debate as something distinct from, say, national unity. Next, I articulate a conception of community that lies at the heart of much African thought about morality and, in the following section, present an account of national reconciliation that is grounded on an Afro-communitarian moral ideal. I then apply the principle to several facets of national reconciliation, demonstrating its explanatory breadth and depth, often in the context of South Africa to illustrate. I conclude by suggesting that it would be worth critically comparing the theory of national reconciliation that I advance with rival theories in future work.

National Reconciliation: Some Uncontroversial Elements

My overarching aim in this chapter is to provide a theory of national reconciliation, and, so, to provide clarity about the subject of this theory, I start by differentiating it from related topics and point out some definitional facets of it that virtually all theorists would accept. I here bring out what competing theories of national reconciliation are *about*. Although I do not intend to be presenting anything particularly controversial in this section, it should be revealing to see what the uncontested facets of the concept include.

First off, national reconciliation, of the sort I theorize about in this chapter, is a kind of relationship between people. One group is thought to reconcile with another group, which differs from a kind of reconciliation that I do not address, one in which a group comes to terms with its past and seeks to "get on with life" (much of the focus in Dwyer 1999; Villa-Vincencio 2000; Hughes 2001; cf. Murphy 2013: 4451–3). The latter sort of reconciliation often does require relating to other people in a particular way in order to eventually "move forward." However, it need not; imagine the culprits have all died, leaving the victims on their own to adjust and to accept. The key point is that being reconciled *to the fact of one's having been mistreated or harmed* differs from being reconciled *with other people who mistreated or harmed one*, where I am interested strictly in the latter, essentially relational condition.

In addition, national reconciliation is an interpersonal relationship that, by definition, follows a period of serious societal conflict, characteristically one in which was there was grave injustice between at least two groups. This is one major respect in which the concept of national reconciliation differs from ones such as national cohesion (*contra* Quinn 2009: 183). Seeking the latter condition does not imply a prior condition of civil war, large-scale oppression, moral atrocity or the like.

Although the "re" in the word "reconciliation" might be thought to imply that there must have been an absence of conflict at some point in the past (Krog 1998: 109), few mean something so

1 There are of course also those who reject reconciliation as something illiberal, too (e.g., Ash 1997), or as otherwise asking way too much of a state or its people (Gerwel 2000).

literal by the term. Instead, nearly all academics, activists and policy makers would agree, upon reflection, that it is conceivable for something they call "reconciliation" to emerge from groups that have always been deeply antagonistic toward each other (as per Dwyer 1999: 83; de Gruchy 2002: 14–15; Hamber and Kelly 2009: 294). Hence, "reunification" is also not an exact synonym of "reconciliation" (*contra* Hughes 2001: 130; Alie 2008: 133).

Another fairly uncontroversial element of national reconciliation is that it is not a socio-political ideal, in the sense of an unsurpassable condition, let alone the "Holy Grail" (as per Gerwel 2000). Achieving a state of national reconciliation hardly implies utopia, or even a somewhat lower standard such as, say, the absence of injustice. Instead, nearly all agree that reconciliation is a way station or a stepping stone toward an even more desirable condition for a nation.

Now, just because national reconciliation is not an ultimate end-state for a society does not mean that it is necessarily to be valued merely as a means. Some do emphasize the instrumental nature of reconciliation as a path toward a better socio-political condition, while others suggest that it is *also* something good for its own sake. Although I think that the sort of national reconciliation most worth pursuing is one the value of which is not merely instrumental, I doubt that this is part of the mere concept of national reconciliation or true by definition. For instance, I balk at the suggestion that reconciliation is *analytically* a matter of justice, whether distributive, transitional, restorative or something else. A desirable sort of reconciliation might well be a form of justice (à la de Gruchy 2002; Philpott 2009), but, if so, it is not the case by definition. It is an open question whether reconciliation is just (see, e.g., Dwyer 1999), and, indeed, some radicals in South Africa are currently calling for doing away with reconciliation as a hindrance to the realization of distributive justice (not the usual suspect of retributive justice).[2] Hence, I simply point out that national reconciliation is by definition neither of merely instrumental worth, nor of inherently final value. It may or may not merit pursuit in itself to some degree, and, if it does, it may or may not be a matter of justice.

For yet another relatively uncontested idea, most would readily say that national reconciliation is the sort of thing reasonably expected to be promoted to some degree by a TRC (or some similarly named body) doing things such as making informed judgments of political wrongdoings, hearing out victims, assisting them with compensation for their losses, and facilitating ceremonies between them and their oppressors in which the latter express remorse or at least accept responsibility for what they have done. Almost no one believes that the workings of a TRC can be sufficient for national reconciliation, but most believe that the former can, under certain conditions, noticeably help to realize the latter.

Finally, national reconciliation is often captured with phrases such as "reestablishing broken relationships" and "healing deep wounds," which are meant to convey something more richly interactive than merely a truce or peaceful coexistence. These characterizations are not inaccurate, but I maintain that it would be intellectually and practically useful not to rest content with them; it would be of interest to articulate a theory of national reconciliation, a principle that articulates the core of a desirable instance of reconciliation at the political level, and then to show how that core accounts for topics such as listening to victims, dealing with emotional trauma, accepting responsibility for misdeeds, offering amnesty, and many other, related practices. In the rest of this chapter, I provide such a theoretical account, one that is informed by characteristic sub-Saharan prizing of community.

2 This is an explicit element of the manifesto of Julius Malema's new party intended to rival the African National Congress (Economic Freedom Fighters 2013: paras 29, 35).

An African Ethic

As is well known, pre-colonial sub-Saharan societies often resolved conflict with an eye toward neither deterrence nor retribution in the first instance, but rather reconciliation or harmony of some kind (Aja 1997; Ramose 2001). The aim when responding to wrongdoing was by and large to resolve conflict between the offender and his victims, or, more precisely, between his family and the families of those whom he had wronged. It has been no accident that reconciliation has figured prominently (even if with varying degrees of success) in responses to widespread conflict taken by countries such as Zimbabwe, South Africa, Rwanda, and Sierra Leone.

In the following, I appeal to salient values in the sub-Saharan tradition to articulate an ethic that is distinct from the dominant ones in the West and that grounds a promising conception of national reconciliation. In doing so, note that I am neither recounting traditional African ethics as they may have been understood *in toto* by a particular people, nor seeking to defend any specific reconciliatory practices that a given sub-Saharan society employed. My aims are instead constructive; I spell out a way of understanding African morality that is philosophically refined and will appeal to an analytical temperament, and then use that to spell out a novel theory of national reconciliation that is revealing. Although I draw on elements of traditional African culture, I am not seeking to describe or mirror the past, but rather to develop something out of it that will be of theoretical use now for sub-Saharan societies, although not only them.

According to one large swathe of sub-Saharan thought about morality, one's basic goal in life should be to realize one's humanness ("*ubuntu*," as it is famously known among southern Africans), which one can do if and only if one enters into community with others. One should strive to live a genuinely human way of life, something that is largely, if not solely, a function of prizing communal relationships with other human persons.

As for what is meant by "community" or the relationships constitutive of it, consider the following statements from a variety of African thinkers. According to the Ghanaian Kwame Gyekye, the most influential African political philosopher of the past 25 years, "The fundamental meaning of community is the sharing of an overall way of life, inspired by the notion of the common good" (2004: 16); Pantaleon Iroegbu, a Nigerian theologian, remarks that "the purpose of our life is community-service and community-belongingness" (2005: 442); the Kenyan historian of African philosophy Dismas Masolo highlights what he calls the "communitarian values" of "living a life of mutual concern for the welfare of others, such as in a cooperative creation and distribution of wealth ... Feeling integrated with as well as willing to integrate others into a web of relations free of friction and conflict" (2010: 240); and, finally, the South African public intellectual Muxe Nkondo notes that if you asked adherents to an African ethic what they live for, "(T)he answers would express commitment to the good of the community in which their identities were formed, and a need to experience their lives as bound up in that of their community" (2007: 91).

As I have spelled out in detail elsewhere (Metz 2011, 2013), implicit in these and other analyses of how to develop one's humanness or what community consists of in the African tradition are two distinct relationships, what I call "identity" and "solidarity." Identity is a matter of sharing a way of life, belonging, feeling integrated, and experiencing oneself as bound up with others, while solidarity consists of working for the common good, serving, expressing concern for people's welfare, and being committed to the good of others.

More carefully, identifying with another is the combination of exhibiting certain psychological attitudes of "we-ness" and cooperative behavior. The psychological attitudes include a tendency to think of oneself as a member of a group with the other and to refer to oneself as a "we" (rather than an "I"), a disposition to feel pride or shame in what the other or one's group does, and, at a higher level of intensity, an emotional appreciation of the other's nature and value. The cooperative behaviors include being transparent about the terms of interaction, allowing others to make voluntary choices, acting on the basis of trust, adopting common goals, and, at the extreme end, choosing for the reason that "this is who we are."

Exhibiting solidarity with another is also the combination of exhibiting certain psychological attitudes and engaging in helpful behavior. Here, the attitudes are ones positively oriented toward the other's good and include a belief that the other merits aid for her own sake, an empathetic awareness of the other's condition, and a sympathetic emotional reaction to the empathetic awareness. And the actions are not merely those likely to be beneficial, that is, to improve the other's state, but also, in the ideal case, are ones done for that reason and for the sake of making the other a better person or for the sake of communal relationship itself.

Notice that community, understood as the combination of identity and solidarity, is more or less what English-speakers mean by the word "friendliness" or even a broad sense of "love." To be friendly with another is pretty much a matter of identifying with him, engaging in joint activities, and acting for his sake, giving oneself and one's resources. As Desmond Tutu has remarked of characteristically African approaches to morality:

> We say, "a person is a person through other people." It is not "I think therefore I am." It says rather: "I am human because I belong." I participate, I share … Harmony, friendliness, community are great goods. Social harmony is for us the *summum bonum*—the greatest good. (1999: 35).

And perhaps at this point one can begin to see why I have argued in recent work that a prescription to prize community *qua* sharing a way of life and caring for others' quality of life forms the basis of a promising ethic that differs from Kantianism, utilitarianism, contractualism, egoism, divine command theory, and the other moral theories which are at the forefront of Euro-American debate (e.g., Metz and Gaie 2010). From the present Afro-communitarian perspective, what makes a person bad or an action wrong is, roughly, that one is not being friendly or is being unloving, as opposed to that one causes harm in the long run, degrades autonomy, violates a social agreement, does what has been forbidden by God, and so on. Notice, too, that this African ethic differs from salient forms of Western communitarianism, which tend to be relativistic, defining wrongness as what flouts its norms and sensibilities (e.g., Walzer 1983; Sandel 1984). In contrast, the opposite of developing humanness from a characteristically sub-Saharan standpoint consists of honoring the contraries of identity and solidarity, viz., relationships of division and ill-will. To engage in crimes against humanity and other gross forms of injustice, that is, the sorts of wrongful behavior that call for national reconciliation, is basically to prize enmity.

It is not my concern in this chapter to defend a new moral theory, but instead a new theory of reconciliation. One readily sees how a concern for reconciliation consequent to conflict would be recurrent in societies that prize community understood as the combination of identity and solidarity or something akin to that. If what is of utmost importance is relating communally or prizing people's capacity for friendly relationships, then one who acts in an unfriendly manner should be responded to in ways that are likely to counteract his unfriendliness and to foster friendliness between him and others. Imposing retribution in the manner of an eye for an eye, with no essential expectation of good to come from the imposition of harm, would be out of place.

A Theory of National Reconciliation as Partial Community

In this section, I appeal to elements of the African ideal of community to articulate the essentials of a desirable kind of national reconciliation.[3] It is only in the following section that I apply it to a variety of topics, in order both to shed light on them and to illustrate and motivate the view.

Above I contended that national reconciliation, generally construed, is a relationship consequent to serious social conflict between people tighter than mere peaceful coexistence that is desirable but not an ideal and that is typically fostered to some degree by a TRC, a body which, for example, makes public characterizations of the conflict upon careful historical enquiry, pays special attention to victims, and facilitates encounters between them and those who wronged them in egregious ways. There are a variety of different ways that such a general idea could be realized in practice. My present aim is to proffer a particular version of reconciliation that is attractive, rich, and informed by the African ideal of community adumbrated in the previous section.

If one major proper aim of the state were to promote communal relationships in its territory, and if national reconciliation were a stepping stone toward such an end-state, then it would be sensible to think of national reconciliation as constituted by only *some* of the elements of community. Reconciliation should be seen as a substantial step on the path toward realizing a society that fully respects communal relationships, ones of identity and solidarity. Specifically, then, a promising conception of national reconciliation would be based primarily on the *behavioral* facets of a characteristically African conception of community, or at least not so much the attitudinal ones. As a first approximation, consider the view that to reconcile is for two parties to engage in cooperative behavior oriented toward mutual aid, and that it need not involve mental states such as thinking of oneself as a "we," taking pride in others' accomplishments, exhibiting sympathetic emotions, and the like.

Including the latter, attitudinal aspects would be expecting "too much" from the concept of reconciliation, veering it too closely to a social ideal. After a period of great conflict between groups, one cannot expect people's attitudes to change quickly, whereas their behavior can. Although immediately after World War II many Germans continued to favor Hitler's policies, they nonetheless conformed to a constitutional order that sought to repair some of the damage done to the Jewish population. What (desirable) changes to mind-set there were came later. Similarly, at a small-scale level of just two people reconciliation intuitively is possible despite an absence of shared pride, altruistic motivation, and the like.

Hence, if reconciliation were a stepping stone toward a society of full-blown community, then it would be plausible to think of it as consisting mainly of the behavioral facets of identity and solidarity, and not requiring all the emotional and motivational ones. Of course, people's hearts and minds would need to change to *some* degree in order to move from a conflict-ridden society, that is, one of division and ill-will, or enmity, to one with the core, behavioral components of identity and solidarity as above. However, they would need to do so to a much lesser degree than they would in order, say, to be motivated by altruism or compassion or to feel a sense of togetherness with former opponents.

Now, since prizing or honoring a final value such as community is not merely a matter of promoting it, but also expressing certain positive attitudes toward it, reconciliation will plausibly involve *something* attitudinal. Specifically, if agents are to prize communal relationships, then an attractive notion of reconciliation would be one that acknowledges when they have been flouted.

3 I first articulated this conception of national reconciliation in Metz (2011a) and applied it to the issue of amnesty for political crimes; I did not there analyze the concept of reconciliation in general or apply my favored conception of it to a wide array of issues beyond amnesty.

That will involve at least public institutions, if not offenders in the first instance, expressing disapproval of the grave injustice, the love of enmity, as it were.

Although sometimes people who have fought and who have been treated wrongly are able to come together and repair the relationship without thinking in terms of wrongdoing, or at least not expressing themselves in those terms, my suggestion is that, in cases of gross and large-scale wrongdoing, such so-called "reconciliation" is not particularly desirable. To honor community means acknowledging when it has been seriously undermined in impermissible ways, and to treat people as special in virtue of their capacity for community means responding to them in light of the way they have greatly misused this capacity.

Putting these two ideas together, I proffer the following principled statement of what national reconciliation is:

> a condition consequent to serious social conflict in which a country's residents interact on a largely voluntary, transparent, and trustworthy basis for the sake of compossible ends largely oriented toward doing what will help one another and in which at least public institutions, if not also substantial numbers of the public and the offenders themselves, disavow grave wrongdoing that had been a part of the conflict.

This account should seem *prima facie* attractive, but in the following section I work to bring out its explanatory power.

Applying the Theory

In this section, my aims are to shed light on several aspects of national reconciliation and to demonstrate the ability of the principle advanced in the previous section to provide compelling accounts of them. I explore eight different facets of discourse about reconciliation, arguing that the Afro-communitarian view provides a unified and plausible explanation of them. By the end of the section, a powerful theory of national reconciliation will have emerged.[4]

Peace, Order, Rule of Law

It is a given that reconciliation requires, and is even by definition constituted by, the cessation of serious conflict. It is interaction that comes after civil war and related forms of enmity. It therefore is instantiated by the presence of peace, law, and order, and, some would add, democratic institutions.

By the Afro-communitarian conception, national reconciliation includes such conditions, but is far from exhausted by them; reconciliation merely as the achievement of institutional stability is "too little." Since social conflict is well understood in terms of people seeking to undermine one another's goal-seeking and to harm each other, that is, the opposites of the behavioral facets of community in the African tradition, the centrality of peace is easily accounted for by the present principle prescribing cooperation and mutual aid. However, the way that the Constitutional Court of South Africa has sometimes thinly understood reconciliation, as more or less a matter of

4 In the following I do not address what Murphy (2010) maintains is a core desideratum for a theory of national reconciliation, namely, the ability to plausibly explain when and why it is called for. However, appealing to the African ethic, my explanation would be founded on the idea that national reconciliation is apt in response systematic, extreme unfriendliness or enmity between social groups, an account that readily captures the routine description of those in need of reconciliation as "enemies."

establishing the "proper rule of law" and "strengthening peace, democracy and justice" (2009: para. 21; but cf. para. 56), fails to capture much of what counts as reconciliation, in at least two respects.

First, reconciliation plausibly involves peace not merely in the sense of the absence of conflict, but also in Thomas Hobbes' (1651: ch. 13) understanding of it as the absence of a tendency toward it. To have reconciled means that the public by and large has a reasonable expectation that conflict will not arise again, and does not significantly act out of fear of such.

Second, if reconciliation were merely the achievement of peace, order, the rule of law, and even related conditions such as democracy, then South Africa, for instance, would be a fully reconciled society, or at least nearly so. However, most in South Africa would deny that claim; there is still much reconciliation to be achieved among different racial groups. It is common, here, to point to stark economic inequalities (e.g., Mgxashe 2000; de Gruchy 2002: 195, 200–1) as glaring evidence of a lack of reconciliation. One could also add, among other things, the clannishness of various groups, by which I mean the tendency not to trust others not of one's race and instead to favor one's own when making appointments, exchanges, friends, and the like.

One proper task of a TRC is to help "normalize" dealings between groups so that they are willing, say, to make economic exchanges, to deliberate together in the media about legislation, and to engage in academic study with one another. A commission can and should promote such relationships by expressing the state's intention that from now on things will be done differently, exhorting the populace to go out of their way to engage with one another, and encouraging by example, for instance, by showing leaders of conflicting groups speaking to one another and expressing a commitment to work to build something new.

Emotions[5]

Some might suggest that another salient respect in which South Africa, for instance, is not fully reconciled is that people's emotions are still negative, ones of anger, resentment, bitterness, and disappointment. According to some, "the essence of reconciliation is a psychological process, which consists of changes of the motivations, goals, beliefs, attitudes, and emotions of the majority of society members" (Bar-Tal and Bennink 2004: 17). In particular, some would suggest that reconciliation consists of replacing negative emotions with "positive attitudes" towards others (Bar-Tal and Bennink 2004: 15; see also Govier 2009a), perhaps ones in which one "feels a sense of belonging" with others, "embracing ... those who are different" (Hamber and Kelly 2009: 292), or in which "others are not seen in merely instrumental terms" (du Bois and du Bois-Pedain 2008: 302). These are of course desirable conditions, and, indeed, are part of the sub-Saharan ideal of community. But are they essential to national reconciliation?

I view reconciliation as a mere stepping stone to the realization of fully communal relationships, and, so, as I have indicated above, I suspect that conceiving of reconciliation as *requiring*, let alone *consisting of*, positive emotions (and related attitudes) is expecting "too much" of this category. Recall the example of two individuals who have had a fight, talked openly about what happened, and are now engaging in joint projects and doing what they expect will be good for one another. Even if they continued to have lingering negative emotions, my intuition is that they can be said to have reconciled if they are "going about their business" in ways that are cooperative and involve mutual aid. If these two also took pride in one another's activities and felt compassion for each other, these would be manifestations of a new category of value, such as full-blown friendship

5 In this chapter I do not address the relationship between belief change and reconciliation (beyond apprehension of facts about the past), though acknowledge that it merits addressing in a fuller statement (cf. de Gruchy 2002: 152–3; Bar-Tal and Bennink 2004: 21–2; du Bois and du Bois-Pedain 2008; Eisikovits 2010).

or community, and not reconciliation. (Or, at most, I suggest they would be instances of a much *better* or *thicker* instance of reconciliation, but not necessary for reconciliation *simpliciter*.) Similar remarks apply at the political level.

Although some dissipation of anger, achievement of closure, and the like are *usually instrumental* for reconciliation to occur, what I deny is that they are essential to it. I accept that it is often the case that one could not have reconciliation without some emotional change, and yet I deny that reconciliation is well understood as consisting of it.

Forgiveness

One might still reasonably suspect that my account of reconciliation leaves out too much when it comes to people's mental states. In particular, forgiveness lies at the heart of national reconciliation not only for many whose views are grounded on the Christian tradition (e.g., Tutu 1999, 2009; Helmick and Petersen 2001; de Gruchy 2002: 170, 178–9), but also for a notable number of those who do not appeal to any religious perspective (e.g., Bar-Tal and Bennink 2004: 19; Philpott 2009; May 2011: 589–90; cf. Auerbach 2004). I therefore devote a separate subsection to accounting for the exact relationship between the two ideas, advancing what I suspect are some under-recognized reasons to believe that forgiveness is not essential to reconciliation (but cf. Govier 2009a: 14).[6]

I want, as much as I can, to avoid the tricky issue of how forgiveness is to be understood; I do not thoroughly address what it precisely is.[7] However it is plausibly construed, it is reasonable to think it has some kind of close tie to reconciliation. I here provide additional reason to think that it is not constitutive of reconciliation, and instead related insofar as it can be a reliable cause of it.

Now, the most straightforward way of trying to show that reconciliation does not require forgiveness would be to show that it can instead come consequent to mere forgetfulness. Suppose that among two people who had been fighting, the victim elects simply to forget, as opposed to forgive. That is, imagine that he simply succeeds in putting out of mind what had happened, instead of continuing to be aware of the wrongdoing and evincing a forgiving disposition toward the wrongdoer. Having removed the offending events from his awareness, he then engages in cooperative projects involving mutual aid with the offender. Hence, it seems that one could fairly conclude that reconciliation without forgiveness is possible, even somewhat common.

Although this is a tempting maneuver, it is not one I can invoke since, as I discuss below, the Afro-communitarian principle of reconciliation implies that it is a process that includes knowing the truth about the past. A proper form of reconciliation, informed by the sub-Saharan conception of community, is one in which people come together consequent to an awareness of the wrongdoing that has occurred between them.

At this point, I could suggest that a desirable form of reconciliation would be possible if the victim and offender first became clear about what had transpired between them, the victim then elected to forget about it all rather than forgive, and then both engaged in the relevant behavioral changes. Perhaps that works to establish my point.

Here, though, is another rationale for thinking that forgiveness is not necessary for reconciliation, one that does not appeal to the idea that reconciliation could come upon the victim forgetting the wrong done to him. I accept that *part of* forgiveness is essential to reconciliation to the extent that forgiveness by definition involves the absence of an inclination to inflict harm or to rebut another's end-seeking. Since reconciliation by the African view is roughly a matter of cooperation and mutual

6 Often those who reject forgiveness as essential to national reconciliation have worries about whether it is a realistic and permissible goal for a state to pursue.

7 I am sympathetic to the account in Allais (2008).

aid, there must not be a behavioral tendency to engage in the opposites on the part of the victim. However, I maintain that forgiveness *as such* is not necessary for reconciliation since forgiveness is invariably understood to be more than merely a change in behavior. Forgiveness plausibly also involves an emotional element such as "a changed view of the wrongdoer as a person in which you cease to have towards her the personal retributive reactive attitudes that her wrongdoing supports, without a change in judgment about her responsibility for the wrong" (Allais 2008: 57). Whatever extra element that forgiveness includes beyond the letting go of conflict, it is something that is not essential to reconciliation. To see this, return once again to a case of two persons. Imagine that the victim remains fully aware of the wrong done to him (instead of forgetting), that the victim and wrongdoer have had it out about what transpired, perhaps with the latter apologizing, that the victim and wrongdoer then successfully embark on cooperative projects involving mutual aid, but that the victim continues to harbor negative emotions toward the wrongdoer. He just cannot shake a feeling of resentment, at least for a long while. To the extent there is the latter condition, there is an absence of forgiveness. However, I submit that the two parties are plausibly described as having reconciled; for there is the *commitment* to commune (cf. Villa-Vincencio 2009: 154). And what applies to a case of two individuals would readily seem to apply to a case involving two large groups.

Of course, it will sometimes be the case that the change in behavior could not come about without a prior or accompanying change of mind. Many times, then, forgiveness will be a particulalry fruitful means to reconciliation. But not always, not necessarily. And it is of course also true that the offender might well want more than merely a change in behavior on the part of the victim, and in addition to be viewed in a positive light. However, emotional change is usually hard to come by in the short to medium term after conflict and therefore is not so clearly a matter of reconciliation, a basic form of which can, in contrast, often be expected in that time frame.

Listening to Victims

Central to most people's thoughts about national reconciliation is the hearing out of victims. It is not enough that, say, a scholar interview victims and report on what they said in a professional journal. Instead, a crucial part of reconciliation is a process by which, in the ideal case, offenders listen to their victims, and, failing that, some kind of public body does so. A satisfactory theory of national reconciliation must entail and plausibly explain why this is so.

Notice that it will not do to appeal to the value of truth, here. Of course, one way to access the truth about the nature of the social conflict would be to listen to victims. However, it appears that the historical facts could also be ascertained behind the scenes by academic interviews that are then published in scholarly forums and newspapers as well. While an interest in truth supports the idea of listening to victims, it does not uniquely do so.

To make sense of why it is important that victims address specific people, such as their offenders or the public in general, one must appeal to something beyond the content of what victims have to recount. For instance, in South Africa, a common explanation given of why victims needed to be heard, by offenders or by the TRC, has been that it would help them to achieve catharsis and obtain closure, which, in turn would enable them to move forward to create a peaceful and democratic order (see, e.g., Constitutional Court of South Africa 2010). In short, it is not just what victims have to say, but the fact that they say it to a certain audience, which promises to produce a desirable outcome.

Such a rationale might be part of the reason to hear out victims, but it cannot be all of it. Suppose, for instance, that such an order could have been created without listening to victims, as basically happened in Chile and Argentina. Or consider a case in which it has already been created, but not all victims have yet been heard; there would be reason to continue to listen to the remaining victims, despite large-scale nation building proceeding on track. Similar remarks apply even if the broader socio-behavioral facets of reconciliation, i.e., cooperation and mutual aid, are considered.

Another reason that reconciliation plausibly requires victims to be heard, beyond the content of what they have to say, is that it is a way for the public, and in the ideal case offenders, to disavow the injustice that was done. Recall that honoring community means expressing disapproval of when it is egregiously undermined. For offenders to take responsibility for their misdeeds and to express contrition for what they have done requires being willing to undergo the discomfort of hearing how one has wrongfully harmed others. And for a public institution such as a TRC, to disavow injustice means coming closer to victims, while tending to distance itself from offenders, where coming closer to victims naturally involves listening to the way they were mistreated and, as I now discuss, offering assistance.

Compensation

Another core element of national reconciliation is the attempt to help victims overcome their plight. Offenders themselves should offer restitution to their victims, or at least express an apology with the aim of easing psychological burdens. And where offenders are unwilling to do that, or unable to cover the extent of victim suffering, it is common to hold that the state ought to step in and use public funds to help compensate victims.

The Afro-communitarian conception of reconciliation naturally accounts for these judgments. If hearing out victims is a way for offenders to disavow their misdeeds, then so is offering victims resources to help make up for their losses. When considering what it is that should be offered to victims, it is natural to consider what was taken away in the first place. If land was stolen, then there is strong *prima facie* reason to think that land should be returned. However, there can be considerations favoring the offer of something other than repayment in kind for what was unjustly taken. National reconciliation is a process that takes time, and the kind of compensation offered should ideally be one that supports an ongoing improvement in the extent to which there is cooperation and mutual aid between formerly antagonistic groups.

For instance, in South Africa, an interest in national reconciliation probably does not, all things considered, prescribe an immediate and systematic transfer of farmland and mineral wealth from whites to blacks.[8] The reason is that whites are primarily the ones with the skills and knowledge to run farms and mines, and it is well known in South Africa that a very large majority of what little transfers of farmland have been made so far has become unproductive. Those who suffered under apartheid, and their descendants, would be unlikely to be better off were South Africa to be no longer able to feed itself or to extract the minerals in an efficient manner. In this context, the right sort of compensation would not be merely the return of land, but also the transfer of the ability to make use of it. Or it might be to provide resources that would enable black people to flourish in urban areas, should they prefer that kind of support.

A commission can help to facilitate compensation for those who have been particularly wrongfully harmed by the conflict. It can identify the latter, for one, and it can make sensible recommendations about whom precisely should take responsibility for working to make up for their losses. Sometimes it should recommend that particular wrongdoers be the ones to do so, a particularly welcome form of reconciliation in which wrongdoers would also be disavowing

8 Here I draw on ideas first published in Metz (2011b: 551–4).

their wrongdoing by working to make restitution to their victims. However, national reconciliation would also be fostered if those not responsible for wrongful harm pitched in to improve the lot of victims, something a commission is in a position to recommend, as it did in the case of South Africa's TRC, which recommended that the government pay a certain amount of public tax money to some individual victims of political crimes.

Truth

Another key facet of national reconciliation, or at least a desirable form of it, is the search for, and dissemination of, truth about the social conflict that occurred. As I now point out, salient accounts of how truth relates to reconciliation conceive of it instrumentally, as something that fosters reconciliation in the long run. In contrast, the theory I support entails that reconciliation is partially constituted by obtaining the truth about the past. From this perspective, to speak of "truth and reconciliation," as per some influential commissions, is ultimately redundant, as the right sort of reconciliation itself includes truth.

Why think that reconciliation, properly conceived, requires digging up the truth about the past? Why not just "move forward," rather than stir up negative memories and emotions, as many white people in South Africa have favored? The standard answer to these questions in the South African context has been that victims can move forward only upon expressing themselves, being heard and releasing negative feelings.

However, while this might be a plausible rationale for listening to victims, it is not a particularly good one for a mandate to get at the truth, which would require much more than obtaining the perspectives of victims. Offenders' stories, too, would add to the truth, as would more impersonal and dry enquiries such as forensic investigations into gravesites and academic scholarship about the negative influences of social conflict on institutions, relationships, and opportunities. While the latter kinds of information might help to foster solace and closure on the part of victims, including ones who were not direct victims of political crimes, they might not. Even if victims had already obtained solace, or even if they never would obtain it, reconciliation intuitively would demand obtaining clarity about what transpired between conflicting groups. This is one way to grasp a recurrent criticism of South Africa's TRC, that it focused mainly on crimes done to individuals, and did not also highlight evidence of more collective wrongdoing and its foreseeable effects.

According to the theory of national reconciliation that I favor, accurate and comprehensive historical awareness is partially constitutive of national reconciliation. Part of genuinely *sharing* a way of life among formerly antagonistic groups, which includes the idea of cooperative behavior between them, is acting consequent to knowledge of what has happened between them. That means not merely the absence of deception, but also the revelation of truth.

If one has a serious fight with one's spouse, reconciliation of a desirable sort would involve clearing the air. It would mean that both parties listen to one another, and that they move forward in light of a clear understanding of what happened, or at least of the various perspectives about what did. A genuine sort of reconciliation would not sweep the fight under the rug. Similar remarks apply at the political level.

One might question the analogy in that it appears merely to require both parties to the conflict to be heard, and not to support the more academic and scientific enquiries that I maintain are central to national reconciliation. However, upon reflection, the analogy is strong. Couples rarely have access to a third-party who has the time, resources, and interest to comment on what happened between them. However, sometimes they do, and when they do, a welcome form of reconciliation would involve taking such a perspective into account. For instance, if a couple has been seeing a counsellor, one would expect the pair to bring up the issue of the fight with her, and to be open to her opinion about what caused the conflict and how it has likely affected a given party. An ideal kind of reconciliation is one in which those who were for a time enemies together seek to get to the bottom of things. To the extent that one party attempts to hide things, or one party fails to acknowledge things, or both parties close their eyes to the input of a sympathetic and informed observer, there is less of a shared way of life, less reconciliation, than there could and should have been.

Orientation toward the Guilty

A possible sort of reconciliation is one in which there is no thought of wrongdoing, or at least no talk of it, or censure for it. However, it would not be a plausible sort, at least by the Afro-communitarian account, which includes the requirement of disavowing injustice, ideally on the part of offenders, and at least on the part of public institutions.[9]

Here is one respect in which I believe the South African Constitutional Court has judged correctly about national reconciliation, when it says the latter must not be understood as permitting the guilty to receive "the lion's share of benefits" or as requiring the state "to ameliorate hardship for the perpetrators of human rights abuses" (2009: 53, 55). If reconciliation did not include judgments of culpable wrongdoing, then guilty parties would have no less of a claim to the receipt of benefits and the lifting of burdens as their victims. For instance, it would apparently mean that, say, a state should allow neither a newspaper to call a perpetrator of an atrocity a "murderer" (see Constitutional Court of South Africa 2011), nor an organization, such as the police force, to take into account a person's political-criminal past when deciding to hire or fire (Constitutional Court of South Africa 2009).

Although such a neutral approach would of course provide the utmost encouragement to the guilty to participate in so-called "reconciliatory" processes, it would come at the expense of a failure to adequately respect the value of community, which, as per above, requires taking account of when this value has been seriously undermined. A better sort of reconciliation is surely one in which offenders themselves acknowledge their wrongdoing, apologize for it, and contribute to making victims better off because of what they have done, and in which, at least if offenders are unwilling to do these things, public institutions step in to stand by victims.

A commission would be well positioned to assist with the public disavowal element. It would have become accurately and comprehensively informed about the wrongdoing, and might well itself express disapproval of it on behalf of the government or the new society more generally. In addition, it could furnish other public institutions, particularly the executive branch of government, but also, for instance, universities and accrediting bodies, the grounds for further expressions of disapproval.

Amnesty

In the previous two subsections, I indicated that the Afro-communitarian conception of national reconciliation implies that the truth about the past as well as disavowal of injustice are both inherent to it. However, as is well known, one cannot expect these two desiderata to be maximally jointly fulfilled. In order to get substantial truth from offenders about their unjust behavior, a state often must reduce the extent to which it otherwise would have responded negatively to them.

---

9 While Bashir (2008) is good about highlighting the idea that reconciliation centrally involves the relevation of truth about misdeeds and the censure of them, I am afraid that he appears to reduce reconciliation to these conditions alone.

This point must not be taken to be a strike against the present understanding of national reconciliation; in fact, I submit just the opposite. It is a plus for the Afro-communitarian view that it plausibly accounts in a new way for a widely recognized tension in reflection about national reconciliation. It explains the tension not in terms of any conditions external to reconciliation, as, say, between truth and justice, but rather as intrinsic to reconciliation itself. A fully reconciled society would be one in which there is *both* a completely accurate picture of the nature of the conflict *and* a systematic disavowal of the extent to which that conflict was unjust. Although such a state of affairs is possible, it is not likely to obtain, and achieving the most reconciliation that a given society can along the two dimensions requires careful judgment about how much to trade off disavowal for the sake of truth.

One salient strategy by which to balance these two elements of reconciliation has been to offer amnesties to offenders in exchange for full disclosure about their misdeeds, as was done by South Africa's TRC. Sensitivity to context will determine whether amnesty, and which sort, is necessary to obtain an adequate amount of truth from offenders.

Conclusion

In this chapter, I have sought to unify several concepts routinely associated with thought about national reconciliation by providing a principle that purports to capture its essential nature. According to this view, reconciliation is a condition consequent to serious social conflict in which a country's residents interact on a largely voluntary, transparent, and trustworthy basis for the sake of compossible ends largely oriented toward doing what will help one another and in which at least public institutions, if not also substantial numbers of the public and the offenders themselves, disavow grave wrongdoing that had been a part of the conflict. I have spelled out this principle, demonstrated that it follows from a *prima facie* attractive ethic informed by sub-Saharan values, and argued that it plausibly accounts for myriad practices such as truth-telling, forgiving, listening to victims, offering amnesty, and the like.

I have lacked the space to defend this theory of national reconciliation systematically against those who would question it. On the one hand, there will be those who doubt the theory because they reject one of its implications, say, that forgiveness is not essential to reconciliation. On the other hand, there will be critics who favor alternate theories (see esp. Murphy 2010; Philpott 2012). I have hoped in this chapter merely to articulate a new theory grounded on African communitarian values and to show that it is attractive enough to merit rigorous comparison with rival perspectives in future work.[10]

References

Aja, E. 1997. "Crime and Punishment: An Indigenous African Experience." *Journal of Value Inquiry* 31: 353–68.

10 I am thankful that Lucy Allais, Alex Broadbent, and Nir Eisikovits who took the time to read an earlier draft and to offer supportive comments. This chapter has also benefited from the input of audiences at a colloquium sponsored by the University of Johannesburg Philosophy Department and at a workshop to honor the jurisprudence of former Constitutional Court of South Africa Chief Justice Sandile Ngcobo organized by Drucilla Cornell's Ubuntu Project at the University of Pretoria School of Law.

Alie, J.A.D. 2008. "Reconciliation and Traditional Justice." In *Traditional Justice and Reconciliation after Violent Conflict: Learning from African Experiences*, Huyse, L. and Salter, M. (eds) Stockholm: International Institute for Democracy and Electoral Assistance, pp. 123–45.
Allais, L. 2008. "Wiping the Slate Clean." *Philosophy and Public Affairs* 36: 33–68.
Ash, T.G. 1997. "True Confessions." *The New York Review of Books* July 17: 33–8.
Auerbach, Y. 2004. "The Role of Forgiveness in Reconciliation." In *From Conflict Resolution to Reconciliation*, Bar-Siman-Tov, Y. (ed.) Oxford: Oxford University Press, pp. 149–75.
Barkan, E. and Karn, A. (eds) 2006. *Taking Wrongs Seriously: Apologies and Reconciliation.* Stanford, CA: Stanford University Press.
Bar-Tal, D. and Bennink, G.H. 2004. "The Nature of Reconciliation as an Outcome and as a Process." In *From Conflict Resolution to Reconciliation*, Bar-Siman-Tov, Y. (ed.) Oxford: Oxford University Press, pp. 11–38.
Bashir, B. 2008. "Accommodating History Oppressed Groups: Deliberative Democracy and the Politics of Reconciliation." In *The Politics of Reconciliation in Multicultural Societies*, Bashir, B. and Kymlicka, W. (eds) Oxford: Oxford University Press, pp. 48–69.
du Bois, F. and du Bois-Pedain, A. 2008. "Post-Conflict Justice and the Reconciliation Paradigm." In *Justice and Reconciliation in Post-Apartheid South Africa*, du Bois, F. and du Bois-Pedain, A. (eds) Cambridge: Cambridge University Press, pp. 289–311.
Bujo, B. 2001. *Foundations of an African Ethic: Beyond the Universal Claims of Western Morality.* New York: Crossroad Publishers.
Constitutional Court of South Africa. 2009. *Du Toit v Minister for Safety and Security and Another* (CCT 91/08) 2009 ZACC 22.
Constitutional Court of South Africa. 2010. *Albutt v Centre for the Study of Violence and Reconciliation and Others* (CCT 54/09) 2010 ZACC 4.
Constitutional Court of South Africa. 2011. *The Citizen (1978) (Pty) Ltd and Others v Robert John McBride* (CCT 23/10) 2011 ZACC 11.
Crocker, D.A. 2002. "Punishment, Reconciliation, and Democratic Deliberation." *Buffalo Criminal Law Review* 5: 509–49.
Dwyer, S. 1999. "Reconciliation for Realists." *Ethics and International Affairs* 13: 81–98.
Economic Freedom Fighters. 2013. *Founding Manifesto of the Economic Freedom Fighters*. Available at: http://www.politicsweb.co.za/politicsweb/view/politicsweb/en/page71619?oid=393903&sn=Detail.
Eisikovits, N. 2010. *Sympathizing with the Enemy: Reconciliation, Transitional Justice, Negotiation.* Dordrecht, the Netherlands, and St. Louis, MO: Republic of Letters Publishing.
Gerwel, J. 2000. "National Reconciliation." In *Looking Back Reaching Forward: Reflections on the Truth and Reconciliation Commission of South Africa*, Villa-Vicencio, C. and Verwoerd, W. (eds) Cape Town: University of Cape Town Press, pp. 277–86.
Govier, T. 2009a. "The Concept of Reconciliation." *Taking Wrongs Seriously*. Amherst, NY: Humanity Books, pp. 9–25.
Govier, T. 2009b. "A Dialectic of Acknowledgment." In *Reconciliation(s)*, Quinn, J.R. (ed.) Montreal, ON: McGill-Queen's University Press, pp. 36–50.
de Gruchy, J.W. 2002. *Reconciliation: Restoring Justice.* Minneapolis, MN: Fortress Press.
Guttman, A. and Thompson, D. 2000. "The Moral Foundations of Truth Commissions." In *Truth v. Justice: The Morality of Truth Commissions*, Rotberg, R. and Thompson, D. (eds) Princeton, NJ: Princeton University Press, pp. 22–44.
Gyekye, K. 2004. *Beyond Cultures.* Washington, DC: Council for Research in Values and Philosophy.

Hamber, B. and Kelly, G. 2009. "Beyond Coexistence: Towards a Working Definition of Reconciliation." In *Reconciliation(s)*, Quinn, J.R. (ed.) Montreal, ON: McGill-Queen's University Press, pp. 286–310.

Helmick, R.G. and Petersen, R.L. (eds) (2001) *Forgiveness and Reconciliation*. London: Templeton Foundation Press.

Hermann, T. 2004. "Reconciliation: Reflections on the Theoretical and Practical Utility of the Term." In *From Conflict Resolution to Reconciliation*, Bar-Siman-Tov, Y. (ed.) Oxford: Oxford University Press, pp. 39–60.

Hobbes, T. 1651. *Leviathan*. Available at: http://archive.org/details/hobbessleviathan00hobbuoft.

Hughes, P.M. 2001. "Moral Atrocity and Political Reconciliation." *International Journal of Applied Philosophy* 15: 123–33.

Huyse, L. 2008a. "Introduction: Tradition-based Approaches in Peace-making, Transitional Justice and Reconciliation Policies." In *Traditional Justice and Reconciliation after Violent Conflict: Learning from African Experiences*, Huyse, L. and Salter, M. (eds) Stockholm: International Institute for Democracy and Electoral Assistance, pp. 1–20.

Huyse, L. 2008b. "Conclusions and Recommendations." In *Traditional Justice and Reconciliation after Violent Conflict: Learning from African Experiences*, Huyse, L. and Salter, M. (eds) Stockholm: International Institute for Democracy and Electoral Assistance, pp. 181–98.

Ikuenobe, P. 2006. *Philosophical Perspectives on Communalism and Morality in African Traditions*. Lanham, MD: Lexington Books.

Iroegbu, P. 2005. "Beginning, Purpose and End of Life." In *Kpim of Morality Ethics*, Iroegbu, P. and Echekwube, A. (eds) Ibadan: Heinemann Educational Books, pp. 440–45.

Krog, A. 1998. *Country of My Skull*. Johannesburg: Random House.

Masolo, D.A. 2010. *Self and Community in a Changing World*. Bloomington, IN: Indiana University Press.

May, S.C. 2011. "Moral Compromise, Civic Friendship, and Political Reconciliation." *Critical Review of International Social and Political Philosophy* 14: 581–602.

Metz, T. 2011a. "Limiting the Reach of Amnesty for Political Crimes." *Constitutional Court Review* 3: 243–70.

Metz, T. 2011b. "*Ubuntu* as a Moral Theory and Human Rights in South Africa." *African Human Rights Law Journal* 11: 532–59.

Metz, T. 2013. "African Ethics." In *The International Encyclopedia of Ethics*, LaFollette, H. (ed.) Malden, MA: Blackwell Publishing Ltd, pp. 129–38.

Metz, T. and Gaie, J. 2010. "The African Ethic of *Ubuntu/Botho*: Implications for Research on Morality." *Journal of Moral Education* 39: 273–90.

Mgxashe, M. 2000. "Reconciliation: A Call to Action." In *Looking Back Reaching Forward: Reflections on the Truth and Reconciliation Commission of South Africa*, Villa-Vicencio, C. and Verwoerd, W. (eds) Cape Town: University of Cape Town Press, pp. 210–18.

Moellendorf, D. 2007. "Reconciliation as a Political Value." *Journal of Social Philosophy* 38: 205–21.

Moosa, E. 2000. "Truth and Reconciliation as Performance." In *Looking Back Reaching Forward: Reflections on the Truth and Reconciliation Commission of South Africa*, Villa-Vicencio, C. and Verwoerd, W. (eds) Cape Town: University of Cape Town Press, pp. 113–22.

Murphy, C. 2010. *A Moral Theory of Political Reconciliation*. Cambridge: Cambridge University Press.

Murphy, C. 2013. "Reconciliation." In *The International Encyclopedia of Ethics*, LaFollette, H. (ed.) Malden, MA: Blackwell Publishing Ltd., pp. 4451–9.

Nkondo, G.M. 2007. "Ubuntu as a Public Policy in South Africa." *International Journal of African Renaissance Studies* 2: 88–100.

Philpott, D. 2009. "An Ethic of Political Reconciliation." *Ethics and International Affairs* 23: 389–407.

Philpott, D. 2012. *Just and Unjust Peace: An Ethic of Political Reconciliation*. New York: Oxford University Press.

Quinn, J.R. 2009. "What of Reconciliation?" In *Reconciliation(s)*, Quinn, J.R. (ed.) Montreal, ON: McGill-Queen's University Press, pp. 174–206.

Ramose, M.B. 2001. "An African Perspective on Justice and Race." *Polylog* 3. Available at: http://them.polylog.org/3/frm-en.htm.

Sandel, M. 1984. "The Procedural Republic and the Unencumbered Self." *Political Theory* 12: 81–96.

Tutu, D. 1999. *No Future without Forgiveness*. New York: Random House.

Tutu, D. 2009. "Foreward." In *Walk with Us and Listen: Political Reconciliation in Africa*, Villa-Vicencio, C. Cape Town: University of Cape Town Press, pp. ix–xii.

Villa-Vicencio, C. 2000. "Getting on with Life: A Move towards Reconciliation." In *Looking Back Reaching Forward: Reflections on the Truth and Reconciliation Commission of South Africa*, Villa-Vicencio, C. and Verwoerd, W. (eds) Cape Town: University of Cape Town Press, pp. 199–209.

Villa-Vicencio, C. 2009. *Walk with Us and Listen: Political Reconciliation in Africa*. Cape Town: University of Cape Town Press.

Walzer, M. 1983. *Spheres of Justice*. New York: Basics Books.

Chapter 10

Restoring Human Capability: Reconciliation and Liberal Multiculturalism[1]

Monica Mookherjee

Introduction

Given the persistence of bitter ethnic conflicts today, a question arises as to whether liberal multiculturalists ought to pursue reconciliation. While this goal has gained prominence in countries ranging from Australia to South Africa, the matter remains highly controversial. Since the 1980s, liberal multiculturalists have emphasized diversity and disagreement as permanent features of the human condition, and might accordingly hesitate to compel the deep engagement between citizens that seems necessary for true reconciliation. While much depends on the meaning of this concept, liberals might instead adopt a value pluralist view that confronts irreducible divergence of perspectives and irreconcilable goods in human life (Berlin 1959). On the other hand, however, to assume that reconciliation has no place in liberalism seems unworkable. Intractable problems of diversity today, from the plight of Australian Aboriginals to the legacy of violence in the former Yugoslavia, seem to call urgently for reconciliatory settlements. As the magnitude of the inequalities resulting from historical conflicts suggests strategies like minority rights will not suffice, a liberal multicultural concept of reconciliation, emphasizing the commemoration of past injustice, thus appears timely, if controversial, indeed.

This chapter defends such a concept by considering the French government's construction in 2001 of a plaque at Paris' Pont St Michel to remember the killing of Algerians in the so-called 'Paris Massacre' of 1961 (Bernard and Gawn 2001). While I postpone the details of the case to my substantive discussion, it bears noting at this early point that the French state's apparent desire to achieve reconciliation with its Algerian communities in this manner prompts a debate about the meaning of the term. One possibility lies in the reconciliatory narrative of the South African Truth Commission, a narrative that focuses on forgiveness and which aims to 'heal' individuals and 'redeem' societies (Tutu 2000; Gobodo-Madikizela 2002). The notion of Reconciliation-as-Forgiveness (RF) may be contrasted with a less demanding conception which merely seeks to institutionalize impartiality and respect. Reconciliation-as-Civic-Trust (RCT) does not require citizens to 'let go' privately, but invites them to build limited public trust through democratic reason. Locating difficulties with both approaches, this chapter defends an alternative informed by Amartya Sen's capability approach (1992, 1999) and which develops from Colleen Murphy's (2010) insight into the role of capabilities in political reconciliation. Drawing on Sen's emphasis on constructive

1 I am grateful to the audiences to which drafts of this chapter were presented, notably at the Centre for Equality and Multiculturalism (CESEM) in Copenhagen, at the UK Peace and Conflict Research Society Annual Conference at Coventry and at the University of Leeds Political Theory Seminar. I am particularly indebted to Kerri Woods for her careful attention to this research and for her encouraging feedback, and to the editors for their kind support and for accepting this chapter for inclusion in the volume.

action in the world with others as the fundamental objective of human development in conditions of cultural pluralism, this conception is labelled Reconciliation-as-Agency (RA).

My discussion proceeds as follows. After outlining problems in defining reconciliation (in the next section), the following two sections unfold the two conceptions above. Finding both inadequate with regard to the French memorial, the chapter then presents RA as the moral heart of political reconciliation under culturally diverse conditions. Plausibly supported by the St Michel commemoration, RA draws on Sen's theory to defend a higher quality, sustainable peace which restores victims' and perpetrators' 'agency-freedom'. Defined as an ability to assess and act in pursuit of one's needs whilst cognizant of others', the concept of agency-freedom locates middle-ground between the ambition of reconciliation based on forgiveness and the weakness of the approach grounded in trust. In questioning liberalism's border between public and non-public reason, moreover, it promises humane responses to historical injustices, in conditions of cultural diversity, not fully achieved by systems of minority rights.

Reconciliation versus Multiculturalism? Dilemmas in Contemporary France

A preliminary difficulty with integrating reconciliation within liberalism is that the former ideal is usually considered most appropriate to the field of 'transitional' justice.[2] In contrast with stable liberal democracies, transitional states seek to move towards the rule of law after atrocity and thus lack an established culture of minority rights. Yet recent political events reveal problems with an absolute distinction between established democracies and transitional states. Kymlicka and Bashir (2008: iv–v) accordingly observe that, while the post-war commitment in developed nations to democratic constitutionalism supports minority rights, exclusions and inequalities persist. However, even if one positively welcomes a liberal concept of reconciliation, a further difficulty is that its meaning is notoriously unclear. While it has been regarded as the '*sine qua non* for democracy' (Ratner 1999: 734), and although some (e.g., Kriesberg 1998; Rigby 2001) define it through various combinations of peace, mercy and compromise, its moral core remains elusive. As Quinn (2009: 182) complains: 'I have never understood just what "reconciliation" is supposed to be. Is it the sum total of what Christians believe about God's saving work? … Or [does it involve] bringing … incompatible descriptions of events into narrative equilibrium?'

The need for a clear definition, in conditions of cultural pluralism particularly, becomes apparent on considering the predicament of immigrants in states such as France today. While the republican government has historically opposed Anglophone multiculturalism, the nation confronts the need to accommodate its minority citizens with respect (Silverstein 2004). After colonial independence in the 1960s, the state practised a form of political amnesia, seldom teaching imperial history in schools; and today it not unrelatedly denies the existence of minorities (Norman and Vidal 2004). Yet institutional silence surrounding colonialism and the legal invisibility of minorities have been questioned on account of conflicts including the urban riots involving many immigrants in 2005. Moreover, as a measure to quell populist security fears regarding Algerian migrants, in 2001 Bertrand Delanoë, Mayor of Paris and himself of Tunisian origin, unveiled a plaque in memory of the 'Paris Massacre' of 1961, during which 40 – some historians say 200 – peacefully protesting Algerians were killed, and their bodies dumped in the River Seine. The action was commanded by Maurice Papon, erstwhile Chief of Police, in an event which was long shrouded in silence (House and McMaster 2006).

2 The literature on transitional justice is eclectic and vast. Multidisciplinary collections include Kritz (1995), Roht-Arriaza (1995) and McAdams (1997).

A comprehensive history of this event is beyond the scope of this chapter. I draw on its legacy and the memorial specifically as lenses through which to consider the meaning of a pluralist approach to reconciliation. And although this chapter cannot address the significant literature on 'the politics of memory' in France (e.g., Lebow, Kansteiner and Fogin 2006), it concentrates on remembrance as a component of multicultural reconciliation. The case itself has proved controversial, as the plaque failed to declare responsibility. The journal *l'Humanité* notably complained that it referred to a bloody repression rather than to a crime against humanity (Ducoin 2011). Delanoë nonetheless insisted that 'there are parts of Paris's history that are painful, but which have to be talked about and which have to be accompanied by acts'. Such commemoration was therefore necessary, he argued, for France to move forward 'with unity'.[3]

A key question is whether this call for inter-ethnic unity amounted to a plea for reconciliation. Even if this is assumed, it seems obvious that a plaque alone cannot resolve all inequalities experienced by the country's minorities today, such as dire housing in shanty-towns, which may be considered in part their colonial legacy (Laachir 2007). As the *héritiers involontaires de la guerre d'Algérie* (involuntary heirs of the Algerian war), France's postcolonial minorities have been deemed outsiders of the grand ideal of republican unity, which traditionally demands integration over dedicated protection for minority identities (Bouamama 2008).

The case thus raises a problem concerning the relationship between reconciliation and egalitarian multiculturalism, and, indirectly, that concerning liberal multiculturalism and French republicanism. While the second issue warrants deeper discussion than space enables here, it bears remarking that some recent French writers articulate a progressive republicanism open to recognizing ethno-cultural differences (Laborde 2008; cf. Wieviorka 1996). While republicanism undoubtedly differs from liberalism with regard to its conceptualization of both self and society (Chabal 2010), some newer voices in the tradition take seriously the way in which social exclusion can motivate or exacerbate the politicization of ethnic differences (Laborde 2008: 11). Indeed, at times these progressive republican writers seem better positioned to defend liberal goals of equality and freedom than some writing within the Anglophone tradition.

While my point in this regard is not ambitiously to re-frame French republicanism, it is to emphasize the plausibility of exploring liberal-multicultural ideals in the French context. More precisely, it is to maintain that Delanoë's call for unity need not imply the suppression of difference that liberals might fear. This point might be considered, whilst proceeding to examine the meaning of multicultural reconciliation and whether state commemorations may support it.

Reconciliation-as-Forgiveness: A 'Deeply Illiberal Idea' (Ash 1999: 38)?

In view of the grave violence of the Paris Massacre, it seems apt to consider whether the state's commemoration contributes to a form of reconciliation often associated with the attractive goal of forgiveness. This idea informed the South African Truth and Reconciliation Commission of the 1990s, a ground-breaking response to an arguably more acute history of inter-ethnic violence, namely that which took place during the Apartheid regime. While there are many ways of understanding forgiveness, in essence it appears to involve the resolution of debt by letting go of resentment (Murphy and Hampton 1998). In this sense, it seems to account for the fundamental change of heart that true reconciliation might require after bitter conflicts in deeply divided, ethnically plural societies.

---

3 Cited in a BBC News Report: 'Paris Marks Algerian Protest Massacre', http://news.bbc.co.uk/2/hi/world/monitoringmedia. Accessed 4 December 2012.

Although South Africa's Commission's Final Report defends reconciliation without referring to forgiveness (see Kiss 2000: 75), the two concepts were linked during the country's transition. For instance, the Chairperson of the Commission, Archbishop Desmond Tutu, alluded to the spiritual dimension of reconciliation in chapter 5 of the report by invoking an image of South African people as the 'Rainbow People of God'. In *No Future without Forgiveness* (1999: 34, 56–7), he further allied the Commission's work with the Catholic 'sacrament of reconciliation', which involves the sinner seeking forgiveness from another, notably the priest, and ultimately seeking absolution from and communion with God.[4] In apparent accord with the liberation theology underpinning the US Civil Rights movement, Tutu wished to establish the Christian notion that humanity, not only the sinner, has distorted its personality such that each of us requires restoration with God, whose goodness is ontologically prior to violence. The co-dependence of forgiveness and in this context reconciliation was reinforced by Krog's moving narrative in *Country of My Skull*, which affirmed that 'the one begins, or opens a process of becoming … the other … The Xhosa word for reconciliation in the concept of Truth of Reconciliation is forgiveness (*uxolelwano*). The TRC literally means in Xhosa: the Truth and Forgiveness Commission' (Krog 2010: 37). Tutu and Krog thus sought the political application of an approach to reconciliation usually belonging to private, spiritual sphere (Philpott 2006: 79–80); and it seems, therefore, that Reconciliation-as-Forgiveness (RF)[5] unofficially underpinned the magnanimity that the Commission extended to some of the protagonists of the Apartheid regime.

Yet, quite apart from the profound dissatisfaction of many South Africans in relation to this ideal, states like France with a strong public–private divide might strongly resist the idea of invoking any, and particularly a religious, notion of forgiveness in politics. This is because any version seems part of a comprehensive vision of the good life or world-view, the political endorsement of which might deny the culturally diverse values that inform responses to wrongdoing. Although Arendt (1958: 236–43) defended the indispensability of forgiveness in politics, she recognized that the version based on Christian love could threaten human 'plurality'. Tutu notably also grounded forgiveness in the African notion of *Ubuntu* or humaneness, which holds that 'a person is diminished when others are humiliated and diminished' (Tutu 1999: 35), without, however, seemingly recognizing that different world-views might specify different conditions for forgiveness; and that if parties to a conflict hold divergent tenets regarding forgiveness, its specific grounding may hinder the reconciliatory process (Auberach 2005: 469). Yet in presuming that a damaged society cannot move forward without deep inward change to break the cycle of revenge, Tutu was not alone in aiming to synthesize forgiveness and reconciliation (Philpott 2006; Gruchy 2004).

However, while the TRC ideal thereafter proliferated (Van Antwerpen 2008), the synthesis proved controversial amongst South African, European and American critics alike. Crocker contends that the moral consensus on which forgiveness is based is an objectionable goal in modern politics (2000: 69). Bhargava (2000) further argues that, while forgiveness is sometimes an appropriate response to historical injury, it is a personal choice beyond the state's responsibility. It is not always clear if these objections relate to a secular as well as a religious notion of forgiveness. The two may differ (Kohen 2009), in that the spiritual version may be unilateral, involving a pure 'act of grace', whereas the secular notion seems to require the perpetrator's atonement or

4 In the report, Tutu paradoxically warned of a 'potentially dangerous confusion' between personal and political reconciliation (Tutu, *Final Report*, cited in Kiss 2000: 87).

5 See also Colleen Murphy's (2010) conceptual distinctions of reconciliation in terms of forgiveness and trust. This chapter aims to outline cultural pluralist reasons in particular for resisting the forgiveness-based concept. Also, whereas Murphy accepts trust as an element of reconciliation, I contend in contrast that recent approaches based on reciprocity and trust are problematic under culturally plural conditions. The versions considered in this chapter seem to expect of diverse citizens confidence in 'the other' that may be too thin or pragmatic to sustain lasting peace after group-based ethno-cultural conflicts.

reparation. In any event, the problem lies in the 'thickness' of forgiveness and its dependence on a moral scheme which liberals might rightly hesitate to impose on all in a pluralist society.

The concern might also be expressed that the backward-looking focus of this approach neglects future political transformation (Kymlicka and Bashir 2008: 14; Murphy 2010: 11). However, as attention to a more peaceable future does not seem logically precluded, and indeed might seem the very point of forgiveness, the liberal multicultural worries arising about this approach may be distilled into the three following concerns. The first may be called *the Objection from Justice*, which emphasizes that RF sacrifices the liberal duty to prosecute, the need for which may be felt particularly acutely in cases of offences by members of one ethnic or cultural group against another. And although amnesty[6] is not necessarily an act of forgiveness (see Bennett 2003), the concern is that RF renounces proportionality between an individual's or community's resentment and punishment for moral wrong, thereby violating retributive justice (Minow 1998: 12). Yet, this objection does not seem decisive: absolving the wrongdoer from suffering may be a humane and liberal aim sometimes, in part because of the historical contestability which diverse liberal societies should acknowledge. Yet, even then, the core worry persists that RF, at least when promoted through truth commissions or memorials, imposes on citizens a requirement to react uniformly to trauma in such a way that might conflict with their private sentiments (Murphy 2010: 11).

What we might call the *Objection from Privacy* thus holds that, if remembrance of past violence is not necessarily healing (Hamber 2007), and if these measures reopen old wounds, the required change of heart may fail to transpire. Furthermore, even if these measures could prove cathartic for some by establishing an official account of past events (Gobodo-Madikizela 2002: 8–10), reasonable people evidently can hold conflicting accounts of the past without anyone being misled. This point suggests a lack of agreement on the appropriate circumstances of the forgiveness-reconciliation synthesis. More specifically, commemoration may counter-productively seek institutional closure on a troubled past without addressing issues of responsibility, reparation or the possibility of multiple histories, which perhaps must be the real grounds of forgiveness. Moreover, and in a different vein, one might doubt whether Algerians today, who wish for equality and respect, have any real interest in forgiving the state or other French citizens. In this sense too, RF might violate their private beliefs.

A final concern regarding this approach addresses the claim that, even if forgiveness is liable not to transpire in practice, reconciliation may be legitimate so long as the aspiration to forgive is its agreed rationale. However, liberals may object that even to justify reconciliation on this basis grounds policy on a comprehensive, 'sectarian' ideal which some may reasonably reject under conditions of diversity. If a justification may be rationally rejected then a given policy will not be stable under liberalism (D'Agostino 1991). Thus, the *Objection from Comprehensiveness* draws attention to the need for common justifications to establish mutual commitment to life according to fair terms of cooperation. These objections suggest that RF would clash in our central case with French republican neutrality (*laïcité*). Even if one grounds reconciliation on a potentially viable notion of political forgiveness, aligned perhaps with judicial clemency or mercy, it seems that the relation between personal and political forgiveness is too controversial to ground a political commitment to reconciliation under conditions of diversity (cf. Digeser 2000). Consequently, in relation to the French state's desire for unity, the risk is that RF would exacerbate an already fraught and unequal situation.

---

6 The Amnesty Provision of the Truth and Reconciliation Commission Charter had the power to extinguish civil and criminal liability. The provision was upheld by the constitutional court in rejecting a lawsuit filed by the families of murdered anti-apartheid activists Steve Biko and Griffith Mxenge. The family members contended that the provision violated their constitutional rights to seek judicial redress (see Kiss 2000, for further elaboration of this point).

Reconciliation-as-Civic-Trust: The Weakness of Democratic Public Reason?

Given France's historic commitments to impartiality and free conscience, it is worth considering an alternative approach which may be called Reconciliation-as-Civic-Trust (RCT). As pluralist societies cannot expect between all citizens agreement on a comprehensive theory of the good, it seems justifiable to turn to a non-sectarian concept based on peaceful coexistence and human rights. This account focuses on trust, which is timely in our case given traditional republican reliance upon this idea (Pettit 1998).[7]

Before unfolding this account, it bears emphasizing that even a thin, democratic approach to reconciliation should address the issue of psychological change, if it is to transcend the moral bankruptcy of a realist compromise, and inaugurate sustainable peace at a higher level. For even if forgiveness proves too demanding, a non-sectarian version of reconciliation should still account for citizens' capacities to attain mental openness to the possibility of a better future after conflict (Hutchinson and Bleiker 2008). As this point will structure the remainder of my discussion, I now contend that RCT is liable perhaps surprisingly to be ethically weak on account of not requiring sufficient psychological change, and in fact may be further debilitated by one-off acts of commemoration of rights-violations against particular ethnic groups in conditions of cultural diversity.

To be sure, however, the approach seems attractive at first. Liberal writers Gutmann and Thompson offer a version of this approach to reconciliation by relying on the related notion of civic reciprocity – 'the capacity to seek fair terms of social cooperation for their own sake' (1996: 229). Gutmann and Thompson appreciate the fact that hostilities after generations of ethnic or cultural conflict are often difficult to overcome entirely. That is, they conceive policies of reconciliation as the output of engagement between civic participants, who offer one another lucid arguments in democratic debate, if only for the sake of their common future (2000: 37). Citizens need not forgive or love one another, but commit at a minimum to a respectful, transparent dialogue. While trust and reciprocity are not synonymous, they seem co-dependent and inter-related in a pluralist society focused on moving beyond past injustices. This is because trust should not be one-sided. It implies the equality involved in reciprocity (Margalit 2002); and, conversely, treating others as equals involves a readiness to view them as contributors to shared political space, which entails at least some reliance or trust. Of course, trust and reciprocity are not easily achieved. Defined as optimism about the prospective good will of others, or as the normative expectation of favourable relations, for Govier trust depends on 'acknowledgement', the content of which is contextually variable (Govier 2009: 49) and could itself be a matter of democratic debate. As the trust-based approach to reconciliation does not seem to require a very ambitious change of heart (cf. Murphy 2010), RCT thus seems reasonable and realistic, conceiving reconciliation as an everyday political concept, rather than as transcendent or morally transformational.

Moreover, RCT does not ignore retribution or reparation but encourages citizens to 'economize' on disagreement about the past and build consensus on justice (Gutmann and Thompson 2000: 40–41). Embedding the development of trust within democratic processes, perhaps relying on memorials to catalyze debate about history, promises to promote participation which is itself an important aspect of liberal justice, because debates about history should not be univocal but must make room for legitimate disagreement (2000 37).[8] These are modest aims based on values that

7 The International Centre for Transitional Justice also explicitly defines reconciliation in terms of civic trust. See ICTJ at wwwictj.org/cn.en/tj.784.html. Accessed 4 January 2013.

8 The work of the organization 'Au Nom de la Mémoire' is influential here, a campaign which from the 1980s reactivated interest in the 'Paris Massacre'. However, arguably further measures would be needed to assist reconciliation.

a diversity of citizens can defend according to public reason, thereby suggesting, at least at first sight, a plausible interpretation of Delanoë's hope that the St Michel plaque might foster inter-ethnic unity.

However, while reconciliation undoubtedly involves trust, questions arise about its robustness under this conception. It seems reasonable that acknowledgement of a fractured history need not connote consensus or self-disclosure, which are problematic in circumstances in which agreement is usually possible only in relation to some aspects of the past. However, even if acknowledgement requires only accepting fellow citizens as equal partners in dialogue and a commitment to locate agreement on what further should be acknowledged and how, this is a strenuous achievement in divided societies (Bhargava 2000: 47). The disaffection of many immigrants in France demonstrates the estrangement that can persist in spite of democratic processes (Geisser 2003; Laachir 2007). Thus, the borderline between the voluntary pragmatic trust involved in committing to procedural democracy and forced compliance borne out of powerlessness is often fine, with continual threats of the former collapsing into the latter (Kelman 2004: 116). More fundamentally, the liberal pluralist deliberative approach seemingly fails to recognize structural power inequalities in assuming that all citizens are equally interested in reconciling through democracy. Furthermore, perhaps only acknowledgements that take responsibility explicitly would facilitate trust. This is in spite of the difficulties with questions of responsibility when perpetrators and victims are dead or when the significance of past events is contested (Bashir 2008: 48; Butt 2006).

These difficulties suggest that in a procedural democracy the limited empathy, at least in the form of recognition of mutual humanity, needed even for pragmatic and 'self-interested' trust may fail to emerge after profound conflict. Citizens, experiencing excessive dissonance between the terms of formal political engagement and their private beliefs, would probably struggle to honour the settlement. Controversies surrounding reconciliation in Australia (Motha 2007) emphasize that after a violent history sometimes refusing to trust in liberal democracy is reasonable, and even that limited democratic cooperation might be possible without trust (Cook, Hardin and Levi 2007). On balance, therefore, Bashir opposes this approach. For one thing, if trust is required for dialogue, deliberation presupposes what reconciliation is supposed to achieve. Therefore, the concept is circular. Moreover, the requirement to offer 'neutral' reasons, whilst broader than in standard liberal theories, may still be too narrow in a polity which has historically dismissed minority claims (Bashir 2008: 66).

One might respond here by openly accepting the development of trust as a central challenge of reconciliation. The deepest conflicts today, including those of Israel-Palestine and Northern Ireland, are marked by widespread disengagement. However, this problem does not necessarily nullify the attempt to build a society of equals through dialogue. The problem is to ensure an equitable basis for facilitating it, as the history of violation makes all persons' views mistrustful, biased and polarised, with all sides claiming victimhood. The intractability of these cases often arises from the fact that 'everyone has done something to somebody else' (Yael Tamir, cited in Minow 1998: 80). However, while the fact that nobody in a damaged society escapes the effects of the past surely makes formally egalitarian democratic structures important (Murphy 2010: 15), the problem remains. For even if RCT addresses the earlier objections from *Justice, Privacy* and *Comprehensiveness*, it remains true that if reconciliation hinges on procedural fairness only, there may be little to distinguish the idea from realist compromise which lacks moral foundations and fails to secure stability. Indeed, RCT may then be indistinguishable even from a settlement which indirectly institutionalizes, by passively tolerating, entrenched social disrespect.

In brief, I contend that the approach based on civic trust, perhaps paradoxically, lacks an essential account of citizens' attitudinal change towards a stable and integrated preference to view others as political equals. This key psychological shift would enable wounded individuals to engage in a sustained and committed way with those they may privately continue to resent. Put differently, a plausible account of mutual engagement through multicultural democracy must account for the intra-psychic change according to which citizens develop a durable mental openness to the possibility of a more cohesive future after conflict, an openness which is internalized and integrated into their own world-view. The concern is that, without such integrated change, democratic institutions can be compatible with gross injustices (Murphy 2010: 17); and that after serious violations, generations of families and communities can remain traumatized, unable to make sense of, let alone articulate views about, the past (Minow 1998: 37). This is true for many Algerians after the Liberation War, who long remained mute regarding the violence (Sebbar 1999). In such circumstances, the danger is that a one-off act of commemoration, in randomly publicizing one aspect of a wider, more complex history, might further debilitate a fragile political situation by exacerbating unexpressed private grievances which are seriously dissonant from the equal relations in law to which democratic citizens subscribe.

In summary: while the deep purpose of RCT may in fact be to encourage positive attitudinal change, the version of it discussed here does not guarantee this shift and may also hinder it; and the moral heart and deep objective of political reconciliation should thus be found elsewhere. The point of reconciliation, I next suggest, resides in internalized change in each party's identity, notably the removal of 'self-negation' and 'negation of the other' as central components of one's self-concept (Kelman 2004: 120). As a movement from victimhood to agency, such change is necessary if the contested idea of reconciliation is to transcend problems with the status quo which initially provoked the conflict, and, ultimately, to contribute to culturally pluralist unity.

Beyond Politics as Usual: Reconciliation-as-Agency and Non-Shareability

The French state's desire for unity indicates the need for reconciliation that is sufficiently universalistic to prescribe attitudinal change but still consistent with liberal diversity. This conception challenges liberal multiculturalists who might hesitate to prescribe private psychological transformation. For Philpott (2006) warns of an enduring tension between liberalism and reconciliation: the former, with its guarded private sphere, cannot yield a warrant to interfere with the personal sentiments of the wounded in a diverse, pluralist society. With this problem in mind, I propose Reconciliation-as-Agency (RA), which responds to the concern that, while reconciliation should neither assert sectarian ideals nor violate privacy, the trust-based approach drawing on democratic procedures alone often fail to deliver high-quality, durable peace.

My proposed alternative prioritizes human choice and action in post-conflict recovery. It focuses on learning about the social roots of inequality and needs-denial which gave rise to conflict, in an approach which has proved indispensable in post-genocide Rwanda (Staub 2006: 868). In focusing on individual psychology, RA strains the normal boundaries of liberal thought. However, it remains receptive to pluralism. It does not impose on citizens a single view of the past or a teleological goal like forgiveness. It conceives reconciliation as a work-in-progress, the moral core of which lies in an evolved understanding of the frequent origin of conflict in frustrated needs for security, effectiveness, control and comprehension of a changing world (Staub 2006: 877), or else in perceived threats to identity, community and justice (Kelman 2004: 112). While developing from her insights, in contrast with Murphy's (2010) contention that the rule of law, trust and human capacities equally underpin reconciliation, I claim that restoring a particular capacity constitutes the heart of the concept, without which forgiveness might connote despair, trust may fail and democratic institutions would be weak. I also argue that the contribution of commemoration to such reconciliation is plausible, but highly dependent on its presentation.

RA draws from Sen's (1985, 1992, 1999) human capabilities approach in order to conceive reconciliation in terms of re-imagining both self and others as complex human beings choosing amidst the structural constraints of a rapidly transforming, confusing world (Staub 2006: 878). This recognition is difficult after atrocity but all-important, because understanding the motives and concerns of others without de-humanizing them is essential to making progress individually and collectively (Haidt 2006). While Sen does not apply his theory directly to the issue of reconciliation, although he writes of identity and violence elsewhere (1998; 2006), he defends an ideal of constructive social action in the world, cognizant and critical of structures of power (1999: 5).[9] If political reconciliation has a moral core, it seems to lie here.

Before considering his account, it bears noting that others also recognize that reconciliation involves extending the 'psychological repertoires' of victims and perpetrators (e.g., Lederach 2011). A memorial such as the St Michel plaque might foster reconciliation in this way because its moral restraint, or its refusal to dramatize, vilify or condemn, might assist to 'unfreeze' perspectives on the past, to help individuals and groups to re-frame traumatic experiences, enabling them to re-categorize others as, at least, not existential threats. This is not to forsake the establishment of responsibility after wrongdoing but to emphasize that the gradual and difficult process of viewing ethnic conflict as the outcome of understandable human processes often requires normatively neutral overtures (Staub 2006: 878). Sometimes victims do require an admission of guilt in order to progress psychologically (Gobodo-Madikizela 2002); but, equally, extreme recrimination in fragile situations can stifle hope of reasonable and constructive understanding of either self or other.

The reciprocal achievement of the (still undefined) ideal of agency seems important *prima facie*, then, because breaking out of endless cycles of revenge, vendetta or condemnation must involve an imaginative paradigm shift that sets in motion a rethinking of rights and coexistence which, as Sen observes in *Identity and Violence* (2006), enables individuals conceive self-realization in non-negating ways. Of course, one objection to this thought is that it 'psychologizes' the predicament of minorities in post-conflict situations without addressing structural injustices and actual suppression of material needs that often underlie the discord.[10] This criticism is highly relevant to the French case; and attention to Sen's capability approach assists to address it.

In an acclaimed theory of human development, Sen counsels a shift of theoretical attention away from a society's human rights record and material resources towards citizens' capacities to 'achieve valuable states of being or doing' (1985, 1992). He distinguishes 'wellbeing capability', which connotes valuable physical and psychological potentialities such as achieving adequate nutrition and appearing in public without shame, from 'agency-freedom', which involves opportunities to pursue valuable goals beyond subsistence or survival. Conceiving the latter as potentially fundamental to life as the former, agency-freedom renders the capability approach attuned to human diversity by emphasizing the multidimensionality and possible non-materiality of human need.

One important well-being capacity is the 'ability to show concern for others and understand their point of view' (Sen 2005: 152), a capacity which is often blunted during ethno-cultural conflict. While multicultural reconciliation is a matter of promoting this objective dimension of well-being,

9 Space does not permit a full examination here of Sen's account of identity, reason and violence (1998, 2006). I undertake such a study in my work-in-progress, *Multiculturalism: From Political Principle to Human Capability*, where I argue that Sen's understanding of identity is continuous with his emphasis on choice in the capability approach.

10 I am grateful to a member of the Leeds Political Theory seminar for indicating this problem and relating it to the debate between Honneth and Fraser (2003) concerning redistribution and recognition.

it also recognizes the diverse ways in which human beings attain it, by re-dignifying themselves and others after atrocity as complex beings confronting difficult choices. Sen emphasizes this point by observing that agency goals and material well-being may conflict interpersonally and within a single life. That is to say, different basic capabilities may 'move in different directions' (Sen 1992: 56). For instance, a person's goals may include national independence, religious enlightenment or retaining an inherited language. Their agency-freedom might involve choosing to sacrifice stability of an authoritarian order to fight for democracy, with the entailed risks to material or bodily security. Briefly, then, agency-freedom connotes the individual's assessment of how to function and their opportunities to act in accordance with this view. Far from ignoring material needs, the approach supports mutual opportunities to live well socioeconomically, but encourages personal assessment of the balance and priority of individual needs after the conflicts that often negate this capacity.

While agency-freedom in Sen's sense seems the indispensable objective human development, it also promises to disrupt an otherwise endless cycle of violence by opening a person mentally to the complexity of human experience, and, thus, towards a re-humanization of the other as a complex being choosing according to their vision of the good. While this mutual capacity is by no means easily achievable in post-conflict situations, particularly where violations have spanned centuries and generations of families are traumatized (Philpott 2006: 39–40), the approach accounts at a sustainably higher level than other approaches for the attitudinal shift required for reconciliation. Although the individual may continue privately to recriminate, they learn not to de-humanize or comprehensively alienate the other as a condition of maintaining identity, exactly because they are enabled to assess, prioritize, trade off and pursue their personal and collective agency goals. Restoring this human capacity means that limited but durable trust in the other might thus become integrated into the person's world-view. In this sense, one changes in order to remain the same (Kelman 2004: 112). Without implying amity or love, the process promises higher-quality reconciliation than that based on the pragmatic trust of the procedural approach.

Pluralist states would therefore consider that the agency-freedom of some may involve choosing to resent past injustices, thereby undermining some well-being through negative affect, in maintaining a separate ethnic identity. This does not mean that they fail to reconcile, as reinforcement of a strong world-view does not logically have to involve negating others or viewing them as existential threats (Kelman 2004: 117). Moreover, in France, agency-freedom might perhaps involve contesting official unitary citizenship and the church-state separation, insisting on maintaining religious dress in public, or institutionalizing education about colonial history, as the conditions of social inclusion. The point is that citizens may only approach the issue of how to reconcile by engaging an unfrozen reflection about the significance of historical group-relations.

A number of dilemmas arise in relation to this conception of reconciliation, not all of which are fully resolvable here. One problem is how, beyond deliberative democracy itself, the agency-freedom of diverse citizens might be cultivated. Also, Sen admits that the relation between agency-freedom and justice is far from settled (Sen 1992: 71). Governments have duties to secure citizens basic well-being and agency but not necessarily to support them in, say, erecting a statue in honour of their political hero (Sen 1992: 73). However, the fact of pluralism induces doubt surrounding the nature and content of state responsibility in this regard, a problem which is most acute where annihilation of others is perceived by some as a basic agency goal, as has been tragically the case in Bosnia-Herzegovina and Israel–Palestine (see e.g., Finkelstein 2003). Agency, thus, constitutes the moral problem and the moral heart of political reconciliation, as Sen indicates indirectly elsewhere (Sen 1998, 2006; Qizilbash 2009). Although the question of public policy to support mutual agency-freedom in a culturally plural society requires further consideration, I refer again to Sen's belief in the progressive potential of education in human development (Sen 1999: xi; 5).

A key observation, and indeed potential difficulty, is that RA challenges standard liberal distinctions between public and non-public reason. Liberals typically hold that public reasons should be intelligible and shareable and that policies and institutions are accordingly legitimized when based on 'reasons for each [which] are reasons for all' (D'Agostino 1991: 391). Yet it remains true that the development of reconciliation might necessitate rights to public expression according to a non-political spiritual ideal, which may be intelligible to others but not shareable. Yet RA's expansion of liberal thought in this regard then raises the difficulty of limiting the domain of disagreement about reconciliation and the problem of dismissing views of the past that are manifestly false or unreasonable, and which may violate the basic moral tenets of some.

As a brief though inevitably incomplete response to this issue, I suggest that, while logically dissonant views evidently cannot be reconciled, liberal multiculturalists would seek reconciliation between persons rather than beliefs. It is human beings who engage civically and who warrant ultimate concern and respect. Moreover, the controversy about liberal reasonableness is neither new nor limited to the concept of reconciliation (Fines 2010). RA suggests that the boundary around reasonableness cannot plausibly be absolute and a-historical, as to assume its metaphysical 'given-ness' would be to count mistakenly on the transparency of all human reason and experience. With this thought, it is at least reasonable to conclude that reconciliation is most sustainable and at its highest quality when, admitting the non-shareability of at least certain human reasons, it supports the agency and humanity of all.

Conclusion

This chapter has outlined different formulations of the contested ideal of reconciliation in the context of liberalism's long-standing commitment to diversity. It has been argued that reconciliation must avoid requiring the demanding personal change involved in forgiveness, notably but not exclusively in plural societies like France. At the same time, conceived in terms of fostering mutual agency-freedom according to Sen's capability approach, reconciliation still asks that liberals unsettle their vaunted boundary between public and private reason. After an unequal or atrocious history, liberal multiculturalists might thus reconceive reconciliation as encouraging attitudinal change towards all persons' re-humanization of others and of themselves, in a mutual pursuit of agency goals that seems the most plausible interpretation of Delanoë's hope with respect to the St Michel plaque. While future elaboration is undoubtedly required, reconciliation so understood anticipates a humane balance between justice and mercy, to which citizens mutually commit on principle, rather than out of the pragmatism of despair, for the sake of a fairer and more compassionate future for all in a culturally plural liberal state.

References

Amiraux, Valerie and Patrick Simon (2006). 'There Are No Minorities Here: Cultures of Scholarship and Public Debate on Immigrants and Integration in France', *International Journal of Comparative Sociology* August, 47(3–4): 191–215.

Arendt, Hannah. 1958. *The Human Condition*. Chicago, IL: University of Chicago Press.

Ash, Timothy. 1999. True Confessions. *New York Review of Books* 17th July: 33–8.

Atria, Fernando. 2007. Reconciliation and Reconstitution. In S. Veitch (ed.), *Law and the Politics of Reconciliation*. Edinburgh: Edinburgh University Press, pp. 33–47.

Auberach, Yehudith. 2005. Forgiveness and Reconciliation. *Terrorism and Political Violence* 17(3): 469–85.

Bashir, Bashir. 2008. Accommodating Historically Oppressed Social Groups. In W. Kymlicka and B. Bashir (eds), *The Politics of Reconciliation in Multicultural Societies*. Oxford: Oxford University Press, pp. 48–69.

Bennett, Christopher. 2003. 'Is Amnesty a Collective Act of Forgiveness?' *Contemporary Political Theory* 2: 67–76.

Berlin, Isaiah. 1959. Two Concepts of Liberty. In *Four Essays on Liberty*. Oxford: Oxford University Press, pp. 121–54.

Bernard, Philippe and Christine Gawn. 2001. Le Massacre du 17 octobre 1961 obtient un début de reconnaissance official. *Le Monde Intéractif*, 17 octobre.

Bhargava, Rajeev. 2000. Restoring Decency to Barbaric Societies. In I. Rothberg and D. Thomspon (eds), *Truth v Justice*. Princeton, NJ: Princeton University Press, pp. 45–67.

Bouamama, Saïd. 2008. *La France: Autopsie d'un Mythe National*. Paris: Larousse.

Bouthilly, Anne. 2009. Minorities in the Republic of Invisibles. *BSIS Journal of International Studies* 69.

Butt, Daniel. 2006. 'Nations, Overlapping Generations and Historical Injustices', *American Philosophical Quarterly* 43(4): 357–67.

Chabal, Emile. 2010. Writing the French National Narrative in the 21st Century. *Historical Journal* 53(2): 495–516.

Cook, Karen, Russell Hardin and Margaret Levi. (eds) 2007. *Cooperation without Trust*. NY: Russell Sage.

Crocker, David. 2000. Truth Commissions, Transitional Justice and Civil Society. In I. Rothberg and D. Thomspon (eds), *Truth v Justice*. Princeton, NJ: Princeton University Press, pp. 99–121.

D'Agostino, Fred. 1991. Some Modes of Public Justification. *Australasian Journal of Philosophy* 4: 390–414.

Digeser, Peter. 2001. *Political Forgiveness*. New York: Cornell University Press.

Ducoin, Jean-Emmanuelle. 2011. *Un Crime d'Etat*. Special Issue of *L'Humanité*, 17 October.

Dwyer, Susan. 1999. Reconciliation for Realists. *Ethics and International Affairs* 13: 81–98.

Fines, Allan. 2010. 'Reasonableness, Pluralism and Liberal Moral Doctrines' *Journal of Value Inquiry* 44: 221–339.

Finklestein, Norman. 2003. *Image and Reality of the Israeli-Palestinian Conflict*. London: Verso.

Fraser, Nancy and Axel Honneth. 2003. *Redistribution or Recognition?* London: Verso.

Geisser, Vincent. 2003. *La Nouvelle Islamophobie*. Paris: La Découverte.

Gobodo-Madikizela, Pumla. 2002. Remorse, Forgiveness and Rehumanization. *Journal of Humanistic Psychology* 42: 7–32.

Govier, Trudy. 2009. A Dialectic of Acknowledgement. In J. Quinn (ed.), *Reconciliation(s)*. Montreal, ON: University of McGill Press, pp. 36–50.

Gruchy de, John. 2002. *Reconciliation*. Minneapolis, MN: Fortress University Press.

Gutmann, Amy and Dennis Thompson. 1996. *Democracy and Disagreement*. Cambridge, MA: Harvard University Press.

Gutmann, Amy and Dennis Thompson. 2000. The Moral Foundations of Truth Commissions. In I. Rothberg and D. Thompson (eds), *Truth v Justice*. Princeton, NJ: Princeton University Press, pp. 22–44.

Haidt, Jonathan. 2006. *The Happiness Hypothesis*. London: Heineman.

Hamber, Brandon 2007. 'Forgiveness and Reconciliation: Paradise Lost or Pragmatism?', *Peace and Conflict: Journal of Peace Psychology* 13(1): 115–25.

Honneth, A. and N. Fraser. 2003. *Redistribution or Recognition?* London: Verso.
House, Jim and Neil MacMaster (2006). *Paris 1961: Algerians, State Terror and Memory*.Oxford: Oxford University Press.
Hutchinson, Emma and Roland Bleiker. 2008. Emotional Reconciliation. *European Journal of Social Theory* 11: 385–99.
Jennings, Jeremy. 1999. *Intellectuals in Twentieth Century France*. London: Routledge.
Kelman, Herbert. 2004. Reconciliation as Identity-Change. In Y. Bar-Simon Tov (ed.), *From Conflict Resolution to Reconciliation*. Oxford: Oxford University Press, pp. 111–24.
Kiss, Elisabeth. 2000. Moral Ambition Within and Beyond Political Constraints. In I. Rothberg and D. Thompson (eds), *Truth v Justice*. Princeton, NJ: Princeton University Press, pp. 68–98.
Kohen, Ari. 2009. The Personal and the Political. *Critical Review of International Social and Political Philosophy* 12(3): 399–423.
Kriesberg, Louis. 1998. *Constructive Conflicts: From Escalation to Resolution* (Lanham, Maryland: Rowman & Littlefield Press).
Kritz, Neil J. 1995. (ed.) *Transitional Justice*. Washington, DC: US Institute for Peace Press.
Krog, Antijie. 2010. *Country of My Skull*. Johannesburg: Random House.
Kymlicka, W. and B. Bashir. (eds) 2008. *The Politics of Reconciliation in Multicultural Societies*. Oxford: Oxford University Press.
Kymlicka, Will and Wayne Norman. (eds) 2000. *Citizenship in Diverse Societies*. Oxford: Oxford University Press.
Laachir, Karima. 2007. 'France's "Ethnic Minorities" and the Question of Exclusion', *Mediterranean Politics* 12(1): 99–105.
Laborde, Cecile. 2008. *Critical Republicanism*. Oxford: Oxford University Press.
Lebow, R. Ned, Wulf Kansteiner and Claudio Fogin. (eds) 2006. *The Politics of Identity in Post-War Europe*. Durham, NC: Duke University Press.
Lederach, John Paul. 2011. Preface. In J.P. and A. Lederach, *When Blood and Bones Cry Out*. Oxford: Oxford University Press, pp. xv–xvi.
Margalit, Avishai. 2002. Is Truth the Road to Reconciliation? In O. Limon et al. (eds), *Experiments with the Truth*. The Hague: Hatje Cantz, pp. 61–4.
McAdams, A. James. 1997. *Transitional Justice and the Rule of Law in New Democracies*. London: Notre Dame University Press.
McCormack, Jo. 2011. Social Memory in (Post-)Colonial France. *Journal of Social History* 44(4): 1129–38.
Minow, Martha. 1998. *Between Vengeance and Forgiveness*. Boston, MA: Beacon Press.
Motha, Stewart. 2007. 'Reconciliation as Domination', in Scott Veitch (ed.), *Law and the Politics of Reconciliation*. London: Ashgate, pp. 69–91.
Murphy, Colleen. 2010. *A Moral Theory of Political Reconciliation*. Oxford: Oxford University Press.
Murphy, Jeffrie and Jean Hampton. 1998. *Forgiveness and Mercy*. Cambridge: Cambridge University Press.
Pettit, Philip. 1998. Republican Theory and Political Trust. In V. Valerie et al. (eds), *Trust and Governance*. New York: Russell Sage Foundation, pp. 295–315.
Philpott, Daniel (ed.) 2006. *The Politics of Past Evil*. Notre Dame, IN: Notre Dame University Press.
Quinn, Joanna (ed.) 2009. *Reconciliation(s)*. Montreal, ON: University of McGill Press.
Qizilbash, Mozafhar. 2009. Identity, Community and Justice: Locating Amartya Sen's Work on Identity. *Politics, Philosophy and Economics* 8(3): 251–66.

Ratner, Steven. 1999. New Democracies, Old Atrocities. *Georgetown Law Journal* 87: 707–48.

Rigby, A. 2001. *Justice and Reconciliation*. Boulder, CO: Lynne Rienner Publishers.

Roht-Arriaza, Naomi. (ed.) 1995. *Impunity and Human Rights in International Law and Practice*. New York: Oxford University Press.

Rothberg, I. and D. Thompson. 2000 (eds). *Truth v Justice*. Princeton, NJ: Princeton University Press.

Sebbar, Leila. 1999. *La Seine Etait Rouge*. Paris: Thierry Magnier.

Sen, Amartya. 1985. Wellbeing, Agency and Freedom. *Journal of Philosophy* 82(4): 169–21.

Sen, Amartya. 1992. *Inequality Reexamined*. Cambridge: Cambridge University Press.

Sen, Amartya. 1998. *Reason before Identity*. Oxford: Oxford University Press.

Sen, Amartya. 1999. *Development as Freedom*. Oxford: Oxford University Press.

Sen, Amartya. 2006. *Identity and Violence*. New York: W.W. Norton.

Silverstein, Paul A. 2004. *Algeria in France*. Bloomington, IN: Indiana University Press.

Staub, Ervin. 2006. Reconciliation after Genocide, Mass Killing or Intractable Conflict. *Political Psychology* 27(6): 867–94.

Tutu, Desmond. 2000. *No Future without Forgiveness*. New York: Doubleday.

Van Antwerpen, Jonathan. 2008. 'Reconciliation Reconceived: Religion, Secularism and the Language of Transition'. In Will Kymlicka and Bashir Bashir (eds), *The Politics of Reconciliation in Multicultural Societies*. Oxford: Oxford University Press, pp. 25–47.

Veitch, Scott. (ed.) 2007. *Law and the Politics of Reconciliation*. Edinburgh: Edinburgh University Press.

Wieviorka, Michel. 1996. Identity and Difference. *Thesis Eleven* 47(1): 49–71.

PART V
Transitional Justice and the Arts

Chapter 11

Transitional Justice and the Arts: Reflections on the Field

Sanja Bahun

On 19 September 2006, the former Director of General Investigations for the Police of Buenos Aires Province, Miguel Osvaldo Etchecolatz, addressed his concluding remarks of the accused to the judges of the Oral Court in the First Federal Court of La Plata, Drs. Horacio Isaurralde, Carlos Rozanski and Norberto Lorenzo. Standing still, defiant and unrepentant, Etchecolatz quoted his compatriot writer Jorge Luis Borges: 'As Borges would say, you are not the judge. The Supreme Judge would judge us after death'. His voice resonated in the tense silence of the courtroom (*Who Am I? The Lost Children of Argentina*, dir. Estela Bravo, 2007) and it was these words that would be given prominence in the late evening and the next day editions of major Argentinean newspapers (e.g., *La Nacion*, 19 September 2006, online edition; *Página 12*, 20 September 2006, online edition).

Etchecolatz had already been tried for illegal arrest and torture in 1983, receiving a 23-year prison sentence, but was subsequently released under Argentina's notorious amnesty laws. Triggered by the growing evidence of Etchecolatz's direct involvement in the murder, torture and illegal deprivation of freedom of a group of 'disappeared' (*los desaparecidos*), his 2006 trial was the first public retrial of those amnestied since the repeal of the Full Stop Law (Ley de Punto Final) and Law of Due Obedience (Law of Obediencia Debida) by the Supreme Court of Argentina in June 2005, as well as the first in the series of penal cases delivered by the Juicio por la Verdad (Trial for Truth, established in 1998).[1] Having heard his final remarks, the judges sojourned and returned to deliver an unprecedented sentence: Etchecolatz was imprisoned for life for what was legally defined, for the first time in Argentina, as crimes against humanity, committed under the framework of a systematic plan of extermination, or genocide.

Remarkably, Etchecolatz's literary remarks struck neither the judges nor the audience as extraordinary on that September day. And they were not. Etchecolatz was simply using, or rather blatantly misappropriating, that inspiring and unsettling proximity between literature and law of which recent critical discussions, including those within the field of transitional justice, are more than aware. In his discussion of testimony provided before the South African Truth and Reconciliation Commission (TRC), Mark Sanders (2007) described the relationship between literature and law as one of 'interdependence' – where law, 'in order to be law … engages, and engages with, cultural explanation, linguistic idiom, and even literary form' (9). Yet Maria Aristedemou (2000) has insisted that this relationship is also oppositional: literature, she writes, presents a 'site of struggle'

1 Etchecolatz was convicted for the first degree murder of Diana Esmeralda Teruggi, the illegal deprivation of freedom, application of torture and first degree murder of Nora Formiga, Elena Arce Sahores, and Margarita Delgado, and the illegal deprivation of freedom and torture of Jorge Julio López and Nilda Eloy. During the trial, the principal witness for the prosecution, a 77-year-old López disappeared on his way to the court hearing; he remains missing. Etchecolatz's was the second public conviction for forced disappearance since the annulment of amnesty laws (the first was that of Julio Héctor Simón, sentenced on 4 August 2006).

where the discourse of law as it manifests itself at a specific historical moment may be contested or confronted (10). More specifically to this case, however, Etchecolatz also invoked a figure that had had a close, if complicated, relationship with the military regime whose governance between 1976 and 1983 and the use of clandestine state terrorism for the kidnapping, torture and death of an estimated 30,000 people (Feitlowtiz 1998, ix) was under public and judicial scrutiny at this trial. Outspokenly 'right-wing', Borges had been known as an acquaintance (of indeterminate intimacy) and supporter of Jorge Rafael Videla.

In stark contrast to these dubitable credentials, the aged Borges, then émigré, also attended as a witness the 1985 junta trials. He gave a humanely outraged interview to *Diario del Juicio*, the ephemeral newspaper dedicated exclusively to covering the trial, and memorably described the experience of the session in his characteristically punctilious language in an essay entitled 'Monday 22 July 1985' ('Lunes, 22 de Julio de 1985'), published in *Clarín* on 23 July 1985. In this expressive account of the trial, read by a vast number of Argentineans (assumedly also by Etchecolatz), an 85-year-old Borges made clear the parameters of both his own unorthodox ethical philosophy and his ultimate conviction in some inalienable rights and concomitant responsibilities: 'Personally, I do not believe in free will. Neither do I believe in punishments or rewards. I do not believe in hell or heaven … However, to not judge and not condemn this crime would mean to foster impunity and to become, in a sense, an accomplice' (Borges 2003: 315). This statement, deprived of the writer's signature ironic tone, yet projecting a characteristically 'Borgesian' vision of the world, amounted to both a personal recognition of accountability and a more general statement on historical obligations of workers in culture. In a conspicuous contrast to the way in which his words would be used by Etchecolatz more than 20 years later, Borges acknowledges and reinforces the credibility of the court and the proceedings.

This constellation of events – of the 1970s, 1980s, and 2000s – in which mass violation of human rights, judiciary proceedings, and creative practice surprisingly converged, illuminates well the complex interaction of the arts and transitional justice and the multifaceted roles that art and art-related practices play in societies in transition. These roles, their meanings, and their heuristic values for the field of transitional justice are the subject of the present chapter.

Charting the Field

The label 'transition' is generally attached to societies that transit from a totalitarian regime, or conflict (where mass atrocities and violations of human rights have taken place), to a more pluralistic type of governance, and peaceful and just society. The questions of justice figure prominently in transitional periods, and they are integrally linked to the society's dual effort to bring justice to the past through redistribution and recognition, and ensure the continued practice of fairness in the future. This is the field of transitional justice, an interdisciplinary area that, while reliant on the discipline of law, rightfully combines insights from a range of other disciplines such as history, psychology, economics, philosophy, sociology, linguistics, and, as this essay argues, the investigation of the arts. The operating paradigm of transitional justice is that any state in transition should engage in judicial and non-judicial activities (e.g., reparation, truth, institutional reform, demobilization, national consultation processes, and others) that would deliver justice for past crimes and establish a rule of law. In that spirit, according to the United Nation Secretary-General's report, transitional justice refers to 'the full set of processes and mechanisms associated with a society's attempts to come to terms with a legacy of large-scale past abuse, in order to secure accountability, serve justice and achieve reconciliation' (Annan 2004: 4). The UN has further highlighted that, in order to properly address the root-causes of conflict, or past political abuses in a society, it is necessary also to tackle violations of economic, social, and cultural rights (OHCHR 2009).

This view is reliant on an experientially supported assumption that culture – including art practices and art heritage – vitally contributes to building just societies.[2] Indeed, the arts (literature, film, visual art, music, theatre, dance, architecture, and other art forms) present both a crucial catalyst mechanism and an important information and reparation tool to support societies in transition. Their actual functioning in a transitional context is, however, multifaceted: as I shall proceed to argue, the works of art play a complex role as both a decisive contributor to and impeder of socio-political recalibration of society.

There is evidence of swiftly growing interest in investigation in this area. In the past decade, arts-based approaches to peace-building have gained the attention of scholars and policy-makers, and to recognize the importance of this inquiry the International Peace Research Association established an Arts and Peace Commission in 2004. An active research-artistic platform in this area is the Peacebuilding and the Arts Program of Brandeis University, USA, whose initiatives include some projects dealing with countries in transition (Search for Common Ground 2012). Recent academic publications reflect a more specific interest in the interaction of the arts and transitional justice, where area-based inquiries dominate the field (Bell and Di Paolantonio 2009; Lenta 2010; Lipscomb 2010). In addition, some aspects, or modes, of the operation of art in transition have received significant critical attention, albeit without explicitly being linked to transitional justice mechanisms. In particular, the essential role of visual art in community-based rehabilitation programmes has been widely documented (e.g., Dokter 1998, Kalmanowitz and Lloyd 2005), and the successes of music and other performative arts in the realm of human and cultural rights have been extensively discussed (e.g., Cohen et al. 2010; Peddie 2011). On the other hand, memorial art and socially responsible place-based artistic practices in post-conflict societies have received renewed attention from scholars working in the interdisciplinary field of memory studies (e.g., Kwon 2004), and institutions like the International Coalition of Memorial Museums in Remembrance of Victims of State-perpetrated Crimes. These and other inquires and initiatives usually revolve around three focal points, art practices, artworks, and artists; one could add to these the tools and the material and symbolic instruments of art-making. Following on these discussions, one may also infer a few observable types of interaction between the arts and transitional justice: representational (representation of, and engagement with justice and injustice, trials, legal proceedings, punishments, and so on in art), memorial (the use of the arts to remember and commemorate), the intrinsic or adopted artistic underpinning of law and law-making practices in transitional societies, and regulation and protection of the arts by (international or domestic) law and law-enforcing practices in transitional societies.[3]

For all their insightfulness, discussions and initiatives in the field have often lacked closer engagement with the actual mechanisms and initiatives of transitional justice as they are being developed domestically and in international criminal law and as they impact the situation on the ground. In addition, because the meanings attached to art and art-based practices, resources and vicissitudes of art production differ in each transitional setting, the researchers have mostly been forced to focus on a single region or a single mode of artistic expression. In effect, such

2 See, for example, the International Covenant on Economic, Social, and Cultural Rights. The importance of culture and cultural practices, including artistic practices, in the context of rehabilitation is specifically highlighted in the Article 14 of the UN Convention against Torture, and Other Cruel, Inhuman, or Degrading Treatment or Punishment and the Draft General Comment on Article 14.

3 Here I partly paraphrase and expand Patrick Lenta's observations on literature and law (2010).

studies sometimes miss a wider picture that would enable them to see the art of their consideration interacting with other types of artistic practices in the same transitional context, and similar practices at other global transitional sites; their restricted scope limits their audience. Finally, in concentrating on the reparative aspects of art production, the arts and transitional justice studies so far have tended to sideline the discussion of the ways in which artistic practices could also hinder or obstruct transitional processes. Due to all these practical and hermeneutic conundrums, the discussions of the interaction between the arts and transitional justice have rarely ventured into interdisciplinary theoretical assessment and hermeneutic correlation of artistic practices in various transitional contexts. Born out of an awareness of the inchoate nature of the inquiry, shortage of methodological frameworks, and the poor dissemination of research outcomes, the following presents an attempt to identify and systematize a few dynamics pertaining to the arts and transitional justice, and to argue for the heightened relevance of their further investigation by both scholars and practitioners.

Operation of Art in Transitional Justice Context

Any inquiry into the operation of art in transitional justice context should probably start with the recognition that symbolic practices like art production are a means to express the *nomos* – that set social narratives and interactions that, according to Robert Cover (1992), locates and constitutes any legal system – and to give observable, emotionally compelling form to its demands (144–5). The arts thus establish a particular rapport with law and justice-related practices in society, a relationship that, as we have seen, is one of both interdependence and opposition, or, rather, suplementarity – for art may 'draw attention to inequities committed by law's exclusions' (Thomas 1991: 537). A regular trial, and even a very comprehensively envisioned series of trials, can host only a limited number of victims, witnesses and perpetrators, and thereby its findings and the truths it exposes are by necessity limited. In transitional contexts, art practices provide important unofficial counterparts for truth-finding, but also reconciliation, civic repair and psychological reparation, lustration, public apology and other mechanisms of transitional justice, often enabling empowerment of underrepresented groups.

Peace-building and just-society building imply a particularly charged relationship with the past, and necessitate attempts at finding the 'path between too much memory and too much forgetting' (Minow 1998: 4); it is in identifying and traversing that path that the function of the arts in transitional societies is most visible. Art practices and artworks both assist recognition of past injustices, their memorialization, and psychological reparation, and testify to the social challenges of transition, measuring satisfaction and evaluating the transitional processes. Their operation tends critically to expose the commensurabilities and disparities between the general reading of the rule of law and its local perception, and the external and the internal practices in place to promote legality in a given community. Yet the ameliorative function of engagement with the arts, and art-based therapies in particular, is also essential in the context that often involves forced displacement of people, the legacy of atrocities and injustice, division of communities, fear of cohabitation, and mistrust of both local and international governing bodies. Artworks furthermore document atrocities committed by abusive regimes in ways and with emotional impact that are unavailable to both governmental policy-makers and non-governmental organizations working in the field of transitional justice or human rights. As such, the arts can give voice to the victims to tell their story: past experiences can sometimes be more fully and more accurately represented via artistic performance (instead of, or in addition to, courtroom testimony) (Stepakoff 2008: 19). In fact, scholars and artists alike frequently insist on just such a function of the arts in a transitional setting: compulsively addressing themselves to the right to remember, the 'transitional arts' often remind us of some surreptitious dangers of the practice and theory of transitional justice, for example, those presented by the diffusion of dialogue and memory of the past in an effort to focus solely on economic development. This insistence is informed by one shared structural property of all kinds of art: the production and reception of art affords one with a unique opportunity to engage historical traumata at the level of a cathartic public action, and under relatively protected circumstances of creative activity. A few days before she was scheduled to testify, a witness before the Special Court for Sierra Leone had asked the Witnesses and Victims Section and the Office of the Prosecutor for permission to perform, in front of the court staff, a play she had created together with other witnesses. In an interview after the court performance and the court testimony, she highlighted the similarities and differences between the two experiences: during their testimony the court was able to hear the experience, whereas the play enabled them also to see it, thus relaying some less easily expressible, or inexpressible, content; in addition, while in the courtroom each witness would speak for himself or herself, in the context of a play participants were able to present their stories simultaneously and to show both to the court and to themselves how different elements of their respective experiences are linked (Stepakoff 2008: 23).

Not to be missed in this account, however, is another property of art-making in a transitional justice setting, in and beyond the court: art production can provide a public platform to restore the dignity of individuals and groups, offering acts of moral and symbolic reparation and enabling the participants to re-vision themselves and their role in both local and wider communities. This function is intrinsically related to the well-recorded power of the arts to shape personal and group identities, and create new identities (Mamdani 2007; Kwon 2004). In societies in transition, such processes involve reckoning with the issues of accountability, responsibility, reconciliation, and the sense of justice, as well as projective thinking about the destiny of a nation, and/or the artist as a member of that nation. Art-making assists creative thinking, which is crucial for negotiating these concerns and the construction of new, collectively imagined future.

The uninhibited, uncensored art production is particularly relevant for what has recently become known as transformative reparations, or 'reparative justice' – those judicial and non-judicial measures and practices of 'repairing' society that aim at transforming or challenging the structures that brought about a conflict or violation of human rights in the first place (Uprimny and Saffon 2009). Typically for this type of operation, an artist would take up an issue in contemporary transitional society (and its legal provision) to reflect on a persistent pattern of structural injustice. The art intervention work *Identification* (*Identificación*, 2007) by the Guatemalan-Dominican artist David Pérez Karmadavis provides an engaging exemplification of this model.[4] For this performance, Karmadavis contracted a tattoo artist to tattoo, free of charge, the name and identity number on the inner lower arms of those who were interested – so that, if they disappeared, there would be a record of their existence, and, should their features be rendered unrecognizable, or they be buried without being identified, there would be a means of identifying them. The result was a series of close-up photographs of tattooed inner arms, including one of Karmadavis's own tattoo.

Identification bridges Body Art and participatory art interventions, and is an affiliate of a range of artistic practices using the insight that body may operate as 'a nodal point or nexus for relations of juridical and productive power' (Butler 1989: 601). But Karmadavis's intervention also has a site-specific target: collusion between state and non-state actors in a preposterous delay to identify the victims of murder/disappearance in transitional Guatemala City. The Guatemalan

4 The following analysis appears expanded in my curatorial research paper, written for the exhibition 'Karmadavis: Art, Transition, Justice' at firstsite Gallery, Colchester, UK (10 November 2012–10 March 2013); see Bahun 2012.

Policía Nacional Civil (PNC, National Civil Police) has long been facing the challenges of institutional corruption, explosion of organized crime, high murder and 'disappearance' rates, and inexplicable delays in its procedures. The procedure which Karmadavis targets in *Identification* is a case in point. Most of the numerous murder victims in Guatemala City are found with no form of identification; if their bodies are not claimed within 72 hours, they are dispatched to the city cemetery and buried as 'XX'. Ironically, Karmadavis highlights in his description of the piece, when a disappearance is reported to the PNC, the report prompts an investigation and search only precisely 72 hours later.

This absurd practice appears against a specific historical background: the aftermath of Guatemalan civil war (1962–96) in which an estimated 200,000 people were killed and about 40,000 people disappeared, and where the state's military operations against the Mayan populace have been judged genocide (CEH 1999). A more immediate context for Karmadavis's intervention includes the lobbying for and preparation of the first domestic trial in regard to enforced disappearances in the civil war, that of former military commissioner Felipe Cusanero.[5] What Karmadavis's photographs of 'identificatory tattoos' intimate, then, is that a state which fails to provide a reasonable environment and efficient procedures for the identification of murder and kidnapping victims is just like the one that perpetrates and covers up forced disappearances. To further reinforce this comparison, Karmadavis's photographed tattoos feature both the serial number and the proper name, probing the semantic and political tension created by the interaction of anonymity and proper name/naming, and drawing attention to a continuing problem with name record and identification in Guatemala. While the latter problem involves all sectors of Guatemalan society, and all forms of record, it particularly affects indigenous Maya people who have not Latinized their names: it presents them with substantial difficulties in such mundane processes as being issued a national ID card – a card, incidentally, indispensable for the purpose of identification. And this is where continuities and collusions in Karmadavis's artwork peak: unidentified victims of gang/state-colluded violence nowadays more often than not belong to the same social group as unidentified victims of the civil war.

As this example has demonstrated, the operation of the arts in transitional societies is inextricably linked to our capacity to generate, mobilize and develop creative vigilance and 'moral imagination'; in turn, these could vitally help our efforts to build enduring peace (Lederach 2005). This important function of the arts stems from their inherent capacity to engage multiple temporalities and to comment on transitional processes in a manner unavailable to other civil and legal mechanisms and practices: at their best, artworks do not state, but invoke and envision. It is in this way that artworks like *Identification* can be jurisgenerative (cf. Bell and Di Paolantonio 2009: 153–4) and serve as potent 'transformative agents' in a transitional society (Taylor 2003: xxviii).

Like Borges earlier, Karmadavis now lives in Diaspora, though, and his art practice reflects as much his concerns with transitional processes in his new domicile as his continuing labours to support the establishment of an honest, equity-based political dialogue between Haiti and the Dominican Republic. Artists working in exile, or Diaspora, often emphatically engage with the transitional processes in their home region. Yet their position and symbolic status are ambiguous and their artistic efforts to assist the work of transition are frequently greeted with animosity by the artists and public in the transitioning country itself: they are accused of 'escape', and/or of losing touch with the realities on the ground, as well as of perpetuating the calls for remembrance at the expense of a focus on economic and social development. At the same time, and precisely because

5 The case of Felipe Cusanero was opened in 2003, when the relatives of six Kaqchikel Maya farmers filed a complaint against him. On 30 August 2009 Cusanero was sentenced by the Criminal Court of Chimaltenango to 150 years in prison for ordering the kidnapping and forced 'disappearance' of at least six people.

of the ambivalence of their status, the Diasporic artists' voices resonate forcefully in transitional settings. Such has been the case of, for example, writers Dubravka Ugrešić and Slavenka Drakulić, two of 'Croatian witches',[6] and Serbian-Montenegrin artist Marina Abramovich. In the context which includes reckoning with the legacy of ethnic cleansing, heightened visibility of certain types of crime such as war rape, and need for structural changes, especially in the domain of gender relations, their unsettling fictional, essayistic and artistic encounters with the past mass atrocities and transitional realities in the region of former Yugoslavia (e.g., Drakulić's *S: The Novel about the Balkans* [2000], Ugrešić's *The Ministry of Pain* [2005], Abramovich's video installation *Balkan Erotic Epic: Banging the Skull* [2005]) provoked heated debates 'at home' – not the least because the public allegations of these female artists, both during and after the conflict, included the charge of insensitivity to war rape. Surfacing the persisting patterns of gender stereotyping, media and sometimes art community itself would pitch these artists against female artists that remained in the region, for example, the Croatian writer Ivana Simić Bodrožić and Serbian playwright Biljana Srbljanović, or those that live between the home-space and Diaspora like Bosnian artist Šejla Kamarić, presumably in an impossible task to identify the more authentic voice of transition and justice. As this case study suggests, the opposition between the artists who have gone into (voluntary or involuntary) exile and those who have remained in the country during and in the aftermath of gross violations of human rights presents researchers in the field with a substantial amount of heuristic difficulties, including the question of whose voice should be isolated for investigation. Such conundrums could be productive, though, insofar as they reveal that our interrogation of the arts and transitional justice must be (a) comparative and (b) attentive to a wider international socio-symbolic network established as a result of transitional processes.

The last example also exemplifies that, far from having an unequivocally positive function, the arts are amenable to both use and abuse in transitional context. In post-genocide Rwanda, for example, theatre has been widely used to re-imagine national identity, through government-sanctioned theatre companies and projects of rewriting history as well as grass-roots theatrical associations often affiliated with the Gacaca courts. Here the role of community-based theatre is particularly fraught with difficulties. As Ananda Breed has found, whereas Rwandese grass-roots theatre associations like 'The Poetry of Rwanda' (Umuhanzi w'u Rwanda) successfully bring together and reconcile perpetrators and survivors, they also 'perform nationalism' through a strategic use of slogans promoting the government's concept of Rwanda as one unified culture with the same language. Such a situation bifurcates the operation of theatre/art in a transitional society: 'Although the use of theatre contributes to individual cases of reconciliation, it can also create dilemmas that impede large-scale or general reconciliation' (Breed 2008: 33).

This dual potential is ostensible in the treatment of artworks and art tools, products which, due to their determinable economic and symbolic value, are strongly operative in transitional settings. In particular, the art-making tools are frequently endowed with strategic cultural resonance that intersects closely with the concerns of transitional justice. In Peru, for example, the recent recognition of the *cajón*, an idiophone from Peruvian coast, as 'Cultural Patrimony of the Nation', may be seen as an outstanding recognition of Afro-Peruvian community in a country where disenfranchisement of ethnic minorities is embedded in the texture of society. But it could also be seen as a state-validation of the greater Peruvian identity without tangible impact on the Afro-Peruvian community itself (León 2009). Similarly, the artworks themselves have capacity to figure as highly ambivalent tokens of

6 Five Croatian female intellectuals (Slavenka Drakulić, Rada Iveković, Vesna Kesić, Jelena Lovrić and Dubravka Ugrešić) came under an orchestrated media attack in Croatia in 1992, because they drew attention to the lack of freedom of speech in the country – and additionally insisted that wartime rapes should be analysed in terms of gender relations in a misogynist society rather than in terms of ethnicity; they were labelled 'conspirators' and 'witches' (Tax 1993).

restitution in litigation, as witnessed in the proliferation of cases dealing with looted artworks in the Holocaust, but also in Argentina, former Yugoslavia, and South Africa.

For all its value as a transformative agent in society, therefore, art can also – and without cancelling its opposite – obstruct transitional processes, or impart ambivalent meanings to them. One of the aims of the following survey is to make this paradoxical operation of the arts more understandable to the reader.

Ars transienti

As previous examples have intimated, a remarkable variety of the arts overtly engage with transitional justice processes. At the same time, while all the arts contribute to transitional justice discourse, there is also a culture-specific preference, in each transitional site, for an art form best suited to convey complex socio-political messages. In relation to their operation in societies in transition, the arts could be provisionally divided into those that function in the 'open' (popular music, certain types of performance, theatre and public space intervention, architecture, monumental art) and those whose reception tends to unfold in the 'enclosed', or 'intimate', public spheres (literature, occasionally film and visual arts). In addition, works of art can have an impact which unfolds over lengthy periods of time (e.g., literature, architecture, film) or can operate most forcefully in limited time spans (drama and performance). So far the scholarly discussions of the interaction between the arts and transitional justice have dominantly concerned themselves with open, limited time, and place-based practices such as art therapy, drama, music and performance, as well as the long-span, site-specific monumental art and architecture.

The role of performative arts in achieving rights such as freedom of expression, equal treatment before the law, rights of assembly and franchise, and the cultural rights of remembering and forging collective identities and histories, especially in the transitional context where public space for debate and outreach is still limited, has rightly been praised (Weintraub and Yung 2009; Cohen et al. 2011). Richard Schechner's (1985) famous definition of performance as 'twice-behaved behavior' (36) gives a good indication why performative arts may be particularly relevant as vehicles for transitional justice. Community-based theatre that deploys participatory exercises and games – where members of the affected community assume protagonist roles, discuss problems and propose solutions without having solutions imposed on them by experts – has provided unique opportunities for sharing the conflict- or state abuse-related experiences in a number of transitional settings, including Afghanistan, Burundi, Peru, South Africa, countries of former Yugoslavia, and others (Siddiqui 2010; Stepakoff 2008; Simić 2010). Moreover, the operation of many transitional justice mechanisms is in itself performative. The South African TRC's live public hearings self-consciously presented themselves as an important public ritual and national (that is, nation-building) theatre (Cole 2010). Some other transitional justice proceedings have similarly suffered the influx of theatricality, even when they did not desire it (e.g., the International Criminal Tribunal for Former Yugoslavia). Such blending of law and an affect-ridden medium has been criticized for impeding due process and resulting in unfair trials (Minow 1998). This critique is not surprising: as we have seen in the case of affiliations between law and literature, the normativity of law depends on the repression of its artistic underpinning, be it its literariness or its performativity. Nevertheless, when introduced with purpose and caution, the practices that purposely activate the artistic element of legal practice seem to be singularly effective in transitional justice precisely because they enable the introduction of emotive and creative components (e.g., the work of the South African and Peruvian TRCs).

Such investigations have fruitfully been extended to the form that embodies 'restored behaviour' in a less direct way – music. This art may operate as a powerful lever of social transformation wherever ethical and social concerns have traditionally been relayed via singing and music-making. In one such context, contemporary or past pieces of music, voices (and personalities behind them), and even instruments can become fetishized tokens in social changes. Through its capacity to speak to wide audiences and disseminate message both via live performances and mass media, popular music gains prominence under these circumstances. Insightfully writing about the complementary roles and discourses of the Peruvian Truth Commission and the *canción social Ayacuchana* ('Ayacuchan social song'),[7] Jonathan Ritter (2006) has pointed out that the discourses of the law ('informative') and popular song ('commemorative') can fruitfully complemented each other in the work of remembering and collecting testimonies. Yet, the actual role of popular music in such situations is never simple. When, on the occasion of the presentation of the final report of the Peruvian TRC to the public on 29 August 2003, Carlos Falconí, one of the pioneers of the *canciones testimoniales*, performed his 1983 song on the plaza of Huamanga (city of Ayacucho), the audience's response was equivocal: while for hundreds of elated fans the event provided a bittersweet sense of closure of an important chapter in transitional history, for a not insignificant group of demonstrators that had marched against the Commission on that very plaza the whole afternoon, this performance marked a beginning: prompted by a media smear campaign, some protesters contested the conclusions of the Commission; others demanded attention to occluded concerns (Ritter 2006: 2–3). All these affects poured out and intermingled before the stage where Falconí performed.

Such a contradictory response to the use of the arts in transitional justice is not limited to performance. Ever since the rise to prominence of 'counter-monument' (*Gegendenkmal*) theory and practice in response to TJ issues pertinent to the Holocaust,[8] artistic interventions in monumental art and memorial art projects have regularly (and, one may add, intentionally) sparked controversy. A good example here is the reopening of the Navy Petty-Officers School of Mechanics (Escuela de Suboficiales de Mecánica de la Armada), the largest detention centre in Argentina from 1976 to 1983, as a human rights museum and cultural centre, which was greeted at once with jubilation, apprehension and repulsion (see Bell and Di Paolantonio 2009). But, perhaps controversy, or the invitation to pose unsettling questions in the public sphere, is exactly what the transitional justice art needs to do: to encourage, prompt, even force, the culture of dialogue.

Researchers in the field have frequently shunned the consideration of the arts that may enable social rehabilitation, memory-work, and capacity-building in less site-specific ways, and over lengthy periods of time, e.g., film and literature beyond testimonial texts. But the arts operating over long spans, and with the possibility of recurring interaction, have their intrinsic values, for they allow time for gradual semantic unveiling and prolonged reflection. Much could be gained, for instance, by simply observing the prominence or sudden resurgence of a genre (e.g., the rise of two opposite but related genres in South African literature: crime fiction and judicial autobiography) or by heeding the changes in literary style and rhetoric of legal decisions in transitional period (Lenta 2010: 3–4). Additional insights could be culled through a perusal of oral literature and its translation into judiciary proceedings (see my previous comments on the work of post-apartheid South African courts). More directly, Leigh-Ashley Lipscomb (2010) has argued that transitional

7 *Canciones testimoniales* ('testimonial songs'), or the *canción social ayacuchana* ('Ayacuchan social song'), is a genre of protest guitar-based song, often written in Quechua, that has been performed in Peru since the 1980s, as an explicit response to the country's 'Dirty War'.

8 'Counter-monument' movement is associated with artists such as Jochen Gerz, Esther Shalev-Gerz and Hors Hoheisel. According to James E. Young (1992), 'counter-monuments' do not console or heal, but 'torment' and perpetuate the loss they memorize. Precisely because of such functioning, they are socially proactive: they combat petrification of memories.

poetry produced by a generation of post-independence Timor-Leste's authors, writing in Tetum, Indonesian and Portuguese, exercises 'a hidden, informal kind of accountability, or an 'aesthetics of accountability', that is entwined with the formal pursuits of the transitional justice sector' (168). Such 'aesthetics of accountability' indeed operates best in art forms like literature which allow us time for reflection, and thereby the critical positioning of ourselves towards the theories and practices we espouse, a meta-stance that is necessary for their improvement. As Goodrich has commented, and writings of Abe Baretto Soares (Timor), Nadine Gordimer (South Africa), Tununa Mercado (Argentina) and many others confirm, literature not only provides alternative testimonies and ways of memorizing but also 'deconstructs law', suggesting 'other possibilities for law, other means of expression of law and, more profoundly, conceptions of value and justice that draw upon a wider variety of gender, sexuality, ethnicity and lifestyle' (Goodrich 1996: 6).

A similar claim could be made with respect to film, one of the main levers of dissemination of messages and meanings in modern society. Film (documentary, commercial, 'art house', amateur, professional) establishes particularly strong rapport with transitional justice processes due to its specific status in contemporary world: the circumstances that digital movies can now be made relatively inexpensively and that the global distribution and reception of films, through both legal and illegal channels, and in both private and public venues, is thriving. Films often commemorate past events and describe contemporary realities from an underrepresented point of view, and thereby give transitional justice experts an insight into cultural groups and opinions they may not access otherwise. Two films made within few years in an interrelated transitional space can serve as evocative examples here: Bosnian film *Grbavica* (2006, dir. Jasmila Žbanić) describes the struggles of a single mother-rape victim of Bosnian war and her daughter in transitional Sarajevo through performances that are both poignant and poetic; in contrast, Serbian subtle and unpretentious film *Tilva Roš* (2010, dir. Nikola Lezaić) employs amateur teenage skaters to depict growing up in economically deprived city of Bor – using skateboarding as both a metaphor and a real lever of forging a more positive vision of the future. As these two examples, and the resurgence of cinema in Argentina, Chile, Peru and other transitional sites, indicate, film art, through its characteristic conjugation of the visual (recording the world), the auditory (listening to the world) and narrative (imagining the world), its drive for documenting, and its often deliberate address to the unrepresentable, is vital for understanding and fostering civil society's active engagement with transitional justice: the film opens the eyes of viewers, both the general audience and those working in TJ sector, to novel ways of understanding, and acting upon, justice.

The above report is not, and cannot aspire to be, comprehensive: most significantly, it limits itself to the most commonly and prominently utilized art forms and does not provide a sufficient account of a great number of hybrid and related art forms. Nevertheless, it can serve as a useful overview, on the basis of which we can now extrapolate a few summary methodological questions and concerns.

Methodologies and Questions

In order to give justice to the complexity and significance of the relationship between the arts and transitional justice, one needs to engage the entirety of types and modes of operation of the arts, and the diverse and variable roles an artwork can play in a transitional context, at the same time focusing this investigation through the specific lens of legality. Hermeneutic frameworks developed by sociolegal scholars (Cover 1992) and experts who work across the divide between the arts and law studies (Felman 2002; Sanders 2007; Cornell and Panfilio 2010) can be of marked use in such an investigation, especially when combined with in-depth knowledge of regional culture. The latter aspect of the equation implies valuable foregrounding of the role of local cultures, means of expression, and visions of development, which directly contributes to the debate about the challenges and limitations of externally driven processes in peace-building and delivering justice (on the need to refocus on the local culture and development, see De Greiff and Duthie 2009). But it appears to be even more beneficial to expand such an inquiry by comparing two or more transitional justice settings, and at various levels. The discipline of comparative literature, and it affiliate, the discipline of comparative arts, thus emerge as well positioned to contribute with methodological correctives to the field of transitional justice itself. In practice, transitional justice initiatives sometimes appear as divisive, top-bottom, institutionalized, externally imposed, and failing to properly understand and address the varied meanings of transitional justice, or justice as such (Nagy 2008). The introduction of frameworks of comparative inquiry that insist on both irreducible specificity of geocultural sites and their simultaneous amenability to comparative discussion may fruitfully expand the existing hermeneutic practices in the field of transitional justice. In terms of altitudinal scope, whereas transitional justice, as traditionally conceived, deals with the legislative frameworks and social dynamics at the level of nation state, an inquiry focalized through the lens of comparative arts addresses transitional processes as they operate also at the subnational (ethnic minority or secluded community) and international levels; and treats as equal in heuristic value governmentally funded, NGO-funded and grass-roots transitional justice initiatives in the arts sector, as well as international and domestic policies impacting them.

Perhaps by necessity, the methodological framework and scope of such inquiries can never be exhaustive or completely precise. One could even argue that there might not be a need for one such overarching framework, as the irreverent multiplicity of contexts would always question it. But there are also other ways to think about the methodology of investigating the arts and transitional justice, namely, as reliant on a weak paradigm, or as generative of an advisory toolkit that is to be readjusted in each particular situation. In fact, such re-constellated hermeneutic thinking is befitting the field of transitional justice that, insofar as the tidiness of tools, practices, outcomes, and theoretical conclusions is concerned, will always be 'incomplete and messy' (Franke 2006: 813).

Such a perspective liberates us not only to appreciate various types of interaction between the arts and transitional justice but also to postulate and systematize three sets of questions relevant to the inquiry:

- *Questions concerning the operation of the arts*: What recognized and unrecognized functions do the arts have in transitional societies? What are 'engaged' arts? Can the arts be understood as significant unofficial agents in ensuring 'meaningful public participation' in transitional processes (Ki-Moon 2010: 9) or even jurisgenerative? How does the fact that the context-based transitional justice mechanisms are also subject to the universalizing human rights discourse impact local artistic practices and their recipients?
- *Representation, or making sense of, justice*: How are the notions of legality and justice represented, in a variety of art practices, produced by 'transitional' artists on site and in Diaspora? What formal means art uses to 'foster a culture of respect for the rule of law' (Ki-Moon 2010: 9)? How do artists envision and represent justice when their interests intersect with those of indigenous justice pressure groups like the environmental justice movement, or when they engage in public debates surrounding transitional justice?
- *Who creates art (and what art)*: How do existing legal provisions in transitional societies protect and promote, or impede, the diversity and freedom of artistic expression, both in terms of contemporary practice and use of cultural heritage? How are the arts censored or auto-censored in transitional societies? How is transitional cultural identity 'practised'

independently from, or in defiance of, what the law guarantees or allows? How artists traverse the unstable, transitional justice mechanism-ridden, trajectory between the local and the global: how they negotiate the need to homologate a certain accepted international style, but also to assert their regional artistic identity, themes and traditions?

It is of essence to address these questions because the arts work with and develop symbolic forms crucial for our understanding of who we are, what our place in society is, who we might be, and what society could be (see Cornell and Panfilio 2010). The consideration of how humans as symbolizing creatures both shape development of and give form to justice is one of the key inquiries for the twenty-first century, and, as this essay has argued, one of the vital issues for transitional justice itself.

References

Annan, Kofi. 2004. *The Rule of Law in Conflict and Post-Conflict Societies*. New York: United Nations.

Aristedemou Maria. 2000. *Law and Literature: Journeys from Here to Eternity*. Oxford: Oxford University Press.

Bahun, Sanja. 2012. *Karmadavis: Art, Transition, Justice. Research Paper*. ESCALA and firstsite Gallery, Colchester, UK.

Bell, Vikki and Mario Di Paolantonio. 2009. The Haunted Nomos: Activist-Artists and the (Im) possible Politics of Memory in Transitional Argentina. *Cultural Politics* 5(2): 149–78.

Borges, Jorge Luis. 2003. Lunes, 22 de Julio de 1985. In *Borges: Textos Recobrados 1956–1986*, ed. Sara Luisa del Carril and Mercedes Rubio de Zocchi, 314–17. Buenos Aires: Emecé Editores.

Breed, Ananda. 2008. Performing the Nation: Theatre in Post-Genocide Rwanda. *The Drama Review* 52(1): 32–50.

Butler, Judith. 1989. Foucault and the Paradox of Bodily Inscriptions. *The Journal of Philosophy* 86(11): 601–7.

Cohen, Cynthia, et al. (eds). 2011. *Acting Together: Performance and the Creative Transformation of Conflict*, Vols 1–2. New York: New Village Press.

Cole, Catherine M. 2010. *Performing South Africa's Truth Commission*. Bloomington, IN: Indiana University Press.

Commission for Historical Clarification, Guatemala (La Comisión para el Esclarecimiento Histórico, CEH). Public report "Guatemala: Memory of Silence." February 1999.

Cornell, Drucilla, and Kenneth Michael Panfilio. 2010. *Symbolic Forms for a New Humanity: Cultural and Racial Reconfigurations of Critical Theory (Just Ideas)*. New York: Fordham University Press.

Cover, Robert. 1992. Nomos and Narrative. In *Narrative, Violence, and the Law: The Essays of Robert Cover*, ed. Martha Minow et al., 95–172. Ann Arbor, MI: University of Michigan Press.

De Greiff, Pablo, and Roger Duthie (eds). 2009. *Transitional Justice and Development: Making Connections*. New York: Social Science Research Council.

Dokter, Ditty (ed.). 1998. *Arts Therapists, Refugees, and Migrants: Reaching Across Borders*. London: Jessica Kingsley Publishers.

Feitlowtiz, Marguerite. 1998. *A Lexicon of Terror: Argentina and the Legacies of Torture*. New York and Oxford: Oxford University Press.

Felman, Shohana. 2002. *The Juridical Unconscious: Trials and Traumas in the Twentieth Century*. Cambridge, MA: Harvard University Press.

Franke, Katherine M. 2006. Gendered Subjects of Transitional Justice. *Columbia Journal of Gender and Law* 15(3): 813–28.

Goodrich, Peter. 1996. *Law in the Courts of Love: Literature and Other Minor Jurisprudences*. London: Routledge.

Kalmanowitz, Debra, and Bobby Lloyd (eds). 2005. *Art Therapy and Political Violence: With Art, Without Illusion*. New York: Routledge.

Ki-Moon, Ban. 2010. Guidance Note of the Secretary-General: United Nation's Approach to Transitional Justice. New York: United Nations.

Kwon, Miwon. 2004. *One Place after Another: Site-specific Art and Locational Identity*. Cambridge, MA: MIT Press.

Lederach, John-Paul. 2005. *The Moral Imagination: The Art and Soul of Building Peace*. Oxford: Oxford University Press.

Lenta, Patrick. 2010. Introduction: Law and South African Literature. *Current Writing: Law and South African Literature* 22(2): 1–18.

León, Javier F. 2009. National Patrimony and Cultural Policy: The Case of the Afroperuvian *Cajón*. In *Music and Cultural Rights*, ed. A. Weintraub and Bell Yung, 110–39. Urbana, IL: University of Illinois Press.

Lipscomb, Leigh-Ashley. 2010. Post-independence Timorese Literature and the Aesthetics of Accountability. In *Hatene kona ba/Compreender/Understanding/Mengerti Timor-Leste*, ed. M. Leach et al., 168–73. Hawthorn: Swinburne Press.

Mamdani, Mahmood. 2007. Amnesty or Impunity? A Preliminary Critique of the Report of the Truth and Reconciliation Commission of South Africa. In *Identities, Affiliations, and Allegiances*, ed. Seyla Benhabib et al., 325–61. Cambridge: Cambridge University Press.

Minow, Martha. 1998. *Between Vengeance and Forgiveness: Facing History after Genocide and Mass Violence*. New York: Beacon Press.

Nagy, Rosemary. 2008. Transitional Justice as Global Project: Critical Reflections. *Third World Quarterly* 29(2): 275–89.

Office of the UN High Commissioner for Human Rights. 2009. Annual Report of the United Nations High Commissioner for Human Rights and Reports of OHCHR and the Secretary-General. Analytical study on human rights and transitional justice. http://www.unrol.org/files/96696_A-HRC-12-18_E.pdf.

Peddie, Ian. 2011. *Popular Music and Human Rights*. Farnham: Ashgate.

Ritter, Jonathan. 2006. Complementary Discourses of Truth and Memory: The Peruvian Truth Commission and the *Canción Social Ayacuchana. Diagonal: Journal of the Center for Iberian and Latin American Music* 2. http://www.cilam.ucr.edu/diagonal/issues/2006/Ritter.pdf.

Sanders, Mark. 2007. *Ambiguities of Witnessing: Law and Literature in the Time of a Truth Commission*. Stanford, CA: Stanford University Press.

Search for Common Ground. 2012. Strengthening Work at the Nexus of Arts, Culture, and Peacebuilding. Report. http://www.brandeis.edu/ethics/peacebuildingarts/pdfs/library-authors/2012_2_13_Cohen-Strengthening_Work_at_the_Nexus_of_Arts-Report_FINAL.pdf.

Schechner, Richard. 1985. *Between Theater and Anthropology*. Philadelphia, PA: University of Pennsylvania Press.

Siddiqui, Nadia. 2010. Theatre and Transitional Justice in Afghanistan. Briefing paper. The International Center for Transitional Justice. http://ictj.org/publication/theater-and-transitional-justice-afghanistan.

Simić, Olivera. 2010. Breathing Sense into Women's Lives Shattered by War: Dah Theatre Belgrade. *Law Text Culture* 14(1): 117–32.

Stepakoff, Shanee. 2008. Telling and Showing: Witnesses Represent Sierra Leone's War Atrocities in Court and Onstage. *The Drama Review* 52(1): 17–31.

Strajilevich, Nora. 2006. *The Art of Not Forgetting: Testimonial Literature in Chile, Argentina, and Uruguay between the 1980s and 1990s*. Buenos Aires: Catálogos.

Tax, Meredith. 1993. The Five Croatian 'Witches': A Casebook on 'Trial by Public Opinion' as a Form of Censorship and Intimidation. *Women's World.* 1 July. http://www.wworld.org/archive/archive.asp?ID=157.

Taylor, Philip. 2003. *Applied Theatre. Creating Transformative Encounters in the Community*. Portsmouth: Heinemann.

Thomas, Brook. 1991. Reflections on the Law and Literature Revival. *Critical Enquiry* 17(3): 510–37.

Weintraub, Andrew, and Bell Yung (eds). 2009. *Music and Cultural Rights*. Urbana, IL: University of Illinois Press.

Uprimny, Rodrigo, and Maria Paula Saffon. 2009. Reparaciones transformadoras, justicia distributiva y profundización democratic. In *Reparar en Colombia: los dilemas en contextos de conflicto, pobreza y exclusion*, ed. Catalina Díaz et al., 31–70. ICTJ Colombia: DeJuSticia.

Young, James E. 1992. The Counter-Monument: Memory against Itself in Germany Today. *Critical Inquiry* 18(2): 267–96.

Chapter 12

Democratic 'Sacred Spaces': Public Architecture and Transitional Justice

Mihaela Mihai

'Transitional Justice' (TJ) covers the institutional mechanisms a society employs in order to deal with a past of violence and injustice. Truth commissions, criminal trials, restitution, compensation, and lustration are frequently used to address the legacies of authoritarianism or civil war. While a large literature examines these mechanisms,[1] less attention has been paid to the symbolic facet of the past.[2] This chapter seeks to explore the architectural dimension of TJ. More precisely, it asks what aspiring democracies should do with public constructions glorifying an undemocratic, i.e. racist, authoritarian or totalitarian, past.

Public constructions attest to political regimes' desire to imprint their version of history on the country's landscape and, more importantly, on the memory of citizens. Statues, memorials and monuments set in stone a certain view of the past, usually in glorious and heroic terms. Hierarchies of all kinds (political, social, racial, gendered) are reflected in – and reproduced through – public art, one of the many 'voices' through which the state speaks. What is celebrated or commemorated is as significant as what is forgotten: defeats, reprehensible deeds by the nation, as well as marginalized groups are usually omitted from the material representation of the official story.

This chapter starts with the assumption that it is liberal democracies, or societies aspiring to become liberal democracies, that invest in TJ. Far from being a universal phenomenon, TJ is normatively and politically linked with a certain kind of regime: one committed to human rights, based on the idea of equal respect and concern for all members of the polity. The main argument advanced here is that condoning public monuments that symbolically humiliate certain groups is normatively inconsistent for a liberal democracy. In other words, the public funding of state-commissioned monuments occupying a society's 'sacred space' is problematic to the extent that it violates the egalitarian and inclusive theory of moral worth that liberal democracy presupposes. In talking about 'sacred space' I follow Sanford Levinson, who defines it as 'public cemeteries, state and national capitol grounds, and other ground that is invested with special meaning within the structure of the civil religion that helps to constitute a given social order' (Levinson 1998: 36–7).

This contribution proceeds in several steps. The first section offers a schematic account of liberal democracy and of what could count as symbolic humiliation in such a regime. I then move on to a critical examination of Sanford Levinson's take on what to do with humiliating monuments. I assess his seminal work on democracy and public monuments and argue that, while liberal democracies can choose from a variety of possible avenues of disavowal, certain ways of dealing with objectionable public constructions are normatively problematic. The third section offers two

1 For some recent contributions to this rich field see Eisikovits 2010, Olsen et al. 2010, Arthur 2011, Corradetti 2012, May 2012.

2 There is a large literature on museums and memorials in history, art history and anthropology, but not much has been written about public art seen through the lenses of TJ. For some seminal texts see: Young 2000, Winter 1995, Michalski 1998, Coombes 2003, Walkowitz and Knauer 2004, Lehrer et al. 2011, Czepczynski 2012.

examples, one of a racist, the other of a totalitarian construction. While this chapter is an exercise in normative theory, I use cases to illustrate my theoretical analysis and show the salience of the issues addressed here. The conclusion deals with some potential criticisms.

Liberal Democracy: Institutional Order, Normative Regime, and Ethos

As mentioned before, this chapter departs from the assumption that TJ is typical of liberal democracies or societies aspiring to become liberal democracies. Liberal democracy is conceptualized here as an institutional order and an ethos guided by a number of normative principles. As a normative regime, liberal democracy presupposes an egalitarian theory of human worth,[3] which determines the limits of state powers, as well as the rights and duties that citizens enjoy. Democratic institutions are supposed to approximate in practice the value of equal respect and concern that moral egalitarianism presupposes. At the same time, institutions need to encourage their citizens to internalize these principles: like any other political regime, liberal democracy depends for its reproduction on the robustness of an ethos of mutual respect and concern.

Given that liberal democracy is the goal of transitional processes, the values it presupposes set the objectives of, as well as the constraints on, TJ projects. In other words, the public affirmation and institutionalization of the value of respect and concern for all requires that certain TJ measures be taken, and that they be taken in certain ways. The commitment to equality demands that institutional steps be taken to address the violations of the past and the concerns of the victims in a way that does not scapegoat the victimizers. While a massive literature has been dedicated to the needs of the victims within the typical TJ processes (Hayner 2001, Stover and Weinstein 2004, Philpott 2006, Torpey 2006, Urban Walker 2006, Verdeja 2009, Leebaw 2011), less has been written on the symbolic humiliation that certain public constructions inherited from a previous regime can inflict on previously oppressed groups (Levinson 1998; Coombes 2003; Bell 2008). This is rather surprising given that statues, flags and portraits are often revolutionaries' first victims. In what follows, I will introduce Christian Neuhäuser's (2011) account of collective symbolic humiliation as a useful tool for understanding what is at stake in doing monumental justice in the aftermath of democratic change.

In Neuhäuser's view, humiliations 'attempt to lower someone below the status of a human being as a person with dignity through an improper attitude or treatment' (2011: 22). While it is undisputable today that individuals have dignity and can be humiliated, it is more controversial to argue that groups can suffer demeaning treatment. Neuhäuser thinks that, by outlining a typology of group humiliations, it will become clear to what extent one can meaningfully talk of group humiliation.

The first form of group humiliation he discusses is *direct*: it targets all the members of the group precisely because they are the members of the group. It is only because they belong to this group that a certain set of characteristics is ascribed to these individuals, characteristics that, in the eyes of the humiliating agent, justify the demeaning treatment. The example the author gives is of imagined – yet not too implausible – police filters being established on airports to exclusively check those who appear to be Muslims. I would add the more mundane examples that could be derived from the historical – and continued – marginalization of women and homosexuals, racial profiling or the 'stop-and-frisk' policies in operation in some parts of the US. Certain groups' exclusion from the protective scope of liberal democratic rights amounts to *direct* humiliation.

Neuhäuser then turns to *representative* group humiliation, which he describes as the humiliation of a whole group through the humiliation of one of its members. For representative group

3 I borrow the concept of 'a theory of human worth' from Murphy and Hampton 1988.

humiliation to obtain, three conditions must be fulfilled: '(I) the humiliation is directed against a collectively shared part of identity; (II) this shared part of identity is constitutive for the self-respect of the members of this group; (III) the humiliation is sanctioned on a social level and/or no appropriate measures against it are taken' (Neuhäuser 2011: 30). Clear examples are Rodney King's beating or the torture of prisoners in Abu Ghraib and Guantanamo Bay. In all these cases, individuals were singled out for their identity and debased by virtue of possessing that identity.

The third type of group humiliation – and the one that is of most importance for this chapter – is *symbolic* group humiliation. In this case, a symbol of the group is defiled and the defiling 'is connected to past humiliations or the threat of present humiliations' (Neuhäuser 2011: 32). Destroying Jewish cemeteries and showing abasing portraits of gays on TV are the two examples Neuhäuser offers for this category. In order to understand the humiliating dimension of these acts it is necessary to examine the intention behind them. If the symbolic act expresses an exclusionary attitude, if it shows that less respect and concern is owed to individuals, if there is a possibility that the members of the group will face threats by virtue of belonging to that group, then we are witnessing *symbolic* group humiliation.

As will become clear later on, this chapter argues that *symbolic* humiliation is perpetuated if successor states leave unaddressed – or continue to sponsor – monuments, memorials and other public buildings that populate a polity's 'sacred space' and transmit a message about (some) citizens' inferiority. Public constructions that contradict moral egalitarianism endanger the normative integrity of a liberal democracy and can, under certain circumstances, negatively impact the institutions' legitimacy. Representing certain groups as less than human, glorifying former victimizers, or excluding the members of marginalized groups from monuments are just three of the ways in which public constructions can symbolically humiliate citizens.

The second section will employ the idea of *symbolic* humiliation to critically engage Sanford Levinson's path-breaking book on the ways in which a democracy can deal with its undemocratic monuments. While Levinson's recommendations constitute a good starting point for reflection on monumental transitional justice, I argue that his preference for a policy of monumental inclusion needs to be tempered by a concern with moral egalitarianism and what it implies for the state as the main memory entrepreneur.[4]

The Limits of Democratic Monumental Inclusion

Levinson's *Written in Stone* (2011) is one of the few works that tries to examine the normative connection between democratic ideals and the public art occupying a country's 'sacred space'. While his book explores a multitude of cases from all over the world in order to highlight the vulnerability of public art to political change, his main focus lies with the South of the United States and the challenges that monuments dedicated to the confederate cause pose for democracy. This section seeks to recuperate the theoretical tools Levinson offers us, while at the same time critically engaging with his account of democratic monumental inclusion.

Levinson's starting point is that 'sacred grounds' serve as the space for public art, art that is never innocent or neutral. He quickly – and correctly, I think – dismisses the idea that the state should remain neutral with regard to the figures and events it celebrates or commemorates. Public constructions constitute the means through which the state seeks to inculcate certain attitudes in the citizens: attitudes favourable to the normative, political, and cultural order the state embodies (2011:

4 The state is the main memory entrepreneur due to the disproportionate amount of resources it usually commands in comparison with private agents.

38–9). The problem is that the public is often divided over who their heroes are. For example, in the case of the United States, many racist monuments punctuate the Southern states, sitting uneasily with the principles the American society currently embraces, at least at the declarative level. The Liberty Monument in New Orleans or the statues of the generals who led the Confederate army in Richmond constitute such examples. The question then is, how should a democratic state deal with racist monuments that can still resonate with a large part of the American citizenry?

In trying to answer this question democratically, Levinson proposes a number of suggestions (2011: 114–23). First, the state can leave the problematic monument as it is, as a testimony of the past and as representative of certain views entertained by sectors of the American public. Since democracy is a regime of inclusiveness, leaving the monument untouched gives voice to the groups who identify with that version of history glorified by the construction. Second, he suggests placing a plaque stating that the state does not identify with the ideas depicted in the monument – a symbolic distanciation from a past of violence. Third, the authorities could install a sign affirming the state's indifference to the message the monument transmits to the public. In this sense, the state would adopt a neutral position towards the various (material) visions of history. Fourth, Levinson proposes that the state explicitly disavow the ideas the construction materializes. A clear-cut discontinuity would thus be marked between the times of inequality and victimization, and the new era of democratic inclusiveness. Fifth, a monument celebrating those who resisted the *ancien régime* could be erected as a counterweight, with or without an explanatory plaque. This would amount to a recalibrating of the balance of symbolic power in the 'sacred space'. Similarly, the sixth idea is to build a multitude of monuments dedicated to the various groups of victims who suffered under the previous regime. Seventh, Levinson recommends the historicization of the monument by means of its museumification. Moving the monument within the precinct of a museum relegates it to the past, at a distance from the present and the values society currently celebrates. Eighth, one could sandblast the text inscribed on the monument and either replace it with a more appropriate one or leave it blank for the viewer's interpretation. Ninth, the most radical solution: destroy the monument.

Levinson's nine recommendations have great potential in terms of formulating a democratically appropriate policy of dealing with democratically inappropriate monuments. Armed with the theoretical tools developed in the previous section, let us now examine them one by one.

Leaving the monument as it is could be a tempting proposal for a state aiming to cultivate a plurivocal 'sacred space', where different and diverging visions of the past can be expressed. Given the contestable character of all 'official stories', it has been argued that a diverse landscape of competing narratives might be a better solution. For example, Duncan Bell writes: '[I]n order to facilitate a pluralistic radical democracy, it is essential to acknowledge multiple and often conflicting pasts, and the intrinsically power-infused and tension-ridden nature of communal mythological construction' (2008: 149). For authors like Bell, excluding some groups' vision of what happened might humiliate the members of those groups (2008: 159). While I find the idea of a pluralist 'sacred space' powerful and plausible as the solution for our conundrum, the versions of the past competing for admission can be radically different in terms of their compatibility with an egalitarian theory of moral worth. Given the commitment to equal concern and respect for all citizens, it is contradictory to opt for an unrestricted policy of 'let a thousand flowers bloom'. Some flowers can poison the democratic public space with their scent. In other words, monuments that symbolically humiliate citizens by relegating them to a subordinate position are problematic from a liberal democratic point of view. Leaving the monument as it is, or adding a plaque that affirms the state's neutrality towards the narrative the monument presents, are two courses of action in tension with the fact that liberal democracy is a normative, political and cultural regime seeking to reproduce itself across generations. Once we honestly admit the partisanship of the liberal democratic creed, we understand that not all ways of relating to the past are compatible with the values of this creed. An attitude of 'anything goes' establishes a problematic equivalence between inclusive and exclusive, racist and respectful, totalitarian and democratic ways of looking at past events. Naturally, deciding which monument belongs to which category is a complex business that requires contextualized judgement. However, a good starting point is to think whether the monuments under consideration could symbolically humiliate certain groups by telling a story about their inferiority or by misrepresenting their contribution to the political past of the nation. If that is the case, then a plaque whereby the state distances itself from such problematic understandings of social relations is the least authorities can do to affirm the state's equal concern and respect to all citizens. A sign that explicitly condemns past abuses is an even better way of marking discontinuity with the violations of the previous regime. If the goal is to instil citizens with a democratic ethos and fight against exclusionary attitudes, efforts must be made to purge the 'sacred space' of monuments that symbolically humiliate certain groups and help reproduce undemocratic views.

Levinson's fifth idea – to build an alternative monument – can be compatible with the normative integrity of a liberal democracy as long as the state explicitly addresses the reasoning behind the new construction. Only in this way can a problematic normative equivalence between the two monuments be avoided and relativist positions on the past discouraged. The same goes for building a multitude of monuments to the various groups of victims of a former regime: giving voice to the silenced victims needs to be accompanied by a public disavowal of the problematic voices of the victimizers.

Museumification can go a long way in ensuring monuments that constitute normatively impermissible glorifications of the past do not continue to humiliate certain groups. Changing the lenses through which we look at such constructions can allow contextualization, a more complex understanding, and even historical learning. However, museumification is not as easy a solution as it appears. As Levinson himself remarks, the burden is on curators to present the monument for what it is and prevent the museum from becoming a place where some are humiliated, while others feed their discriminatory views.

The eighth suggestion – to rewrite the text of the monument – depends on the interpretive malleability of the monument, which is a matter of degree. Some monuments can be more easily appropriated by a democratic regime than others. Should the monument allow for multiple readings, changing the text could be a productive avenue, one that nonetheless requires creativity and careful judgement.

Last but not least, destroying the monument. Levinson accepts the fact that some monuments are so infamous because of their association with a history of atrocity that it is no wonder they should be destroyed. However, I would like to propose that, should the state decide to destroy the monument, an important didactic opportunity might be lost. Rather than razing the monument – and thus risking a backlash form those enamoured with the narrative the monument tells – it might be better to choose from the options discussed above one that clearly disavows political oppression and reaffirms the commitment to fight against anybody's exclusion from without the scope of liberal principles.

Illustrations

This section offers an analysis of two cases, meant to highlight the challenges facing any attempt to deal with materialized symbolic humiliation. I have chosen to examine the Voortrekker

Monument south of Pretoria in South Africa and the People's House in Bucharest, Romania. The reason for choosing these two monuments is that they illustrate two forms of symbolic humiliation: *racial* and *political*. The former symbolically humiliates Black South Africans through its portrayal of their ancestors as treacherous killers in need of white civilization, while the latter degrades an entire people by symbolically expressing the society's subordination to an almighty state and the transformation of citizens into hostages. The two constructions belong to two different transitional contexts: in one case democracy followed a cruel regime of racial segregation, in the other a 'sultanistic'[5] form of totalitarianism. In addition, they are both particularly large constructions that dominate the 'sacred space' of their home societies, thereby posing particularly difficult practical challenges to the successor elites.

The Voortrekker Monument

In 1931, riding on a wave of growing Afrikaner nationalism, the Federation of Afrikaner Cultural Associations proposed a monument dedicated to the Great Boer Trek of 1838. The state provided most of the finances for the monument but, because of the economic crisis of the 1930s and the

Figure 12.1 The exterior of the Voortrekker Monument

Source: © Iolanda Vasile.

5 The term was coined by Linz and Stepan (1998) to refer to a particularly robust and personalized form of authoritarianism.

breakout of the Second World War, it was inaugurated only in 1949, a few months after one of the nationalist Afrikaner parties won the elections on the apartheid platform (Delmont 1993: 78). The inauguration was a spectacle of obscene ethnic feeling and aggrandizing myth-making, gathering thousands of pilgrims in Boer costumes who symbolically joined the great Trek of white Christian heroes (Coombes 2003: 26). Thus, the political and symbolic triumph of Afrikaner Calvinist Nationalism was emphatically celebrated.

The monument stands on a hill outside Pretoria, directly visible from the South African parliament. It is a large structure in the middle of a wild piece of land – a symbol of white mastery over the vast African veld. Its dimensions were meant to reflect the Afrikaners' contribution to South Africa: it measures 40 metres in length and width and 41 metres in height (Crampton 2001: 237–40). The upper hall – the Hall of Heroes – features a frieze representing the obstacles the heroic trekkers had to overcome on their quest to bring white Christian civilization to the *terra nullius* of in-land South Africa (Beningfield 2006). The frieze shows the Boers as God-fearing, upright, family people, peacefully negotiating their way through the territory, in contradistinction with the barbarous, murderous Zulus, stealth killers subject only to the law of the jungle. Inter-tribal conflict is starkly contrasted with the harmony of the trekkers and is used – as in many places around the world – as a justification for colonization: the indigenous population was not 'fit' to rule the harsh, yet bountiful territory (Delmont 1993: 96; Beningfield 2006: 58). On each 16 December – the day of the 1838 Battle of Blood River against the Zulus, when the trekkers made their vow to honour

Figure 12.2 The Cenotaph

Source: © Iolanda Vasile.

God if they won – at midday, a ray of sunlight falls on the cenotaph in the centre of the monument, shining on the inscription 'We for thee, South Africa'.

This optical effect is considered a sign that God endorsed the trekkers' mission (Delmont 1993: 88). Such narratives of divinely sanctioned civilizing missions were subsequently instrumental to the legitimization of apartheid.

Before the 1994 elections, the monument became the rallying point of those who resented the impending end of racial segregation. Right wing Afrikaner groups met and voiced their fear of losing their linguistic and material culture at the hands of the ANC. In 1993, the main association for Afrikaner culture invoked cultural preservation so as to buy the right to manage the monument from the outgoing National Party Government. This was a prudential decision and a cynical move to claim a right that had been systematically refused to the indigenous population (Coombes 2003: 32–3).

After 1994, a public debate about the fate of the monument ensued. Some suggested it should be preserved as a reminder of the past violations, while others wanted it demolished. The ANC decided that all apartheid monuments should be preserved and continued to provide funding to all of them. According to the website of the monument, it still receives up to 16 per cent of its finances from the state today.[6] The idea of a massive construction in the shape of Nelson Mandela's hand was proposed as a counterweight, but was soon discarded due to the sculptor's association with apartheid, the totalitarian style of the drawings, and the source of the funding: two companies specializing in skin whitening products (Coombes 2003: 20–22).

Private actors tried to subvert the political message of the monument after 1994. Ironic pornographic photos were taken at the site in 1995. The idea of painting the monument pink and organizing a gay rave inside it was discussed, provoking the outrage of those still enamoured with the version of the past immortalized in the construction. Several other applications to use the monument as a venue for dancing events were rejected by the managing organization (Coombes 2003: 50–51).

Commentators disagree about the power the monument still has today. Some think it holds many Afrikaners captive and insults those Blacks who come to see its distorted representation of colonization (Coombes 2003). Others proposed that Blacks now look on the monumental landscape of apartheid from a position of power and that, consequently, they are no longer affected by it (Grundlingh 2001). The fact remains, however, that he Voortrekker Monument is still one of the most visited in South Africa, with hundreds of thousands of tourists flooding its gates every year (Gauteng Tourist Attractions). The democratic regime did not interfere with the privatization deal, probably in an attempt to relativize the monument's symbolically humiliating representations. However, the post-apartheid state made impressive efforts to counterweigh such racist monuments, District Six and the Robben Island Museums being the clearest examples. Rather than destroying or explicitly censoring the problematic monument, the newly elected officials appear to have embraced the idea that democracy requires a polyphonic public memory. It might be that, given the discourse of national reconciliation promoted by the Truth and Reconciliation Commission (TRC) and inscribed in the South African Constitution of 1994, the ANC did not want to further antagonize certain groups and opted for a policy of even-handedness: sponsoring both old and new monuments alike.

While acknowledging its pragmatic value, many have criticised the approach to reconciliation promoted by the TRC. The reason is that it set on an equal footing the crimes of the apartheid police and the crimes of those fighting for political emancipation. I argue that the same problem plagues the policy of even-handedness the ANC governments took towards material public memory. The fact remains that some of the beneficiaries of the state's even-handedness still tell an exclusionary, racist, and truncated version of history. Nothing in the construction has changed – representationally

6 See Voortrekker Monument 2007.

and narratively – since the end of apartheid: the same story of heroic white civilizers is retold to groups of school pupils and foreign tourists alike. In spite of the counterweight museums, failing to explicitly disavow the skewed version of the past materialized in the Voortrekker Monument establishes a problematic equality between the story of Afrikaner heroism and that of Black suffering under apartheid, thus showing the limits of the state's strategy.

The People's House

Between 1965 and 1989, Romania lived under the most oppressive communist regimes in Eastern Europe, Nicolae Ceauşescu's 'personal neo-Stalinism' (Tismaneanu 1991). The grip of the party-state over society was exceptional. The secret police – the infamous 'Securitate' – annihilated dissidents and 'facilitated' the dictator's programmes of forced urbanization and industralization, the destruction of the cultural patrimony, the persecution of certain unaligned religions, and a megalomaniac cult of personality (Tismaneanu 1993, Judt 2005).

After the mock trial and execution of the dictator and his wife in 1989, a newly formed organization, the 'Front of National Salvation' (FSN) took over the main institutions of the state. It was made up of former top communist apparatchiks who had been marginalized by the dictator in the last years of the regime. They won the first free elections and stayed in power (as the Social Democratic Party, PSD) until 1997, when the forces of the new (the liberal democrats, the Democratic Convention) won the elections. However, with economic disaster plaguing the liberal democrats' mandate, PSD won the 2000–2004 mandate, and again in 2012.

Beside the reproduction of the communist elite under different guise, the architecture brutally imposed on the country is one of the most enduring legacies of Romanian totalitarianism. After a massive earthquake struck in 1977, the dictator decided to embark on a massive architectural project for the country's 'sacred space'. The project meant to impose his megalomaniacal tastes on the capital and, at the same time, to 'mould' citizens into politically insignificant, abject subjects. The brutal transformation of Bucharest constituted a manoeuvre to affirm the power of the ubiquitous, all-knowing, and all-powerful state and its leader.

The Civic Centre – the official title of the complex – comprises the House of the Republic and The Victory of Socialism Boulevard, which can be seen from any corner of the capital.[7] The House of the Republic is the second largest building in the world and carries an estimate price tag of 1.5–4 billion USD (O'Neill 2009). About 20,000 conscripted workers contributed to the building that, in line with the rabidly nationalistic variety of communism that Ceauşescu embraced after 1968, was made exclusively of Romanian materials (Ioan 2009). The adjoining boulevard is longer and wider than the Champs-Élysées and is lined with apartment blocks for the members of the party nomenclature and the state bureaucrats. It also features 42 large, ornate fountains.

Work on the complex began in 1984 and the building is still today incomplete. 9,300 homes were destroyed and 40,000 people were displaced to make room for the project. Numerous churches, some of them medieval, were either demolished or relocated (Danta 1993). The statistics are staggering: the building is 270 metres long and 240 metres wide, measuring 86 metres above ground and 92 metres underground. It has 1,000 rooms and a total surface of 330,000 metres^2 (Light 2000: 7).

7 In my discussion of this case I rely on secondary sources but also on my own experience as an intern with an NGO that organized guided visits for high-school pupils in the Romanian Parliament (2002–2003).

Figure 12.3 The Victory of Socialism Boulevard

Source: © Mihaela Mihai.

Figure 12.4 Exterior of the People's House

Source: Mihaela Mihai.

The materialization of this project coincided with the most difficult years for the Romanian population, years marred by intensified political terror and by a humiliating, artificially induced famine[8] that ultimately led to the fall of the regime. While millions of citizens lived in inhumanly small, crowded, poorly lit and cold apartments – the infamous 'match boxes', the staple of the abusive urbanization project – and struggled to survive on strictly rationed food, the House of the Republic was eating up immense financial and labour resources. In Neuhäuser's terms, the tyrant humiliated the people, both directly and symbolically.

After the violent overthrow of 1989, there was a public debate about what to do with the building. Its name changed to the People's House, in recognition of the fact that it was the people's work that brought it into existence. Because of its association with political oppression, many wanted it demolished; others proposed that a Museum of Communism should be housed in it; some even argued that it could be transformed into a casino (Salecl 1999). Given the reproduction of communist elites after 1989, it was finally decided that work should resume on the building, with a view to relocating the parliament, the Ombudsman and the Constitutional Court to the newly renamed Palace of the Parliament. Ironically enough, this was Ceauşescu's plan: to gather all central institutions in one, extraordinary building.

Guided tours in several languages are currently available to a public mostly composed of foreign tourists (Light 2000). The narrative focuses on the extreme dimensions of the palace and on the Romanian provenience of the construction materials. The bleak story of the labour that went into this project, as well as the discrepancy between this construction and the uncomfortable flats ordinary citizens inhabited before 1989 – and that most Romanians continue to inhabit today – is left out in an effort to present the country in brighter colours (Light 2001).

The main attempt to detoxify the construction was the opening of the National Museum of Contemporary Art (MNAC). It occupies one of the wings of the building and was inaugurated with a series of exhibitions exploring the relationship between art, the history of communism, and of the building itself.[9] Two new glass elevators flank the unit in which is the museum is housed, partially muting the heavy external adornments. On the inside, some ornaments were removed and while panelling was installed to neutralize the space for the future exhibitions. Access to the museum remains, however, difficult, as sharing the same building with MPs implies heavy security controls (Ioan 2005).

While the MNAC could be read as a partially successful attempt to change the register of the building, I want to suggest that it is, on its own, insufficient. The main problem lies with the fact that the successor regime continued to fund work on this building and then relocated to the old seat of power. Such a move cancels all efforts to show discontinuity with a vision of the state as all-powerful, unaccountable, and inaccessible. As the expression of authoritarian politics, the complex marks the 'sacred space' in a way that places citizens in a relation of subordination to the state. During communism, citizens were transformed into subjects, humiliated politically, physically, and symbolically. The disproportionate relationship between the Civic Centre and the rest of the city, as well as the sense of remoteness and fear that one gets when looking at the building form the outside, clearly point to an idea of an absolute, durable state dominating society. In Light's words, the building is 'No sane government would build such an edifice' (2001: 1064).

The question is, what sane *democratic* government would inhabit it in the wake of totalitarianism. The decision to continue injecting funds in the building diverted important resources from a population impoverished and brutalized by the long years of repression. By placing democratic

8 The famine was the result of an effort to rapidly acquit Romania's sovereign debt and thus affirm international economic independence.

9 For an overview of the opening exhibitions, see MNAC 2004.

institutions in a construction that sits uneasily with democratic values, the successor elites continue to symbolically humiliate citizens. This is aggravated by the fact that in 2014 Romania still does not have a monumental counterweight or a national museum dedicated to the communist period.

Unfortunately, after 1989, the humiliation of the citizens by the state is not just symbolic, it is also direct: the high levels of systemic corruption marring the central institutions, the generalized public disillusionment with politics and the feebleness and impotence of public protest have been the constant markers of post 1989 politics.[10] In spite of the country's admission to the European Union and meaningful progress in the area of human rights and economic development, Romania remains a country where the political elite does not act responsibly towards its citizens. While the people built the house, while attempts have been made to give the house back to the people by opening it to the public for visits and by the creation of the MNAC, the people are still politically left outside their house.

Conclusion

While schematic due to space constraints, the empirical analysis highlights the challenges that monumental legacies raise for democracy. South Africa's approach to the Voortrekker Monument seems to follow the line of national reconciliation advanced by the TRC, thus reproducing its normative shortcomings. By continuing to partially sponsor the monument and by not instigating any recalibration of the skewed message written in the stones of the monument, the policy of even-handedness obscures the differences between the suffering of the colonizers and that of the colonized. The message about the immorality of the Zulus and their inferiority to the Trekkers gets reproduced unmodified even today, thus symbolically humiliating those who see their ancestors portrayed as treacherous savages in need of the disciplining force of white civilization. In the wake of apartheid, it is difficult to see how such a narrative could legitimately occupy the democratic 'sacred space'. While counterweight monuments go a long way in levelling the monumental playfield, more needs to be done to prevent the continuing symbolic humiliation and challenge the racist attitudes the monument expresses and encourages.

The Romanian case highlights a more extensive form of symbolic humiliation, one that encompasses the entire population. The continued use of the People's House as the seat of democratic institutions, as well as its financing by the state during the painful years of the transition, fail to mark discontinuity with a past where citizens were nothing more than hostages of the almighty state. The opening of the MNAC could be interpreted as a first step in the direction of disavowal. Yet, the failure to establish a credible counterweight public project and to change the register of the Civic Centre reveal the reproduction of a problematic vision of the relationship between the state and society.

Before I conclude, a few potential criticisms. First, a realist might claim that, during transitional times, there are more urgent imperatives than monumental justice. I agree with such prudential concerns, but I would argue that they only justify the postponing, but not the irrelevance, of disavowal. Plus, given what happens to statues of former leaders and heroes during dramatic moments of political transformation there are reasons to believe that citizens do care about public monuments they deem humiliating.

Second, one might object that not all monuments are clearly humiliating. Oftentimes, the narrative told is rather ambiguous. This is indeed, a valid observation: some monuments are subtle, allowing multiple interpretations and democratic appropriations. Less radical approaches can be

10 Recent polls show that over 60% of Romanians have very little trust in the democratic institutions and that the perception of institutionalized corruption is very high (Transparency International 2012, INSCOP 2013).

successful in such cases. What to do with such monuments will ultimately remain a contextual, political decision, guided by the aspiration to protect citizens in the present.

Last but not least, one might ask whether democracies need monuments at all. A plausible argument could be made to the effect that a commitment to equality and the glorification of heroic figures are inconsistent. This chapter has taken a less radical route and argued that democracy sets a limit to the kind of monuments democracies can accept as appropriate. Besides normative integrity, transitional societies must also face the functional imperative of historical continuity as cohesive political communities. And, provided monuments are inclusive and do not humiliate anyone, they can play an important role in cultivating a sense of solidarity and stability.

Bibliography

Arthur, Paige. 2011. *Identities in Transition: Challenges for Transitional Justice in Divided Societies*. New York: Cambridge University Press.

Bell, Duncan. 2008. "Agonistic Democracy and the Politics of Memory." *Constellations: An International Journal of Critical and Democratic Theory* 15(1): 148–66.

Beningfield, Jennifer. 2006. *The Frightened Land: Land, Landscape and Politics in South Africa in the Twentieth Century*. Abingdon: Routledge.

Coombes, Annie E. 2003. *History after Apartheid: Visual Culture and Public Memory in a Democratic South Africa*. Johannesburg: Wits University Press.

Corradetti, Claudio. 2012. 'Transitional Justice and the Truth-Constraints of the Public Sphere'. *Philosophy and Social Criticism* 38(7): 685–700.

Crampton, Andrew. 2001. 'The Voortrekker Monument, the Birth of Apartheid and Beyond'. *Political Geography* 20: 221–46.

Czepczynski, Mariusz. 2012. *Cultural Landscapes of Post-Socialist Cities: Representations of Powers and Needs*. Farnham: Ashgate.

Danta, D. 1993. 'Ceausescu's Bucharest'. *Geographical Review* 83(2): 170–82.

Delmonth, Elizabeth. 1993. 'The Voortrekker Monument: Monolith to Myth'. *South African Historical Journal* 29(1): 76–101.

Eisikovits, Nir. 2010. *Sympathizing with the Enemy: Reconciliation, Transitional Justice, Negotiation*. Dordrecht, the Netherlands, and St. Louis, MO: Republic of Letters Publishing.

Gauteng Toursit Attatractions. 2013. 'Voortrekker Monument'. Accessed 23 August 2013. http://www.sa-venues.com/attractionsga/voortrekker-monument.htm.

Grundlingh, A.M. 2001. 'A Cultural Conundrum? Old Monuments and New Regimes: The Voortrekker Monument as Symbol of Afrikaner Power in a Postapartheid South Africa'. *Radical History Review* 81: 95–112.

Hayner, Priscilla B. 2001. *Unspeakable Truths: Confronting State Terror and Atrocity*. New York: Routledge.

INSCOP. 9 April 2013. 'Încrederea în instituţii'. Accessed 20 August 2013. http://www.inscop.ro/aprilie-2013-incredere-in-institutii.

Ioan, Augustin. 2008. 'Bucharest's National Museum of Contemporary Art in the Bog House'. *ArtMargins*, 28 April. Accessed 20 August 2013. http://www.artmargins.com/index.php/2-articles/102-bucharests-national-museum-of-contemporary-art-in-the-big-house.

Ioan, Augustin. 2009. *Modern Architecture and the Totalitarian Project: A Romanian Case Study*. Bucharest: Institutul Cultural Roman.

Judt, Tony. 2005. *Post-War: A History of Europe since 1945*. London: Penguin.

Leebaw, Bronwyn. 2011. *Judging State-Sponsored Violence, Imagining Political Change*. Cambridge: Cambridge University Press.

Lehrer, Erica, Cynthia E. Milton and Monica Eileen Patterson (eds). 2011. *Curating Difficult Knowledge: Violent Pasts in Public Spaces*. Houndmills: Palgrave Macmillan.

Levinson, Sanford. 1998. *Written in Stone: Public Monuments in Changing Societies*. Durham, NC: Duke University Press.

Light, Duncan. 2000. 'An Unwanted Past: Contemporary Tourism and the Heritage of Communism in Romania'. *International Journal of Heritage Studies* 6(2): 145–60.

Light, Duncan. 2001.''Facing the Future': Tourism and identity-building in post-socialist Romania'. *Political Geography* 20: 1053–74.

Linz, Juan and Alfred Stepan. 1998. *Problems of Democratic Transition and Consolidation: Southern Europe, South America and Post-Communist Europe*. New York: New York University Press.

May, Larry. 2012. *After war Ends: A Philosophical Perspective*. Cambridge: Cambridge University Press.

Michalski, Sergiusz. 1998. *Public Monuments: Art in Political Bondage, 1870–1997*. London: Reaktion Books.

MNAC. 2004. 'Inaugurare'. Last modified 29 April 2004. http://www.mnac.ro/archives/category/history/inaugurare.

Murphy, Jeffrie G. and Jean Hampton. 1988. *Forgiveness and Mercy*. New York: Cambridge University Press.

Neuhäuser, Cristian. 2010. "Humiliation: The Collective Dimension." In *Humiliation, Degradation, Dehumanization: Human Dignity Violated*, edited by P. Kaufmann, H. Kuch, C. Neuhäuser, and E. Webster, 21–36.Dordrecht: Springer.

Olsen, Tricia D., Leigh A. Payne and Andrew G. Reiter. 2010. *Transitional Justice in Balance: Comparing Processes, Weighing Efficacy*. Washington, DC: United States Institute of Peace.

O'Neill, Bruce. 2009. 'The Political Agency of Cityscapes: Spatializing Governance in Ceausescu's Bucharest'.*Journal of Social Archaeology* 9: 92–109.

Philpott, Daniel (ed.). 2006. *The Politics of Past Evil: Religion, Reconciliation and the Dilemmas of Transitional Justice*. Notre Dame, IN: University of Notre Dame Press.

Salecl, R. 1999. 'The State as a Work of Art: The Trauma of Ceauşescu's Disneyland'. In *Architecture and Revolution: Contemporary Perspectives on Central and Eastern Europe*, edited by N. Leach, 92–111. London: Routledge.

Stover, Eric and Harvey M. Weinstein (eds). 2004. *My Neighbor, My Enemy: Justice and Community in the Aftermath of Mass Atrocity*. Cambridge: Cambridge University Press.

Tismaneanu, Vladimir. 1991. 'The Revival of Politics in Romania'. *Proceedings of the Academy of Political Science*. 38(1): 85–99.

Tismaneanu, Vladimir. 1993. 'The Quasi-Revolution and Its Discontents: Emerging Political Pluralism in Post-Ceausescu Romania'. *East European Politics and Society* 7(2): 309–48.

Torpey, John C. 2006. *Making Whole What Has Been Smashed: On Reparation Politics*. Cambridge, MA: Harvard University Press.

Transparency International. 2012. 'Corruption Perception Index 2012'. Accessed 20 August 2013. http://www.transparency.org/cpi2012/results.

Urban Walker, Margaret. 2006. *Moral Repair: Reconstructing Moral Relations after Wrongdoing*. New York: Cambridge University Press.

Verdeja, Ernesto. 2009. *Unchopping a Tree: Reconciliation in the Aftermath of Political Violence*. Philadelphia, PA: Temple University Press.

Voortrekker Monument. 2007. 'Who is the Voortrekker Monument Group?' Accessed 23 August 2013. http://www.voortrekkermon.org.za/who.php.

Walkowitz, Daniel and Lisa Maya Knauer (eds). 2004. *Memory and the Impact of Political Transformation in Public Space*. Durham, NC: Duke University Press.

Winter, Jay. 1995. *Sites of Memory, Sites of Mourning: The Great War in European Cultural History*. Cambridge: Cambridge University Press.

Young, James E. 2000. *At Memory's Edge: After-Images of the Holocaust in Contemporary Art and Architecture*. New Haven, CT: Yale University Press.

PART VI
Defining the Parameters of Transitional Justice

Chapter 13

Transitional Times, Reflective Judgement and the 'Hōs mē' Condition

Claudio Corradetti[1]

'The Time that Remains' as the Circumstance of Transitional Justice

The temporal dimension of justice has been very often a neglected aspect of standard normative theories. Nevertheless, time is an unavoidable condition for determining whether political and/or judicial decisions are taken appropriately. Indeed, more than any other 'factual' externalities, temporal dimensions do incorporate a normative aspect. This suggested link directs the investigation of what seems to be an inherent interconnection between time and normativity also into what is a more benevolent understanding of Hume's 'circumstances' of justice. Following this initial move, the understanding of transitional justice as a normative paradigm must be understood as a domain affected by time.

With regard to such preliminary considerations, the present contribution aims to provide a rejoinder to the recent debate on the ideal/non-ideal conditions of justice with the introduction of the intermediate notion of 'the transitional'. It also wants to achieve this goal by expanding on the judicial aspect of Kantian *reflective judgement* [*reflektierende Urteilskraft*] as according to Arendt's interpretation.[2] This will be pursued through the definition of a hypothesis of (dialectical) complementarity between Kantian orienting principle for the purposiveness of judgement and the transitional reading of the Pauline 'Hos me' (as not) condition as suggested by Agamben which has been also recently extended to the transitional justice context by Meister in his recent work.[3] One of the major assumptions that I will consider includes the notion of how transitional conditions play a

1 Paper presented at the General Conference of the European Consortium of Political Research, Sciences Po – Bordeaux 4–7 September 2013. For comments and suggestions on earlier versions, I would like to thank A. Follesdal, R. Maliks, Ø. Stokke, A. Ferrara, L. Zerilli, A. Berg-Sorensen, M. Thaler and M. Mihai. All remaining errors are mine. This chapter was prepared under the auspices of MultiRights, European Research Council Advanced Grant #269841 at the University of Oslo, Norway.

2 Arendt points out a too often overlooked connection between Kant's notion of judgement regarding the impartial spectator and the idea of endless human progress in history: 'Perpetual progress toward freedom and peace, the latter guaranteeing free intercourse between all nations on the earth: these are the ideas of reason, without which the mere story of history would not make sense' … 'One judges always as a member of a community, guided by one's community sense, one's *sensus communis*. But … one is a member of a world community by the sheer fact of being human; this is one's "cosmopolitan existence." When one judges … one is supposed … of being a world citizen and therefore, also a *Weltbetrachter*, a world spectator'. In H. Arendt, *Lectures on Kant's Political Philosophy*, ed. R. Beiner, Chicago, IL: The University of Chicago Press, [1982] 1992, p. 59 and pp. 75–6. It is under this historical profile that I will develop a revised version of the role of judgement in transitional times.

3 As Agamben says: 'Che cosa ha a che fare Paolo con tutto questo? Il messianico è per lui il luogo di un'esigenza, che concerne precisamente la redenzione di ciò che è stato. Esso non è un punto di vista, dal quale si possa guardare al mondo come se la redenzione fosse compiuta. L'avvento del messia significa che tutte le cose – e con esse il soggetto che le guarda – sono prese nel *come non*, chiamate e revocate nello stesso gesto. Non vi è più alcun soggetto che guarda e che potrebbe, a un certo punto, decidere di fare *come se*'. In G. Agamben, *Il tempo che resta. Un commento alla Lettera ai Romani*. Turin: Bollati Boringhieri [2000] 2005, p. 44ff. See R. Meister, *After Evil: A Politics of Human Rights*, New York: Columbia University Press, 2011.

fundamental role in defining backward-and-forward orientations within the normative function of judgement, as well as how such inherent dialectic will prevent any meaningful separation between purely retributive and purely restorative judgements under transitional circumstances of justice.[4]

In recent times a predominant philosophical attitude has shaped our understanding of justice. This has mainly consisted of an 'objectifying' tendency on normative thinking resulting, among other things, in a separation of the principles of justice from the same conditions under which justice aims to achieve its purposes.

Is the saying according to which 'it is never the time for justice' to be interpreted as meaning that 'there is not a time that properly belongs to justice'? Is justice a condition external to any temporal dimension of existence? If this is so, how illuminating could such an understanding be for us as subjects regulating our interests within contingently given political communities? For whom would such principles be instructive if conceived independently from our agent-capacity embedded in time?

In order to answer these questions, I will start from the discussion of Hume's understanding of the circumstances of justice and propose to expand the list with the inclusion of the notion of 'time' as the mode in which other scarcities are presented and historically accountable.

In his *Treatise of Human Nature*, Hume claims that it is: ' ... from the selfishness and confined generosity of men, along with the scanty provision nature has made for his wants, that justice derives its origin'.[5] This same point has also been reconsidered later by J. Rawls who in *A Theory of Justice* has noticed how the circumstances of justice ' ... may be divided into two kinds. First ... objective circumstances which make human cooperation both possible and necessary' such as primarily 'moderate scarcity' and then ... the case of 'subjective circumstances' such as 'conflict of interests' both forcing men to cooperate.[6] The concern over clarifying those factual elements entrenched within theories of justice indicates that the matter of justice arises only in case the scarcity of goods is not too severe and conflicts of interest not too harsh. Any factual condition moving beyond such boundaries would prevent even the arousal of any question concerning justice. This middle ground terrain for justice also sets the level that standards within theories of justice should be apt to achieve, that is, the capacity they must show to account for empirical aspects of the world while proposing normative criteria. Yet, it seems from this picture that something still remains unconsidered, namely the fact that both subjective interests and objective externalities do indeed occur within a certain time frame, as well as the fact that *the mode* in which they occur (sequence, urgency etc.) is not indifferent to the *normative relevance* they assume situationally. Time seems, thus, a necessary prerequisite for the understanding of all other features depicting the circumstances under which justice-questions do indeed arise. At a closer look, one might also notice how Hume himself had accounted for 'less urgent necessities' and 'special circumstances' as externalities positively affecting property acquisition. These cases, though, avoided a proper explanation of the core features defining the circumstances of justice.[7] All this has resulted, accordingly, into a narrow reading of the thresholds of justice and, more importantly, in a lack of *perspectival* understanding of justice as an explicatory pattern for the actual circumstances of justice. In this regard, it is worth noticing in passing how the normative relevance of time has played a crucial role in Nozick's distinction between historical and end-result principles, and particularly how, in the first case, a just distribution has been seen as dependent

4 It must be observed that already in Arendt judgement was not only analysed in the context of still initial transitional processes as with the Eichmann's trial, but that precisely because of this it was seen as strictly dependent upon circumstances of justice. As R. Beiner notices: 'According to Hannah Arendt, "thought itself arises out of incidents of living experience and must remain bound to them as the only guideposts by which to take its bearings"'. R. Beiner, Interpretive Essay, in H. Arendt, *Lectures on Kant's Political Philosophy*, p. 97.

5 D. Hume, *A Treatise of Human Nature*. London: Thomas & Joseph Allman, 1817, vol. 2, part II, p. 202.

6 J. Rawls, *A Theory of Justice*. Cambridge, MA: Harvard University Press [1971] 1999, p. 110.

7 On this point see S. Hope, 'The Circumstances of Justice', *Hume Studies*, vol. 36, no. 2, 2010, p. 130.

'upon how it came about'.[8] Nozick's distinctions are only one of the several ways in which time-constraints can be said to be incorporated into justice. Relevant for discussion here is the idea that time bears normative implications on principles for whatever theory is adopted. However, Nozick's polarization of diachronic and synchronic distinctions for justice seems defective precisely in view of the explicatory force that this bears on explaining the normative import on the circumstances of justice. As a matter of fact, no sharp separation can be usefully drawn between the reason *why* the adoption of certain principles is justified at a time T1, that is, given any configuration X; and *how* such a specific distributional configuration came about on the basis of certain historical circumstances. On the contrary, it is rather the case that redistributive accounts of justice intervene at a time T1 by assuming the historical results of previous redistributive patterns.[9] In addition, the same notion of time appears to be open to a wider philosophical investigation than an over-simplistic distinction between synchronic and diachronic axes would suggest. In fact, time is a culturally thick notion the diachronic rather than circular understanding of which can be grounded upon specific metaphysical views. In view of the present purposes, therefore, I will consider the role that *certain determinants* of time play in disclosing transitional justice phenomena and their related adjudication.[10]

I will do so by proposing an interpretation of Kant's judgement theory through the suggestion coming from Paul's *Letter to the Romans* in Agamben's interpretation .[11] Agamben's remarks on Pauline text will not be considered here in view of their specifically theological insights, but rather with regards to the contemporary philosophical relevance they assume on the circumstances that inform any theory of justice *qua* theory. The interest in Paul's text, therefore, consists in the fact that in analogy to the collapse of state-order (either historically ideal or pre-authoritarian), post-revelatory times point to a new way of experiencing and thinking – a way which cannot pretend either that a previous system of norms never existed nor that this can suffice to provide a conclusive answer to what is yet to be done.[12] The eschatological time of the second descent of Christ on earth can thus be taken to represent a political metaphor for the definition of the circumstances characterizing transitional justice phenomena. This is, indeed, the time of 'inverted tenses' of the past and future – 'the time that remains' – where the apparently concluded past turns into an

8 R. Nozick, *Anarchy, State, and Utopia*. Oxford: Blackwell, 1999, p. 153.

9 This consideration is well reflected in the: ' … distinction like that made by some modern Humean writers on ethics between *deliberative* reflection (what I have reason to do) and *explanatory* reflection (why things are as they are). However, it is not plausible to suppose that any such distinction cuts sharply in all cases. Sound deliberative reflection contains an explanatory element: an account of why things are as they are, in addition to an accurate account of how things are in the worlds in which one acts, is typically an important input into sound practical deliberation'. S. Hope, *The Circumstances of Justice*, *Hume Studies*, 36(2), 2010: p. 140.

10 On a parallel reflection on the semantic of time through the metahistorical categories of experience and expectation, Koselleck writes: 'We shall elaborate this thesis in two stages. First, we outline the metahistorical dimension: the degree to which experience and expectation are, as anthropological givens, the condition of possible histories. Second, we try to historically demonstrate that the classification of experience and expectation has been displaced and changed during the course of history. If the proof is a success, it will have been shown that historical time is not simply an empty definition, but rather an entity which alters along with history and from whose changing structure it is possible to deduce the shifting classification of experience and expectation'. R. Koselleck, *Futures Past*, New York: Columbia University Press, 2004, p. 259.

11 G. Agamben, *Il tempo che resta*.

12 'Com'è noto, Paolo scompone l'evento messianico in due tempi: la resurrezione e la *parousía*, la seconda venuta di Gesú alla fine del tempo. Di qui la paradossale tensione fra un *già* e un *non ancora* che definisce la concezione paolina della salvezza: l'evento messianico si è già prodotto, la salvezza è già compiuta per i credenti e, tuttavia, essa implica, per compiersi veramente, un tempo ulteriore … *Parousía* significa in greco semplicemente: presenza (*para-ousia*, letteralmente: essere accanto; nel presente, l'essere sta, per così dire, accanto a sé stesso). Essa non indica né un complemento, che si aggiunge a qualcosa per renderlo completo, né un supplemento, che si aggiunge ulteriormente senza giungere mai a compimento. Paolo se ne serve per designare l'intima struttura uniduale dell'evento messianico, in quanto composto da due tempi eterogenei, un *kairós* e un *chronos*, un tempo operativo e un tempo rappresentato, congiunti, ma non addizionabili'. G. Agamben, *Il tempo che resta*, pp. 69–70.

unexhausted present and a yet to be realized moment of salvation (the *parousía*, the second descent of Christ) is anticipated *now* in what is left of time before its end, that is, before salvation.[13]

Out of the theological framing, the circumstances under which transitional justice judgements are taken reflects a duplicity of inverted tenses – a *transitional time* in a cognitively thick way – a time which incorporates the paradoxical condition of being something that has both been already, but that is not anymore, and not been yet, but still to come.[14] It is the time – as I will later demonstrate – of the double negation of the 'not-not this', where Kant's orienting principle of the 'as if' cannot work independently from the circumstance of the 'as not' for transitional justice (the 'Hōs mē' for Paul).[15] Once connected to a reformulated notion of judgement, the perceived factual externality of the 'as not' provides a starting point for the orienting function of Kant's reflective judgement. As previously observed, the relevance of time in providing an understanding of synchronic and diachronic framing of justice theories applies similarly in transitional contexts in as far as the understanding of how the evaluative role of reflective judgement represents the way in which transitional time submits its objects to reflective judgement.

Reflective Judgement Detranscendalized: The Transitional Import

Since Arendt's reading of Kant's *Critique of Judgment* and the debate which it generated, scholars have referred to a 'political turn' in Kantian theory of (reflective) judgement.[16] What has been noticed as particularly significant for the interpretation of the standards advanced by judgement is a pretence to look for a universal agreement on the basis of both a subjective feeling of pleasure and the assumption of a publicly shareable *sensus communis* as a meaningful form of interconnectedness among human beings. It is in view of such anticipation of a *sensus communis*

13 On the significance of the *parousía* of Christ as literarily signifying an 'accompanying being, a being that is next' see G. Agamben, *Il tempo che resta*, p. 70.

14 As for the inversion of messianic time and the linguistic function of 'waw' in Hebrew see G. Agamben, *Il tempo che resta*, p. 74.

15 'Da un punto di vista epistemologico, si tratta piuttosto di tagliare la partizione bipolare Ebrei/non-Ebrei per passare in questo modo a un'altra logica, di tipo intuizionista, o, meglio, del genere di quella usata da Cusano nel suo *De non aliud*, in cui l'opposizione A/non-A ammette un terzo, che ha la forma di una doppia negazione: non non-A. L'evocazione di questo paradigma logico ha un fondamento nel testo stesso di Paolo, nel passo di *I Cor.*9, 20–23, in cui egli definisce la sua posizione rispetto alla divisione Ebrei (*hypó nomon*, 'sotto la legge')/non-Ebrei (*anómoi*, 'senza legge') con la singolare progressione: 'come senza legge, non senza legge di Dio, ma nella legge del messia' (*hōs ánomos, mē ōn ánomos theoúall'énnomos christoú*). Colui che si tiene nella legge messianica è non-non nella legge'. G. Agamben, *Il tempo che resta*, p. 53.

16 H. Arendt, *Lectures on Kant's Political Philosophy*. For a critical appraisal of Arendt's conception of communicative power, Habermas and McCarthy notice that: 'Arendt's concept of communicatively generated power can become a sharp instrument only if we extricate it from the clamps of an Aristotelian theory of action. In separating praxis from the unpolitical activities of working and laboring on the one side and of thinking on the other, Arendt traces back political power exclusively to praxis … ' in J. Habermas and T. McCarthy, 'Hannah Arendt's Communications Concept of Power', *Social Research*, 44(1), 1977: 15. Later it is clarified that the generation of legitimate power arises only through communicative action (which contains a critical profile) whereas its maintenance can include strategic action. A further critical stance is the ultimate contractarian pedigree of Arendt's conception of power. In other words, for Habermas and McCarthy, the power-legitimating force is placed on the contract/promise aspect and not on judgement itself which, as mentioned, is conceived by Arendt as grounding praxis in terms of opinion exchange but not as a form of power legitimation (p. 23). Among the several relevant contributions on the topic, it is worth mentioning particularly A. Ferrara (ed.), 'The Uses of Judgment', special issue of *Philosophy and Social Criticism*, 34(1–2), 2008 and L. Zerilli, 'Value Pluralism and the Problem of Judgment: Farewell to Public Reason', *Political Theory*, 40(1), 2011: 6–31.

on all others' modalities of representation that exemplarity of judgement provides an aesthetic dimension of politics through the reflectivity of judgement.[17]

Nevertheless, the political reading of Kantian judgement is not complete if an account of the principle of the purposiveness of nature as transferred to the political – what I have previously referred to as the 'as if' condition – is not also properly conceptualized. Yet, Arendt was not inclined to recognize the full political implications of the notion of purposiveness, and considered the regulative function of this principle as limited to a different type of judgement – the teleological judgement.[18] Accordingly, in the following section I will attempt to clarify the use of reflective judgement on the basis of the encroachment of the 'as if' principle of purposiveness with the 'as not' condition for transitional justice already introduced.

To begin with, Kant's analysis of reflective judgement proceeds from the 'principle of purposiveness [Zweckmäßigkeit]' in natural zoology and in the aesthetic sphere. Through reflection, judgement brings into unity the causal laws of nature and the accord of imagination and intellect springing from the pleasure of the beautiful. For Kant, such purposiveness is purely 'formal' and it is assumed a priori as a way to direct reflectivity.[19] To reinforce the thesis according to which the political reading of Kant's principle of purposiveness is textually plausible, it might be instructive to draw a parallel with his writing on *The Perpetual Peace* where the never ending process of approximation of peace is said to rely on the principle of purposiveness.[20]

Further, as anticipated, the overcoming of a purely subjective condition of pleasure for reflective judgement points to a claim of intersubjective agreement through the pretence of universal communicability. As in Kant's 'Antinomy of taste', the problem was to reconcile the non-conceptual and therefore indisputable subjective status of judgements of taste with the pretence to universal communicability and reasoned agreement.[21] Moreover, in the model of political judgement formulated here, the regulative principle of purposiveness provides a sufficient ground for the never ending disputes of other people's judgements. The reflective element of aesthetic judgement grounded in the free play of imagination and intellect – for what regards its formal purposiveness – shows to the adjudicating body – the 'We' – a possibility of non-biased and unself-interested judgements.

Pleasure in reflective judgements lifts our minds from subjective interests and directs its universally sharable content to a community of fellow human beings. This means that the reflectivity of political judgement is not itself a judgement on a particular something but discloses, rather, a condition of possibility for publicity – the possibility of non-instrumental coordination. This point is of particular interest for connecting Kant's theory of reflective judgement with his political theory in general.[22] As a matter of fact, if in Kant's aesthetic judgement the implicit moment of publicity aims at overcoming a merely subjective condition in favour of an intersubjective universal pretence

17 Cf. I. Kant, *Critique of Judgment*, trans. James Creed Meredith. Oxford: Oxford University Press, [1790] 2007, §18.

18 As noted by Goldman: 'Arendt recognizes that Kantian reflective judgement (the general term for aesthetic, teleological, and now with Arendt, political judgement) depends upon the regulative principle of "purposiveness"; and yet she rejects it in the name of a political deliberation that makes use of only the negative criteria of the moral law'. A. Goldman, 'An Antinomy of Political Judgment: Kant, Arendt, and the Role of Purposiveness in Reflective Judgment', *Continental Philosophy Review* 43(3), 2010: 331–52, at p. 348.

19 I. Kant, *Critique of Judgment*, §11.

20 I. Kant, 'Perpetual Peace: A Philosophical Sketch', in H. Reiss (ed.), *Kant's Political Writings*, Cambridge: Cambridge University Press, [1795] 1970. As Goldman correctly points out: 'in designating the principle of purposiveness as the guarantor of progress towards perpetual peace Kant is describing the 'transcendental principle of public right' as dependent upon the regulative principle of reflective judgment', A. Goldman, 'An Antinomy of Political Judgment', p. 344.

21 I. Kant, *Critique of Judgment*, §56.

22 I refer, here, mainly to I. Kant's *Perpetual Peace* and to the *Doctrine of Right* [*Rechtslehre*] in the *Metaphysics of Morals* [1797], 1970.

of communication, in his legal and political theory (in particular in his transcendental formula of public rights) it provides a negative standard for ruling out non-universalizable maxims.[23] It is this latter point that Arendt emphasizes in the political reading of Kant's judgement, even though she does not draw a connection between Kant's universal condition of communicability of reflective judgement (as the overcoming of the antinomy of the subjective element of taste in the *Third Critique*), and the condition of publicity as a universality test in Kant's political writings. According to the interpretation suggested here, the two aspects are strictly related, particularly since the first represents a preliminary condition for the second. Thus, it is only on the basis of a pretence to universal communicability that those non-universalizable maxims can be disqualified.

To see this point from a different angle it might be useful to claim that the intersubjective validation of maxims is grounded in the subjectively universal aspiration of communication. The overcoming transformation of the merely subjective element of aspiration into a universal form of communication can be seen as a converging element in what Kant defined in the *Critique of Judgment* as a form of 'enlarged mentality'. In this respect, reflective judgement, in as far as it anticipates a *sensus communis*, is bound to consider other peoples' perspectives from within the formulation of a subjectively universal standard.[24]

Overall, the political reading of reflective judgement also highlights another often overlooked component of contemporary theories of justice. Reflective judgements do, indeed, incorporate within their adjudicative standards what Quine has referred to as the collapse of the analytic/synthetic distinction. These judgements show the inadequacy of all those attempts pretending to formulate analytically true a priori statements.[25] Kant, in fact, holds faith to a functional – not a structural – distinction of the threefold partition of judgements as to the a priori, a posteriori, analytic and synthetic distinctions, and he assimilates reflective judgement to the synthetic a posteriori condition. Furthermore, whereas synthetic a priori judgements are connected to determining judgements for which a universal is given and is a priori, in the case of a posteriori judgements and specifically in the case of reflective judgements, the particular is given but the universal is yet to be found. What is crucial here is that following Kantian functional differentiations, it appears that a posteriori judgements possess the status of judgements of knowledge, both in accordance with their empirical-descriptive version, as in the case of the judgement of experience, as well as in accordance with their paradigmatic version, as in the case of scientific-normative judgements constructed on synthetic a priori judgements. Scientific judgements are not, therefore, constituted on the basis of synthetic a priori principles, since the latter provide only a priori conditions. Synthetic a posteriori judgements, on the other hand, require the functional conditions provided

23 As Arendt puts this point: 'The very act of approbation pleases, the very act of disapprobation displeases. Hence the question: How does one choose between approbation and disapprobation? … The criterion, then, is communicability, and the standard of deciding about it is common sense', in H. Arendt, *Lectures on Kant's Political Philosophy*, p. 69. On this final point see I. Kant, 'Perpetual Peace'.

24 I. Kant's notion of 'enlarged mentality' has received a moral interpretation by Benhabib: 'It is in this context that Kant's formula for reflective judgment, the only ground of whose validity is its universal communicability with the hope of winning the assent of all, and Arendt's reading of this as a procedure of "enlarged mentality" become relevant. "Act in such a way that the maxim of your actions can always be a universal law of nature" can be reformulated as "Act in such a way that the maxim of your actions takes into account the perspective of everyone else in such a way that you would be in a position to 'woo their consent'"', in S. Benhabib, 'Judgment and the Moral Foundations of Politics in Arendt's Thought', *Political Theory*, 16(1), 1988: 43. The connection between Kant's reflective judgement of the Third Critique and his political writings helps to answer some of the scepticisms towards a political reading of Kant, as in L.M.G. Zerilli, '"We feel our freedom": Imagination and Judgment in the Thought of Hannah Arendt', *Political Theory* 33(2), 2005: 158–88.

25 Cf. W.V.O. Quine, 'Two Dogmas of Empiricism', in *From a Logical Point of View*, Cambridge, MA: Harvard University Press, [1951] 1964, pp. 20–46. For a contemporary revival of the debate see G.A. Cohen, 'Facts and Principles', *Philosophy & Public Affairs*, 31(3), 2003: 211–45.

by reflective judgement, and thus necessitate a specific 'as if' purposive principle which reflective judgements prescribe to themselves in order to proceed further in their investigations.

As a result of the overall discussion on the connection between fact-sensitivity and normativity of justice – the a priori and the a posteriori properties of judgement – it seems that a contemporary update of the Kantian project on judgement requires a more precise reconstruction of the circumstances for the use of reflective judgement.

If one turns to the (hopefully virtual) circularity of the 'as if' and the 'as not' condition for reflective judgement, it also becomes relevant to consider the importance of this interconnection for the self-constituting process of identity-construction of a political community. What seems interesting here is the subtle dynamics taking place in the construction of an adjudicating collectivity on the basis of the overcoming of non-identitarian elements within the 'as not'. One could say that the 'as if' principle, in order to suggest a viable perspective for the future, should be capable of embedding within itself the same presuppositions for the validity of its own standard – an 'as not' condition – and transform the apparent incommensurability of individual perspectives into a newly reformulated notion of a collective body as a 'not-not being this'. The co-implication proposed here of the 'as if' and the 'as not' as part of a reformulation of Kant's reflective judgement bears, again, important connections to Agamben's analysis of Paul's *Letter to the Romans* where redemption is both a calling and a revoking action on a community and its history. What is claimed is that as a result of the first descent of the Messiah on earth, individual fellow beings are revoked from their socially unrelated bonds and called on to enter a new community. As Agamben argues, with the descent of the Messiah, redemption is no longer a point of view on things 'as if' they had occurred. On the contrary, both things and persons are taken starting from an 'as not' condition which is far from being ideal.[26] The ideal of the 'as if' also found in the transitional reading of time as according to Pauline text, is something grounded in the non-ideal condition of a lost collective self. The 'as not' precedes the 'as if' and the ideal moment of purposiveness is grounded, accordingly, into the non-ideal transitional condition. The Pauline '*klesis*' ('call'), following Agamben's analysis, reminds us that the positive moment for the reflectivity of judgement lies in the negativity and transitionality of the 'as not' as a self-constituting moment.

To return, then, to the disclosing force of a detranscendentalized view on judgement, it can be argued that the political perspective on the world presupposes a non-ideal formation of a self-constituting body placed in between a past which has not yet passed and a future which has already occurred. It is from the encroachment of these two moments that one should locate the transitionally relevant founding aspect of the Pauline 'Hōs mē' ('as not') as a condition of reflective judgement. This is the time which allows to conceive identity as a third possibility beyond the mere opposition between A and non-A or, as Agamben suggests,[27] that of the identity-condition of Jews after revelation as no longer being Jewish or not Jewish, that is, as being not-not-Jews. What then does it mean not to be not Jew? Is this only a not being something or other, or is it also a being something else, even if not something which can be positively described?

There is, indeed, a way to refer to such double negative characterization of 'not-not being something', and this is the case of being in the condition of a transitional identity as 'that which remains'. The transitional identity of a yet-to-be-formed community still in the process of being constructed but no longer in the condition of scattered and unrelated identities generates a community of 'survivals', namely, of identities who cannot be defined in other terms than in the double negative. However, for a people to be in a self-reflective relation to themselves as a 'survival people' – as a 'rest' – implies to be always in a differential relation. This means that they

26 G. Agamben, *Il tempo che resta*, p. 44.
27 Ibid., p. 53.

are a part of a whole which can never be completely coincidental with itself either as a minority or as a majority: thus as a 'not-whole'.[28] This same relation, the double negation standard, applies also to transitional law when seen through the eyes of Messiah's law as negatively relating to the law of God. In such a case there is not a nullifying effect on God's law which thus explains why Paul can define his position in respect to the separation between Jews and not Jews with the formula of the double negation for which messianic law is not-not law.[29]

From this treatment of identities, it seems that there is not a substantive and unbridgeable divide between transitional identities in post-conflict societies – transitional identities, that is, in preconstitutional contexts – and transitional identities within particularly significant legal transformations revolving around particular 'constitutional moments'.[30] Both cases represent either pre or infra constitutional identity crises and ask for a reshaping of collective identities along a mutual interconnection between the 'as if' and the 'as not' standards.

The Paradox of Judgement and its Hermeneutical Turn

In addition to the difficulties noticed in §1, there is indeed a further problem connected to standard normative theories concerning an unresolved tension caused by distinguishing 'the independence of moral principles from … actual political practice [which] makes the model [of standard normative theories] too demanding to be politically useful'.[31] This is what can be defined in terms of the paradox of judgement. It amounts to the unresolved tension of demanding normative standards and a consequential loss of political explanatory force, on the one hand, and an increasing factual accountability and relaxation of critical standards, on the other hand.[32] This seems to have motivated Rawls to elaborate within his work *Political Liberalism* a more stringent analysis of the interconnection between the plurality of reasonable comprehensive views of the good and a publicly justified view of the right, where the first have been progressively included into the justificatory process – and not simply into the legitimacy process – of a public view of the right.[33]

This same difficulty appears in the Habermasian attempt to avoid the risks of empty formalism, as Hegel had noticed in Kant's theory and in the clarification of the role played by the presuppositions of rational justification in discourse theory, not so much in terms of truth validity standards of moral discourses (criteriological standards), but rather as enabling presuppositions for orienting participants towards validity-claims and mutual understanding.[34] If the latter is the relevant case to consider, then it follows that the communicative model remains incapable of accounting for context-specific communicative experiences by assuming that 'every valid norm must satisfy the condition that the consequences and side-effects of its *general* observance can be anticipated to have for the satisfaction of the interests of *each*' as well as that it 'could be freely accepted by *all* affected'.[35] Here the paradox

28 Ibid., pp. 57–9.

29 Ibid., ivi.

30 On the historical analysis of American constitutionalism according to specific constitutional moments see B.Ackerman, *We the People: Foundations*, vol. 1, Cambridge, MA: Belknap Press of Harvard University Press, 1993.

31 A. Azmanova, *The Scandal of Reason: A Critical Theory of Political Judgment*, New York: Columbia University Press, 2012, p. 28.

32 A. Azmanova, *The Scandal of Reason*, p. 239.

33 J. Rawls, *Political Liberalism*, New York: Columbia University Press, 1993.

34 For Hegel's criticisms of Kant's moral theory and for a rebate of analogous criticisms to discourse theory see J. Habermas, 'Morality and the Ethical Life: Does Hegel's Critique of Kant Apply to Discourse Ethics?', *Northwestern University Law Review*, 83(1–2), 1989: 38–53.

35 J. Habermas, *Justification and Application: Remarks on Discourse Ethics*, trans. C.P. Cronin, Cambridge: Polity Press, 1990, p. 197.

of judgement reappears in the form of a conceptual entrapment between the situational relevance of the adjudicating subject and the condition of universalizability of the deliberative result: 'as if' all possible affected agents would have endorsed that same result. If, however, the situational validity of the discursive agreement were to be measured through an idealized discursive standard, then, the cogency of the context would lose its salience; whereas, were the contextual appropriateness of judgemental validity not subjected to universalizable validating ideal conditions, then, the same orienting function of ideal speech presuppositions would become obsolete.

It is to this paradoxical conclusion that the revisitation of judgement suggested here aims to contribute by focusing on two interconnected aspects. The first concerns the relevance of the pre-discursive level of phronetic orientation for discursive agency in which, as I have noted, time represents one additional presupposition for the shaping of discursive reasons. It is though only at a later stage of conceptualization that time turns, then, into a cognitively 'thick' concept as with the Pauline notion of transitional time. Yet, this discursively elaborated view has its external and pre-linguistic origins in the more abstract and undefined postulation of time as that which provides the *way* for a reformulated view on 'world disclosure'.[36]

The second aspect, instead, regards the role played by indexicals along the discursive exchange of reasons. Here the intuition regards the special role and status that indexicals have in action-theory and which – to my knowledge – has never been properly conceptualized. The idea is that indexicals like 'I', 'we', 'here' etc. reflect a pre-discursive level of phronetic orientation. As recently emphasized by contemporary linguistics, the meaning-component of such elements is, strictly speaking, mental and connected to the pre-discursive experiential level.[37] This, in turn, orients agents in engaging into a bi-directional hermeneutical enterprise (such as providing and asking for accounts) rather than entering into a competitive construction of the best argument. In addition, it reinforces the idea of 'a phronetic constitution' and a 'hermeneutical level' as a broader agents' stepping-in level of public reasoning.[38] At this stage, agents orient their views on the basis of indexicals as 'mental dossiers'.[39] These function as starting 'reference points' for articulating views on justice claims on the basis of the significance that they *implicitly* bring about in the discursive exchange of reasons. The hermeneutical turn of communicative reason is required in

---

36 This point is well captured by S.R.S. Finke when he writes 'Since the possibility of the application of the rational presuppositions of discourse is dependent upon pre-reflective modes of *world-disclosure*, an orientation towards reasons must be guided by particular commitments and orientations which are not themselves recoverable solely in terms of discursive reasons. This amounts to saying that in the application of norms and rules of communication generally, in generating novel perspectives upon ourselves, and in producing individual and collective self-identities in relations of mutual recognition, we must rely upon modes of *reflective judgement* that are not themselves transparent, but which must be presupposed in order to provide the orientations towards validity with meaningful communicative experience'. S.R.S. Finke, 'Habermas and Kant: Judgment and Communicative Experience', *Philosophy and Social Criticism*, 26(6), 2000: 38.

37 On the mental status of indexicals and their embeddedness into time see F. Recanati: 'Contrairement à ce qu'on a longtemps cru, l'indexicalité n'est pas une propriété exclusive des représentations linguistiques – on trouve quelque chose d'équivalent du côté des représentations mentales … Notons que le concept démonstratif 'ce type' n'est pas le seul élément indexical figurant dans la pensée 'Ce type va se casser la figure'. En tant qu'événement mental, cette pensée se produit à un certain moment *t*, et le future proche dans 'va se casser la figure' s'interprète comme renvoyant à un moment *t'* postérieur à *t* mais peu distant'. F. Recanati, *Philosophie du language (et de l'esprit)*. Paris: Éditions Gallimard, 2008, pp. 198–9.

38 A. Azmanova, *The Scandal of Reason*, pp. 205ff.

39 The discursive shift into hermeneutics is grounded also on the semantic richness of indexicals as 'mental dossiers' and as 'semantic histories': 'Les concepts indexicaux, ainsi analysés, sont le paradigm des modes de présentation non descriptifs. On peut se représenter un concept non descriptif comme un "dossier" mental … Le dossier, en tant que structure de donné, a une existence propre et, en particulier, une histoire. Un dossier est ouvert à l'occasion d'un épisode cognitif impliquant un objet sur lequel le sujet acquiert des informations. Les informations recueillies dans le dossier peuvent être plus ou moins correctes, et plus ou moins identifiantes. Elles determinent les "conditions de conformité" – les conditions qu'un objet doit remplir pour "correspondre" au dossier … Le dossier, en tant que structure de données, a pour fonction de stocker les informations qui parviennent au sujet *en vertu d'une certain relation au referent*'. F. Recanati, *Philosophie du langage*, p. 207.

order to make explicit the situational/experiential assumptions that indexicals can reveal on the basis of a persistent activity of 'rendering account … as giving reasons for having reasons'[40] as a way to construct and deconstruct reasons and pseudo-reasons through a genealogical investigation on how these convictions came about in personal experience.

If the considerations above are sound, it follows that the reconstruction of the normative significance of judgement in transitional contexts has to prove itself capable of accounting for the notion of time as an unavoidable presupposition which becomes, then, a linguistically shaped experience of transitionality. In this respect, the 'as not' condition introduced at the beginning identifies, first of all, time in terms of a communicative presupposition – as a reference point for the orientation of judgement. It follows that a cognitively elaborated experience of transitional time is only subsequently connected to the use of reflective judgement. Accordingly, the presupposition of the temporal circumstances of justice represents a requirement for the same grasping of the reflectivity of judgement itself. In particular, this means that reflective judgement can aim at being critical only in so far as it proceeds to construct reasons from a situationally grounded point (the 'as not' of transitional time as one of the circumstances of transitional justice), and when it proceeds from the recognition of this condition to the organization of its concepts on the basis of the principle of the 'as if' (as Kant had already recognized in the *Critique of Judgment*).

Consequently, a reformulated view of the critical import of reflectivity in judgement along hermeneutical lines has to take its moves from within a circular co-implication between the 'as not' and the 'as if'. I define this relation as a form of 'virtual circularity' – not as 'vicious circularity' – since in the paradoxical condition of the double negation there can never be a complete coincidence/overlapping of a reflectively constructed universal with its circumstances of emergence. 'The time that remains', as used in Paul's *Letter to the Romans*, represents therefore a formula for defining transitional time as a non-exhaustible standard, or as a non-closure between the critical element of reflective judgement and the conditions for its formulation. The reason why the critical element of reflectivity in judgement emerges from an encroachment of the 'as if' with the 'as not' is because to think in terms of 'as if' something is the case implies, under transitional circumstances, to see it 'as not' being exhaustible by one specific case.

The generalization of messianic time as the disclosing dimension of a sense paradoxically entrapped in a past that has yet to be exhausted and a future that has already occurred seems, indeed, the condition which belongs to several attempts of meaning-construction for a transitionally situated agency. Given transitional circumstances of justice, the agent, in order to regain for the future a sense in the present, must have experienced in the past a form of temporary loss of meaning – a sense which remains – as a surplus of sense that is never completely nullified nor realized. If this is how sense appears paradoxically through time, then, messianic time aims at being a proxy for the suggestion of a universalizable condition in which sense manifests itself along an ontochronic dimension of history. Yet, messianic time is only *one* of the possible representations of the inherent paradoxicality of sense and of its temporal unveiling. Other developments in critical theory have insisted, for instance, on the interconnection between time and disclosure, a return to a notion of 'world disclosure' in Heideggerian terms.[41] But while it is certainly the case that the view of world disclosure presents itself as within a time-constrained framework, it is not certain that it can also show the normative value of time as experienced justice.

Overall, both aspects discussed on the reflectivity of judgement and the general conditions as circumstances of transitional justice provide also a connection to further insight into the

40 A. Azmanova, *The Scandal of Reason*, p. 236.

41 On this connection see N. Kompridis, *Critique and Disclosure: Critical Theory between Past and Future*, Cambridge, MA, and London: The MIT Press, 2006, pp. 21ff.

co-implication – rather than dichotomy – between objectivity and subjectivity, that is, the intersubjective standard of adjudication that reflective judgement advances through its claim on 'universal communicability' and search for agreement. Yet, we are here beyond the standard of ideal agreement, since what is at stake is the same transformative role of reason that is somehow missing in the a-temporal model of Habermas's communicative theory.[42] Similar to the view in which 'dialectics is the consistent sense of nonidentity',[43] the circularity between the transcendental condition of purposiveness in reflective judgements and that of the 'as not' aims at advancing the Habermasian project for a detranscendentalization of Kant's philosophy. This includes a tighter reconnection to Adorno's criticism of Kant's separation between phenomena and noumena and his Hegelian solution to the dialectical tension of identity and non-identity with the non-identical (*das Nichtidentisch*), rather than with the 'speculative'.[44] In this respect, the non-identical is on a par with the Pauline idea of 'that which remains' as a self-reflective form of understanding of an indexical subject (either an 'I' or a 'we'), as well as of transitionally filtered entities. 'That which remains', in other words, is that which cannot be exhausted by any objectifying form of identity-categorization and which resists, accordingly, any attempt of noetic crystallization of dialectical thinking. 'That which remains' is the Adornian notion of the non-identical, as a sense which always exceeds its possible conclusive definition, and which turns into its opposite as a form of endless movement of dialectic contradiction. These are the conditions for a reformulated notion of reflective judgement which, also in the case of Adorno, do not proceed simply towards an extrinsic unification of the subjective and the objective, but do incorporate these elements as their ineradicable preconditions.[45]

Reflective Judgement and the Reconciliation of the Actor-Spectator Divide

So far, it has been argued that a reformulation of reflective judgement would see an interconnection between the principle of purposiveness – the 'as if' – and the 'as not' condition for transitional contexts. Questions following from this point concern the legal and institutional impact that this view has for a definition of transitional law as well as for the understanding of the operationalization of transitional justice. One way to suggest a reunification of such a dichotomy is by looking at it in terms of the Arendtian role for reflective judgement along the actor/spectator divide. This connection is grounded in the view that if the spectator, as a supposedly impartial judge, evaluates the past in terms of an 'as if' standard of fairness, the actor, conversely, when deciding on alternative options, redefines her own identity on the starting assumption of an 'as not' condition. The rationale for this final paragraph considers that advancing an interpretation of Arendt's actor/spectator divide requires the formulation of a standard that institutional settings should respect when operating within transitional justice contexts.

According to the view defended here, transitional reflective judgement and the functions it displays, includes a specific, normatively justified view of legal and institutional functionalities that would be lost in those accounts emphasizing the dichotomy between the 'actor' and the 'spectator' –

42 On this criticism see also N. Kompridis, *Critique and Disclosure*, p. 29.

43 T.W. Adorno, *Negative Dialectics*, New York: Continuum Press, [1966] 2007, p. 5.

44 Ibid., pp. 146ff. T.W. Adorno, in a paragraph instructively titled 'disenchantment of the concept', argues that '… no philosophy, not even extreme empiricism, can drag in the *facta bruta* and present them like cases in anatomy or experiments in physics … '. *Negative Dialectics*, p. 11.

45 'Judgments are not a mere synthesis of concepts, for without judgment there is no concept … Every analysis of a judgment takes us to a subject and an object, but this fact does not create a region beyond those moments, a region that would be "in itself" in T. Adorno, *Negative Dialectics*, p. 105.

as for instance in the recent interpretation of Arendt's notion of judgement proposed by Leebaw.[46] On the contrary, even if not always consistently, there seems to be the possibility of interpreting Arendt as suggesting a unified view where the 'position of the spectator ... is the position of the judge'.[47] A helpful indication, in this respect, is Arendt's controversial analyses of Eichmann's trial in Jerusalem where an 'enlarged view' of reflective judgement is granted, with the possibility of an intersubjective understanding of the 'banality of evil' by an (impartial) spectator, and the critical trespassing of Eichmann's defence in terms of abidance to Nazi law. Here, judges are called to endorse a reflective use of judgement for something which was completely new at that time – the crime of genocide – and which for Arendt could not be understood on the basis of an 'evil nature'. Eichmann, Arendt claims, was neither a fanatical anti-Semite nor a legal positivist. He acted as a diligent servant and bureaucrat of a totalitarian system where any form of critical morality was annihilated. Eichmann was not simply a 'murderer' as a determinative use of judgement would suggest based on the only available application of the legal category of that time. He was instead a 'mass murderer', a new category that only a 'reflective' use of judgement could have helped to understand. The relevance of reflectivity for judgement is also significant in as far as time contributes to shaping both the spectator's and the actor's evaluations.[48] Just as the spectator in judging the past does not have access to a final point of observation according to which history can be judged – so that her judgement can never be conclusively retrospective – the actor, likewise, as a timely situated agent cannot articulate prospective judgement as a non-revisable anticipation of final end-points.[49] The same structure which I have presented as part of the normative-conceptual level might also provide a viable explanation for justifying the actor-spectator import at the legal-institutional level.

Indeed, the forward and backward orientation of transitional judgement is reflected in the same retributive and transformative function that transitional law shows, particularly in its inclusion within contexts of institutional and social change.[50] Transitional law, as opposed to so-called standard law, aims at advancing both a retributive and a restorative function which blurs the possibility of drawing a clear-cut distinction between the two areas. If it is assumed as normatively binding the internal interconnection of the 'as if' (forward-looking) with the 'as not' (backward-looking), then it becomes apparent why the social transformative aim of the transitionality of law and the prosecutionary aspect represent, at different levels, a Janus-faced condition for the implementation of legal transitionality itself. Such operationalization is polarized into the functional differentiation of the role that Criminal Tribunals and Truth Commissions do indeed fulfil. In addition, while a strict dichotomization of the two institutional functions in these cases does not provide an adequate account of how trials alone contribute to the recording of truth and to the securing of victims' *fora*, it is nevertheless important not to conflate partial overlapping between the two with a clearly definable backward-and-forward-looking functional differentiation. The account of judgement proposed here prioritizes and links the roles of transitional justice institutions by starting from a normative account of the nature of transitional reflective judgement as an inherent interconnection of both dimensions.

---

46 As Leebaw claims: 'These are not exactly two entirely different theories of political judgment. Arendt is consistent in arguing that "enlarged mentality" is the basis of good judgment for political actors as well as spectators. However, her analysis does illuminate two distinctive *stances* or forms of political judgment that are implicit in theoretical debates on transitional justice – that of the actor and that of the spectator', even though she then recognizes their co-implication when she writes: 'These two forms of political judgments are mutually constitutive'. In B. Leebaw, *Judging State-Sponsored Violence: Imagining Political Change*, Cambridge: Cambridge University Press, 2011, pp. 91–108.

47 H. Arendt, *Lectures on Kant's Political Philosophy*, pp. 55–6.

48 On this point see also L.Y. Bilsky, 'When Actor and Spectator Meet in the Courtroom: Reflections on Hannah Arendt's Concept of Judgment', in *History and Memory*, 8(2), 1996: 160ff.

49 See H. Arendt, [1982] 1992: 79ff.

50 See R. Teitel, *Transitional Justice*. Oxford: Oxford University Press, 2000.

To argue for a single judgemental model the differentiation of which is only subsequent and contextually justified means to defend, on a normative basis, the duplicity function of retributive and restorative aims as unavoidable and inseparable goals for transitional justice. This also implies that other transitional measures such as amnesties, memorialization or lustration processes are to be placed subordinate to the core axis of the retributive/restorative continuum represented by the backward-and-forward-looking action of the Courts and Truth Commissions, respectively. This model might still seem quite abstract. Indeed, the specific advantages and/or disadvantages of sequencing in either way retributive measures and/or truth telling restorative processes are to be left to the contextual evaluation of how and by whom a conflict has been ended. The argued connection between a backward-and-forward dimension of transitional justice wants only to show to be capable of defending the necessity of a *holistic* approach to the overcoming of state-sponsored violence, and the activation of a process of democratization.[51]

Conclusion

Throughout this essay, I have argued in favour of a reformulated view of judgement in transitionality. Accordingly, I have proposed an understanding of the 'as if' in terms of a co-dependent variable of the 'as not' (the 'Hōs mē' according to Paul's *Letter to the Romans*). Additionally, I have defended the view by which reflective judgement presupposes, in a sort of virtual circularity, a sense of appropriateness according to time as an all-encompassing property of manifestation for the subjective and the objective circumstances of transitional justice; that is, what I have referred to in the first paragraph as 'moderate scarcity' and 'conflict of interests'. The reformulation of the 'onto-chronic' conditions of validity for reflective judgement integrate under relevant respects Searle's and Habermas's models of speech act theory and communicative action respectively, through an emphasis on the role of indexicality for the validity of discourse-claims.[52] Among other aspects, the provision of a 'transitional' understanding of justice has incorporated within reflective judgement the dialectical 'negation of negation' synthesized by the identity dynamics expressed with the Pauline formula of 'that which remains'. Differently from the 'speculative' moment of Hegelian dialectic, the outcome of the double negation defines its object only through subtraction. 'That which remains', as a negatively defined result, opens the space for a judgement as a critical enterprise of world disclosure distancing itself from a conceptually unmediated – and thus normatively extrinsic assumption of a *Dasein* – as in Heidegger. Contrary to this view, the thesis suggested here provides a rejoining also to Benjamin's asymmetric idea of past and future, as well as to his notion of a transitory present as a 'rescuing critique' (*rettende Kritik*). In so far as time becomes connected with social critique, new disclosing possibilities are inconceivable outside 'the notion of a present which is not a transition, but in which time stands still and has come to a stop'.[53]

The double negative delimits only the external contours of what is not, without predetermining the positive content of a contextual normative arrangement for a self-interpreting community. Overall, this wide internal margin of positive but 'yet to be defined' identity-construction mediates between the indexicality of reflective judgement and the contingency of a collective self-determining

51 On the evaluation of the pros and cons of transitional processes either anticipating, posticipating or coordinating simultaneously restorative justice with retributive justice measures, see A. Dukalskis, 'Interactions in Transition: How Truth Commissions and Trials Complement or Constrain Each Other', *International Studies Review*, 13(3), 2011: 432–51.

52 See J. Searle, *Speech Acts*, Cambridge: Cambridge University Press, 1969.

53 W. Benjamin, *Illuminations, Essays and Reflections*, ed. H. Arendt, New York: Harcourt Brace Jovanovich [1950] 1969, p. 255.

action through the use of reflectivity in judgement. The clarification of the circumstances of transitional justice also bears important legal and institutional consequences for the understanding of the double functionality of transitional law. The backward-and-forward perspective opened by transitional times shapes not only a duplicity function of law in its retributive and restorative identity-construction process, but it also grounds the core axis of transitional institutions into the interdependency of the Courts and Truth Commissions as part of a single and holistic institutional and policy framework.

Chapter 14

Further Explorations of the Social Death Hypothesis

Claudia Card

If genocide is the *murder*, not simply the destruction, of a people, then genocide can never be justifiable but is always an evil. I will defend the view that genocide is a kind of murder, even when it is non-homicidal. It is not obvious what it means to murder a people. Neither is it obvious that genocide can never be justified, especially on my hypothesis that social death is central to genocide. For, the vitality lost in social death can surely include evil forms. And so, I am led to explore further than I did a decade ago the implications of the social death hypothesis. I aim to show also its helpfulness for making progress with such commonly asked questions as:

1. How do genocides differ from non-genocidal mass atrocities?
2. As a crime, is genocide redundant, given other war crimes and crimes against humanity in International Humanitarian Law? Does it identify something distinct?
3. Is genocide the worst crime, or greatest evil, imaginable?
4. Against whom or what can genocide be committed? Could there be a gay genocide? Is femicide a kind of genocide? What about people with disabilities? Evil groups?
5. What kinds of acts can be genocidal? What about expulsion? Mass rape?

I borrow the social death concept from historian Orlando Patterson (1982: 5–9). He used it to describe the plight of slaves captured in Africa who survived the middle passage to the Americas. They had been torn from their roots, chained together with captives who spoke other languages, and in the New World were continually robbed of the security of family connections through the practice of selling off children, spouses, and other kin. In the Americas, Patterson argued, relationships among slaves had no social sanctions or security. Slaves were, as he put it, *socially dead.* Later generations born to a condition of social death he called *natally alienated*—cut off from social ties in both directions, to ancestors and to progeny (Patterson 1982: 7). These hypotheses are controversial among historians who take seriously the idea of slave culture (Stuckey 1987). If Patterson's critics are right, genocides may offer clearer instances of social death than was offered by slavery in the Americas.

I begin with the idea of social vitality and then understand social death as a major deprivation or loss of social vitality. By social vitality I understand the meanings, shapes, and contents given the lives of individuals by social relationships, personal and institutional, contemporary and inter-generational, that unite them into a people or other significant community. Social vitality takes many forms: linguistic, educational, political, economic, artistic, and religious practices all contribute, as do friendship and kinship networks. Major loss of social vitality is a loss of social identity, consequently, a serious loss of meaning for one's existence. Putting social death at the center of genocide takes our focus off body counts and directs it instead to relationships and interactions. Social death has degrees, and it typically also has stages. Sometimes social vitality is recoverable or re-creatable. Often it is neither. Or the new forms of vitality are impoverished, as compared with what was lost.

Social death sounds like something suffered by a group. It is. But what makes it *morally* significant is that it is suffered by individuals, as members. Major loss of social vitality often robs one even of the ability to give meaning to one's life, thereby destroying a fundamental aspect of one's humanity. Social death can have other sources—slavery, banishment, disfigurement, illness, self-chosen isolation (becoming a hermit). These need not cut one off from a shared language, history, traditions, and the like. Causes of social death are not always violent, as they typically are in genocide.[1] In genocide, social death is extreme. And massive.

I leave the notion of being "central" relatively undefined. But when I say that massive social death is central to genocide, I mean at least that it is an organizing core of the most paradigmatic instances. Also, that it is key for appreciating the kind of evil genocide is. It suggests a certain approach to answering the commonly asked questions. It helps to distinguish genocide from other mass atrocities. It is useful for explaining how genocide differs from other murders. It helps us identify which groups can be victims of genocide, a matter of some consequence in international law. It should be useful for identifying a genocide-in-progress, where interventions might interrupt it before it ran its course.

It is a gross understatement to say genocide is wrong. Genocide is not just wrong; it is an evil—not in the popular loose sense of "evil" that applies to *anything* bad or wrong but in that stricter, narrower, more specific sense in which "evil" is a very strong term of opprobrium. For many years, I have focused my work on particular evils, such as torture, and on the meaning of the concept of evil (Card 2002, 2007, 2010), taking on two tasks. The first is to distinguish evils from lesser wrongs. I no longer say "from ordinary wrongs" because that implies that evils are not ordinary. On my view, evils are not just more extreme than other wrongs. They are more complex. My second task has been to work through tough moral and conceptual questions about notorious evils of our time, especially, torture, terrorism, and genocide. Neither torture nor terrorism is wrong by definition. So there is room to argue about justifiability or excusability. But if genocide is the *murder* of a people, there is no room for that kind of argument. Homicide can be justified (in self-defense, for example); *murder* cannot. This is a conceptual point. Killing in justifiable self-defense is not murder. Confronting genocide morally is analogous, in a certain way, to confronting rape. The question is not when, if ever, it is justified. Rather, the questions are how to recognize it, how grave it is relative to other crimes, how it is justifiable to respond, and so forth.

It has seemed to some of my students an arbitrary stipulation to say that genocide is a kind of *murder*, implying that it is wrong by definition, rather than simply a kind of *killing*, leaving open the possibility of justification. I know no scholars or politicians trying to define genocide who have taken the view that it could be anything but wrong. The Convention on the Prevention and Punishment of the Crime of Genocide of 1948 (hereafter, "the genocide convention") took as its task the definition of a crime not previously defined in international law. Still, it is philosophically interesting to inquire how, apart from size of the target, destroying an evil group would differ from genocide. If social death is central, it should be natural to ask why it would not be committing genocide to destroy an *evil group* that gave its members social identity and vitality. If that were genocide, too, some genocides would appear justifiable. This is not how the concept is used. But is common usage arbitrary? Or is there a basis for refusing to call any justified destruction of a group "genocide"? I will argue that there is such a basis. I call this issue "the Murder, Inc. problem."

Consider the organization known in the 1940s as "Murder, Inc.," later as "the Syndicate" and "the Mob." Authors of the book *Murder, Inc.* describe it as a "fantastic ring of killers and extortionists" that constituted organized crime in the United States (Turkus and Feder 1951: 1–2,

1 For more on violence, see note 3 below.

xi). In one decade, they report, Murder, Inc. was responsible for a thousand murders "from New England to California" (Turkus and Feder 1951: 1–2). If Murder, Inc. seems too small or too thin to constitute a people, consider the Ku Klux Klan, a group larger and perhaps more complex. When sociologist Kathleen Blee interviewed women who had been Klan members in the 1920s, they described it nostalgically as a way to socialize with like-minded others (Blee 1991: 1). Or, consider the Nazi Party. The vitality contributed to members of these groups may have been as important to their lives as that contributed by a national or religious culture is to others' lives. Must we grant the possibility of a good genocide? Is imposition of social death necessarily an evil? To make progress on these questions, it is necessary to explain the conception of evil in play here. I turn to that next.

My book *The Atrocity Paradigm: A Theory of Evil* (Card 2002) develops a theory of evil that takes large-scale mass atrocities as paradigms. By a "paradigm," I mean an uncontroversial instance, something uncontroversially an evil. My approach is secular. I do not presuppose a theological context, although my theory is compatible with most aspects of the theological problem of evil, which ponders how an omnipotent perfectly good creator could produce a world as flawed as ours.

My initial definition was that evils are reasonably "foreseeable intolerable harms produced by culpable wrongdoing" (Card 2002: 3, 16). I changed "culpable wrongdoing" to "inexcusable wrongs" in my second evil book, *Confronting Evils: Terrorism, Torture, Genocide* (2010: 16ff.), to yield the definition that evils are reasonably foreseeable intolerable harms, produced by inexcusable wrongs. Thus, evils have two basic, irreducibly distinct components: an agency component and a harm component, connected by reasonably foreseeable causality. I take the noun "evils" (plural) as basic, but am not interested in the idea of evil as a metaphysical force. I treat adjectival uses of "evil" as derivative. An evil intention, for example, is an inexcusably wrongful intention to do reasonably foreseeable intolerable harm. An evil practice inexcusably does reasonably foreseeable intolerable harm. A practice inexcusable today might have been excusable in the past, not then an evil but an evil today. (Slavery?) My motivating interest is in identifying deeds, practices, even environments that are evils, not in labeling evil perpetrators, although I think that can sometimes be done. My approach highlights the plight of victims and resists immersion in perpetrator psychology.

My conception of evils is ethical in that it presupposes the idea of moral wrongs. Atrocities do not include natural catastrophes (such as earthquakes), although such catastrophes can be as harmful. Although I do not specify a definition of "wrongs," my definition of evils is compatible with many non-utilitarian theories of the distinction between right and wrong. Key concepts to clarify are "intolerable" in "intolerable harm" and "inexcusable" in "inexcusable wrongs."

By intolerable harms I mean substantial deprivations of basics ordinarily necessary for a life (or death) to be decent for the person whose life (or death) it is. Such basics, in a life, include access to non-toxic air, water, and food; the ability to move your limbs and to sit, stand, or lie down, to make choices and act on some of them, to have affective bonds with others and interaction with some of them, to be free from severe and unremitting pain or humiliation, and so on. These basics cut across cultural differences and stem from our common needs not only as members of a species but as mammals. How much deprivation? Enough to make a life or death indecent and so, intolerable, for the person whose life or death it is. Being intolerable is not simply a matter of subjective preference, even if preferences are not totally eliminable. This conception of the intolerable is normative—not what you cannot in fact tolerate but the absence of conditions required for your life (or death) to be decent. Millions tolerate the intolerable daily. Next, consider inexcusable wrongs.

Wrongs can be inexcusable in two ways. Evils are inexcusable in both. First, what I call a *metaphysical* excuse exists when you act under diminished capacity, such as physical disability or mental illness. Second, what I call a *moral* excuse exists when you have a partial moral justification. There is some excuse, morally speaking, when you have some good moral reason for what you did, even though it was not good enough to justify your deed on the whole (what is justified needs no excuse). There is usually some reason for any deed, but not every reason carries moral weight. When your reasons carry no moral weight, then, if your deed is wrong, there is no *moral* excuse for it. A reason that carries moral weight for some deeds may carry none for others. For example, the fact that someone's feelings would be hurt if you did not do something carries some moral weight as a reason not to always speak frankly, but no moral weight as a reason to kill someone. Evils are inexcusable both metaphysically and morally.

The etymology of the components of Raphael Lemkin's coined term "genocide" seems to leave open whether genocide is necessarily an evil.[2] If the Greek "genos" meant "clan or race," the Latin "cide" is from a verb that meant "to cut down." It could be applied cutting down trees but was also used to mean both "to kill" and "to murder." Clearly Lemkin's intent was not to leave open the question of justifiability. I find it clear enough that genocide satisfies the harm component of evils, that for those who suffer it, social death is an intolerable harm. What is at issue in the Murder Inc. problem is the agency component: could agents be justified in inflicting social death on a people or other significant community? If so, would genocide not necessarily be an evil? Or, would the infliction not be genocide?

When Lemkin agitated for international recognition of genocide as a distinct crime in the 1930s, his paradigm was the Turks' slaughter of the Armenian Christians in 1915 (Power 2002: 1–30). Turkey has rejected the charge of genocide. The United States has officially agreed, perhaps to avoid questions regarding the US in Vietnam (Balakian 2003). Still, there is widespread consensus among scholars that the slaughter of the Armenians was a genocide. An account of the meaning of genocide and how it differs from other mass atrocities should illuminate how Turkey could soberly maintain its denial. The most widely cited definitions do not settle the issue.

Most widely cited is the definition in the 1948 Genocide Convention, which says:

> Genocide means any of the following acts committed with the intent to destroy, in whole or in part, a nation, ethnical, racial, or religious group, as such:
>
> (a) killing members of the group;
>
> (b) causing serious bodily or mental harm to members of the group;
>
> (c) deliberately inflicting on the group conditions of life calculated to bring about its physical destruction in whole or in part;
>
> (d) imposing measures intended to prevent births within the group;
>
> (e) forcibly transferring children of the group to another group.[3]

Every clause of this definition is controversial: the scope and content of "intent," the meaning of "in whole or in part," and the scope of the whole definition: is it too narrow in naming only four kinds of groups and only five kinds of activity? Is it too broad, because of the non-homicidal acts

2 The Latin "caedo" could mean "I kill, slay, murder" but also "I cut down, fell (trees, etc.)" (Glare 1982, p. 759). The suffix "-cida" meant "one who cuts or kills" (Glare 1982, p. 313). The ancient Greek "genos" could mean "race, stock, kin" or "clan, house, family" (Liddell and Scott, 9th edn, p. 344).

3 For the full text of the genocide convention, see website http://www.hrweb.org/legal/genocide.html (accessed August 22, 2013).

it includes as apparently sufficient when coupled with the right sort of intent? Why does it fail to mention violence?[4]

"Intent" was not defined at the genocide convention. If intent is understood narrowly to mean aim, or ends and means, then destruction of a people as a reasonably foreseeable consequence that was neither an aim nor a means would not count as genocide (but merely as "collateral damage"). The deaths of millions of Native Americans from diseases brought by Europeans would not count as genocides except where those deaths were aimed at. Using this narrow understanding of "intent," Hugo Adam Bedau (known for his campaigns against the death penalty in the U.S.) wrote an essay defending the U.S. in Vietnam against the charge of genocide raised by the 1967 Jean-Paul Sartre/Bertrand Russell genocide convention held in Stockholm and Copenhagen (Bedau 1974; see also Sartre 1958). This kind of argument might underlie Turkey's denial of genocide against the Armenians. But if we understand more broadly as part of intent *the reasonably foreseeable consequences* voluntarily accepted as the *price* of attaining an aim, though not instrumental toward its attainment, then the slaughter of the Armenians and the deaths of at least some Native American nations from European diseases is not so clear.[5] On this broader view of intent, it has been argued that Joseph Stalin's economic policies that resulted in the starvation of millions of Ukrainian peasants in 1932–33 were genocidal, because those consequences were utterly foreseeable. Starvation was not a means but a price Stalin willingly accepted for achieving his aims. In Kantian terms, that price is part of the morally relevant maxim (statement of intent), just as my foreseeing that I cannot keep my promise is included in the maxim of Kant's most famous illustration, though it is neither an end nor a means.

Regarding the scope of the UN definition, the question of narrowness has been raised in regard to the acts and in regard to the groups enumerated. Some ask why only these acts and not others, such as forcible expulsion or rape aimed at enforced pregnancy (Allen 1996). But the UN definition, as stated, does not preclude continuing the list of acts. Since Yugoslavia and Rwanda, mass rape is widely acknowledged as among acts that can be constitutive of genocide. Those wars also raise the issue of mass expulsions, which should get us to ponder whether Spain's expulsions of the Jews in the late fifteenth century and the Moriscos in the seventeenth were genocides. Much social vitality was lost and entire communities destroyed.

In regard to *groups*, many ask, why limit genocide to "national, ethnical, racial, or religious" groups? Why not political groups? What about the disabled? Or gays? females? evil groups? The UN definition does not say what the groups it enumerates have in common.

Whether to include political groups was controversial at the convention. Like religious communities, political communities give meaning and shape to the lives of their members. Some said the definition should include only groups into which one is born. Although religious and national groups can be joined and exited voluntarily, they are commonly an inherited aspect of one's identity, which is less true of political groups. Some prefer the term "politicide" for destruction of political groups (even if the destruction is massively homicidal) and "ethnicide" for cultural genocides not massively homicidal (Chalk and Johnasson 1990). A commonly cited example of

4 Thanks to Martin Shaw for pressing me on the question of violence, and to my colleague Steven Nadler for getting me to think about whether the gradual suppression, without the use of force or violence, of customs that once defined a valuable way of life would be genocidal. There are, historically, good reasons to include violence in the definition of genocide, although neither the U.N. definition nor Lemkin's definition explicitly does. But then we should want a generous understanding of violence. I would regard a mass poisoning, on the scale of the Jonestown massacre, as genocidal. If a whole people died from deliberate poisoning of its water or other essential elements of its environment, would that not be genocide? What if they were gassed instead? Is gassing violent? Gas is deliverable by missiles, commonly regarded as weapons, which suggest violence.

5 For divergent views on the mass deaths of Native Americans, see Stannard 1992 and Katz 1994.

"politicide" is Stalin's purges of his political opponents. A commonly cited example of cultural genocide is the transportation and reeducation of children, as done to Native American children in the U.S. and mixed race children in Australia, both forbidden to use their native languages and to communicate with their families of origin. Those who favored including "politicides" lost at the 1948 convention whereas those who favored including forced cultural assimilations won their point. That inclusion means that, on this definition, a genocide need not be massively homicidal.

The Murder, Inc. problem was apparently not considered at the convention, which regarded its task as to define a *crime*. But what if a religious group that gave meaning and shape to the lives of its members centered on the practice of human sacrifice? Would the intentional destruction of that religion by non-homicidal means be a genocide?

The Southern Poverty Law Center (SPLC) in the U.S. destroys white supremacist groups by bankrupting them with lawsuits. One reason to regard this as not a genocide is that it relies on non-violent means. Another is that it does not produce massive social death, despite its curbs on certain forms of social vitality. Likewise, a reason not to regard de-Nazification as genocidal is that its means, too, were lawful non-violent procedures, and they did not leave those de-Nazified socially dead. Still, lawful procedures can lead to legally sanctioned violence in enforcement. And dismantling those groups sounds something like condition "c" of the UN definition: deliberately imposing conditions of life calculated to bring about its [the group's] destruction. And so one might want to press the question whether there is anything about the group destroyed that distinguishes, in a non-arbitrary way, the projects of the SPLC and de-Nazification from genocidal projects?

Here is a way to think about that issue. It is not just that the groups are too small or too thin to constitute a people, even if they are. Some peoples are larger and richer, more layered, than others. Rather, there is an interesting disanalogy to be explained between killing an evil person and destroying an evil group: Why is destroying an evil *group* not necessarily murder (i.e., it can be justifiable), even if it produces social death in former members, whereas killing an evil *individual* is still murder (unjustifiable), unless done in self-defense, understood fairly narrowly? Being an evil person does not justify others in killing you. But it can be justifiable to destroy a group on the grounds that it is evil, that it inexcusably does intolerable harm.

A rationale that makes some sense to me, and is inspired by Stoic values, is that the principles or projects a person endorses at a particular time do not define or determine the worth of the person, whereas they can define or determine the worth of an organization. The person is capable of evaluating principles and projects, adopting and rejecting, discovering errors, correcting mistaken judgments and identifying other mistakes. With a new set of principles, I am the same person, morally speaking, who did what I did when I espoused different ones. I may *feel* like a new person. But that past is still mine. In contrast, for *some* human groups—e.g., some evil organizations—principles and projects really do define the organization. There is no way to reject those defining principles while preserving the organization. Other groups, such as states with a constitution and organized religions with processes for re-evaluating their positions or policies, are, like individuals, capable of self-correction. A people is the kind of group that has within itself resources to evaluate its members' positions, and so the worth of a people, like the worth of a person, is not simply a function of particular projects found within it.

But organizations like Murder, Inc. have as their *raisons d'*être the perpetration of such deeds as murder for hire and extortion. There was no way to eliminate those policies without the organization's ceasing to have its reason for existing. There is no meaningful distinction to be drawn here between the principles and projects that define the organization and the organization itself. That does not imply that *all* its projects were evil, only that essential ones were. Regarding the religion of human sacrifice, we should ask whether it could survive without that evil project.

Arguably, the Third Reich had too little capability of self-correction. Within Germany, some tried to get rid of Hitler. Thirteen failed assassination attempts are known, according to the documentary film *Operation Valkyrie: The Stauffenberg Plot to Kill Hitler* (2008). But there was no effective internal mechanism to remove Hitler from power. What is destroyed when such a group is destroyed are the inhumane projects to which it is committed. Likewise with Murder, Inc. and the Ku Klux Klan.

The defensible idea that it can be justifiable (thereby not genocidal) to destroy some evil groups (those lacking the capability of self-correction) may partly explain how neighbor can turn on neighbor in genocidal slaughter. If an authority, such as government, sponsors propaganda that portrays the neighbor's group as "purely evil," killers might regard their actions simply under the description "eliminating a purely evil group."

However, propaganda such as that portraying the Jews or the Hutus as a purely evil group could at best only partly explain the willing complicity in genocide of ordinary German or Rwandan citizens. For it matters *how* a group is destroyed. The SPLC does not kill white supremacists in the US. It bankrupts their organizations with law suits. Individual members of evil groups still have human rights. The SPLC's methods of destruction and those of de-Nazification aimed to respect the human rights of individuals. Genocides do not. This point, I think, is more fundamental than the use of violence and should be made explicit today in a definition of genocide. Although the concept of human rights was not well defined in international law until 1948 (also the year of the Genocide Convention), it had entered the common moral consciousness in Europe. I do not know whether human rights was a concept in the common moral consciousness of Rwandans in 1994. But where it is, the belief that one's neighbors belonged to an evil group could not plausibly explain willing complicity in the killing of the individual neighbor (or stranger, for that matter).

I consider next some groups not mentioned in the UN definition that today are widely regarded as deserving protection. What about the idea of a gay genocide? Would that make sense? Gays are not a people or clan. Yet, the men identified as homosexuals and forced to wear the "pink triangle" in Nazi camps suffered profound losses of social vitality specific to their being gay if they had been members of gay communities. Does such a forcibly imposed loss constitute a gay genocide? The case is interesting in that it was not exactly that the men's social identities were destroyed. The men continued to be identified, more conspicuously than ever, as homosexual. Rather, the meanings they had created for their identities were altered and devalued.

The men of the pink triangles resemble victims of genocide to the extent that their lives had importantly gained decent meaning from the gay communities to which they belonged. Yet those communities were far younger, transitory, in flux and inevitably less richly textured and layered than communities constituted by sharers of a natural language, religion, and multigenerational traditions. Furthermore, those communities were only part of what gave shape and meanings to the lives of their members, who had other communities of origin. Gay communities can have a life-saving impact on those who are otherwise cultural rejects. But many gays then, as now, did not belong to gay communities. Most likely to be rounded up and sent to concentration camps were those who met at gay bars or parties or were activists. Ludwig Wittgenstein's idea of family resemblance concepts is useful for thinking about whether the idea of a gay genocide makes sense (Wittgenstein 1958: 31–3). Destruction of gay communities is hardly a paradigm of genocide. But it bears some relevant similarities and so, when the assault is systematic, violent, and violates human rights, it might find a place in the extended family of genocidal assaults. Ways to think about it, on the social death hypothesis, are to consider to what extent the destroyed community had contributed decent sorts of social vitality to its members, and whether the loss of those meanings would leave those individuals socially dead.

The idea of a genocide of the disabled stretches the concept of genocide further. Yet there are communities built around the needs of persons with specific impairments, some to prevent the impairment from becoming a disability (Brownlee and Cureton 2011). Hitler's euthanasia program targeted disabled individuals. A tyrant with similar ambitions today might target communities.

"Femicide," the systematic murder of females, is not always a form of genocide. But it can be part of a genocidal project, a means of bringing about social death in a group to which females are essential. The practice of allowing infant females to die from exposure, for the purpose of population control, is not genocide, even if it is violent and violates human rights. And when Marc Lépine entered a Montreal classroom in 1989, announced he was "fighting feminism," separated the men from the women, shot nine women (killing six), and then roamed hallways shooting more women (fourteen all told), he became a misogynous mass murderer but not a perpetrator of genocide.

Females and feminists are classes or categories, not themselves communities, although they are essential to the reproduction of certain kinds of communities. Classes or categories, considered simply as such, are not the right sorts of groups to be candidates for genocide. The class of all the individuals (of many nationalities, religions, and ethnicities) in the Twin Towers on 9/11 does not define a community. It might be argued that the 9/11 bombings seen as part of a larger project could be regarded as *part* of an intended genocide, if the larger project had the right sort of target. The class of those in the downtown Federal building in Oklahoma City on April 19, 1995, or those in the targeted Tokyo subways on that fateful day in March the same year, might better illustrate groups that are not of the right sorts to be targets of genocide.

A cadet at the US Air Force Academy posed the following question after I had presented a version of this chapter: "Was Hitler's destruction of the Czech city of Lidice, in response to the assassination of Reinhard Heydrich, a genocide?" An astute question. If destruction of the city of Carthage was a genocide, why not that of Lidice? Again, a helpful way to think about it is to consider to what extent that city defined the social vitality of its members. The city of Lidice was part of the larger Czech state that was surely also a contributor to the social vitality of the inhabitants of its cities, which makes the case more complicated than that of Carthage.

A member of another audience asked about the Cambodian slaughters of the 1970s by the Khmer Rouge. In questioning whether genocide had to target a whole people, I had noted that in the Cambodian slaughters by the Khmer Rouge, victims who were identified as intellectuals because they wore glasses belonged to *the same people* as the perpetrators. My questioner asked whether those who wore glasses were not also a category, or class, rather than a community, and as such, not the right kind of group to be a target of genocide. My first response was that, yes, that was a good reason to question whether the Cambodian slaughters were a genocide. However, it can be argued, as Daniel Bultmann did later at the Potsdam genocide conference (August 2013), that destroying intellectuals was a means of destroying the larger community to which they belonged. It broke up families. It brought down social institutions and practices that had given meaning and identity to the lives of the Cambodian people, not just to its intellectuals. The Cambodian case is more complicated than a focus on immediate targets suggests.[6]

And so, what about Stalin's "politicides"? Political groups are not just categories. They create social vitality. The point of calling Stalin's politicides genocides might be that they imposed social death (not just physical death) on their victims, culminating in the show trials. However, they did this not *en masse* but by isolating targeted victims individually from families, friends, anyone and any social institution or practice that might have helped or sustained them. Still, the consequences

6 Hearing Bultmann's application of the social death idea to the Cambodian slaughters led me also to the more nuanced view that I currently hold on whether femicides can be genocidal.

may have included the social death of others to whom they were related or with whom they interacted socially in ways important to how they identified themselves. Stalin's politicides may have some of the features Bultmann identified in the Cambodian slaughters.

I turn next to the worry that the UN definition may be too wide, because of the phrase "in whole or in part." On the commonest interpretation, that phrase invites the question, "How big does the part have to be?" How many need be killed? One person is a part of a group. Yet the murder of one, or even a handful, is not a genocide, although it can be a hate crime. And how severe must the harm be? How many need be harmed or transferred? And so on. A proviso with which the U.S. eventually accepted the genocide convention was that the "part" had to be "a substantial part" (Charny 1999, vol. 2: 597). There seems no way to draw a line between genocides and less massive atrocities that is not arbitrary.

Lemkin's approach to defining genocide fits better with the social death hypothesis (thus specifying the kind of harm) and does not so naturally invite these unanswerable questions. In his view, genocides harm members of a group generally. Instead of interpreting "in whole or in part" as a matter of how many individuals are killed or harmed, what I call the Lemkin approach looks at the relationships and social institutions that define a group as a people—its educational institutions, child-rearing practices, language, economic practices, political practices, religion. Lemkin calls these the group's *essential foundations*. He defines genocide as "a coordinated plan of different actions aiming at the destruction of essential foundations of the life of national groups, with the aim of annihilating the groups themselves" (Lemkin 1944: 79). He attaches the aim of annihilating the group to the overall plan that aims to destroy foundations of the life of the group. In contrast, the UN definition attaches that aim to enumerated kinds of actions, thereby inviting the question how many such actions need be performed.

On the Lemkin approach, the group is destroyed by destroying the relationships, contemporary and inter-generational, created by social institutions that are foundational for defining its members as a people. This destruction typically takes place in stages as more and more social restrictions and prohibitions are imposed. It is not as though religious, ethnical, and national groups are different kinds of targets. Rather, religious, ethnic, and political institutions are what bind individuals together into a people, and it is the people that is the target. Like the UN definition, Lemkin's understanding allows for degrees of genocide. But the degrees are kinds and ranges of social vitality destroyed, which tends to affect individuals in the group generally, not just a part of the group, even if not all are affected in the same way or to the same degree. Lemkin also understands a genocide as having two phases: first, the destruction of a people; second, the imposition of a new people on the land *or individuals* remaining (Lemkin 1944: 79). Destruction of a people does not always require mass slaughter. Hitler reserved that measure for those he considered un-Germanizable.

To illustrate the difference between the UN approach and the Lemkin approach, consider US President Bill Clinton's explanation of why he had not intervened to stop the Rwandan genocide. In saying he did not realize "the depth and speed with which [Rwandans] were being engulfed by this unimaginable terror" (Power 386), he seemed impressed mainly by how many were killed and how fast, as though body counts were key to its being a genocide. On Lemkin's approach, one would have looked for destruction of social vitality in terms of practices, institutions, and relationships, a destruction that began well before and facilitated the bloodbath.

Given what is commonly not known outside Rwanda about that genocide, it might appear to onlookers as though Rwanda were a counter-example to the social death hypothesis. Most salient to onlookers was the rapid mass slaughter by machete. Where was there even time for social death? But, in fact, the mass slaughters were preceded by a series of social restrictions and prohibitions that destroyed the social vitality of those perceived as Tutsis, making it easier for Hutus to kill them and harder for survivors to rebuild. Samantha Power writes that the Hutu newspaper *Kangura* published in December 1990 a list of “Ten Commandments of the Hutu,” governing relations between Hutu and Tutsi (Power 2002: 338–9). Included were such statements as that any Hutu who marries, befriends, or employs as a secretary or concubine a Tutsi woman shall be considered a traitor, and likewise for any Hutu who makes a business partnership with a Tutsi, invests money in a Tutsi enterprise, or lends to or borrows money from a Tutsi, and the list goes on (Power 2002: 228–9).

Similarly, she writes, in the town of Celinas in northern Bosnia non-Serbs were given “special status” prior to expelling them or concentrating them in camps. A curfew was imposed from 4: 00 in the afternoon to 6:00 in the morning. Non-Serbs were prohibited from (1) meeting in cafes, restaurants, or other public places, (2) bathing or swimming in the nearby rivers, (3) hunting or fishing, (4) moving to another town without permission, (5) carrying a weapon, (6) driving or traveling by car, and the list goes on (Power 2002, 250). The restrictions were less dramatic, less perceptible to outsiders, than the subsequent mass slaughters. But what is most dramatic or perceptible is not necessarily core.

In conclusion, I return to two of the most commonly asked questions with which I began.

1. How do genocides differ from non-genocidal atrocities?

First, non-genocidal mass murders can victimize aggregates or classes of individuals whose deaths are not a means to social death in their societies. Second, genocides aim to destroy peoples or other groups that have basic capacities for choice that we value in persons and that create decent forms of social vitality in their members. But genocides need not aim to destroy every member of the group. Scholars regard the destruction of the people of the island of Melos by the Athenians in the fifth century BCE as a genocide. But the Athenians killed only men and enslaved women and children, common practice then. The people of the island was destroyed as a people, although many individuals survived.

Some worry that the concept of genocide is diluted in an unfortunate way if mass killing of individuals is not considered essential. In response, first, it is not obvious that physical death is *always* graver than social death. Consider the mass rapes aimed at enforced pregnancy perpetrated in the former Yugoslavia in the 1990s. They left many female survivors little more than gestating corpses, social outcasts, unmarriageable, their offspring unassimilable. What had those survivors to look forward to other than life-long post-traumatic stress? Would their fate have been worse had they been killed? The worst harm Immanuel Kant imagined was to have one’s humanity *disrespected*, to be treated as if one were a thing, treated only as a means (Kant 1996a, 80; 1996b, 77–8). Hannah Arendt identified an even worse harm in her description of “living corpses,”namely, the *erosion or destruction* of one’s humanity, being reduced to an automaton, not just treated *as if* one were a thing (Arendt 2004: 582–92).

2. Is genocide the worst crime, or the greatest evil, imaginable?

If massive social death, a matter of degree, is central to genocide and mass homicide is not necessary, the answer has to be, as Larry May argued recently (2010), “not necessarily.” Further, not every genocide could be the worst atrocity if only because some genocides are worse than others. Forced assimilation and transportation of children can result in great losses of social vitality. But if there remains the possibility of regeneration, or there are substantive remnants of social vitality, it would probably have been worse to kill the children or enslave them.

Finally, because of their complexity, evils can defy ranking. Severity of harm is only one basic element of an evil. The other element is the inexcusable wrong behind the harm. Some evils, including some genocides, have worse motives than others. Some do worse harm. And the ones with worse motives need not be the ones that do worse harm. The same applies to comparisons of genocides with other atrocities.

Acknowledgments

I owe many thanks for helpful discussion of earlier drafts of this essay to audiences at the United States Air Force Academy, the University of Wisconsin, and the International Genocide Conference of philosophers and sociologists in Potsdam, Germany, August 2–3, 2013, organized by Roy Knocke. I am especially grateful to Daniel Bultmann for his perceptive application of the concept of social death to the Cambodian slaughters. I am especially grateful also to Martin Shaw both for his comments in Potsdam, stimulating me to think about the role of violence, and for his illuminating work on war and genocide (Shaw 2003 and 2007).

References

Arendt, Hannah. 2004. *The Origins of Totalitarianism*. Introduction by Samantha Power. New York: Schocken Book.

Allen, Beverly. 1996. *Rape Warfare: The Hidden Genocide in Bosnia-Herzegoviona and Croatia*. Minneapolis, MN: University of Minnesota Press.

Bedau, Hugo Adam. 1974. "Genocide in Vietnam?" In *Philosophy, Morality, and International Affairs*, ed. Virginia Held, Sidney Morgenbesser, and Thomas Nagel. New York: Oxford University Press.

Balakian, Peter. 2003. *The Burning Tigris: The Armenian Genocide and America's Response*. New York: HarperCollins.

Blee, Kathleen. 1991. *Women of the Klan: Women and Gender in the 1920s*. Berkeley, CA: University of California Press.

Brownlee, Kimberly and Adam Cureton, eds. 2011. *Disability and Disadvantage*. New York: Oxford University Press.

Bultmann, Daniel. 2013. Unpublished. "Commentary: Claudia Card On 'Genocide and Social Death'." Presented at the International Genocide Conference, Potsdam, Germany, August 2–3.

Card, Claudia. 2002. *The Atrocity Paradigm: A Theory of Evil*. New York: Oxford University Press.

Card, Claudia. 2010. *Confronting Evils: Terrorism, Torture, Genocide*. Cambridge: Cambridge University Press.

Card, Claudia and Armen T. Marsoobian, eds. 2007. *Genocide's Aftermath*. Malden, MA: Blackwell.

Chalk, Frank and Kurt Jonassohn, eds. 1990. *The History and Sociology of Genocide: Analyses and Case Studies*. New Haven, CT: Yale University Press.

Charny, Israel (editor in chief). 1999. *Encyclopedia of Genocide*, 2 vols Santa Barbara, CA: ABS-CLIO, Inc.

Glare, P.G.W. 1982. *Oxford Latin Dictionary*. Oxford: Clarendon Press.

Kant, Immanuel. 1996a. *Practical Philosophy*. Trans. and ed. Mary J. Gregor. Cambridge: Cambridge University Press.

Kant, Immanuel. 1996b. *Religion and Rational Theology*. Trans. and ed. Allen W. Wood. Cambridge: Cambridge University Press.
Katz, Steven. 1994. *The Holocaust in Historical Context, vol. 1: Mass Death before the Modern Age*. New York: Oxford University Press.
Lemkin, Raphael. 1944. *Axis Rule in Occupied Europe*. Washington, DC: Carnegie Endowment for International Peace.
Liddell, Henry George and Robert Scott. 1940. *Greek-English Lexicon*, 9th edn, rev. and augmented by Henry Stuart Jones with Roderick McKenzie. Oxford: Clarendon Press.
May, Larry. 2010. *Genocide: A Normative Account*. Cambridge: Cambridge University Press.
Patterson, Orlando. 1982. *Slavery and Social Death*. Cambridge, MA: Harvard University Press.
Power, Samantha. 2002. *"A Problem from Hell": America and the Age of Genocide*. New York: Basic Books.
Sartre, Jean-Paul. 1968. *On Genocide*. Boston, MA: Beacon Press.
Shaw, Martin. 2003. *What Is Genocide?* Cambridge: Polity.
Shaw, Martin. 2007. *War and Genocide: Organized Killing in Modern Society*. Cambridge: Polity.
Stannard, David E. 1992. *American Holocaust: The Conquest of the New World*. New York: Oxford University Press.
Stuckey, Sterling. 1987. *Slave Culture: Nationalist Theory and the Foundations of Black America*. New York: Oxford University Press.
Turkus, Burton B. and Sid Feder. 1951. *Murder, Inc.* New York: Manor Books.
Wittgenstein, Ludwig. 1958. *Philosophical Investigations*. Trans. G.E.M. Anscombe. Oxford: Blackwell.

Chapter 15

Making Reparations Possible: Theorizing Reparative Justice

Margaret Urban Walker

To hold that redressing a wrong is an obligation of justice is to hold that some remedial action is (at least *prima facie*) necessary, something that morally *must* be done. The requirements of justice are usually understood to be ones that we are required to meet in all cases in which practical circumstances are not so dire or chaotic as to prevent our performance, and in which no other obligations of comparable gravity or urgency conflict. It is curious, then, how often arguments in recent theoretical literature on reparations for massive violence and abuse aim to show that reparations are impossible (or nearly impossible)—logically, morally, or practically—to make. Some claim to show that, regrettably, the very worst among actual injustices—atrocity, genocide, slavery, dispossession, and the like—are ones for which just repair is simply impossible. Yet these are the very cases for which we invoke the concept of reparations.

The absence of theory concerning justice in repair is curious as well. Despite vast and varied theoretical literatures on distributive and retributive justice, with competing positions grounded in philosophical commitments and tested by practical implications, the contemporary theoretical literature on reparative justice remains relatively slight. To begin with (and not inconsequentially), there is no uniformly agreed-upon terminology for the kind of justice in question. While many authors speak of corrective or (in an older tradition) commutative justice, others speak of compensatory, rectificatory, reparatory, or reparative justice, without clarification about whether these are labels for the same kind of theory or principle. There is relatively little in the way of genuine theories of reparative justice. Instead, many writers assume or invoke some version of the principle that justice requires a victim of wrongdoing to be returned by the wrongdoer to the state the victim enjoyed prior to, or would have enjoyed in the absence of, the wrong. This is, of course, Aristotle's conception of commutative (or corrective) justice. But whatever luster of authority that philosophical pedigree imparts to corrective justice, its more immediate referent is legal practice concerning remedies for unjust harms and losses, where responsible parties are required to make restitution to wronged individuals, or pay them compensation in proportion to harm or loss, in cases of tort or breach of contract. The principle of corrective justice is for the party at fault to restore the prior condition of the wronged party as nearly as possible by wiping out the consequences of the wrong.

To illustrate the poverty of such narrow thinking about reparative justice, I begin with a number of arguments in very recent theoretical writing on reparations that aim to show that justice in repair is defective or deceptive, where it is possible at all. I call them "impossibility arguments." They share the assumption that justice in repair is identical to or exhausted by corrective justice: justice in repair consists in cancelling out or reversing wrongful harms, typically by means of restitution or proportionate compensation. I propose that we see impossibility arguments, resting on the corrective justice premise, as reductio arguments: if reparations are necessary as obligations of justice, they must typically be possible; if certain assumptions about the nature of reparative justice make them (nearly or commonly) impossible, then those assumptions must be incorrect. Reliance on the corrective justice assumption represents a failure to pursue an adequate theory of (what I will call) 'reparative justice', the broadest genus of justice in repair. A theory of reparative justice must expose its core concerns, guiding aims, and implications in practice. A useful theory would also identify the specific challenges and limits, including sources of resistance, to justice in repair.

I will offer in broad outline an account of the nature and guiding aim of reparative justice. My view takes as a reference point the new contemporary practice of political reparations for mass violence and systemic human rights abuse that emerged in the mid-twentieth century. This nascent practice, I will argue below, is an important reference point for the theory of reparative justice. It has resulted (and will no doubt continue to develop) through tests and struggles that can be seen as a set of experiments in discovering what constitutes and signifies justice in repair, however imperfect, for massive human rights crimes. An adequate account of reparative justice ought not only to cohere with but to explain prominent features of this new practice, especially for my purposes here, the diversity of measures that embody justice in repair. Finally, corrective justice ought to find a place within this broader account; I think it can be seen as one implementation of reparative justice within a certain institutional framework under certain political conditions.

Impossibility Arguments

A surprising number of current arguments concerning reparations for mass violence and political repression aim to show that reparative justice is impossible or irrelevant. A number of very recent papers illustrate common ways of thinking about reparative justice that result in impossibility arguments (Du Plessis and Peté 2007; Williams et al. 2012). Some arguments aim to deflate or abuse the idea of corrective justice in response to massive harms while others aim to displace the application of reparative justice in favor of "prospective," "forwarding looking," or distributive justice. All of these arguments assume that justice in repair of wrongs is corrective justice, so whether the standard of corrective justice is fulfilled determines whether reparations, envisioned or made, are true, real, "first-best," adequate, serious, or meaningful as attempts at justice. The conclusion in various versions is that reparations are doomed to inadequacy; in the benign case they fail at doing justice while in the worst case they impede justice or violate it.

Gary Bass argues that reparations are at best a "noble lie," since atrocity or genocide "cannot be undone" and compensation for such crimes "can never be adequate if measured against the depth of the wound" (Bass 2012: 167 and 171). Bass places reparations in parallel to war crimes tribunals, calling reparations a kind of war tort. By the corrective justice standard of "normal tort law" (169) that requires compensation in proportion to injury, reparations cannot be other than a "tokenistic measure ... to mollify the victims ... " (167). While he recognizes that in some cases victims seek admissions and apologies instead of or in addition to compensation, justice demands proportionate compensation (171). This argument may seem simplistic, but I have heard versions of it on many occasions in discussion: reparations are inherently wrong-headed or incoherent because we cannot change the past or undo what has been done. It is worth remarking this kind of argument, not only for its equation of money payments with "real" justice, but because it is problematic in two other ways. No one is more acutely aware than victims of grave wrongs that there is no undoing many of them; what they seek as reparations can hardly be that. On the other hand, in some cases what has happened in the past may indeed be "undone" and is exactly what victims seek: return of land, restoration of rights and status, or the correction of false history.

Jon Elster, in the same volume, shares the idea that only material reparations are real reparations. But while Bass sees symbolic gestures as noble, or at least kindly, Elster scorns them. In the aftermath of widespread abuses, he argues, there are demands of distributive, retributive, restitutive, and compensatory justice to be met (Elster 2012: 80). When it comes to reparations, "Unless governments are willing to put their money where their mouth is," it is nothing but "cheap talk," including official apologies, which are likely to be "meaningless," "absurd," or "empty" (86). If, on the other hand, governments do fund reparations, they might unjustly "punish" non-victims or collateral victims if reparations draw resources away from compelling distributive justice demands (92–3). In any case, "full reparation at a large scale may be economically unfeasible" (93). Reparations, seen as corrective compensation, are probably unwise if not unjust, and often impossible.

Adrian Vermeule also assumes that reparation means compensation and that corrective compensation in reparations is chronically inadequate. But it is no more "disastrously unprincipled" than the ordinary legal system of corrective justice (Vermeule 2012: 163). In many such cases, Vermeule argues, inadequate and non-individuated compensation fails to satisfy justice but responds to an unprincipled sense of "rough justice," an intuition that some compensation is better than none at all (151). While reparations are "indefensible on any plausible first-best criterion of justice," and although there may be problems of unequal treatment among the compensated, and between the compensated and the uncompensated, this second-best is *not more* objectionable than what goes on in ordinary corrective justice. Vermeule thus defends reparations, but not because it answers to any principled idea or conception of justice appropriate to its own aims and demands. In other words, to say that it is rough justice is to say it's not really justice at all, and to say that arbitrary compensation is better than none at all suggests that compensation, and only compensation, is at issue in the justice of repair.

Other arguments claim that reparations are not really best understood as an exercise of backward-looking justice at all, or that if they are so understood, they are superseded or preempted by forward-looking distributive justice demands. These arguments say, in effect, that if we seek justice in addressing wrongs we should adopt forward-looking or distributive justice as our guide (see also Wenar 2006 and Pierik 2006).

Writing on expropriated land in former communist countries, Christopher Kutz argues that corrective justice is a distinct and valid normative ground for justice in repair, and one that embodies ideals of accountability, but it is often "the wrong framework for considering reparative claims" (Kutz 2004: 302). Because corrective justice rectifies wrongful invasions of entitlements it is dependent for its force on a distributively just scheme of entitlements (297). As a consequence, a state has "no business" meeting reparations claims in those cases where it is unable to ensure minimally adequate standards of living generally (301). Applied generally, Kutz's claim for the priority of distributive justice would put material reparations—and possibly symbolic ones that too have their cost—out of bounds in most cases. Given the serious distributive injustice of most societies even by minimal standards, limited resources should be put to the more fundamental work of distributive justice. If there is an argument for return of expropriated land, he argues, that argument will be one of distributive justice, where a group is entitled to its land as a condition of continuing its tradition and culture (310). Kutz sees the reparative value of symbolic recognition, including symbolic monetary payments, as acknowledgment of "the legal and moral subjectivity of the victims" (284). But he seems to see these as forward-looking questions of national identity being reconstructed or transformed (281–3). It is unclear what space is left in his scheme for a kind of reparative justice—neither corrective nor retributive—that grounds independent claims of redress for victims of specific grievous wrongs in the past.

Jeremy Webber argues that reparations (and other transitional justice measures) are often about "prospective justice" that seeks to bring parties into relationship on a just foundation for the future (Webber 2012: 104). Retrospective corrective justice, on the other hand, involves a "narrow optic" that simply seeks to reverse a wrongful transaction without addressing broader questions (121). Even payment often functions symbolically, as an "earnest" to lend weight to apologies or other measures that look forward to better future relations. (105). While reparations programs can partake of both backward-looking corrective compensation of individuals and constructively forward-looking reconstruction of relationships, these forms of justice operate by "very different logics" (107). They pose choices, and potentially dilemmas, about whether "to focus on the nature of past wrongs" or "to manage parties' relations from here on" (108). So, where Kutz finds a dependency of corrective justice on distributive justice, Webber finds a tension between two independent and competing principles.

Webber illustrates this claim with the case of indigenous peoples, who may seek redress through actual land restitution but also seek to reconstitute their relationship through prospective claims to greater resources and autonomy (111–12). Indeed, Webber points out, they might be willing to forego retrospective remedies to secure self-determination (112). While this claim about some indigenous peoples might be correct, it establishes only that cases of profound, multifaceted, extended, and deeply destructive histories of relationship between people or peoples may give rise to multiple justice claims of distinct types that compete for resources, practical priority, and political traction. What it does not show is that reparative justice is exhausted by corrective justice and its modes of redress for the past are confined to that "narrow optic" of reversing an unjust transaction. If corrective justice alone redresses the past, then where corrective justice cannot be done the past cannot be the focus of justice, and justice claims must look to the future instead. What is missing is an examination of diverse ways, beyond corrective justice, that reparative justice can engage the past and attempt redress. In the choice between past and future, the actual scene of reparations struggles—the present—is not in view.

While Kutz has corrective and distributive justice as distinct normative principles with a priority ordering, and Webber sees them as principles with divergent temporal orientations that can be in tension, Michael Freeman sees corrective justice as a proper part of distributive justice, because it "specifies rightful (re)distribution" (Freeman 2012: 39). Surprisingly, however, Freeman argues that the focus on rectifying past wrongs makes reparative justice "conceptually distinct" and its claims possibly incompatible with distributive justice, especially in cases of historical injustice (14). The claim that reparative justice is a part of distributive justice, however, turns out to be no more than nominal, for reparative justice for Freeman is simply corrective justice, expressed in the principle, "If A wrongfully harms B, then in the absence of overriding considerations, A should compensate B for the wrong" (29); or, more concisely, "The first principle of reparative justice is that the wrongdoer pays" (39). Freeman rehearses many familiar objections to reparative justice so conceived. His paper ends, however, with the acknowledgment that "We have no comprehensive and integrated theory of reparative justice" (50). Given this, one wonders why Freeman is sure what its first principle is. In any case, he concludes that " ... the more difficult it is to achieve reparative justice, the more it should be dominated by distributive justice" (49).

Current impossibility arguments echo a famous prototype, Jeremy Waldron's argument that claims for repair of historical injustices such as land theft are likely to be "superseded" by present and future distributive claims. Waldron says, " ... it is the impulse to justice now that should lead the way in this process, not the reparation of something whose wrongness is understood primarily in relation to conditions that no longer obtain" (Waldron 1992: 27). In variations on a theme, current impossibility arguments purport to show that what is done as reparations is deceptive or wrong-headed; that it is merely "symbolic" in a deflationary sense; that what might be done is actually a different kind of justice, something other than justice, or something contrary to justice; or that reparative justice should be left aside in favor of another kind of justice. Most of all, it looks in the wrong direction, to an inert and unrecoverable past.

I don't mean to suggest that there are no constructive arguments concerning reparations that are rooted in a corrective justice approach (see Winter 2006 and 2014, Bernstein 2009, and Sammons 2012 for diverse examples). Yet many have argued that a "juridical," or "tort," or "corrective justice" model is often inadequate or unhelpful applied precisely to the kinds of cases that reparations are meant to address, including mass violence in conflict, genocide and crimes against humanity, systemic gross human rights violations, severe political repression, or extreme intergenerational injustices with long histories (Thompson 2002; Brooks 2004; De Greiff 2006b; Walker 2006a; Yamamoto et al. 2007; Satz 2007; Verdeja 2007; Gray 2010a; Philpott 2012). Here I add the point that corrective justice not only fails to guide understanding or action in many such cases, but can function affirmatively as a lever to deflect, demote, or dismiss reparations claims as hopeless, wrong-headed, or destructive. Impossibility arguments serve a kind of reparations skepticism at a time when a distinctive new global practice and "reparations ethos" has been taking form (Falk 2006: 485; see also Barkan 2000).

A New Practice of Reparations

If we think that reparations for these massive and complex wrongs are indeed a requirement of justice, we need alternative ways of theorizing the concerns, aims, and measures of reparative justice. In doing so, I believe we should study the new practice of reparations that emerged in the later twentieth century, a practice that has been shaped by activities by and on behalf of victims of human rights violations and historical injustice around the globe. The multiform character of reparations in this new practice sets a task for the theory of reparative justice: to understand what are the underlying concerns that explain the complexity and diversity of reparations.

It is widely agreed that the payment of reparations by West Germany to individual survivors of the Holocaust after WWII introduced a genuinely new practice, treating individuals, and not only nations, as the subjects of claims against states for reparations for grave violations (Colonomos 2006). Extensive programs of reparations for victims and families were instituted in waves in the aftermath of brutal military governments in Latin American countries, especially Chile and Argentina, that engaged in repression, torture, disappearance, and illegal detention of their citizens. The United States legislated a reparations program in 1988 for Japanese-Americans interned during the World War Two, over 40 years after the events. After two decades of study, the United Nations General Assembly in 2005 endorsed the "Basic Principles and Guidelines on the Right to a Remedy and Reparation for Victims of Gross Violations of International Human Rights Law and Serious Violations of International Humanitarian Law" distilling a set of measures for making full and effective reparation, understood as a human right in the case of severe abuses (United Nations 2006). The Basic Principles did not invent this new practice of reparations. It has developed out of popular and civil society movements representing the needs and expectations of victims and their societies as well as the work of domestic and international institutions. The Basic Principles consolidated a wide-ranging and accelerating set of developments in many places: actual programs of reparations; recommendations of appropriate reparations by truth commissions; decisions by international courts (especially the Inter-American Court of Human Rights); reparations by private entities; reparations proposals and demands by NGOs and victim advocacy groups; domestic and international lawsuits seeking compensation; and legal and academic scholarship (see De Greiff 2006; Johnston and Slyomovics 2009; Du Plessis and Peté 2007).

Section IX of the Basic Principles stress five categories of reparations measures. The first two are the familiar ones of *restitution*, interpreted broadly to include liberty, legal standing, residence, citizenship, and employment, and *compensation* for both economically assessable and moral damage. A third is medical, psychological, social, and legal *rehabilitation* services. The last two categories involve very diverse interventions. *Satisfaction* includes eight distinct measures: to stop ongoing violations; to verify and disclose the truth publicly; to search for and rebury those disappeared or abducted; to officially declare the reputation and rights of victims; to apologize publicly; to sanction responsible parties administratively or judicially; to commemorate and honor victims; and to include an accurate account of violations in educational materials. The final category, *guarantees of non-repetition*, includes various preventive measures including institutional reforms: an independent judiciary; due process guarantees; civilian control of the military; training and education of public officials; monitoring; and institutional and legal reforms. These are all measures that have been recommended repeatedly in truth commission reports and are increasingly ordered by some international courts (Schonsteiner 2007).

I want to call attention to three features of the practice described. First, the Basic Principles are addressed to states, and state responsibility for reparations is assumed. Several kinds of measures mentioned can only be provided by state institutions. Where other persons or entities are liable, they should provide reparations; if other liable parties are unable or unwilling, states should establish national programs. Second, the Principles expressly recognize that victimization of individual persons may also be directed against groups of persons who are targeted collectively, and that states should develop procedures to allow groups of victims to pursue reparations. These two features are not my principal concern here, but they suggest significant dimensions in which the corrective justice model—with its individualized picture of injury and liability to compensate—does not capture or explain distinctive features of the practice.

It is the third feature I want to emphasize here. The Basic Principles do not rank the different categories of reparations measures. Restitution and compensation are paradigmatic legal remedies, but practice has revealed that acknowledgment, responsibility-taking, truth telling, apology, and memorialization, as well as credible guarantees of non-repetition, often turn out to be foremost in importance to individuals and groups who have suffered human rights abuses (in contrast, for interstate remedies, see Shelton 2002). The common distinction between "material" and "symbolic" reparations, while useful for some purposes, can be very misleading here. A symbol or symbolic gesture is what stands in for or represents something else that is absent or only indicated. To call some reparations—such as apologies, truth telling, or commemoration—"symbolic" is to imply that they are not the real thing. Yet one thing learned in contemporary reparations attempts is how essential it is to victims of wrongs that money be accompanied by, or be part of, truth telling, responsibility-taking, and gestures of respect toward victims. Even where it is necessary, money is not sufficient (see Hamber 2009 and Mazurana et al. 2013). Money may be refused or understood as insulting in the absence of honest accountability, respectful recognition, and clear admission of wrongs. The "material/symbolic" distinction also fails to capture the concrete but expressive role played by preventive reforms. To undertake major change in societal institutions is costly in money as well as social and political capital; but as part of a program of reparations it also sends to victims and to society at large the message that what happened to the victims is simply intolerable and cannot be allowed to happen again.

The diversity of measures that constitute reparations is striking; these measures recognize, respect, enable, and support victims not only materially, but psychologically, legally, civically, and politically. Restitution and compensation have a central role, and in many cases there can be no substitute for material redress. But there are other essential dimensions of reparations, including gestures and actions that dignify and empower victims and that stress a societal commitment to structural reform so that the suffering of victims is not repeated. While some of these reparative measures could in principle be implemented by individuals responsible for wrongs, most of them are or entail societal responsibilities for publicly communicating the dignity and deservingness of victims and society's obligation to create the conditions in which victims can not only deal with their injuries but continue their lives as full civil and political actors. These measures thus address a problem larger than discrete injury; they recognize a problem of social and political standing that may be both a cause and a result of gross violations. A theory of reparative justice should try to illuminate what the multiform reparations agenda is seeking to address.

Rethinking Reparative Justice

Several new approaches in theorizing reparative justice have emerged. They have in common a focus on the roles of reparations (and other post-conflict or transitional measures) in reconfiguring or reconstituting the flawed moral and political relationships that invite abuses and are revealed by the specific forms abuses take. The point is not restoring the status quo ante but affirming a new baseline for moral and political engagement going forward. These accounts are not uncritical concerning reparations efforts; they offer normative perspectives from which reparations attempts can be found more or less apt or adequate. They are not skeptical of the project of reparations as such; instead, they are prompted by new and diverse forms of reparations and by renewed attention to questions of historical injustice. Many of these theories see reparations as establishing new relationships of recognition, trust, equality, respect, atonement, or reconciliation (on civic recognition and trust, see De Greiff 2006b; on relations of respect and reciprocity, see Thompson 2002, Satz 2007, Verdeja 2007, and Murphy 2010). The central idea of my own view is that reparations are about demonstrating (rather than establishing) relations of accountability and reciprocity that no process or program of reparations can itself guarantee. Reparations are a medium for the contentious yet hopeful negotiation in the present of proper recognition of the past and proper terms of relation for the future. As such they require mutually reinforcing commitments in multiple registers of relationship: money, acknowledgment, public ritual, social change.

Corrective justice—the idea that one party or group can hold another to account for wrongful harm suffered, can pose terms of restitution or compensation, and can seek a resolution in that way—*presupposes* that parties stand in relations of effective accountability and reciprocity, and can activate these relations through institutional channels when they seek correction or redress. Where, for example, a legal system gives its citizens rights to a remedy for unjust harms or losses they have suffered and where citizens in fact have access to the institutions that can provide or enforce those remedies, corrective justice describes one standard implementation of justice in repair. Even in societies that provide this legal avenue, however, not all citizens may have equal access to these institutions and some may have none. Some citizens may not have reason to expect a fair hearing or may find that a legal system that historically permitted or enforced their oppression, dispossession, or subordination now sets terms for remedies that disqualify their claims, as unsuccessful legal actions by African-Americans for corporate reparations have found (Brophy 2006 and Sammons 2012). Yet it is the *absence* of precisely these relations that lies at the root of many of the profound harms and gross abuses where reparations are sought. Relationships of accountability and reciprocity may not have obtained at the root historically, as in the case of chattel slavery in the United States and its aftermaths of segregation, domination, and racial violence. They might have been inconsistent and fragile, as in the case of treaties and alliances made with indigenous peoples and then quickly and willfully discarded for conquest, genocide, and dispossession. They might be shallowly or selectively functional until historical resentments, current power struggles, or competition for resources gives political opportunists an opening with violent consequences, as in Germany in the 1930s, or in the former Yugoslavia or Rwanda in the 1990s. The details in all their variety are crucial for reparations in any particular case. But a common factor is that reparations typically seek repair in a context where accountability and reciprocity themselves are at issue (Walker 2014).

Accountability is the relationship in which we see each other as answerable to each other under some common standards—whether I can reprimand you for your table manners, or insist on an apology for your lack of consideration, or take you to court for a breach of contract. Accountability relations can take formal legal or institutional forms, but upholding common standards of *any kind*—from etiquette to human rights—requires accountability between us. If you have the power to be unmoved by my demands, to be indifferent to the harms you cause me, or even to retaliate against me for presuming that I can hold you to account, we do not stand in this most basic moral and social relations. And if I have the privilege of assuming that what goes for me need not go for you—that I deserve protection but you deserve none; that I can demand your respect, but you may not expect mine—we are not in a relationship of reciprocity at some level, perhaps even at the level of human decency. It is the absence of accountability and reciprocity that lies at the root of the kinds of gross violations and profound harms to which programs of reparations respond. I suggest that *signifying the possibility of a relationship of accountability and reciprocity* where there has been none, or where it has been dangerously unreliable, is the fundamental task of reparations—to which all its varied measures are a means. In some cases substantial material restitution or compensation will be indispensable but it will never by itself be enough unless it is accompanied by other measures that signify clear acknowledgment, responsibility, and the intent to do justice (Walker 2013). This is something we can begin to see in the new practice of reparations.

It is also visible in a spreading rejection of the corrective justice or "tort model" of reparations and in the emergence of related but contending accounts of reparative justice. Erik Yamamoto, Sandra Kim, and Abigail Holden see international practice as a model of "remaking societal understandings of who is worthy of redress" (Yamamoto et al. 2007: 74). David Gray writes that the reparations must aim at new social and material conditions in order to "achieve a sustainable new equilibrium among members of groups," and to situate victims "as individuals capable of being wronged" (Gray 2010b, 1101–102). Pablo De Greiff argues that reparations must aim at recognition of victims as bearers of rights, and at reestablishing trust between citizens and in their institutions, based on confidence that shared values and norms are real and regarded as binding on all (De Greiff 2006b). In these views and others we see the beginning of a genuine project of theorizing reparative justice, creating a field of contending approaches with potentially different explanations of, and implications for, reparations practice.

My own view of reparations emphasizes the central but neglected role of hope (Walker 2006b). Since reparations can only ever be particular measures or programs at particular times, they cannot bear the whole weight of actually remaking understandings, bringing about a new equilibrium, or establishing trust. They can only inspire a hopeful willingness for victims of injustice to believe in and to try for better relationships, *if* others will struggle towards an understanding of past wrongs and failed relationships, and accept the need for adequate gestures of amends for the past and strong guarantees for the future that truly reflect an engagement among equals. If others become accountable—by actually accounting and making amends—then hope is reasonable, and it becomes possible to seek equilibrium, build trust, and operate on a premise of basically respectful treatment.

Reorienting reparations to the issue of reconstructing relationships—socially, legally, and economically—might in turn let us look more clearly at the real practical problems of reparations rather than at a set of repetitive academic debates. The real problem is what I will call the "reparations deficit."

The Reparations Deficit

Despite ever more refined and complex understandings of reparations that are reflected in the Basic Principles, not much, and not much that is truly attuned to actual needs, perceptions, and desires of victims of mass violence and injustice, is being done in the world in the way of reparations. The main reparations deficit is that reparations are the least favored among measures that are seen as "transitional justice." A recently published data-base on transitional justice measures around the globe finds that financial reparations trail far behind either criminal trials or truth commissions; all trail miserably behind some forms of amnesty—an official policy to just the close books and move on (Olsen et al. 2010, Appendix 4). Ruben Carranza, Director of the Reparative Justice Program of the International Center for Transitional Justice, comments: "Reparations are arguably the most victim-centered of the various approaches to fighting impunity; but in recent years, most of the international resources meant for transitional justice and peacebuilding has gone to operating war crimes tribunals, occasionally to truth commissions, certainly to reintegrating ex-combatants, but seldom, if ever, to directly benefit victims of human rights violations" (Carranza 2009: 4). Reparations are a low priority domestically and internationally in both stable and transitional societies. The other deficit is one *within* current practices of reparations. Victims of violence and severe injustice who receive reparations receive little, have what they receive determined by others, and receive what those others decide it is affordable or efficient to provide (see Johnston and Slyomovics 2009 and Rubio-Marín 2009).

If we ask why reparations happen so infrequently, amount to so little, and often fail to engage with actual needs and perspectives of the individuals and groups who seek justice, we need to understand what is at stake in reparations struggles, and it is by no means only money. I have suggested that restitution and compensation are often crucial instruments of reparations, but they are not, as the corrective justice model would have it, what is exclusively at stake. It is a renegotiation of relationship that reparations always symbolize and promise: they are an attempt *in the present* to acknowledge and repudiate what happened before, and to begin a transformation by attempting a first step, here and now, toward defining and creating relations of accountability and reciprocity.

If a nation, institution, or group avoids making or refuses to make reparations in cases of gross abuse or manifest histories of severe injustice, they hold themselves, even now as before, beyond *accountability* to the people they have injured or whose mistreatment it falls to their society to repair. They see themselves as having the power to refuse demands of justice from those who deserve reparations. Since compelling calls for reparations come from those who have suffered histories of injustice that have degraded their status socially and economically, or who have borne the brunt of conflict because their economic or social vulnerability, they are generally not in a strong position to compel the fulfillment of their claims. If a nation, institution, or group attempts reparations without seeking to hear and understand the needs and perspectives of those who would receive reparations then there is a failure of *reciprocity*. Those who would decide reparations based solely on their own perspective and assessment of what is due and what they are willing to offer, reserve the right to decide *for* others rather than with them the nature and meaning of the victims' losses. Even now as before, they do not show a willingness to meet the others on the ground of shared standards and mutual responsibility.

Accountability and reciprocity are the basic terms of moral relationship, and they are what reparations, whatever form they take, must try to *signify*. If a struggle for reparations begins to engage, it is a medium for beginning to move forward toward a picture of what relationships of accountability and reciprocity might look like where they have not existed before. Unlike an exercise of corrective justice that "settles up" and closes the case, reparations open that passageway. They are the beginning, not the end, of a different history. But they are only a beginning and it is beyond the scope of reparations themselves to do more than exemplify, through meaningful and costly deeds, a promise to reconstruct relations; the achievement may take decades or generations to secure. To understand the resistance within societies to negotiating *in the present* a mutual understanding of just relations—taking responsibility for a shameful past and making uncertain but hopeful commitments to a better future—is to appreciate what a remarkable, if fragile and limited, achievement reparations are.

References

Barkan, Elazar. 2000. *The Guilt of Nations: Restitution and Negotiating Historical Injustices*. Baltimore, MD: Johns Hopkins University Press.

Bass, Gary. 2012. "Reparations as a Noble Lie." In *Transitional Justice*, *Nomos LI*, edited by Melissa Williams, Rosemary Nagy, and Jon Elster, 166–79. New York and London: New York University Press.

Bernstein, Anita. 2009. "Tort Theory, Microfinance, and Gender Equality Convergent in Pecuniary Reparations." In *The Gender of Reparations: Unsettling Sexual Hierarches While Redressing Human Rights Violations*, edited by Ruth Rubio-Marín, 291–323. New York: Cambridge University Press.

Brooks, Roy L. 2004. *Atonement and Forgiveness: A New Model for Black Reparations*. Berkeley, CA: University of California Press.

Brophy, Alfred L. 2006. *Reparations Pro & Con*. New York: Oxford University Press.

Carranza, Ruben. 2009. "The Right to Reparations in Situations of Poverty." New York: International Center for Transitional Justice.

Colonomos, Ariel. 2006. "German Reparations to the Jews after World War II: A Turning Point in the History of Reparations." In *The Handbook of Reparations*, edited by Pablo de Greiff, 390–419. New York: Oxford University Press.

De Greiff, Pablo, ed. 2006a. *The Handbook of Reparations*. New York: Oxford University Press.

De Greiff, Pablo, 2006b. "Justice in Reparations." In *The Handbook of Reparations*, edited by Pablo De Greiff, 451–77. New York: Oxford University Press.

Du Plessis, Max and Stephen Peté, eds. 2007. *Repairing the Past? International Perspectives on Reparations for Gross Human Rights Abuses*. Antwerp: Intersentia.

Elster, Jon. 2012. "Justice, Truth, Peace." In *Transitional Justice*, *Nomos LI*, edited by Melissa Williams, Rosemary Nagy, and Jon Elster, 78–97. New York and London: New York University Press.

Falk, Richard. 2006. "Reparations, International Law, and Global Justice: A New Frontier." In *The Handbook of Reparations*, edited by Pablo de Greiff, 478–503. New York: Oxford University Press.
Freeman, Michael. 2007. "Back to the Future: The Historical Dimension of Liberal Justice." In *Repairing the Past? International Perspectives on Reparations for Gross Human Rights Abuses*, edited by Max Du Plessis and Stephen Peté, 29–51. Antwerp: Intersentia.
Gray, David C. 2010a. "Extraordinary Justice." *Alabama Law Review* 62: 55–109.
Gray, David C. 2010b. "A No-Excuse Approach to Transitional Justice: Reparations as Tools of Extraordinary Justice." *Washington University Law Review* 87: 1043–103.
Hamber, Brandon. 2009. *Transforming Societies after Political Violence: Truth, Reconciliation, and Mental Health*. Dordrecht: Springer.
Johnston, Barbara Rose and Susan Slyomovics, eds. 2009. *Waging War, Making Peace: Reparations and Human Rights*. Walnut Creek, CA: Left Coast Press.
Kutz, Christopher. 2004. "Justice in Reparations: The Cost of Memory and the Value of Talk." *Philosophy & Public Affairs* 32: 277–312.
Mazurana, Dyan, Teddy Atim, Ariane Brunet, and Helen Kezie-Nwoha. 2013. *Making Gender-Just Remedy and Reparation Possible: Upholding the Rights of Women and Girls in the Great North of Uganda*. Somerville, MA: Feinstein International Center, Tufts University.
Murphy, Colleen. 2010. *A Moral Theory of Political Reconciliation*. New York: Cambridge University Press.
Olsen, Tricia D., Leigh A. Payne, and Andrew G. Reiter. 2010. *Transitional Justice in Balance: Comparing Processes, Weighing Efficacy*. Washington, D.C.: United States Institute of Peace.
Philpott, Daniel. 2012. *Just and Unjust Peace: An Ethic of Political Reconciliation*. New York: Oxford University Press.
Pierik, Roland. 2006. "Reparations for Luck Egalitarians," *Journal of Social Philosophy* 37: 423–40.
Rubio-Marín, Ruth, ed. 2009. *The Gender of Reparations: Unsettling Sexual Hierarches While Redressing Human Rights Violations*. New York: Cambridge University Press.
Sammons, Diane E. 2012. "Corporate Reparations for Descendants of Enslaved African-Americans–Practical Obstacles." In *Transitional Justice, Nomos LI*, edited by Melissa Williams, Rosemary Nagy, and Jon Elster, 315–58. New York and London: New York University Press.
Satz, Debra. 2007. "Countering the Wrongs of the Past: The Role of Compensation." In *Reparations: Interdisciplinary Inquiries*, edited by Jon Miller and Rahul Kumar, 176–92. New York: Oxford University Press.
Schonsteiner, Judith. 2007. "Dissuasive Measures and the 'Society as a Whole': A Working Theory of Reparations in the Inter-American Court of Human Rights." *American University International Law Review* 23: 127–64.
Shelton, Dinah. 2002. "Righting Wrongs: Reparations in the Articles on State Responsibility." *The American Journal of International Law* 96: 833–56.
Thompson, Janna. 2002. *Taking Responsibility for the Past: Reparation and Historical Injustice*. Cambridge: Polity Press.
United Nations. 2006. "Basic Principles and Guidelines on the Right to a Remedy and Reparation for Victims of Gross Violations of International Human Rights Law and Serious Violations of International Humanitarian Law," United Nations Document A/RES/60/147, March 21.
Verdeja, Ernesto. 2007. "A Normative Theory of Reparations in Transitional Democracies." In *Genocide's Aftermath: Responsibility and Repair*, edited by Claudia Card and Armen T. Marsoobian, 166–85. Malden, MA: Blackwell.

Vermeule, Adrian. 2012. "Reparations as Rough Justice." In *Transitional Justice, Nomos LI*, edited by Melissa Williams, Rosemary Nagy, and Jon Elster, 151–65. New York and London: New York University Press.

Waldron, Jeremy. 1992. "Superseding Historic Injustice." *Ethics* 103: 4–28.

Walker, Margaret Urban. 2006a. "Restorative Justice and Reparations." *Journal of Social Philosophy* 37: 377–95.

Walker, Margaret Urban. 2006b. *Moral Repair: Reconstructing Moral Relations after Wrongdoing*. New York: Cambridge University Press.

Walker, Margaret Urban. 2013. "The Expressive Burden of Reparations: Putting Meaning into Money, Words, and Things." In *Justice, Responsibility and Reconciliation in the Wake of Conflict*, edited by Alice MacLachlan and Allen Speight, 205–25. Dordrecht: Springer.

Walker, Margaret Urban. 2014. "Moral Vulnerability and the Task of Reparations." In *Vulnerability: New Essays in Ethics and Feminist Philosophy*, edited by Catriona MacKenzie, Wendy Rogers, and Susan Dodds, 110–33. New York: Oxford University Press.

Webber, Jeremy. 2012. "Forms of Transitional Justice." In *Transitional Justice, Nomos LI*, edited by Melissa Williams, Rosemary Nagy, and Jon Elster, 98–128. New York and London: New York University Press.

Wenar, Leif. 2006. "Reparations for the Future." *Journal of Social Philosophy* 37: 396–405.

Williams, Melissa, Rosemary Nagy, and Jon Elster, eds. 2012. *Transitional Justice, Nomos LI*. New York: New York University Press.

Winter, Stephen. 2014. *Transitional Justice in Established Democracies: A Political Theory*. Basingstoke: Palgrave Macmillan.

Winter, Stephen. 2006. "Uncertain Justice." *Journal of Social Philosophy* 37: 342–59.

Yamamoto, Eric K., Sandra Hye Yun Kim, and Abigail M. Holden. 2007. "American Reparations Theory and Practice at the Crossroads." *California Western Law Review* 44: 1–85.

PART VII
Case Studies

Chapter 16

Trust and Commitment: How Athens Rebuilt the Rule of Law

Paul Gowder

> Indeed men too often take upon themselves in the prosecution of their revenge to set the example of doing away with those general laws to which all alike can look for salvation in adversity, instead of allowing them to subsist against the day of danger when their aid may be required.
>
> Thucydides[1]

Introduction

Much literature about democratic transitional justice focuses on the content of post-conflict law, particularly the tension between reconciliation and accountability; that is, when a democracy takes power from a dictatorship that has violated human rights, should the leaders of the previous regime be prosecuted, or should they be granted amnesty? Let us call questions like that, collectively, "the substance question."

Once a democracy has arrived at an answer to the substance question, however, it will sooner or later be faced with a second question: should it stick to its first answer? If it has publicly and legally committed to some treatment of its previous leaders, may it change its mind?

The citizens of a transitional democracy may decide that they were originally mistaken. Perhaps their original choice caused too much political unrest, or circumstances may have changed. For example, their original choice may have been made in order to mollify some powerful interest group. But the balance of power has shifted, and that group no longer threatens the democracy; the *demos* is only now freely able to pursue its conception of justice.[2] Should it? Let us call this "the commitment question."

In answering the commitment question, the *demos* must consider not only issues of abstract political morality—must a democracy keep its promises?—but also structural issues. Should the *demos* create institutions, such as courts and constitutions, to reinforce its transitional commitments? If the demos breaks or keeps those commitments, what effect will that choice have on the success of its democratic political institutions? Call this "the structure question."

This chapter is a call to pay more attention to the structure and commitment questions. It will argue that transitional democracies have reasons to stick to their transitional commitments, regardless of their substance.[3] And they have reasons to prospectively build structures that allow

---

1 Thuc. 3.84, as translated by Strassler (1996).

2 Nobles (2010: 171–5) helpfully collects the scholarship about the impact of changing circumstances on transitional justice decisions.

3 Distinguish the democracy breaking its own commitments from breaks imposed on it by law. Sometimes, domestic or international courts strike down transitional justice measures; to the extent those rulings are consistent with preexisting law, a demos does not undermine the rule of law by following them (and ordinarily political actors ought to be able to predict this risk when negotiating transitional measures). Consequently, this kind of commitment-breaking ought not to pose the same kind of danger to transitional democracies as (I argue below) would the *demos* ignoring its own legal commitments. (I thank Mark Osiel for raising this worry).

them to do so.[4] In consequence, we should understand the rule of law as an element of transitional justice, *independent* of the substantive choices transitional democracies make about how to handle the past.[5]

This chapter is divided into three sections. The first is narrative: I tell the story of one of the first transitional justice problems in recorded history: the reconciliation and amnesty within the Athenian democracy after the brief but infamously brutal regime of the Thirty Tyrants (403 BCE). The second is analytic: I give an account of how the Athenians learned from their prior experience in successfully maintaining their transitional commitments and rebuilding the political community. The final section generalizes to make some theoretical claims about the relationship between public and visible mass commitment to the rule of law and the success of transitional democracies, and from there to the role of courts, civil society, and truth commissions.

Before beginning, a word of disclaimer. Necessarily, this chapter is tentative and partially speculative. It's almost certainly wrong in more ways than it's right. In the space of a single chapter, I cannot do anything even remotely approaching full justice to the political complexities of the one case I examine, let alone the greater universe of transitional justice circumstances. Nor can I give a strategic account that captures the multiple and shifting interests necessarily reduced, here, to the binary of "mass democrats" and "elite oligarchs." The object is not to declare "this is what made the Athenian amnesty successful, and this is what contemporary democracies must do," but to explore new territory with a plausible but tentative hypothesis, and, in doing so, encourage future scholars to map it more closely.

Transitional Justice in the Golden Age of Athens: A Chronology[6]

In the late fifth century BCE, two oligarchies, known to history as the Four Hundred and the Thirty Tyrants, overthrew the Athenian democracy and were overthrown in turn. Those oligarchies, the events leading up to them, and the way the restored democracy handled the fallout, are the subjects of this section.

As the end of the fourth century neared, Athens was mired in the Peloponnesian War against Sparta. By the standards of the time, Athens was a democracy: although citizenship was a hereditary status, held by around 10 or 20 percent of the residents, and women, foreigners, and slaves held inferior legal status and no direct say in politics,[7] political rights were distributed largely without reference to socioeconomics class, and three mass institutions—the jury, the council, and the assembly—ruled the city.[8]

In 415 BCE, the assembly decided to invade Syracuse, a powerful city on Sicily. The expedition was probably hopeless on its own, but internal politics made matters worse. Just before the invasion began, the citizens discovered that a number of *hermai*—statues of the god Hermes—had been

4 Of course, even strong reasons may be overridden. Sometimes a democracy should abandon profoundly unjust commitments.

5 To be clear, I mean to say that the *prospective* rule of law is important to transitional democracies: they must run their own governments under law. This is not the same as the claim made by many scholars that the rule of law requires punishment for the *past* violations of the prior regime (for example, Mendez 1997: 6); I take no position on that.

6 In the interest of brevity, I have refrained from giving extensive citations in the historical narrative, which is generally standard knowledge to those who study ancient Athens. The main classical sources are Thucydides, Xenophon's *Hellenika*; Andocides's *On the Mysteries*, and Aristotle's *Constitution of Athens*. The secondary sources on which I've most heavily relied are Ostwald (1986), Lanni (2010), and Hansen (1999). I have given more precise references for all of the elements of the narrative below in Gowder (2014a).

7 Accordingly, I will use the male pronoun to refer to politically active Athenian citizens.

8 An excellent summary of Athenian government is in Blackwell (2003).

mutilated. At the same time, it was alleged that some citizens had privately parodied an important religious ceremony, the Eleusian mysteries. Both were believed to associated with an oligarchic plot against the democracy.

Faced with these events, the legal system utterly broke down. Andocides (not, admittedly, a disinterested source) recounts that those making denunciations were given a financial reward; unsurprisingly, some 300 citizens ended up being denounced. At least some of those denunciations were false, and one Diocleides was ultimately executed for making false accusations. Before the hysteria died down, a number of citizens were executed or went into exile as a result of the denunciations, others were summarily thrown into prison on suspicion, and at one point the council called the whole city to arms and considered torturing citizens in order to extract more names. Alcibiades, one of the generals of the upcoming expedition, fell under suspicion. His opponents waited until he had set sail, and then accused him *in abstensia.* Upon being recalled from the invasion as a result, he turned traitor, joining up with the Spartans.

In 413 BCE, the entire Sicilian expedition was destroyed. The loss of men, money, and ships was devastating. The "allies" (client states) went into revolt. Athens seemed doomed.

Somehow, Athens survived to continue the war for a few more years. Meanwhile, Alcibiades and others conspired to overthrow the democracy. They followed a two-pronged strategy. First, they tried to persuade the Athenians that the Persians would give them a much-needed alliance if they installed an oligarchy. Second, they called on clubs of the rich and powerful within the city, the *hetaireiai* (who had widely been believed to be behind the sacrileges of the herms/mysteries), to carry out acts of violence and intimidation in order to support an oligarchic coup. Thucydides reports that the terror campaign was successful: the democrats were unable to resist the oligarchs because they were too afraid to speak against them or organize their own collective action. (I will suggest below that some of this is attributable to failures of the rule of law.)

In 411 BCE, the democracy voted itself out of existence, turning over power to the Four Hundred, the first of two Athenian oligarchies. The Four Hundred ruled relatively mildly—Thucydides reports that they killed "not many" people—but were not strategically sustainable. The lower classes controlled the bulk of (what was left of) Athenian military might, the navy at Samos. Consequently, within a few months, the oligarchy collapsed and the democrats regained control of Athens, thus facing their first problem of transitional justice. Their choice was legal accountability: they convicted a number of oligarchs for their crimes during the regime. Moreover, in order to build a more solid legal basis for deterring and punishing future oligarchs, they enacted the decree of Demophantus, which allowed anyone to kill with impunity any person who attempted to overthrow the democracy or took office in an oligarchy.[9]

The war continued. In 406 BCE, Athens won its last major victory, the naval battle of Arginusae. Unfortunately, a storm prevented them from rescuing the sailors from their disabled ships afterward. Outraged by the mischance, the people of Athens again crashed their legal system, executing the (victorious!) generals *en masse* by *diktat* of the assembly. The hysteria and disregard for law reached such a fever pitch that one citizen, who tried to put a stop to the illegal proceeding, was himself threatened with execution.[10]

Predictably, after killing its generals Athens lost the war. In 405 BCE, Lysander obliterated the Athenian fleet at the battle of Aegospotami, and in 404, under siege and starving, Athens capitulated. Among the terms imposed by the Spartans was the rule of another oligarchy, the Thirty Tyrants.

According to Xenophon, the Thirty began with a popular move, persecuting some alleged *sycophants*—reputedly frivolous litigants who used the Athenian courts to extort money from

9 Particularly, see Ostwald (1986: 414–22).

10 Gowder (2014a) and Gowder (2014b) go into more detail on this.

their opponents. (Classicists debate whether sycophancy actually occurred.) But the Thirty quickly expanded their violence, executing numerous citizens and expropriating an immense amount of property.

A rebellion arose and began to win battlefield victories against the Thirty. Sparta sent troops to reinforce the Thirty, but the commander of the relief troops grew tired of the conflict and imposed a peace on the warring factions. The Thirty were forced to step down, but the Athenian people were forced to grant an amnesty to their collaborators, forbidding the restored democracy (for the most part) from prosecuting them for any crimes except murder, and forbidding individuals from taking revenge outside the legal system. The solution to Athenian democracy's second problem of transitional justice within a decade was imposed on it from the outside.

Shortly thereafter, Athens comprehensively revised its legal system. A new court procedure, *parahraphe*, was created, allowing a citizen to immediately challenge a lawsuit alleged to violate the amnesty. Athens also prohibited laws targeted against individuals as well as the enforcement by magistrates of unwritten laws. Finally, a distinction was created between laws, which were to be difficult to amend, and decrees of the assembly, making it clear that the former were to supersede the latter—in effect constitutionalizing the existing legal system, and, with the help of the long-standing procedure of *graphe paranomon*, creating a system of judicial review to challenge unconstitutional decrees. The overall effect of these changes was to entrench the existing laws and shift power from the assembly to the juries.

The amnesty held. Those who collaborated with the oligarchs were not legally punished for their crimes, and the council summarily executed the only citizen whom history records as attempting extra-legal revenge. Having successfully reintegrated the oligarchic opposition into the community and reformed its legal system, Athens swiftly rebuilt, and, within a few years, transformed from a crippled and conquered city into a major power once again.

What Changed in Athens?

After the Four Hundred fell, the democrats prosecuted the oligarchs for their misdeeds. After the much more brutal regime of the Thirty, the democrats observed an amnesty, even though that amnesty, while imposed by Spartan military might, wasn't propped up by it.[11]

The obvious explanatory hypothesis is that Athens learned. Their behavior after the Four Hundred led to continued class conflict, impeded the war effort, and brought on a second oligarchy eight years after the first. Their behavior after the Thirty, by contrast, contributed (along with other changed circumstances) to a speedy return to military significance after a devastating defeat, and to no further oligarchies.

But that believable hypothesis is also ambiguous. Did Athens learn only to refrain from punishment and revenge, or also about the importance of keeping their legal commitments?

Suppose the Athenians learned that in an unstable external political environment, it's better to give an amnesty to one's former rulers than to prosecute them?[12] This seems like a good lesson for them to have learned, since Athenian class conflict, carried out in part through legal prosecutions, probably contributed to their military defeat: the affair of the *hermai*/mysteries helped turn the Sicilian expedition into a disaster, and then the trial of the generals decapitated the army just

---

11 As proof of the latter, note that less than a decade after the overthrow of the Thirty, Athens joined another war against Sparta—hardly what we would expect if the democrats kept the amnesty out of fear of Spartan punishment.

12 This is the hypothesis given by Elster (2004) and Loening (1987: 149).

in time to lose the war altogether.[13] Moreover, there is reason to believe that the upper classes wanted to topple the democracy in part because they were unhappy about the way they were treated by the legal system: consider that the Thirty started off by eliminating alleged frivolous litigants who targeted the rich, and that a letter attributed to Plato claims that their rule was a result of general dissatisfaction with the laws.[14] Consequently, the democrats after the Thirty had good reason to pursue an amnesty strategy rather than a retribution strategy, in order to reintegrate their socioeconomic elites into the community, gaining the benefits of their resources and talents against external competitors as well as giving them less reason to plot against the *polis*. There is strong evidence on the side of those who have argued that

Athens learned that it could not go on without reconciling the rich and powerful to the democracy.[15]

However, that version of the hypothesis is incomplete. An unreliable amnesty would not have achieved the democrats' ends. If the elites had reason to fear that the restored democracy would disregard its promises and punish them for their crimes, they still would have had reason to plot for a future oligarchy. If the democracy did, in fact, continue to eat its own elites, it would have again deprived itself of their services in international conflict. Consequently, in order to have learned the right answer to the substance question, it also must have learned the right answer to the structure and commitment questions. In the jargon of political science, the Athenians must have learned to *credibly commit* to the amnesty: to enforce it in support of their long-run interests even in the face of a short-run desire by aggrieved democrats to the contrary.[16]

Moreover, in order to successfully fight off *future* oligarchic threats, the democrats of Athens must have learned to trust one another. The elite, like all elites, were more powerful than members of the mass on a one-to-one basis; they had the capacity to do things like bribe or intimidate assemblies and juries. They also had greater capacity to coordinate their own actions to magnify their individual power, due to their smaller population, and preexisting organizational capacity in the form of the *hetaireiai*.[17]

In order to counteract these advantages, the masses would have had to make full use of the only advantage they had: numbers. They would have to have been able to trust one another for support to punish future elite coups, even though elites would have had the power to do them harm on a one-on-one basis. This need for support is reciprocal and extends across the political community. A depends on B's support, but B, in order to be able to support A, depends on A's reciprocal support, and both also depend on the support of citizens C, D: each individual democratic, non-elite, citizen, in order to be willing to stand up to a member of the oligarchic elite, must be able to rely on the support of each other individual democratic citizen.

13 Many classicists think the trial of the generals was motivated by class animosities. See Asmonti (2006).

14 The Seventh Letter, 324.c in the standard Stephanus numbering. Lysias's 25th speech tells a similar story.

15 Moreover, a year after the trial of the generals, and before the Thirty took over, the Athenians tried to end the cycle of retaliation by enacting a belated amnesty which covered some of the prior political conflict (Boeghold 1990). Although this amnesty of 405 was too late to prevent the Thirty, it does indicate that the Athenians had come to see the importance of reconciliation. See also Lys. 18.17–18, in which a litigant argues the importance of a return to civic harmony after the Thirty. However, several times, the democrats carried out acts of retaliation against former oligarchs—acts which were consistent with the law, and hence could be conducted without undermining what I argue is the lesson of the Athenian amnesty, namely the importance of the rule of law. For example, when called upon to send troops off to a foreign war where they would be likely killed, Athens deliberately sent cavalrymen who had been associated with the oligarchs. It also cut the pay of the cavalry and quadrupled the pay of the lower-class archers. And, incidentally, it reconquered an oligarchic enclave at Eleusis (though that last one might have been illegal—the circumstances are lost to history). On all of this, see Wolpert (2001: 46) and Loening (1987: 117–19).

16 On the idea of credible commitment, see North (1993).

17 On the advantage of small groups see Olson (1971).

Otherwise, doing so is too dangerous. Thucydides tells us that they were unable to so trust one another when the Four Hundred took over, suggesting that they must have had to build this trust out of nothing after the Thirty.

In the jargon of game theory, the democracy has a coordination problem: each non-elite citizen wants to be doing what each other non-elite citizen does. He wants to punish future elite transgressions if and only if each other citizen will do so—then he gets his most-preferred outcome, a functioning democracy. However, he wants to refrain from attempting to punish elite transgressions if other citizens won't do so, because so refraining allows him to avoid his least-preferred outcome, being crushed by an overwhelmingly powerful member of the elite, although it forces him to accept his second-least-preferred outcome, living under an oligarchy.[18] This is a class of problem that has been extensively studied in political science and economics.[19] One thing we've learned in those disciplines is that law, understood as a common-knowledge mapping of conduct to evaluations ("legal" or "illegal"), with some mechanism for producing authoritative decisions about those mappings, is instrumental to the success of coordinated sanctioning systems (Law 2009, Hadfield and Weingast 2012, Hadfield and Weingast 2014). In order to achieve coordinated punishment against some transgressor, the democratic masses must have some settled way of determining when a transgression has occurred. And they must be able to trust one another to apply it faithfully. The upshot is that the Athenian democracy after the Thirty Tyrants critically depended on each citizen's ability to predict each other citizen's behavior; the law was the instrument for this prediction just to the extent that citizens knew one another could be depended on to uphold it.

Enter the jury. The chief institution of Athenian litigation, the jury was composed of several hundred citizens who were selected at random. Any citizen could bring an indictment against any other, without regard to class or wealth, and the jury too was selected without regard to class. Its decisions were final. The jury provided the necessary authoritative resolution of disagreements about whether a given course of conduct was sanctionable under law or not, and thus made it possible for the democracy to coordinate itself by law in the first place.

It is this jury that would have heard charges against oligarchs, both amnesty-violating charges for crimes committed under the Thirty Tyrants, as well as charges for new oligarchic crimes committed after the Thirty; it is also the jury that would have heard charges against self-help amnesty violators, had any (other than the one we know of) happened. And—this is the key point—this gave the jurors reason to support the amnesty, because by doing so they could signal their willingness to one another to stand up for the law, and hence solve their coordination problem, and protect their democracy.

Because it was a *mass* institution, filled with hundreds of randomly selected citizens, the jury could serve as an excellent informational proxy for the extent to which the citizen body was willing to enforce the laws. Trials were conducted under a glare of publicity; citizens would know what happened there (Lanni 2012). A jury that ruled for a clearly legally correct outcome, especially when that outcome was contrary to the short-run self-interest or preferences of many of its members, and where that jury was drawn from a large and fairly representative sample of the population, demonstrated a widespread commitment to enforcing the laws, and, consequently, the extent to which the laws were likely to be enforced in the future. Finally, because individual votes were secret, each individual citizen was not in danger of retaliation from voting to enforce the law, even if the vote was against the interest of powerful members of society. In short, the jury could build a record of lawful behavior without presupposing it: by safely allowing citizens to demonstrate their

18 This is a simplification: it may require the cooperation of fewer than all democrats to effectively resist threats. Nothing turns on this.

19 Classic on the subject is Weingast (1997).

willingness to sacrifice individual preferences to support one another and the law with their votes in the jury room, it allowed them to trust one another enough to be willing to take the risk to do so elsewhere, and hence allowed them to credibly threaten to resist future oligarchic coups in the streets as well as in the courts. The mass jury served the dual role of resolving legal disputes and demonstrating that the populace was committed to following the law.

This explains (at least in part) why the amnesty succeeded, and why the democracy itself succeeded. The people of Athens learned that it was important to rule according to the law, rather than according to their short-run political preferences, even if that means letting some oligarch go scot-free for crimes committed during the time of the Thirty Tyrants; by voting in accordance in the jury, they signaled to one another that they were willing to swallow their personal interests to enforce the law, and this, in turn, allowed them to trust one another to enforce other laws and to stand together in solidarity against future oligarchic coups.[20]

This commitment-signaling function was critical to the success of the restored democracy. The jury established a record of consistent conduct upon which each citizen could rely in predicting the behavior of his fellow citizens; this, in turn, made it less risky for each democrat to use the legal system to resist any oligarchic threats that might arise. And this, in turn, suppressed those threats: in the jargon of game theory, attempting future oligarchic coups was off the equilibrium path, because the democrats could credibly threaten to collectively respond with overwhelming force against any such attempts.[21]

The commitment to law was useful not only to the masses, but also to the elites. Even those with oligarchic sympathies, many of whom had committed crimes under the Thirty, would have reason to uphold the law—even to the extent of prosecuting their political allies for future oligarchic crimes—because if the law collapsed, the amnesty would cease to hold, and there would be nothing protecting them from mass vengeance. This is quite a trick: the law could reconcile the elites to the legal system by protecting them from punishment for their past misconduct, and at the very same time, to the extent the masses actually extended that legal protection to elites, it strengthened their own power to prevent future elite misconduct.

With this strategic analysis in hand, it becomes clearer that the best explanation for the success of the amnesty is that the democrats obeyed it because maintaining the law—even a law they didn't want in the first place, that had been imposed on them by Spartan sword—was more important to the strength of their democracy than getting rid of a few oligarchs. Aristotle confirms this hypothesis. In the Constitution of Athens, he recounts the argument given for summarily executing the one citizen who tried to disregard the amnesty: "[h]e argued that [the council's] actions would show whether they intended to preserve the democracy and stand by their oaths; if they let the man go, they would encourage others, while if they executed him, they would establish an example for all."[22] Evident in this passage is first the idea that keeping their legal oaths (the amnesty) was necessary to preserve the democracy, and second that if the council (representing the *demos*) didn't act (and thus didn't signal their commitment to enforcing the law), the law would break down.

I submit that they had learned this in part thanks to their experience in the fifth century. It is quite natural to suppose that the failure of trust before the Four Hundred, that Thucydides reported, included a failure of trust in the laws, thereby preventing the democrats from prosecuting those

20 In Gowder (2014a) I give evidence that the Athenians recognized, at least by the fourth century, the importance of a functioning legal system to the strength of the democracy.

21 Nor would we need any trials of amnesty-violating charges to get this happy result; it is enough that everyone believed the jury would make the right decision, and hence never brought such charges. (The real danger would be if someone brought an amnesty-violating charge and succeeded.)

22 *Constitution of Athens* XL.2, translated by Everson (1996).

who would subvert the democracy. After all, the coup followed shortly after the terrible affair of the herms/mysteries. Then, shortly before they again lost control, the legal system yet again revealed its deficiencies in the trial of the generals; widespread dissatisfaction with the performance of the legal system was evidenced both by the popularity of the Thirty's initial persecution of alleged *sycophants* and by Plato's ability to claim that the coup had come about because of legal dissatisfaction rather than Spartan force.

No surprise, then, that with the amnesty the democrats also reformed the legal system, building institutional structures to help ensure that it would be stable and enforced, and, in doing so, deterring future violent attempts at political power. They'd learned their lesson.

We have a term for the control of state power by law: "the rule of law."[23] The rule of law was the keystone in the success of the final restoration of the democracy in classical Athens, and the real difference—the answer to the structure and commitment questions, not the substantive question between amnesty and punishment—between the failed restoration after the Four Hundred and the successful restoration after the Thirty.[24]

The Structure and Commitment Questions in Contemporary Transitional Justice

The lessons of Athens can apply to contemporary political communities. The structure and commitment questions are independent of the substance question. Whether a nascent democracy wishes to punish those who collaborated with the prior regime, or whether it wishes to forgive and forget and reintegrate the perpetrators into society, it must be able to commit to the solution that it has decided upon, and it must build constitutional institutions to support that commitment. It must, in short, create the rule of law. These are two separate claims, one about the commitment question, and the other about the structure question. I will take them in turn.

First, the commitment question. Contemporary transitional democracies are likely similar to Athens in that, whether they choose reconciliation or punishment, they will have to be able to credibly threaten to mobilize mass collective action to prevent future attempts to regain power by the interest groups who previously ruled the state. After all, such groups often will have had some unusual, and perhaps persistent, advantage (wealth, troops, international support, etc.) in order to have been able to seize power in the first place. All democracies rely on the collective power of the individually weak masses; all oligarchies and autocracies rely on the individual power of discrete and unusual individuals or small groups; therefore, all democracies need to figure out how to coordinate to resist the powerful. And this means that the citizens of all democracies need to be able to rely on their fellows' demonstrated commitment to uphold the law. Whether they choose forgiveness or justice, they must all establish the rule of law.

This leads to the structure question. What can transitional democracies do to bring about the rule of law, and demonstrate their collective commitment to it? Today's large-scale states don't have the natural advantages of Athens: they can't so easily run mass juries in which a significant proportion of the population participates, and which are visible to the community as a whole. Thus, contemporary democracies typically rely on something like a constitutional court to enforce their

23 In Gowder (2013) and Gowder (2014c) I give an account of what the rule of law is.

24 This chapter operates at right angles to the usual discussion in the transitional justice literature on the rule of law, which often focuses on whether different substantive choices are consistent with or required by the rule of law, e.g., the controversy over the extent to which punishing the previous regime is necessary to establish a norm of legal justice, or forbidden by legal norms against retroactivity. All of this is orthogonal to my question of whether a democracy should stick to whichever choice it makes.

transitional choices. This serves the first function of the Athenian jury, the authoritative resolution of disputes, but does not necessarily serve the second—a small, elite, court does not have a built-in way for ordinary citizens to signal their commitment to enforcing the law. In fact, the power of constitutional courts depends on, rather than establishes, widespread knowledge of a popular commitment to the law.[25]

Observe the continuity between this account of the structure and commitment questions and the existing literature on the substance question. Some scholars have suggested that an aim of the substance of transitional justice arrangements should be to publicly and collectively reaffirm the values of the society in question (e.g., to display and demonstrate disapproval of the crimes of the previous regime), in order, inter alia, to rebuild "civic trust" that those norms will be enforced in the future.[26] I have suggested that the structure and commitment questions are intrinsically connected to such civic trust: the rule of law requires maintaining transitional commitments, and the rule of law is necessary for civic trust, insofar as it constitutes a pattern of collective support for law, giving citizens some warrant to believe that they will reliably defend one another. At the same time, civic trust is necessary for the rule of law, since citizens will only be willing to risk their individual interests to enforce the law on behalf of the rights of others to the extent they trust other citizens to join them in collective enforcement. The solution is the Athenian one: create structures to give citizens some forum in which they can costlessly demonstrate their collective commitment to law.

Even though contemporary transitional democracies don't have mass juries, they do seem to often have active civil society organizations. Moreover, those organizations do seem to play a prominent role in demanding yet another outlet for demonstrating collective commitment: the many iterations of the truth and reconciliation commission.[27]

Perhaps these commissions can mimic the function of the Athenian jury. Rather than simply demonstrating the substantive commitments of the people—we condemn these crimes of the previous regime, we say that they are not how we operate—they may also demonstrate a commitment to the rule of law in the same way as in Athens. They may give citizens who wish to pursue accountability for the crimes of the previous regime a riskless way to do so, and to do so within the law. A citizen who chooses to take her grievances to the truth commission rather than to pursue private justice has signaled her commitment to lawful means of dispute resolution; the citizens who operate the truth commissions and campaign for their use send a similar signal. At the same time, civil society organizations that represent citizens, by advocating for and participating in these processes, may also help signal a broad-based commitment to using lawful means to resolve disputes with the previous regime.[28]

Athens, too, had its truth and reconciliation commissions. The Thirty Tyrants themselves, though not their collaborators (with a handful of exceptions), were required to subject themselves to formal *euthunai*—judicial examination of former officeholders, which posed the prospect of punishment for their conduct—in order to return to Athenian citizenship. And if collaborators

25 Law (2009); Gowder (2014b).

26 "Civic trust" comes from De Greiff (2012: 44–8). Similarly, Dyzenhaus (2012) has, drawing from Hobbes, has suggested that a function of transitional justice is to provide a civic education in the rule of law. I agree, but submit that what is being taught is not the importance of the rule of law in the abstract, but that citizens may rely on one another to support it: the education is collective and interdependent rather than individual.

27 Examples are given in Popkin and Bhuta (1999). Hayner (2011: 223ff.) details numerous roles of civil society in truth commissions, including offering political support and expertise, advocacy for improvement in commission operation, providing access to victims, and providing access to files and information.

28 Allan (1999) argues that one function of the truth and reconciliation commission is to provide a forum for public recognition of the values of the rule of law, but he seems to limit this recognition to an expression by the state; this chapter argues that the most important kind of expression is that of the people participating in such institutions.

wanted to take office under the restored democracy, they, like all candidates for office, were subject to *dokimasia*, formal examination of a prospective official's character, at which their crimes could be considered.[29] Lanni (2010: 584) argues that those institutions operated as a "safety valve for local resentments," allowing some measure of revenge to be exacted. The analysis in this chapter suggests that her account is correct but incomplete: these measures also gave citizens an opportunity to choose the lawful method rather than some other method to seek accountability for past crimes, and hence to affirmatively and publicly show their commitment to the accountability mechanisms provided by law.[30]

These are the lessons that the Athenian experience with transitional justice suggests.[31] Transitional democracies should establish the rule of law, and build institutions to enable the masses to signal their willingness to uphold the law, even against their own short-run political preferences. Doing so can support their continuation *as* a democracy, which is a precondition for the implementation of those substantive choices. Additionally, the literature on transitional justice should pay less attention to the perennial tension between reconciliation and punishment, and more to the institutiols that allow democracies to effectuate their newfound rule.[32]

References

Allan, Jonathan. 1999. "Balancing Justice and Social Unity: Political Theory and the Idea of a Truth and Reconciliation Commission." *University of Toronto Law Journal* 49(3): 315–53.

Asmonti, Luca. 2006. "The Arginusae Trial, the Changing Role of Strategoi and the Relationship between Demos and Military Leadership in Late-Fifth Century Athens." *Bulletin of the Institute of Classical Studies* 49(1): 1–21.

Blackwell, Christopher. 2003. "The Council." in *Demos: Classical Athenian Democracy*, ed. Blackwell, http://www.stoa.org/projects/demos/council.pdf.

Boeghold, Alan. 1990. "Andokides and the Decree of Patrokleides." *Historia: Zeitschrift für Alte Geschichte*, 39(2): 149–62.

De Greiff, Pablo. 2012. "Theorizing Transitional Justice." In *Nomos LI: Transitional Justice*, edited by M. Williams, R. Nagy and J. Elster, 31–77. New York: NYU Press.

Dyzenhaus, David. 2012. "Leviathan as a Theory of Transitional Justice." In *Nomos LI: Transitional Justice*, edited by M. Williams, R. Nagy and J. Elster, 180–217. New York: NYU Press.

Elster, Jon. 2004. *Closing the Books: Transitional Justice in Historical Perspective*. Cambridge: Cambridge University Press.

Everson, Steven, ed. 1996. *Aristotle: The Politics and The Constitution of Athens*. Cambridge: Cambridge University Press.

29 Both were pre-coup institutions.

30 In one respect, Lanni is mistaken. She suggests that the Athenians lacked the rule of law, and that this lack was helpful in their reconciliation efforts. Elsewhere (Gowder 2014a) I have argued that Athens did have the rule of law; here I have argued that it was instrumental in their successful reconciliation.

31 Several prior scholars (McAdams 1997, Halmai and Scheppele 1997) have highlighted that other states have learned the lesson that the prior regime must be prosecuted (if at all) in accordance with the rule of law. However, these accounts have not focused attention, as I do, on the importance of a visible mass, not elite, commitment to the rule of law in transitional democracies.

32 Recently, there has been empirical research attempting to discern the relationship between a state's substantive transitional justice choices and its success in developing the rule of law (Weiffen 2012). (Nobles 2010 highlights a few others.) This chapter suggests that there may be a missing variable in Weiffen's analysis: the extent to which a state stuck to its transitional choices, whatever they may have been.

Gowder, Paul. 2013. "The Rule of Law and Equality." *Law and Philosophy* 32(5): 565–618.
Gowder, Paul. 2014a. "Democracy, Solidarity and the Rule of Law: Lessons from Athens." *Buffalo Law Review* 62(1): 1–67.
Gowder, Paul. 2014b. "The Countermajoritarian Complaint." *Transnational Law and Contemporary Problems* 23(1): 7–34.
Gowder, Paul. 2014c. "Equal Law in an Unequal World." *Iowa Law Review* 99(3): 1021–81.
Hadfield, Gillian and Barry Weingast. 2012. "What is Law? A Coordination Account of the Characteristics of Legal Order." *Journal of Legal Analysis* 4(2): 471–514.
Hadfield, Gillian and Barry Weingast. 2014. "Constitutions as Coordinating Devices." In *Institutions, Property Rights, and Economic Growth: The Legacy of Douglass North*, edited by Sebastian Galiani and Itai Sned. Cambridge: Cambridge University Press, 121–50.
Halmai, Gabor and Kim Lane Scheppele. 1997. "Living Well is the Best Revenge: The Hungarian Approach to Judging the Past." In *Transitional Justice and the Rule of Law in New Democracies*, edited by A. James McAdams, 155–84. Notre Dame, IN: University of Notre Dame Press.
Hansen, Mogens. 1999. *The Athenian Democracy in the Age of Demosthenes*. Norman, OK: University of Oklahoma Press.
Hayner, Priscilla. 2011. *Unspeakable Truths: Transitional Justice and the Challenge of Truth Commissions*. Oxford: Routledge.
Lanni, Adriaan. 2010. "Transitional Justice in Ancient Athens: A Case Study." *University of Pennsylvania Journal of International Law* 32(2): 551–94.
Lanni, Adriaan. 2012. "Publicity and the Courts of Classical Athens." *Yale Journal of Law and Humanities* 24(1): 119–35.
Law, David. 2009. "A Theory of Judicial Power and Judicial Review." *Georgetown Law Journal* 97(3): 723–801.
Loening, Thomas. 1987. "The Reconciliation Agreement of 403/402 B.C. in Athens: Its Content and Application." *Hermes* 53: 1.
McAdams, A. James. 1997. "Introduction." In *Transitional Justice and the Rule of Law in New Democracies*, edited by A. James McAdams. Notre Dame, IN: University of Notre Dame Press.
Mendez, Juan. 1997. "In Defense of Transitional Justice." In *Transitional Justice and the Rule of Law in New Democracies*, edited by A. James McAdams, 1–26. Notre Dame, IN: University of Notre Dame Press.
Nobles, Melissa. 2010. "The Prosecution of Human Rights Violations." *Annual Review of Political Science* 13: 165–82.
North, Douglass. 1993. "Institutions and Credible Commitment." *Journal of Institutional and Theoretical Economics* 149(1): 11–23.
Olson, Mancur. 1971. *The Logic of Collective Action*. Cambridge, MA: Harvard University Press.
Ostwald, Martin. 1986. *From Popular Sovereignty to the Sovereignty of Law: Law, Society and Politics in Fifth Century Athens*. Berkeley, CA: University of California Press.
Popkin, Margaret and Nehal Bhuta. 1999. "Latin American Amnesties in Comparative Perspective: Can the Past be Buried?" *Ethics & International Affairs* 13: 99–122.
Strassler, Robert ed., Richard Crawley, trans. 1996. *The Landmark Thucydides*. New York: Anchor Books.
Weiffen, Brigitte. 2012. "The Forgotten Factor—The Impact of Transitional Justice on the Development of the Rule of Law in Processes of Democratization." *Zeitschrift für Vergleichende Politkwissenschaft* 6(2): 125–47.

Weingast, Barry. 1997. "The Political Foundations of Democracy and the Rule of Law." *American Political Science Review* 91(2): 245–63.

Wolpert, Andrew. 2001. *Remembering Defeat: Civil War and Civic Memory in Ancient Athens*. Baltimore, MD: Johns Hopkins University Press.

Chapter 17

Transitional Justice in Post-Genocide Rwanda: An Integrative Approach

Lynne Tirrell

> Whether dead or alive, the victims must be recognized as victims and must know that we consider them as victims. Whether dead or alive, the guilty must be declared guilty and recognize themselves as guilty. Whether dead or alive, the innocent must also be declared innocent. Justice does not have several faces; it has only one, and it must be the same for everybody.
>
> Andre Sibomana 1996[1]

> Delivering justice would mean killing the killers ... Justice finds no place after genocide, because it surpasses human intelligence. Priority must be given to the fields, the harvests, the country, and so to the killers as well and to their families, who are many and strong. What would become of a nation lying fallow, without schools or sturdy houses, eyed greedily by neighbouring countries? This is not a human justice, it's a politics of justice. We can only regret that they never show either sincerity or sorrow.
>
> Berthe Mwanankabandi, survivor of '94[2]

An imperfect "politics of justice" is inevitable in the aftermath of genocide. An even-handed justice, Andre Sibomana emphasizes, requires recognizing victims as victims, the guilty as guilty. In Rwanda, an even-handed justice has proven elusive, given the scale of the atrocities, the breadth of participation, and the need to build a justice system from scratch while establishing security and restoring the rule of law. Like many Rwandans, Berthe Mwanankabandi's resignation to less than perfect justice is matched with determination to live again. Rebuilding individually and collectively in the aftermath of the apocalyptic events of April-July, 1994, Rwandans know that a non-ideal "politics of justice" will be incomplete justice, that despite efforts to build a new criminal justice system, major *génocidaires* have escaped punishment and small fry have served only short terms. They also know that distributive justice will be hard to achieve. And all along they have been hearing their government and churches stressing the importance of reconciliation without anyone really knowing how to bring it about, despite heroic efforts.

There can be no perfect justice for atrocity. The very concept of transitional justice carries with it diminished expectations and a sense of compromise, and unfortunately suggests that justice has "several faces" (Sibomana). This is, in part, because transitional justice cannot presuppose a stable society, and must have a variety of goals. Gerald Gahima defines transitional justice as comprising the "policies, practices and mechanisms with which societies seek to confront and deal with legacies of past violations of human rights and humanitarian law in the context of political

1 Sibomana, Andre, Hervé Deguine, and Laure Guilbert. 1999. *Hope for Rwanda: Conversations with Laure Guilbert and Hervé Deguine*. Translated by Carina Tersakian. London: Pluto Press, 105.

2 Hatzfeld, Jean. 2009. *The Antelope's Strategy: Living in Rwanda after the Genocide*. Translated by Linda Coverdale. New York: Farrar Strauss, & Giroux. Quote, 130–31.

transition with a view to restoring or establishing social cohesion and securing durable peace."[3] The twin goals of transitional justice—social cohesion and durable peace—are broad social goals, not limited to systems of justice. In his recent book Gahima, who was Rwanda's Attorney General from 1999–2003, nevertheless argues that Rwanda's intensive emphasis on prosecution may have undermined these important unifying goals. Understanding the complex systems of transitional justice embarked upon in Rwanda is too large a project for this brief chapter, so here I examine the ways different mechanisms yield distinctive forms of recognition, each crucial to Rwanda's transition.

Learning from Rwanda's post-'94 transitional justice, broadly construed, I shall argue that without development, neither official occasions for testimony nor the meting out of punishment yields sufficient recognition to survivors. The social cohesion that arises in the aftermath of silence about injustices done to survivors is bought at the expense of those who have already paid too high a price. Official contexts for survivor testimony and corresponding perpetrator punishment are crucial for establishing shared norms and narratives, but these processes can destabilize social relations in important ways. Survivors are often reluctant to come forward, for fear of retaliation from neighbors on whom they depend. Accordingly, without development, these justice mechanisms can undermine social stability and emerging cohesion. The converse is also true: without official contexts of testimony and judgment, development is only material support, and lacks the recognitive force we saw Sibomana demanding in our epigraph. The crucial interdependence of development, which provides distributive justice, with criminal proceedings, which offer retributive and restorative justice, has the potential to secure a lasting and stable peace.

A nation comprised of so many survivors and killers, locked into proximity by economic necessity, is beset by special challenges. Elsewhere, I have argued that genocide is not only mass murder writ large in the attempt to exterminate a people, but it is also what I call *recognition harm*.[4] Genocide's incomprehensible violation of self and community leaves survivors, bystanders, and even many perpetrators, truly and deeply bereft. These world-shattering wrongs leave survivors feeling cast out of humanity, for as persons we depend on the recognition—cognitive and moral regard—of others to develop our distinctively human capacities. Of course material harms must be repaired (bodies healed, homes rebuilt, wells cleaned, property restored) but social and psychological damage needs repair as well. Being recognized by others as each being a self—a being with plans and projects, a life to live in all its particularity—is an important part of moving away from genocidal terror and into social life and so back into a life of one's own. Human rights articulate material and social protections of the self as well as the community, with an emphasis on individual well-being.

There has been significant discussion weighing the relative merits of retributive justice versus restorative justice, and there is a burgeoning literature on this topic. Following the genocide, the new government, led by the Rwandan Patriotic Front, decided that prosecuting the *génocidaires* was necessary, rather than offering blanket amnesty to low-level offenders or a South African-style Truth and Reconciliation Commission (TRC). As Schabas observed in 2005, "The Rwandan experiment is contributing a new element to the ongoing debate between those who brook no compromise in dealing with impunity, and others who argue that reconciliation, cultural differences, or simple

3 Gahima, Gerald. 2013. *Transitional Justice in Rwanda: Accountability for Atrocity*. New York: Routledge, 2. Gahima was chief of staff to Rwanda's Justice Minister '96–'99, and Attorney General 1999–2003.

4 Tirrell, Lynne. 2013. "Apologizing for Atrocity: Rwanda and Recognition." In *Justice, Responsibility and Reconciliation in the Wake of Conflict*, ed. Alice MacLachlan and Allen Speight, 159–82. New York: Springer.

pragmatism militate in favour of moderation."[5] In our epigraph from Berthe Mwanankabandi, we hear a resigned pragmatism, perhaps stemming from her conception of justice as requiring a life for a life. Moderation in Rwanda might have meant prosecuting only planners, but more is needed to help the Tutsi widow whose husband and children were killed, and who now lives alone on a hill alongside those who killed her family. Impunity for those who killed her family sends a message of disregard for their lost lives, which is why all accounts of survivor attitudes say they support punishment for all perpetrators.[6] When 25,000 were released from prison in 2003, survivors lived in fear of further violence. As REDRESS reports: "Violence and intimidation, physical as well as psychological, overt and indirect, have been a central and recurrent theme of genocide justice for survivors, whether they take their cases to the established courts, to *Gacaca*, Arusha or to foreign jurisdictions."[7] Criminal justice, reparations and repair, and fair distributive justice must all work together to enact transitions to justice.

In real-life situations, political agents must decide how to allocate time and money to issues of punishment, restoration, security, and development. In the aftermath of atrocity, survivors need to know that their communities, states, and nation take seriously the wrongs done to them. This is a matter of offering recognition to those who have suffered horrible crimes, and in suffering those, suffered the recognition harms inherent in those crimes. Repairing recognition harms requires moral repair, establishing shared social values that restore lost standing and include those who had been cast out. Punishment of offenders and material repair are each individually insufficient for this task, but when combined with economic development and enhanced protection of human rights, there are better odds of creating a social and political system in which all have a voice, one which offers a shared narrative that fosters mutual recognition.

The case of post-genocidal Rwanda is worth examining because of the complexity of their challenges, and particularly because the new government gave priority to punishing génocidaires, in contrast to the strategy of South Africa's TRC, which traded judicial amnesty for information. With this decision, Rwanda's goals necessarily combined strong backward-looking and forward-looking elements which often conflicted. Looking backward to past wrongs required finding and punishing the killers and others who committed genocidal crimes. All this took place within a context of massive physical and social destruction. A distinctive aspect of Rwanda's genocide was the number of civilian participants—literally hundreds of thousands were mobilized to hunt and kill their neighbors. During my research in Rwanda, an ICTR prosecutor warned me to bear in mind that "the entire country is a crime scene."[8] This dramatic yet helpful admonition reminds us that for survivors, there is no place that offers respite. Seemingly innocent moments—like seeing a child playing in a roadside ditch, or a woman walking with a giant hoe or a man carrying a machete as he approaches—can cause concern to anyone who has studied the genocide, so just imagine the effect of such moments on a survivor who saw the ditches filled with Tutsi, and who saw machetes and hoes used to kill. Starting in August 1994, Rwanda set about cleaning up its crime scenes, finding those responsible, and rebuilding a system of justice.

Rwanda's genocide of the Tutsi left its judiciary decimated, its citizens traumatized and polarized, and its penal system overwhelmed. The new government needed to create safety and security within the country, and reestablish the rule of law. These initial steps include what is often

5 Schabas, William. 2005. "Genocide Trials and *Gacaca* Courts." *Journal of International Criminal Justice* 3: 879–95. Available at: doi: 10.1093/jicj/mqi062 Quote: 895.

6 See, e.g., REDRESS. 2008. *Survivors and Post-Genocide Justice in Rwanda: Their Experiences, Perspectives and Hopes*. Available at: http://www.redress.org/downloads/country-reports/Rwanda%20Survivors%2031%20Oct%2008.pdf.

7 REDRESS 2008: 25.

8 Conversation, ICTR, Arusha, Tanzania, July 2011. Notes on file.

spoken of as "DDR," the disarmament, demobilization, and reintegration of offenders, but there was also a desperate need to find people to take jobs left vacant by the victims or by those who fled.[9] Rwanda needed to rebuild its material infrastructure, rebuild institutions left desolate, and kick-start an economy. They needed to clean up a countryside strewn with the dead, find mass graves, identify and properly bury remains, and disinter people who were cast into smaller yet inappropriate "graves" (latrines, wells, etc.). These were huge and horrific tasks. Rwanda also faced social and economic challenges, with so many Tutsi men killed and so many Hutu men fugitives, with exiled Tutsi returning from neighboring countries, Hutu now in exile to avoid reprisals, and far too many citizens who had recently been in refugee camps, now without homes. Four languages were now common, marking social locations in troublesome ways: Kinyarwanda, French, English, and to a lesser degree, Swahili. Creating unity out of this chaos required great fortitude, and Rwanda's strength in doing this in the early years was held up as a model.[10] For the first decade or more, Rwanda's situation was clearly transitional. Now, approaching 20 years on, questions arise, within Rwanda and amongst international agents, about which measures are transitional and which are permanent.

Mechanisms of Justice

Post-genocidal Rwanda had three official justice mechanisms: The International Criminal Tribunal for Rwanda (ICTR), operating in Arusha, Tanzania, the Rwandan National Courts, and since 2001, Rwanda's local *gacaca* courts. Multiple mechanisms are appropriate, for as Waldorf argues, "Transitional justice requires legally pluralistic solutions, with innovative and context-specific combinations of formal and informal mechanisms operating at the international, national, and local levels."[11] Rwanda's mechanisms reflect this legal pluralism, from the highly formal ICTR to the much less formal *gacaca* hearings. These multiple mechanisms send distinctive recognitive messages.

Each of the judicial mechanisms has distinct methods and cases. The ICTR was established to handle Category 1 cases, concerning high-level perpetrators: leaders, especially those who planned and led the genocide, and those who committed widely known, especially heinous murders and rapes. Rwanda's traditional European-style judiciary system at first took all cases that were not referred to the ICTR, but later took only Category 2 cases, concerning those who killed with intent and who were low-level leaders, perhaps of a death squad. Starting in 2001, a long-abandoned traditional dispute-resolution mechanism, *gacaca*, was restored (and modified) to handle Category 3 and Category 4 cases. Category 3 cases involved participation in killings and mayhem (gross bodily harm) without the actual attempt to murder, including, for example, those who participated in death squads but who claimed lack of intent. (This would cover those who said they went along

9 See Sharp, Dustin. 2012. "Bridging the Gap: The United Nations Peacebuilding Commission and the Challenges of Integrating DDR and Transitional Justice." In *Transitional Justice and Peacebuilding on the Ground: Victims and Ex-Combatants*, ed. Chandra Lekha Sriram, Olga Martin-Ortega, and Johanna Herman. New York: Routledge. Also: Waldorf, Lars. 2009. Transitional Justice and DDR: the Case of Rwanda. Report for the International Center for Transitional Justice. Available at: https://www.ictj.org/sites/default/files/ICTJ-DDR-Rwanda-CaseStudy-2009-English.pdf.

10 Think not only of the myriad academic and legal articles on the subject, but also the glowing praise in Philip Gourevitch's 1998 bestseller *We Wish to Inform You That Tomorrow We Will Be Killed with Our Families* (New York: Picador), and a decade later, Steven Kinzer's 2008 *A Thousand Hills: Rwanda's Rebirth and the Man Who Dreamed It* (Hoboken, NJ: John Wiley & Sons).

11 Waldorf, Lars. 2006. "Mass Justice for Mass Atrocity: Rethinking Local Justice as Transitional Justice." *Temple Law Review* 79(Spring): 86. Also see Max Rettig 2008, "*Gacaca*: Truth, Justice, and Reconciliation in Postconflict Rwanda?" *African Studies Review* 51(3) 25–50.

to save themselves but tried not to kill.) Category 4 cases primarily concerned crimes against property. In fact, the reality is more complex, and with the National courts moving very slowly, the lines between Categories 2, 3, and 4 often got blurry in practice. This matters, because the open-air public nature of *gacaca* lacks important protections to witnesses that the trial courts offer, as became starkly evident when rape cases were referred from the national Courts to *gacaca* in 2008.[12]

The ICTR was the first court to be established in the months following the genocide. Established by the United Nations Security Council on November 8, 1994, the ICTR's mission is to prosecute Rwandan citizens (and those of neighboring states) for the crime of genocide in the genocide of the Tutsi in 1994.[13] The ICTR's establishing focus is on high-level leaders and perpetrators, and their broader purpose is "to contribute to the process of reconciliation in Rwanda by helping to restore a sense of justice and playing a role in development of a lasting peace in the Great Lakes region."[14] This statement reveals an important dimension of the ICTR: although its cases are specifically from the 1994 genocide of the Tutsi, its mission is not only about Rwanda. Its purpose was international and distinctly regional in scope and impact, and the court has been responsible for charting new paths in international law. In 2013, the trial cases are over, and, with only Appeals still pending, the ICTR's closure predicted for 2015. Ninety-three cases were brought and processed, with some recently being referred to other jurisdictions, most especially the Rwandan national courts.

A common complaint I heard in Rwanda was that the ICTR was too expensive, not just internationally, but for Rwanda itself, and was therefore diverting much-needed funds from Rwandan development. Waldorf articulates the practical conflict between prosecution and development during Rwanda's post-genocide transition, saying:

> The RPF's insistence on mass (often arbitrary) arrests and extensive criminal prosecutions only worsened an already terrible situation: it saddled a devastated justice sector with the impossible task of trying some 120,000 Hutu suspects and it fostered a culture of denunciation, both of which have undermined efforts to establish the rule of law. Most cruelly, it diverted resources away from survivors: instead of providing reparations to genocide victims, the government and international donors have spent millions of dollars incarcerating (and occasionally trying) genocide suspects.[15]

In my recent research in Rwanda, I spoke with many Rwandans dedicating their lives to rebuilding the country, improving health and education, and increasing economic productivity. Most would agree with Waldorf. One woman expressed annoyance that I was travelling to Arusha to meet with attorneys at the ICTR. She argued that the ICTR is useless to Rwanda, costs the government significant money that could be used for social services or national prosecutions, and that my time should be spent only in Rwanda. Stay in Rwanda, she said, and support Rwanda.

This argument is compelling in many ways, but overlooks the international significance of genocide, a crime that requires international response, both in prevention and in prosecution. The international argument does not carry much weight with Gahima, who writes: "victims of genocide and Rwandans, in general, still primarily view international criminal justice as a self-serving act of atonement to cover up the international community's failure to come to their rescue."[16] Perhaps this view is widespread. Although *post-hoc*, international prosecutions do serve to spread the

---

12 HRW 2011: 112–18.

13 Available at: http://www.unictr.org/About /GeneralInformation/tabid/101/Default.aspx.

14 Joensen, Vagn (Judge and President of ICTR). 2013. "Address to the United Nations Security Council: Six-Monthly Report on the Completion Strategy of the International Criminal Tribunal for Rwanda." Presented June 12. Available at:http://www.unictr.org/tabid/155/Default.aspx?id=1355.

15 Waldorf 2006: 85.

16 Gahima 2013: 301.

responsibility beyond Rwanda. As Francois-Xavier Nsanzuwera argues, "By recognizing that atrocities perpetrated against Tutsi civilians, and their Hutu sympathizers in 1994, were a crime of genocide and crimes against humanity, the ICTR rendered human dignity back to the survivors of the genocide, who had been robbed of it by the perpetrators." This is an important form of recognition. Nsanzuwera adds that in testifying, survivors not only pay "a final homage" to the dead, but they also ask the court "to recall, by meting out such justice, that crimes which shock the universal conscience cannot go unpunished, regardless of where they were committed."[17]

The ICTR, as an international tribunal, recognizes the gravity of genocidal crimes and their international significance.[18] Also, as an international tribunal, it recognizes that genocide is a crime against humanity, not just against those directly wronged. It constitutes a *post-hoc* taking of responsibility, both backward-looking to decide punishment, and forward-looking to set precedents (as in *Akayesu* which for the first time recognized rape as an act of genocide).[19] In a 2001 report on the ICTR, primarily lamenting its slowness and expense, the International Crisis Group nevertheless highlights the important recognitive role of the court: "It has provided indisputable recognition of the Rwandan genocide and has politically neutralised the 'Hutu Power' movement's agenda of Tutsi extermination."[20] Practitioners at the court are surely aiming for more, but this recognition is an important moral and political achievement, one that an international tribunal is well situated to provide.

Beyond the resources complaint, a second sort of worry focuses on the limits of recognition that the ICTR can achieve, and in so doing highlights the value of multiple mechanisms of justice. For many survivors, testifying before the ICTR is logistically impossible and for those that do testify, they find that the process of ICTR trials is excessively formal and alien. Some see the ICTR as letting the "big fish" escape the gaze of the communities they harmed. One survivor says "they should face us, the Rwandan family, but they avoid us by being there." Another emphasizes the importance of face-to-face encounters between accused and accuser: "A person who testifies in another's absence, it is easy for them to lie but if you see each other, it is much more difficult to lie."[21] These survivors gave priority to local justice, giving little value to the international perspective of the ICTR.

The Rwandan National Courts provide the nation with its own formal mechanisms, saying, "we judge and punish our own, seriously and fairly." Some survivors report feeling that the ICTR takes genocidal crimes seriously but their own government would prefer to sweep them aside.[22] The truth is more complex, but the message that "we judge and punish our own" conveys a message of national autonomy. These national courts were not up to international standards even prior to '94 and then were devastated by the killings of so many judges and attorneys. In the early years of the new regime, restoring the rule of law required reconstructing a judiciary; in the decades that followed that judiciary needed guidance and training to bring the courts to international standards of fairness.

One measure of the success of the Rwandan National courts can be seen in the approval given by a panel of judges, called the Referral Bench, to transfer 11 cases from the ICTR to Rwandan

17 Nsanzuwera, Francois-Xavier. 2005. The ICTR Contribution to National Reconciliation. *Journal of International Criminal Justice* 3(4): 944–9. Available at: doi: 10.1093/jicj/mqi066.

18 See REDRESS 2008: 55.

19 *Case No. ICTR-96-4-T*: The Prosecutor versus Jean-Paul Akayesu. Available at: http://www.unictr.org/Portals/0/Case/English/Akayesu/judgement/akay001.pdf.

20 ICG (International Crisis Group). 2001. "International Criminal Tribunal for Rwanda: Justice Delayed." ICG Africa Report No. 30, June 7. Available at: http://www.crisisgroup.org/~/media/Files/africa/central-africa/rwanda/International%20Criminal%20Tribunal%20f.or%20Rwanda%20Justice%20Delayed.pdf.

21 Both quotes from Clark, Phil and Nicola Palmer, for REDRESS. 2012. *Testifying to Genocide: Victim and Witness Protection in Rwanda*. Available at: http://www.redress.org/downloads/country-reports/1301testifying_to_genocide.pdf.

22 Conversations in Rwanda, 2011 and 2012. Notes on file.

National courts under Rule 11 *bis*. Prior attempts all failed, hung up on two main sticking points: (1) a lack of assurance that the accused would get a fair trial, and (2) Rwanda still imposed the death penalty.[23] With judicial improvements and with the death penalty off the table, on June 28, 2011, the Bench ruled that Rwanda could try these 11 high-level cases itself. I was visiting the ICTR when this ruling came down, and it was cause for celebration there, signaling a new phase in the distribution of responsibility. The goal of transfer, to UN nations as well as Rwanda, was partly to move toward closing the ICTR, but also to promote interaction across the many jurisdictions, each taking responsibility not only for their assigned cases, but also for observing proceedings elsewhere to ensure fair trials everywhere. With different nations comparing trials, there is also hope that higher standards will be followed. For Rwanda to receive responsibility for these cases was a significant vote of confidence from the ICTR and the Referral Bench.

Time will tell whether the Referral Bench was overly optimistic. Jennifer Morris warns that the transfer of these cases may send "a dangerous false message to the international community: that the transformation of the Rwanda's judiciary is complete, and Rwanda can be counted on to handle all of its cases in accord with international standards of justice."[24] Perhaps, but the ICTR monitors the cases it sends out to national courts and can retrieve any cases (in Rwanda and elsewhere) if courts do not follow appropriate standards. This overseeing by the ICTR has the potential to continue to improve the Rwandan judiciary. The very fact that Morris sees the transfer as sending this message is the key. Nearly 20 years after the genocide, it is an important message to consider. If Rwanda can indeed try these cases fairly and well, then that will be significant progress not just since '94, but an improvement over pre-1994 standards. Recognition from the ICTR, in the form of these transfers, can foster further improvements.

Gacaca courts were initiated in 2001, primarily for practical reasons. The National courts moved slowly: 1292 cases between 1996 and 1998, with 130,000 awaiting trial.[25] The government quickly became aware that such a backlog could be not completed during the lifetimes of the prisoners. Prison conditions were appalling; with overcrowding, poor sanitation, lack of food, and more, prisoners were dying before ever coming to trial. Recounting a horrific visit to Gitarama prison in 1996, Andre Sibomana calls the prisons "inhuman death traps" in which prisoners would literally rot away before their cases were heard.[26] Conditions have improved since those early years, but overcrowding is still an issue, along with inadequate nutrition and sanitation. *Gacaca*'s 2001 revival was, in part, to allow for rapid release of as many cases as possible.[27] Instead of literally rotting away in prison, these men could get back to work, and so stoke the economy.

It was also hoped that *gacaca* would reveal important information about the genocide, and promote reconciliation. The new *gacaca* resurrected a traditional dispute-resolution practice that had fallen into disuse during the colonial period when formal courts were instituted. Traditionally, people would gather in a clearing (on the grass) with their elders to hear two sides to a dispute, say over a cow or a property line, and collectively discuss the issues and find a solution. Thus

23 Morris, Jennifer Wren. 2012. "The Trouble with Transfers: An Analysis of the Referral of *Uwinkindi* to the Republic of Rwanda for Trial." *Wash. U.L. Rev*. 90(2): 505–41. Available at: http://digitalcommons.law.wustl.edu/lawreview/vol90/iss2/6. See also Amelia S. Canter. 2008. "'For these Reasons, the Chamber Denies the Prosecutor's Request for Referral': The False Hope of Rule 11 BIS," *Fordham International Law Journal*. 32(5): 1614–55.

24 Morris 2012: 541.

25 Human Rights Watch. 2011. *Justice Compromised: The Legacy of Rwanda's Community-based Gacaca Courts*, 2. Available at: http://www.hrw.org/node/99189.

26 Sibomana 1999: 108–9.

27 Ruvebana, Etienne. n.d. "*Gacaca*: A Rwandan Original and Realistic Justice as a Solution to Social and Legal Problems—Its Achievements and Challenges." In *16 Years After the Genocide Perpetrated Against the Tutsi (1994–2010): Handling its Consequences*, 319–45. Available in person from CNLG Headquarters, Kigali.

practiced, *gacaca* offered relief in cases of micro-level crime by one neighbor against another, such as property disputes. Community participation in the adjudication made it clear that one neighbor's offense against another was of social consequence, but the crimes did not rise to the level of atrocities. In 2001, *gacaca* held out the prospect of keeping justice very local, allowing neighbors, friends, and family, to decide what is right and just. So this justice 'in the grass' (the literal meaning of '*gacaca*') conveys and respects the intimacy of the crimes done, neighbor against neighbor. *Gacaca* promised the opportunity to blend the recognitive functions of testimony and confession along with restorative justice in the form of reparations. As a modified return to "old ways," *gacaca* stands as an invocation of shared history and united identities.

Problems beset the reconceived *gacaca* from the start. As a hybrid between the traditional local hearing and a more formal court, it had official judges and rules, but these did not secure the fair trial rights that defendants found in the national courts or the ICTR. The first implementation problem was the need to find 200,000 judges—*inyangamugayo* (those who love truth)—to serve the nation's 11,000 districts. Many of those elected were not seated, either because they were illiterate or because they were suspected génocidaires. Preparation for the job was "a thirty-six hour crash course."[28] The judges were not trained in rules of evidence, and the government assumed that common sense and the transparency of the context would lead to appropriate outcomes. The imbalance of sheer numbers between perpetrators and their families and survivors, who were a minority within the Tutsi minority, led to substantive problems gathering testimony and adjudicating it appropriately.

Gacaca was indeed speedier than the National Courts. The trials were slated to run from 2005 to 2007, but the closing date was extended several times. A 2011 Human Rights Watch report notes that in 2010, the government announced that the courts were completed, but then a few months later announced their reopening to consider what amount to appeals and reconsideration in cases of "suspected miscarriage of justice."[29]

Gacaca helped both individual and collective healing in a variety of ways. It brought members of the local community together to discuss the recent history and take ownership of the atrocities. It sped up the judicial process and so got a lot of people out of prison, issuing sentences of time served plus community service ahead. *Gacaca* motivated confession (for more leniency) and thereby revealed facts about where and how loved ones died. But again, incompleteness rules the process: survivors know that the accounts are incomplete and report feeling that confessions are often self-serving. Sometimes the local nature of the hearing, touted as an asset to justice, was itself a problem, because the judges were local too; this led to allegations of bias, corruption, intimidation of witnesses and "other serious procedural irregularities"[30] All in all, *gacaca* does leave "a mixed legacy."[31]

Assessing Justice in Transition

Protecting human rights fosters practices of recognition in a society. Since 1994, the Rwandan government has been praised by international observers for its dedication in prosecuting *génocidaires*, for its economic development, and advances in health care and education. Partnerships with NGOs have been undertaken with explicit provisos that the Rwandan government is the primary decider

28 Temple-Raston, Dina. 2005. *Justice on the Grass*. New York: The Free Press, 135. See also Westberg, Megan M., 2011. "Rwanda's Use of Transitional Justice after Genocide: The Gacaca Courts and the ICTR" *U. Kan. L. Rev*. 59: 331.

29 HRW 2011: 3.

30 HRW 2011: 4, 105–11.

31 The phrase is from HRW 2011.

of what the Rwandan people need. In speeches, President Kagame often remarks that international assistance is very welcome, as long as it comes on Rwandan terms.[32] As a society in transition from genocide, one in which internal division was fostered for economic and political ends, Rwanda has, under the Kagame regime, promoted national unity and national self-determination. National autonomy is an important value and goal. Recently, however, praise for Rwanda has been tempered by criticism, as expectations have risen in light of many social and economic achievements. Many outside Rwanda have been critical of its less-than-free press, elections in which over 90 percent of the voters vote for the sitting president, the arresting of political opponents on grounds of their promoting 'genocide ideology', and more. Longman argues that "Rwanda is effectively a one-party state with a corporatist civil society and a leader elected by plebiscite" and worries that political inequality is leading to unequal development with a concentration of wealth in a small group—"primarily Anglophone returnees from Uganda."[33] This is a recipe for instability. In an otherwise laudatory speech in Kigali, the former US Permanent Representative to the United Nations, Susan Rice, said that the next big developmental challenge for Rwanda will be to create a politically open society. She called for the "deepening and the broadening of democracy" and observed: "In Rwanda, economic development and political openness can reinforce each other."[34]

Evaluating a post-conflict government as it works toward justice includes not only evaluating its judiciary, but also its support for human development and human rights. When these are richly protected, citizens are well served. In the early part of a transition, restrictions on freedom are expected as part of the DDR process, but 20 years later, expectations change and the promotion and protection of human rights becomes more urgent. What I heard from many Rwandans in response to criticisms like Longman's and Rice's was that 20 years is still not enough time, and the transition is still young.

Justice in the aftermath of atrocity is, paradoxically, both necessary and impossible. The horrific nature of genocidal crimes cries for punishment and yet reveals the inadequacy of punishment. Every sentence seems too short to a survivor, and yet too long to a prisoner. Survivors need recognition of the harms done to them and their families, and yet the atrocity's scale renders their experience nearly unintelligible, not only to others, but also often to themselves as well.[35] Critics view the achievements of courts and tribunals as eclipsing their limitations, and survivors are often left without a sense that their experiences have been given due measure. Some have pointed out that the mechanisms themselves require testimonial forms that are alien to survivors and witnesses, making them reshape the structure of their memories, and hence serving as an added mode of alienation. In Rwanda, there are those who think the ICTR is all about making international law, and a waste of Rwandan time and money. There are those who think *gacaca* courts were too demanding of those who testify and too lenient on *génocidaires*. These complaints frame an adequacy problem, which poses a challenge to the very concept of transitional justice, narrowly construed.

Although the criticisms point to important improvements that should be made, such narrow construals of transitional justice should be avoided. Assessing transitional justice requires a broad,

---

32 e.g., Kagame, Paul. 2012. Speech at Rwanda Day, Boston, MA, Sept 22. Available at: http://www.paulkagame.com/2010/index.php?option=com_content&view=article&id=792%3Aspeech-by-he-paul-kagame-president-of-the-republic-of-rwanda-at-rwanda-day&catid=34%3Aspeeches&Itemid=56&lang=en.

33 Longman, Timothy. 2011. "Limitations to Political Reform: The Undemocratic Nature of Transition in Rwanda." In *Remaking Rwanda: State Building and Human Rights After Mass Violence*, ed. Straus, Scott and Lars Waldorf, 25–47. Madison, WI: University of Wisconsin Press.

34 Rice, Susan E. 2011. U.S. Permanent Representative to the United Nations. "Building a New Nation: Rwanda's Progress and Potential." Speech at the Kigali Institute of Science and Technology, November 23. Available at: usun.state.gov/briefing/statements/2011/177743.htm.

35 Arendt, Hannah.1973. *The Origins of Totalitarianism*. New York: Harcourt, 439–41.

integrative conception of justice, including distributive justice, and a system-wide analysis of official and unofficial mechanisms of restoration, social and economic development, and restoring respect for human rights. Transitional justice narrowly conceived as the action of courts (in Rwanda, from the local *gacaca* courts, to the national courts, to the ICTR) or of truth commissions, tribunals, and other official forums, should be seen as only one part of the transitional process. For instance, a witness who is secure in her safety, who is economically independent, who is protected by her family and her government, will be better able to articulate her experience in court. Protection of human rights though development is key in achieving transitional justice. The ICTR is a 30-hour bus ride from Kigali, and the cost of airfare is out of the question for most Rwandans, so testifying in Arusha is a burden. By the time witnesses arrive, their vulnerabilities are enhanced. Improving distributive justice can create conditions to mitigate these vulnerabilities. Understanding transitional justice broadly helps to apportion responsibility appropriately, allowing us to see the valuable contributions of the many agents seeking to rebuild a severely damaged and divided society.

Distributive justice is about achieving a fair and moral distribution of the goods and services and opportunities across a society. For our purposes, we need not assume any rich theory of distributive justice; we need only note that every society has some such distribution of goods, services, and opportunities, and that some of these are more fair and just than others. Some promote general flourishing, while others promote widespread oppression. Given these general facts, it is easy to see that the goal of a transition away from conflict toward a more just state will necessarily involve issues concerning the distribution of income, wealth, property, access to education, employment opportunities, and more. These are not matters for the punishment of *génocidaires*, but such punishment might impact judgments about distributive justice just the same.

Land reform is one key area of distributive justice, and illustrates a way that the post-genocide government is reorganizing economic and social stability. From 2005 to 2009, for the first time in its history, Rwanda devised and began to implement a process of registering properties. During my research in Rwanda, several survivors explained their distress at losing their family property to those who killed their families, only to be told by local leaders that the current occupants now have the right to occupy land that had been in the survivor's family for generations. With a title or deed, legal recourse would be a viable option, and one would not have to ask the friends of your brother's killer for the favor of the return of your family home.[36] The government has a bigger picture in mind, and returning land to survivors is not the heart of the reform. In addition to security of tenure, Paul Gready notes:

> Granting value to land is seen as a way of generating investment, a land market, and tax revenue—which will in turn, it is argued, increase land value and public funds ... Other objectives include reining in land fragmentation and promoting plot consolidation, equality and non-discrimination in access to land, and optimizing land management and productivity.[37]

Issues about equality of access, security of tenure on the property, and consolidating wealth across generations, are all matters of distributive justice. Ensuring "equality and non-discrimination in access to land" would be an important step in creating a more just society, particularly in a nation with so many depending on small subsistence farms for survival. If done with care, land reform has

---

36 Conversation, Kigali, July 2012. Notes on file.

37 Gready, Paul 2010. "'You're Either with Us or against Us': Civil Society and Policy Making in Post-Genocide Rwanda." *African Affairs* 109(437). Quote, 647. See also Ann Ansoms. 2009. "Re-Engineering Rural Society: The Visions and Ambitions of the Rwandan Elite." *African Affairs* 108(431): 289–309.

the potential to protect important human rights. Gready adds a concern that the government may be envisioning "a privatized, market-driven, modernized and mechanized agricultural sector,"[38] and we can see that if this is so, considerations of distributive justice should be brought to bear on such a plan.

Restoring Recognition

Talk of recognition requires clarity about the many different forms it can take. There are substantive social and epistemic aspects to it, as well as a performative function. In political theory, this concept is most thoroughly articulated by Axel Honneth, who sees recognition as taking different forms in different arenas, but as fundamentally tied to our personhood, to our own understanding and appreciation of our personhood, and to others' respect and appreciation of our personhood and the particular person that we are. Honneth identifies three patterns of recognition: love, rights, and solidarity. These correspond to three arenas of social life: family, state, civil society. Recognition promotes and protects a person's dignity and integrity. The political implications of this concept should be clear from Honneth's explanation: "Morality, if understood as an institution for the protection of human dignity, defends the reciprocity of love, the universalism of rights, and the egalitarianism of solidarity against their being relinquished in favor of force and repression. In other words, morality inherently contains an interest in the cultivation of those principles that provide a structural basis for the various forms of recognition."[39] Transitional justice, through its many mechanisms, seeks to defend human rights, and aims to promote broader social solidarity.

Recognition can be a psychological concept, as it often is in Honneth's work. The concept I am working with is more social and behavioral, making room for psychological states but not always presupposing them, which is why performative recognition matters. To think of a performative recognition, for example, consider when a judge walks into a courtroom and a bailiff calls out "All rise" and everyone stands. This rising is a form of recognition of the judge's status and role. Someone can be in the court, understand neither what was said nor why it was said, and yet in rising with the others, shows a performative recognition of the judge. Survivors of atrocities want performative recognition from the state and from individuals, regardless of their individual views and epistemic limitations, but they need more substantive recognition too. The substantive recognition comes from cognitive elements missing in the person who merely stands. Someone "gets it" about you—they understand your experience, your situation, your achievements, and your goals. This comprehension depends upon a grasp of shared norms and it has its own normative force. On this view, recognition is respect for the other *as* a person, stemming from an understanding of that person as being a being like oneself (even if differently situated). This is often what former intimates wish for, neighbors whose lives were intertwined prior to '94 who now want to know how the killers could have turned against them. Some assailants also want their victims to know how it was for them. This treats recognition as a moral outgrowth of epistemic clarity. Such a high standard is important for stable mutual recognition, but is unlikely to be possible in cases of atrocity. Consider Adalbert Munzigura, head of a death squad in '94, who was sentenced to 12 years and released in May 2003. Addressing the need for each side to understand the other, and the chasm that lay between them, he said:

38 Gready 2010: 647.

39 Honneth, Axel. 1992. "Integrity and Disrespect: Principles of a Conception of Morality Based on the Theory of Recognition." *Political Theory* 20(2): 187–201. Quote, 197.

> There are people in Kibungo who will be able to understand me, but only those who plied their machetes like me or more than me. The Tutsis though—its unthinkable for them to learn and understand. You just can't ask them to see our actions as we did. I believe their suffering will reject any kind of explanation. What we have done is unnatural to them. Perhaps patience and forgetting will win out; perhaps not.[40]

To remember or imagine what it was like for the killer in the killing situation is profoundly threatening to someone who was hunted. That exercise of empathy asks for a complex exercise that is potentially self-mutilating. Politics cannot demand this. Adalbert is right that "You just can't ask them to see our actions as we did." Neither can the killers truly grasp the despair of being hunted, to be hiding in the muck of the Bugesera's papyrus swamps or fleeing into the depths of Nyungwe Forest. So how can mutual recognition be fostered? It cannot be based upon an empathetically reached epistemic clarity about the other's experience of the past. Perhaps a more forward-looking recognition could be possible, one that at least at first respects each other's rights. With time, it could potentially expanded through undertaking shared projects, in line with Honneth's conception of solidarity (rather than love).

For justice to take hold in the aftermath of atrocity, like genocide, a society cannot rely only on its explicit vehicles of justice; these must be supported by carefully aimed development projects, which are neither reparations nor random. Reparations are the purview of the courts. Development shores up the social standing and economic prospects of survivors, spreading the responsibility for showing recognition beyond the context of court. Well-targeted projects give substance to the symbolic, legal, and social messages issued by courts and tribunals, giving survivors necessary means to help rebuild their lives. Alone, these development projects are insufficient for recovery, because recovery requires ensuring that the context for the projects are made clear. In tandem with judgments, made explicit in court proceedings, such development can be a powerful force.

The question arises of balancing explicit mechanisms of justice against mechanisms of development, but this is a false dichotomy. Development projects must be part and parcel of transitional justice. Amongst Rwandan survivors of '94, there is a tension between wanting *génocidaires* to be brought to justice, on the one hand, and on the other, thinking that the money such processes cost would be better spent on development for the poorest and most damaged people within the country. This tension is not simply economic, but economic concerns, in health care, education, and land reform, for example, highlight the potential for distributive structural changes that should be counted as strengthening the recognitive force of transitional justice.

To some, seeing development as part of justice might seem like a category mistake, but justice is not just about punishing or rewarding individual deeds, but pertains to the arrangement of a legal and social system as a whole. Development has the potential to foster distributive justice, recognizing the structural dimensions of social situation that reproduces violence. As Mark Drumbl remarks:

> By treating genocidal violence as an individualized, pathological, and deviant transgression of social propriety, the criminal justice system may do the dualist postgenocidal society a disservice by blanketing and perpetuating the structural nature of this violence to the detriment of survivors and future generations.[41]

40 Jean Hatzfeld. 2003, 2005. *Machete Season: The Killers in Rwanda Speak*. Preface by Susan Sontag. Translated by Linda Coverdale. New York: Farrar, Straus and Giroux, 194.

41 Drumbl, Mark A. 2000. "Punishment, Postgenocide: From Guilt to Shame to *Civis* in Rwanda." *NYU Law Review* 75: 1221–326. Quote, 1324–5.

Criminal justice individualizes responsibility, which is often appropriate, but hardly the whole truth when the crime is genocide. Distributive justice addresses social and material structures, offering survivors improved prospects of a social, political, and economic life. Taking a structural approach to change respects the limits of individual capabilities while simultaneously offering the means to expand them.[42]

Reflecting on the path Rwanda has taken since '94, Gahima calls for "linking accountability with prevention and protection" (302). I am arguing that prevention and protection require mechanisms of distributive justice, which promote the mutual recognition that fosters healthy civil society. Offering an overview of the current state of transitional justice, Dustin Sharp explains:

> The most iconic mechanisms associated with transitional justice are undoubtedly prosecutions and truth commissions. Beyond this, however, the field has broadened a great deal since the early 90s to include a range of mechanisms and practices designed to encourage reconciliation and differing forms of accountability. Thus, fostering community-level dialogue between former perpetrators and survivors of human rights abuses and the construction of public memorials to preserve memory of the conflict are today as much a part of transitional justice as a prosecution before a war crimes tribunal.[43]

Accountability can take many forms, not just criminal justice and reconciliation work. Substantive changes to distributive justice counts too. In Rwanda, the government did not only pursue prosecution of génocidaires. They established watchdog agencies, a Human Rights Commission, the National Commission for the Fight Against Genocide (CNLG), the IRDP (Institute of Research and Dialogue for Peace), and more, as well as domestic development projects like Girinka (One-cow-per-poor-family), small business microloan projects, and more. So although my focus has been on the typical concerns of transitional justice (courts and tribunals), there is also a story to tell about the strengths and weaknesses of Rwanda's internal and internationally assisted development projects.

My aim has been to show that consideration of the recognitive functions of criminal justice and distributive justice argues for an integration of the two in contexts of transitioning away from genocide and toward a more stable civil society. Rwanda's post-genocidal transition to a more just state is underway but incomplete. Rwanda's integration of several layers of prosecutorial justice, from the ICTR, to the national courts, to *gacaca*, offered a way to prosecute more cases more quickly than might otherwise have been done, and offered distinctive types of recognitive messages and the repair they bring. Government actions, particularly in economic development, health, and education, show that even with limited resources, Rwanda is aware that trials are insufficient for putting the country back on its feet and making its citizens closer to whole again. Development projects are a necessary part of the process. So when we examine the progress that Rwanda has made in transitional justice, neither prosecutions nor development should be considered in isolation. Boosters and critics should both take account of the whole picture. The "practical politics" of which Berthe Mwanankabandi spoke in our second epigraph is a complex phenomenon, not automatically a sell-out. Rwanda has made tremendous strides in imposing the rule of law, prosecuting *génocidaires*, and in getting accounts of the genocide onto the public record in myriad ways. It has improved in economic development in some sectors, and its HDI average has increased 57 percent from 1980 through 2012. It is still in the low development

42 See Zorbas, Eugenia. "Aid Dependence and Policy Independence: Explaining the Rwandan Paradox." In Strauss and Waldorf 2011: 103–17.

43 Sharp 2012: 6.

group and ranks 166th out of 187 countries. Most Rwandans still live in dire poverty, and the HDI does not take account of disparities in income, which are extreme in Rwanda.[44] Access to education and health care has improved, but access will be uneven until education is public and free. Greater access to education and greater freedoms of expression with strengthen citizens and should enhance the strides made in building institutions and in cultural reforms. Considering the recent history of Rwanda, we can see that overcoming recognition harm requires recognition, in the form of punishment of *génocidaires*, but also, importantly, in strengthening the social, cultural, and economic prospects of survivors and of the country as a whole. Attention to recognition, performative and substantive, should be part of any discussion of transitional justice.

References

Ansoms, Ann. 2009. "Re-Engineering Rural Society: The Visions and Ambitions of the Rwandan Elite." *African Affairs* 108(431): 289–309.

Arendt, Hannah.1973. *The Origins of Totalitarianism*. New York: Harcourt.

Canter, Amelia S. 2008. "'For these Reasons, the Chamber Denies the Prosecutor's Request for Referral': The False Hope of Rule 11 BIS." *Fordham International Law Journal* 32(5): 1614–55.

Clark, Phil, and Nicola Palmer, for REDRESS. 2012. *Testifying to Genocide: Victim and Witness Protection in Rwanda*. Available at: http://www.redress.org/downloads/country-reports/1301testifying_to_genocide.pdf.

Drumbl, Mark A. 2000. "Punishment, Postgenocide: From Guilt to Shame to *Civis* in Rwanda." *NYU Law Review* 75: 1221–326.

Gahima, Gerald. 2013. *Transitional Justice in Rwanda: Accountability for Atrocity*. New York: Routledge.

Graybill, Lyn and Kimberley Lanegran. 2004. "Truth, Justice, and Reconciliation in Africa: Issues and Cases." *African Studies Quarterly* 8(1): 1–18.

Gready, Paul 2010. "'You're Either with Us or against Us': Civil Society and Policy Making in Post-Genocide Rwanda." *African Affairs*, 109(437).

Hatzfeld, Jean. 2003. 2005. *Machete Season: The Killers in Rwanda Speak*. Preface by Susan Sontag. Translated by Linda Coverdale. New York: Farrar, Straus and Giroux.

Hatzfeld, Jean. 2009. *The Antelope's Strategy: Living in Rwanda after the Genocide*. Translated by Linda Coverdale. New York: Farrar, Straus and Giroux.

Honneth, Axel. 1992. "Integrity and Disrespect: Principles of a Conception of Morality Based on the Theory of Recognition." *Political Theory* 20(2): 187–201.

Human Rights Watch. 2011. *Justice Compromised: The Legacy of Rwanda's Community-Based Gacaca Courts*. Available at: http://www.hrw.org/node/99189.

ICG (International Crisis Group). 2001. "International Criminal Tribunal for Rwanda: Justice Delayed." ICG Africa Report No. 30, June 7. Available at: http://www.crisisgroup.org/~/media/Files/africa/central-africa/rwanda/International%20Criminal%20Tribunal%20f.or%20Rwanda%20Justice%20Delayed.pdf.

ICTR. 1998. *Case No. ICTR-96–4-T*: The Prosecutor versus Jean-Paul Akayesu. Available at: http://www.unictr.org/Portals/0/Case/English/Akayesu/judgement/akay001.pdf.

44 United Nations Development Programme. 2013. HDI Index for Rwanda. Available at: http://hdrstats.undp.org/images/explanations/RWA.pdf.

Joensen, Vagn. 2013. "Address to the United Nations Security Council: Six-Monthly Report on the Completion Strategy of the International Criminal Tribunal for Rwanda." Presented June 12. Available at: http://www.unictr.org/tabid/155/Default.aspx?id=1355.

Kagame, Paul. 2012. Speech at Rwanda Day, Boston, MA, September 22. Available at: http://www.paulkagame.com/2010/index.php?option=com_content&view=article&id=792%3Aspeech-by-he-paul-kagame-president-of-the-republic-of-rwanda-at-rwanda-day&catid=34%3Aspeeches&Itemid=56&lang=en.

Longman, Timothy. 2011. "Limitations to Political Reform: The Undemocratic Nature of Transition in Rwanda." In *Remaking Rwanda: State Building and Human Rights after Mass Violence*, edited by Scott Straus and Lars Waldorf, 25–47. Madison, WI: University of Wisconsin Press.

Morris, Jennifer Wren. 2012. "The Trouble with Transfers: An Analysis of the Referral of *Uwinkindi* to the Republic of Rwanda for Trial." *Wash. U.L. Rev.* 90(2): 505–41. Available at: http://digitalcommons.law.wustl.edu/lawreview/vol90/iss2/6.

Nsanzuwera, Francois-Xavier. 2005. The ICTR Contribution to National Reconciliation. *Journal of International Criminal Justice* 3(4): 944–9. Available at: doi: 10.1093/jicj/mqi066.

REDRESS. 2008. *Survivors and Post-Genocide Justice in Rwanda: Their Experiences, Perspectives and Hopes*. Available at: http://www.redress.org/downloads/country-reports/Rwanda%20Survivors%2031%20Oct%2008.pdf

Rettig, Max. 2008. "*Gacaca*: Truth, Justice, and Reconciliation in Postconflict Rwanda?" *African Studies Review* 51(3): 25–50.

Rice, Susan E. 2011. "Building a New Nation: Rwanda's Progress and Potential." Speech at the Kigali Institute of Science and Technology, November 23. Available at: usun.state.gov/briefing/statements/2011/177743.htm.

Ruvebana, Etienne. n.d. "*Gacaca*: A Rwandan Original and Realistic Justice as a Solution to Social and Legal Problems—Its Achievements and Challenges." In *16 Years After the Genocide Perpetrated Against the Tutsi (1994–2010): Handling its Consequences*. Kigali: CNLG, 319–45.

Schabas, William. 2005. "Genocide Trials and *Gacaca* Courts." *Journal of International Criminal Justice* 3: 879–95. Available at: doi: 10.1093/jicj/mqi062.

Sharp, Dustin. 2012. "Bridging the Gap: The United Nations Peacebuilding Commission and the Challenges of Integrating DDR and Transitional Justice." In *Transitional Justice and Peacebuilding on the Ground: Victims and Ex-Combatants*, edited by Chandra Lekha Sriram, Olga Martin-Ortega, and Johanna Herman, 23–40. New York: Routledge.

Sibomana, Andre, Hervé Deguine, and Laure Guilbert. 1999. *Hope for Rwanda: Conversations with Laure Guilbert and Hervé Deguine*. Translated by Carina Tersakian. London: Pluto Press.

Straus, Scott, and Lars Waldorf, eds. 2011. *Remaking Rwanda: State Building and Human Rights after Mass Violence*. Madison, WI: University of Wisconsin Press.

Temple-Raston, Dina. 2005. *Justice on the Grass*. New York: The Free Press.

Tirrell, Lynne. 2013. "Apologizing for Atrocity: Rwanda and Recognition." In *Justice, Responsibility and Reconciliation in the Wake of Conflict*, edited by Alice MacLachlan and Allen Speight, 159–82. New York: Springer.

United Nations Development Programme. 2013. HDI Index for Rwanda. Available at: http://hdrstats.undp.org/images/explanations/RWA.pdf.

Waldorf, Lars. 2006. "Mass Justice for Mass Atrocity: Rethinking Local Justice as Transitional Justice." *Temple Law Review* 79(Spring): 86.

Waldorf, Lars. 2009. Transitional Justice and DDR: The Case of Rwanda. Report for the International Center for Transitional Justice. Available at: https://www.ictj.org/sites/default/files/ICTJ-DDR-Rwanda-CaseStudy-2009-English.pdf.

Westberg, Megan M., 2011. "Rwanda's Use of Transitional Justice after Genocide: The *Gacaca* Courts and the ICTR." *U. Kan. L. Rev*. 59: 331.

Zorbas, Eugenia. 2011. "Aid Dependence and Policy Independence: Explaining the Rwandan Paradox." In *Remaking Rwanda: State Building and Human Rights after Mass Violence*, edited by S. Strauss and L. Waldorf, 103–17. Madison, WI: University of Wisconsin Press.

Index

For Product Safety Concerns and Information please contact our EU representative GPSR@taylorandfrancis.com Taylor & Francis Verlag GmbH, Kaufingerstraße 24, 80331 München, Germany

Batch number: 10726294

Printed by Printforce, the Netherlands